Schools in Transition

SCHOOLS IN TRANSITION

Essays in Comparative Education

Edited by
Andreas M. Kazamias
Erwin H. Epstein
The University of Wisconsin

Allyn and Bacon, Inc. *Boston*

Library of Congress Catalog Card Number: 68-12344

Printed in the United States of America

Preface

This book is a collection of articles on topics often discussed when education is examined from a comparative or international perspective. Its focus is on formal education, which is examined from the political, the economic, and the socio-cultural standpoints. As to method, the compilation reflects the various concepts and techniques that have been used in the field. These have either been restricted to one discipline (such as history, political science, sociology, economics, or anthropology) or have combined elements of several. In short, the volume reflects the flexibility of the field it is designed to serve.

In compiling the anthology, the editors relied heavily on material already published in scholarly journals devoted to comparative education and related fields. However, many of the essays were solicited, and appear here for the first time. A few of these latter contributions are revised versions of papers presented at the Midwest Regional Meeting of the Comparative Education Society, which was held in April, 1966, at the University of Wisconsin.

Comparative studies enhance one's perspective on the interrelationships between school and society. It is fitting to point out, however, that these essays and topics can do little more than introduce the reader to a young and exciting field. Rather than delineate frontiers, they should stimulate a search for the new and fertile areas which lie beyond.

The editors are especially indebted to the following authors of the solicited essays: Chaim Adler (The Hebrew University of Jerusalem), C. Arnold Anderson (University of Chicago), Munir Bashshur (The American University of Beirut), Sterling Fishman (University of Wisconsin), Warren Hagstrom (University of Wisconsin), Phyllis Goldblatt (University of Chicago), Ken Kehrer (Yale University), Herbert Kliebard (University of Wisconsin), and Arthur J. Rubel (The University of Notre Dame). They also wish to thank the authors and publishers of those articles that have appeared elsewhere for permission to reprint.

A. M. K.

E. H. E.

Contents

* Asterisks indicate original contributions.

Part Three. Equity, Efficiency, and Educational Planning

Part Four. Sub-Cultural Variations and Education

Part Five. Religion and Education

PART SIX. LANGUAGE AND EDUCATION

Introduction

COMPARATIVE EDUCATION, like most other fields that examine social phenomena through comparison, is characterized by controversy and ambiguity. There is a fairly general agreement that the content of comparative education is largely concerned with formal education, or schooling, in a variety of countries or societies. A general understanding has also developed that schools do not function *sui generis,* that if they are to be viewed meaningfully they must be examined in their social context. Yet "school-society relationships" are found to be elusive. There is lack of agreement over which aspects of society relate most significantly to education and are therefore potentially most worthy of investigation and comparison. Moreover, like the content of the field, approaches to comparative education have been diverse.

At one extreme, comparative education has been pursued in terms of the methods, concepts, and techniques of history, philosophy, or one of the social sciences (such as sociology, political science, or economics). When it is so identified, as a branch of educational history, educational sociology, or the like, specialization in comparative education has implied expertise in a particular "discipline."

At the other extreme, comparative education has been viewed as a field employing the research tools of more than one discipline. The assumption is made that few if any educational subjects can be treated adequately when limited to a single set of concepts and methods. Education, being bound to culture, ramifies into social, political, and economic spheres and is always affected by historical antecedents and traditions. Problems in comparative education, therefore, are seen as best treated from several disciplinary vantage points.

Somewhere in between, there is what may be called the "interdisciplinary" approach to comparative education, one that has had perhaps the widest following. This approach emphasizes the blending of several disciplines rather than their boundaries. It assumes that academic fields can be integrated without necessarily being diluted, presumably because all of them use to some extent the "scientific method" as a mode of investigation.

The present volume does not intend to encompass all the dimensions of comparative education, to vindicate a particular approach, or to demarcate the proper contours of the field. Nevertheless, certain assumptions and points of view have entered into the organization and content of the volume and these must be made explicit.

1. Formal education or schooling entails deliberate instruction. Such instruction is a conscious and orderly, rather than a spontaneous, activity. Formal education displays patterns or characteristics which are more clearly discerned than what is usually referred to as "socialization."

2. Schools, as integral parts of culture, are never inert; they are susceptible to culture change and in turn contribute to it.

3. Although change is characteristic of schools and societies, its tempo and direction vary. For example, the tendency of pre-industrial countries to modernize has influenced political, economic, and social institutions differently. Studies of the dynamics of educational change in a variety of cultures increase our knowledge about modernization in general and the role of schools in particular.

4. Changes in the various aspects of human activity (intellectual, political, social, and economic) make common demands upon schooling. For example, as the form of a political organization changes to that of a nation-state, social integration, a characteristic function of schools, may become more national in scope and emphasis. In the same manner, the content of the culture that is being transmitted through schools varies as societies are affected by modernization, the advance of science, realignments in the power structure, and similar forces.

5. Comparisons can be either explicit or implicit. Aspects of education can be investigated through explicit comparisons involving a variety of contemporary societies that display reasonably similar characteristics or problems. Comparisons can also be made between problems in societies separated in time or between problems in different historical periods in one society. Yet it is not imperative that every comparative study give equal attention to two or more societies. An inquiry into problems of a particular society may indeed qualify as being comparative if the analytic scheme can be extended to problems in other societies.

6. Generalizations about education can be related to various kinds of schooling, past and present. Comparison implies that phenomena can be approached as not being inherently unique; fundamental identities underlie human activity regardless of time, space, and context. This view contrasts with strict historical interpretations which examine historical or contemporary events as unique and therefore not amenable to comparative analysis.

7. The theoretical and practical aspects of education are interrelated. Questions of educational application or policy can be examined fruitfully only if they are grounded in a body of knowledge that has been systematically accumulated. Policy making involves choosing among alternatives; theory provides an understanding of the potential consequences of alterna-

tive courses of action and is the foundation of intelligent choice. If not grounded in theory and analysis, policy statements may be nothing more than normative decrees.

8. A discussion of schooling in a particular society entails a description of the structural or institutional aspects of education. Yet a major purpose of comparison is to establish generalizations which derive from studying relationships cross-culturally and through time. This suggests the value of systematic inquiries that focus less on comprehensive descriptions of particular systems of education and more on the analysis of relationships.

In view of the interrelated dimensions of education, clear-cut classifications of schooling into political, economic, or sociological aspects are always arbitrary. The efficient allocation of resources, for example, has political as well as economic implications. It is also influenced by values and other social-psychological factors. The categories or topics under which the essays in this volume have been classified illustrate variations in emphasis both as regards subject-matter and approach; they should not be viewed as self-sufficient and exclusive units. Parts II and III, "Education and the Polity" and "Equity, Efficiency, and Educational Planning" should be interpreted as *predominantly* political and *predominantly* economic aspects of school-society relationships. Similarly, Part IV, "Sub-cultural Variations and Education," which focuses on the interconnections of several factors—social class, ethnicity, race, demography, and education—should be considered as *predominantly* sociological in method and orientation.

Part I, "Culture Contacts and Educational Transfer," seeks to illuminate a particular aspect of educational change. As a result of contacts between cultures, there is often a transfer of institutions and practices from one society to another, and features of indigenous schooling are adapted to newly created social conditions.

The selections in Parts V and VI, dealing with the religious and linguistic aspects of schooling, could easily have fitted in other sections. Religion and language, being mediated in social interaction, are bound to the topics in other parts. Yet the significance of religion and language transcends economic, political, and sociological boundaries. Insofar as religion has metaphysical implications and language is essentially an organization of symbols, they have a distinctiveness which is more than merely social. Moreover, as social activities, religion and language are often viewed as distinct cultural units.

Part One

Culture Contact and Educational Transfer

The school is an agent in shaping people's values and preparing them for satisfactory participation in society. However, schools do not reflect immutable goals; they are as susceptible to change as other institutions. The school is a recipient as well as a promoter of social, political, and economic changes.

Fundamental changes in the goals of a society often arise from contact with outside cultures. Contact can be gradual, originating from trade, migration, and simple communication, or it can be revolutionary, resulting from war or colonial conquest. When gradual, contact encourages social and technological change. When revolutionary, it tends, at least initially, not so much to generate positive attitudes toward change as to impose cultural transformations.

Inasmuch as education is susceptible to culture contact and change, methods and patterns of schooling are frequently transferred from one society to another. In turn, such educational transfer tends to stimulate other institutional changes. A discussion of the transfer of educational forms can touch on questions of political power, nationalism, economic growth, social equality, cultural integration, religion, and language. In this respect, the opening essay, by Andreas Kazamias, serves to introduce the volume as well as the section. It describes how two countries, Greece and Turkey, experienced parallel lines of social and political development, and how differences in tradition, ideology, and resources have contributed to disparities in the tempo and character of their development. Kazamias views change and development generally as reflected in events surrounding education and illustrates how aspects of schooling can be "borrowed" or imposed. He illustrates also how the school "systems" of certain nations tend to become referents in satisfying the aspirations of other nations for "better" schooling.

Although transfer can be predominantly borrowed or predominantly imposed, the mixture of the two methods can be considerable. Erwin H. Epstein suggests that an ambivalent mixture is apt to arise when one country maintains an uneasy dominance over another, as when the metropole is self-conscious about forcing a transfer of its institutions, and the subordinate country is not passive in the face of imposition. In Puerto Rico, an

American-style school system was superimposed soon after occupation in 1898, but conflicting aims of American policy makers and resistances to change by Puerto Ricans have resulted in some aspects of education being adapted to Hispanic tradition and in a curious truce between American and Latin ideas of schooling.

Uganda also has experienced a colonial type of educational transfer. In that country, however, the metropole sustained transfer more resolutely than in the case of Puerto Rico, and the population rather more passively accepted the institutions of the dominant power. Yet although transfer has occurred less as a compromise between cultures in Uganda than in Puerto Rico, the reception given new ways of education has been no less ambivalent. According to F. Musgrove, Uganda secondary school boys tend to view schooling as a means by which whites can consolidate their ascendancy. While they esteem their British-like education, they are also suspicious of it. They often believe, for example, that "they are taught English so that they can more easily understand and readily obey the orders of Englishmen."

Puerto Rico and Uganda exemplify cases in which transfer occurs rather abruptly in a kind of vacuum, in the absence of long and cherished educational traditions. However, abrupt transfer has been attempted even when the recipient country has had an established and respected educational history. As Robert Lawson suggests, education in Germany immediately after the Second World War was influenced by two powers, Britain and the United States, that vied to impose their own views of schooling. Significantly, educational reorientation had a lasting influence only insofar as it provided for a flow of information from the outside world and reawakened early progressive trends. Lawson concludes that where transfer was in terms of a particularly British or American characteristic, there was little residual effect after outside controls were removed.

These essays suggest the variety of ways educational transfer can occur. They suggest also some of the key considerations that are relevant to any assessment of transfer: the resolve of dominant powers to impose their ways, the receptivity of recipient societies to outside influences, and the educational tradition and prestige of both parties. Most important, these essays illustrate the need to view education not merely as integral to a particular culture and its past but as susceptible to innovation introduced from without.

Transfer and Modernity in Greek and Turkish Education

ANDREAS M. KAZAMIAS

ANY STUDY of education in Greece and Turkey in terms of the concepts of transfer and modernization must necessarily set up certain arbitrary historical limits. Here we shall be concerned mainly with the emergence and development of Greece and Turkey as nation-states since the second half of the eighteenth century. Greece emerged as a nation-state after its War of Independence in 1821-1829; but the "challenge to modernity" was manifested during the half-century or so preceding the decisive event of the revolution. The process of modernization in Turkey, culminating in the Young Turk Revolution of 1908 and the Atatürk Revolution of 1919-1923, for all meaningful purposes began with the reforms of Sultan Selim III (1789-1807). In both cases, educational change or readjustment, as cause and effect of the larger process of socio-political and cultural change, was influenced by foreign ideas and institutions. In Greece the major foreign influences came from France and Germany; in Turkey, from France.

THE TRADITIONAL SETTINGS: AN OVERVIEW

Prior to the attainment of statehood, both Greece and Turkey were parts of the amorphous, multi-racial, and multi-religious entity known as the Ottoman Empire. Ottoman power and authority, centering in Constantinople (later Istanbul), were wielded by the Sultan and his palace clique and stretched over the multiple regions and provinces of the Empire through an administrative and military bureaucracy. As a province of that Empire, mainland Greece was administered in this fashion. Greek Christians (in essence, virtually all ethnic Greeks) constituted one of the several religious communities, known as *millets* (nation or religion), of the Empire. As such, their religious and local affairs were regulated by the Greek Orthodox Patriarch of Constantinople through the Orthodox hierarchy and the local parishes. There the Greeks had considerable autonomy in the religious, educational, and social spheres and in local administration.

There were some general similarities in the social and cultural backgrounds of the Greeks and the Turks in the decades prior to the advent of modernity. First, they were primarily rural, many of them in fact living in isolated and self-sustaining small villages. Second, this rural population was engaged largely in subsistence agriculture. Third, religion, both as doctrine and an organized institution, exerted an important influence on the society in general, and on education in particular. And fourth, both the Greeks and the Turks valued education and accorded the educated a favored position in the society, although the majority of the people were illiterate or semi-educated, and there were sharp variations in the educational level of those who went to schools.

But there were also significant differences. The Greeks in general were unwilling subjects, while the Ottoman Turks were the masters. The latter were Moslems, while the former were Christians. By and large the Ottomans were military leaders and administrators, while the urban Greeks cultivated their entrepreneurial and commercial interests. In some parts of the Empire, notably Constantinople, the Greeks virtually controlled banking, commerce, and small business. Moreover while the Turks, for religious, political, and historical reasons, considered European ideas and culture alien and threatening, the enlightened Greeks, despite some qualifications, indentified themselves with Western civilization. What contacts the Ottomans had with Europe were largely of a diplomatic or military nature with little, if any, appreciable impact upon their way of life, institutions of government, or culture. In contrast, numerous Greek communities existed in all the major European capitals and cities, maintaining lines of communication with the Greeks of Anatolia, Constantinople, and the mainland. Greek contacts with the Western world were further strengthened by certain Greek subjects, the so-called *Phanariotēs,* who, because of their education and socio-economic status, had attained high administrative positions—dragomans of the Porte, diplomatic emissaries in foreign countries, rulers of principalities under Ottoman suzerainty—in the Ottoman political hierarchy. Further, the Christian character of European countries provided cultural links between their peoples and the Greeks, which were reinforced by a common anti-Turkish attitude. The Venetians made frequent forays into the Greek mainland and the islands, while the Russians, in the guise of Orthodox redeemers, constantly harassed the Sultans, aroused the Greeks, and sprinkled the Empire with imperial agents.

When one probes beneath the general similarities of the influence of religion and the value attached to education, one discerns variations in the functions of Orthodoxy and Islam and the schools. The Orthodox patriarchs, bishops, and priests were both spiritual saviours and evangelists, and custodians of "nationality" or ethnicity (Greekness), as well as of "national" culture. Under the Ottomans, the Orthodox Church, in addition to its religious functions, carried the burden of the entire Greek patrimony. The *ulema,* the *mollas,* and the *imams*—the Ottoman religious functionaries—on the other hand, were subjected to the authority of the Sultan-Caliph, the temporal and spiritual leader of all the Moslem faithful. The learning of the *ulema* was mostly Arabic and Persian, not Turkish, and Islam was not associated with "nationality" or ethnicity.

Both religious institutions exerted a profound influence in education. The Ottoman Moslem hierarchy had complete control over educational facilities, the content of the curriculum, and the general orientation of the schools (the *mektebs* and *medreses*), except in the case of the famous Palace School, which was located within the Grand Seraglio of Constantinople. In the lower schools (the *mektebs*), religious instruction, centering in the Koran, formed the staple of the curriculum. Hence the *mektebs* were generally known as Koranic schools. In the higher schools (*medreses*), religion and religious law were the main subjects taught, but Persian, Arabic, astronomy, natural science, mathematics, and even medicine were also included. Both levels of schools were attached to mosques; they were supported by pious foundations (*Evkaf*); and their teachers were members of the religious institution. The Koranic schools provided the rudiments of knowledge, but, in large part they were agencies for the "socialization" of the child in the teachings of the Islamic faith. The *medreses* trained the religious leaders (the *ulema*) of the Empire.

Similarly, the Greek Orthodox Church controlled much of the education of the Greeks in the Empire. Schools attached to the Patriarchate in the Phanar Section of Constantinople, notably the Great National School (*Hē Megalē tou Genous Scholē*), were regarded as the training grounds of the intellectual and religious elites, as well as of many of the school teachers, both of the captive Greeks and of the diaspora. Local communities or parishes in greater Constantinople and in most cities and towns of Anatolia and the Greek mainland maintained "common" (*koina*) and/or hellenic (*hellenika*) schools from church contributions and private donations. In the villages the local priest was also a teacher.

Important differences between the Ottoman Islamic schools and those of the Greek Orthodox *millet* lay in the type of instruction given and in their general outlook. The many years of contact and interaction between Byzantine Greek and Ottoman Turk inevitably affected certain cultural patterns of both. But Christianity and Islam were diametrically opposed to each other and remained so throughout the Ottoman period of Greek history (1453-1821). Also the cultural heritages of the two societies differed. Since the Ottoman overlords allowed autonomy in education, the Greek schools sought to imbue the young with the Orthodox principles and precepts; in addition, they taught the Greek language, Greek philosophy, and Greek literature. Although an oversimplification, one could say that education in the Greek schools, in contrast to that in the Islamic, opened up wider intellectual and cultural horizons for the children. One thing is certain, however. Greek education was "dysfunctional" insofar as Ottoman social and cultural cohesion were concerned. The movement for national independence from the Ottomans, which culminated in the revolution of the 1820's and set Greece on the road to social and political modernization, found ready followers and leaders among the priests and other products of such Greek schools. As the Greeks have always believed, the schools had kept the ashes of the Greek feeling for ultimate self-determination and national liberation burning throughout the long period of Ottoman rule.

THE GREEK EXPERIENCE

The Challenge of Modernity: Neo-Hellenic Revival. The pre-independence period of Greek modernization was influenced by a concatenation of forces and events external, and internal. Of the external conditions, there was first a cultural and intellectual revival stemming largely from Greek emigrés and from the several Greek communities in European cities. Intellectual emigrés, through word and deed, sought to rejuvenate Greek national *paideia* (the ideals of Greek culture), and provide a sense of national continuity and identity. Nurtured in French Jacobinism and the spirit of the Enlightenment, they exhorted the Greeks to regain their liberty through armed revolt, recapture the spirit of their illustrious ancestors, and "resurrect" the Greek "nation."

A second major external influence was the power struggle among the major European countries for influence in Southeastern Europe and the Eastern Mediterranean. In the face of Ottoman decay and the possible disintegration of the Empire, Russia, in particular, wanted the lion's share of the spoils. National independence movements were aided and abetted, and Russia assumed the protector's role over their downtrodden Greek coreligionists. She provided refuge for Greek emigrés; it was through Catherine the Great's encouragement and military support that the first abortive uprising of 1770 took place; and it was in Odessa that the secret revolutionary society known as *Philikē Hetaireia* was first organized in 1814.

Of the internal conditions, there was first a weakening of the Sultan's power over the provincial governors, in the Peloponnese and Epirus in particular, and over the local government authorities, who were mostly Greek. Insurrectionist plots became more frequent. On the open seas, naval units manned by Greeks virtually controlled the Aegean. Second, there was an unprecedented economic and commercial vitality in village, cities, and ports on the Greek mainland and certain of the islands. Villages in Thessaly (e.g., Ambelakia), the Volos region north of Athens, and the Zagori region in Epirus prospered in local manufacturing, and became commercial thoroughfares between Greece and Germany, Venice, Constantinople, even Moscow. The volume of shipping in Salonika, and such islands as Hydra and Spetsai, off the coast of the Argolis region in the Peloponnese, increased considerably. After the French Revolution, the Greek merchant marine became the commercial carriers of most shipping in the Eastern Mediterranean and the Black Sea.

Such political and economic developments affected the traditional socio-economic structure of the Greek *millet.* The clerical hierarchy around the Patriarch of Constantinople and the *Phanariotē* aristocracy continued to occupy a central position in the general power structure. But a local landed aristocracy rooted in the Greek soil began to emerge. With this also, a new "middle" class of cosmopolitan merchants was being formed. Moreover, the lines of communication between isolated rural villages and towns were widened.

Cutting across the boundaries of Western Europe, Russia, the Greek mainland, Constantinople, and Anatolia, was what might be called an awakening of Greek national *paideia*. The intellectual and cultural revival discussed earlier was accompanied by a marked increase in the number of schools established, particularly in the commercially active cities, towns, and villages. Schools, literary societies, and commerce became channels of communication of ideas of national revival. By 1821, when the war of independence broke out, a new generation of Greeks had come of age, influenced by the French revolutionary ideology and the new ideas of the Enlightenment. Their immediate aim was clear: independence. What was not clear, however, was what the political and social organization of an independent Greek state should be. After 1829 the task was to restructure social and political institutions in order to adjust them to the new functions that national independence had created. It is at this juncture that the German influence, especially in education, began.

Education in the New State: The Bavarian Plan. The institutional structure, the ideas and ideals that emerged in Greek education after independence reflected a variety of traditions and influences. First there were the interrelated ideologies of Orthodoxy and Hellenism which pervaded the cultural revival discussed above and the Greek concept of nationalism. To be a member of the new state and to be educated as such implied immersion in the Greek heritage, chiefly the classical, and the doctrines of Orthodox Christianity. In its institutional expression, however, the emerging concept of Greek *paideia* was colored by the nineteenth-century German pattern. This was introduced into the new state immediately after a monarchical system of government was imposed, with young prince Otto of Bavaria as the first king.

Under the influence of Maurer, one of the three Bavarian regents for young Otto, elementary education was declared compulsory for children between the ages of five and twelve and the responsibility of local municipalities. The elementary law, enacted in 1834, bore strong resemblance to the French Guizot Law of 1833. The secondary education law, passed in 1836, bore the imprint of the German system. It provided for two successive "cycles" of schools: a three-year *hellenic* school (grades 5-7) similar to the German *Lateinschule,* and a four-year *gymnasion* (grades 8-11), which was a watered down version of the German *Gymnasium.* The hellenic school prepared for the *gymnasion* and for the "business of life"; the *gymnasion* mainly for higher studies in the Othonian University at Athens, established by royal decree in 1837. The university was modelled on the Northern German universities and several of the professors (all of whom were appointed by the King) were Germans. It consisted of four faculties—theology, philosophy, law, and medicine—and the sequence of studies, indeed the very content, was similar to that of the German prototypes. Colored by contemporary German scholarship and neo-humanism, education in the new state became solidly grounded in the classical literary studies. Classical Greek, for example, was included even in the curriculum of the elementary schools; in the *hellenic* schools and the *gymnasia* it constituted by far the largest portion of weekly hours spent.

In matters of administration also the evolving system bore the imprint of Western influences. During the Ottoman period, there was considerable "decentralization" and local autonomy in educational provision. Under the "Bavarian Plan" authority shifted, and education became a state responsibility, although neither the compulsory attendance law nor state control and supervision became effective until later in the century.

Continuing a tradition going back to the Byzantine period, Orthodoxy was declared the established religion of the new state. With the state stepping into the educational sphere, the Church's role in that field was considerably restricted, although by no means eliminated. Religious instruction (cathechism) continued to be required in all schools; each school day began with a collective act of worship; and students were required to attend church services on Sundays and on other religious holidays. In many localities the priest continued to be the teacher (a priest was also called *daskalos*, i.e., teacher), schooling was carried out in the church, and the local bishop was on the "school committee." The position of the Greek Orthodox Church as a social organization was much more complex; and, in view of its significance in the development of modern Greece, merits further comment.

As mentioned above, by tradition and historical circumstances the scope of activities of the Greek Church extended beyond the religious domain into the educational, political, and cultural spheres. The Church played an active part in the neo-hellenic national revival, and priests carried banners and guns during the revolution. Thus the Church became an integral part of the evolving concepts of Greek "nationality" and culture. To use a modern term, it constituted a powerful interest group in the affairs of the new nation. Although, unlike Ottoman Islam which will be discussed later, it was a "Western" Church, it did not accept all the Western features of the neo-hellenic revival. For example, the Patriarch of Constantinople (Gregory V) condemned the French Revolution and in a special encyclical (1819) criticized strongly the introduction of mathematico-scientific studies into the schools.

True education, according to the Church, must be directed towards the spiritual and moral development of youth. For the Greek youth, in particular, love of God and country were inseparable and should be the foundation of all education. The emphasis upon "man rather than matter," coupled with its traditional ethnic role, placed the Church in close alliance with the classical national humanists. Both groups considered the non-material aspects of man's nature as unchanging and eternal, and more worthy of cultivation. In education this meant greater emphasis upon literary and religious studies than upon technical, scientific, or practical ones. The Church reinforced the entrenchment of classical Greek as the staple of the curriculum for another reason; it was closer to the Church language, i.e., that of the New Testament. Finally, the Church allied itself with those who supported the purist form of the modern Greek language, an issue which has plagued modern Greek *paideia* up to the present time.

"Diglossy," as the issue is commonly known, had its roots prior to the revolution. It has meant two linguistic forms, the pure (*katharevousa*) and the popular (*demotikē* or demotic). A rather simplified description would be that the former was closer to ancient and New Testament Greek while the latter combined elements of popular speech, ballads, and folklore. Despite the fact that the majority of the people spoke in the demotic—the *katharevousa* was written but rarely spoken—and some of the noted cultural revivalists wrote in it, soon after independence the pure form was declared the official language of the new state and the medium of instruction in schools.

The Bavarian Plan created the structure and the mechanism for the formation of an intellectual elite with a common training and common ideologies who gradually assumed the guardianship of modern Greek culture and development. Nourished mostly in the classical literary humanistic tradition and Orthodox Christianity this modern Greek intelligentsia solidified itself into a powerful political and social reference group which articulated the goals and ideals of Greek *paideia* and for the most part controlled access into leadership positions. This continued to be the case even after the expulsion of King Otto (1862) and the emergence of a purely indigenous leadership. In its structure, functions, and orientations, the Bavarian Plan—from elementary school to the University—remained essentially unchanged until 1929.

Stress and Consolidation. With the accession of another stranger as king, George I (1863-1913) of the Danish Royal House, we enter another phase of Greek development. In the political realm this was the period of ultranationalism, internal upheavals, intermittent wars, territorial expansion, victories, and defeats. An underlying ideological motive of the period up to 1923 was the so-called "Grand Idea" (*Megalē Idea*), the idea of ultimately creating a Greek state with Constantinople as its capital, that would include all ethnic Greeks, particularly the many thousands living under the Ottomans. In the economic sphere, up to 1920 the economy remained fundamentally a small agricultural-commercial economy. Manufacturing, limited largely to small domestic industries, occupied a rather minor place. Over 70 percent of the population was rural and agricultural (small farmers and shepherds). Yet, considering where it was in mid-nineteenth century, the Greek economy did register a degree of progress. By the First World War, manufacturing contributed about 10 percent of the national income and towns such as Athens, Patras, Volos, and Piraeus grew to be important commercial outlets for the agricultural products of the hinterland.

Developments in education were uneven. The dramatic growth of the population—within 50 years it had more than tripled—offset gains that had been made in the literacy rate and school attendance. The overwhelming majority of the newcomers, acquired through territorial expansion, were illiterate. At the International Conference of Vienna in 1873 Greece won the second prize for school attendance and Western Europeans praised the Greeks' love for education. But by the First World War Greece fell far behind most European countries in rates of literacy and school attendance. In general, schooling continued to be essentially literary and classical and to perform the same educational and social functions as previously. Indeed during this period there was greater emphasis placed upon the "archaic" and purist aspects of language and culture. This has been described as the era of Atticism, namely, the unadulterated imitation of the ancient Attic models. But there was also a most significant reaction to Atticism, which was destined to have far-reaching social and educational consequences. This was Demoticism, a movement which was part of the *diglossy* issue referred to above but which transcended linguistic boundaries.

Demoticism received its impetus from Greek intellectuals residing abroad. In a sense, therefore, it illustrates another type of cultural transfer. Its turning point is often taken to be 1888, when Psycharis (living in Paris) published his famous book *The Journey*. In the introduction Psycharis wrote:

> Two things are required for a nation to become a nation: extension of its territorial boundaries, and the creation of its own literature. When it demonstrates that it knows what the value of the popular language is and when it is not ashamed of this linguistic form, then we'll see that it has become a nation.[1]

Ostensibly the purpose of Demoticism was to vindicate the value of the popular language as a linguistic medium and to elevate its position and prestige. But as Psycharis implies, Demoticism was also envisaged as a medium of social integration and nation-building. It was felt that the emphasis on classicism and the pure form of modern Greek to the exclusion of the demotic, which was the spoken language and the language of modern literature, created cultural and social splits and thus inhibited Greek national development. Such cleavages were exacerbated by the fact that the schools ignored completely the popular tradition and sought to transmit the heritage through an archaic, and to many, a rather artificial medium. Education, in short, was not grounded in the living experience of the people. Demoticist pedagogues attacked the content of the curriculum, particularly the literary aspects. And their followers produced versions of the Bible and the Greek classics in the popular form.

The counter reaction to Demoticism was fierce and bloody. The movement was attacked by clerics, politicians, and intellectuals. The Church branded it as an expression of atheism and as a threat to the pillars of Greek culture, namely, religion, language, and nationalism. Similar accusations were made by the powerful University of Athens. And when the Bolshevik Revolution erupted in Russia in 1917, Demoticism was linked by some with communism and nihilism.

The Demoticists did not recoil. An aggressive group of educators and intellectuals, supported tacitly by the Liberal government of Venizelos, was able to push through Parliament the reforms of 1917 whereby the demotic was declared the language of the elementary schools. Since then the fortunes of Demoticism in the schools have ebbed and flowed. The ranks of its supporters have thickened and unquestionably the demotic language has dominated literature. But the pure form has continued to be the official language of the state; the purists are deeply entrenched in the University of Athens in which all secondary school teachers are trained, and they continue to draw strong support from the Church and from leading intellectuals. In 1964, through the influence of leading demoticist educators, the demotic language was declared the language of elementary schools (grades 1-6) and was accorded parity of status at all other levels of education.

After the defeat of the Greeks by the Turks in 1923 and the consequent collapse of the Grand Idea, Greece and Turkey agreed to an exchange of populations. For Greece this meant an influx of more than one million ethnic Greeks from Anatolia. Some of these refugees possessed technical and entrepreneurial skills which boosted the Greek economy. But many of them were untrained, illiterate, and destitute. The gains to the Greek economy were offset by vast expenditures to rehabilitate them, to provide houses, schools, hospitals, and similar facilities. Once again the consequences of political events called for changes in the educational system. As a result, a major educational reform package was introduced between 1929 and 1932. Heretofore, the general system of education was to consist of six-year elementary schools (general and vocational), and secondary schools (six-year classical or practical scientific *gymnasia,* lower teacher training schools, two-year *semi-gymnasia,* and four-year middle schools for girls). Sporadic educational reforms were initiated in the following years, but it was not until the late 1950's that serious efforts were made at change.

Post-War Developments. In the post-war decades it was felt that the schools were not geared to the demands made upon them by the changing structure of the economy and by the general goals of socio-economic modernization. Criticisms were levelled against the *gymnasion* which dominated post-elementary education and controlled access into the universities. It was contended that the *gymnasion* perpetuated a narrow conception of humanistic education (exclusively classical and literary); that because of its curriculum emphasis it contributed to unemployment and underemployment among its graduates; that it channeled a disproportionate number of students into already crowded university faculties, e.g., law, theology, and philosophy, and thereby into already crowded occupations; and that it stultified the development of scientific, technical, and vocational education. Technical and vocational education in turn were found to be deplorably lacking. In general it was felt that if Greece were to develop economically, it must pay more attention to the production of technical skills and redress existing educational imbalances and bottlenecks. This climate of opinion led to a series of reports and measures of which three were perhaps the most significant: (a) a report issued in 1958 by a special non-partisan education committee, (b) seven pieces of legislation passed in 1959, and (c) the Education Act of 1964.

One of the novel features of the recent reform movement is the attempt to view education not solely in moral, spiritual, nationalistic, and cultural terms, but in socio-economic terms as well. Economic development plans, and manpower studies and reports by foreign experts stressed education's role in economic growth and development, and education as a form of investment. The 1964 reforms went even further.

> This law (decree) stems from the conviction that the basis and the guarantee of a true democracy rest on equality—without discrimination—of all citizens to acquire the benefits of education. There is no worse form of social inequality than an educational system which is the privilege of the well-to-do. . . . More than that, it would be injurious to the welfare of the nation if its human resources—the most precious "capital"—remained unexploited and inactive through lack of education. At a time when Greece is facing stiff competition in the international economic arena, she has only one sure hope for national survival: through education to equip her citizens with the means to exploit her natural resources and to develop the material and intellectual civilization of the country.[2]

All reform plans stressed the need for a more coordinated and expanded system of technical and vocational education. It was assumed that the burden on education of the techno-economic needs of the country rested with the development of technical and vocational skills in schools.

There was little controversy over this aspect of the reform movement. What opened up a Pandora's box of vested interests, conflicting ideologies, and sheer pedantry were the proposals for the reorganization of schools and changes in the curriculum. The supporters of classicism objected to any curtailment of the study of ancient Greek and Latin in the secondary schools, particularly for students preparing for the universities. And they were extremely critical of the 1964 Act's provision to have ancient Greek texts taught in translation in the first stage of secondary education (grades 7-9, now called the *gymnasion* stage).

The 1964 reforms were justified not only on the principle of economic efficiency but also on that of social justice or equity. Free, compulsory, and uniform education was extended to the age of 15 and from there on a diversified pattern was established to meet the varied interests and abilities of students. Critics found these provisions premature and unrealistic. Some went even further and accused the government of conspiring to set up a popular cultural revolution similar to those of countries behind the Iron Curtain.

The movement to alter the educational system and to bring it in line with techno-economic needs may be seen in the context of the world-wide impact of technology and the world-wide push for modernization. Greece's connection with NATO and its recent association with the European Common Market have made policy makers more aware of inadequacies in the socio-economic structure as well as in skill and manpower development. Economic planning and "human resource development" acquired a more important place in public policy after 1960 when the Center for Economic Research (supported by the Greek Government, the United States Mission in Greece, and the Ford and Rockefeller Foundations) was set up. Foreign scholars, including American-trained economists, participated in the activities of the Center and the formulation of development plans. Through Greece's association with the Organization for Economic Cooperation and Development, Greek and European economic and educational experts cooperated in research studies, reports, and memoranda. On numerous occasions educational reformers drew much of their material from the findings and suggestions of such enterprises. But on other burning educational issues such as curriculum, language, humanistic education, and organization of schools the interplay of foreign or external and indigenous forces was more subtle and complex. Intellectuals and political leaders who played key roles in the formulation of plans and policies were products of what may be called the continental European tradition of intellectualism and classical humanism in education, which was fostered in the University of Athens. Their models, where analogies were drawn, were the German and the French, not the English or American. Some of them had studied in German or French universities, and their views were supported by the Church hierarchy. By and large these people were critical of attempts to curtail the classical aspects of the secondary schools, or to establish parity of status for the two language forms.

It is difficult to put all the more "progressive" reformers into one category, or to identify the influences upon them. Some of them studied in the same Greek schools as the "conservatives." Yet one can discern the impact of non-continental European ideas on their thinking. Educational psychologists introduced the work of American and English writers; Antonakaki, who played an important part in the 1959 reforms, was clearly influenced by American administrative theory; and Papanoutsos, the architect of the 1964 law, sought to combine American and European ideas and patterns. Based on rather fragmentary and impressionistic evidence, one could say that since the Second World War American influences have made large inroads into several aspects of Greek culture. English has challenged

French as a major foreign language and as a symbol of intellectual eliteness. With the increased American tourist traffic to Greece, the various cultural exchange programs between the two countries, and the greater number of Greek students in American universities, one can predict that the transfer of ideas will gather greater momentum in the years to come.

THE TURKISH EXPERIENCE

Unlike Greece, the Ottoman modernization may be looked at as a process of reforming certain features of the existing polity. In the face of Western superiority in the political and military spheres, reforming Sultans and their followers sought to introduce Western techniques, institutions, and ideas to strengthen the Empire and to consolidate the dissipated authority and efficiency of the government.

The Challenge of Modernity. Ottoman modernization started with the military institutions. But gradually it filtered into other spheres, particularly the administrative apparatus of the Empire and education. A major aim was to consolidate the powers of the central government and generally to establish a more efficient bureaucratic machinery. This was done by the elimination of certain traditional institutions (e.g., the feudal military fiefs and the Janissaries); the modification of others (the placing of *Evkaf* under the jurisdiction of the government and the reform of ministerial departments); and the establishment of new ones (the Translation Chamber for the training of government interpreters; police, health, and postal services). During the period of "reorganization" or "regulation," known as the *Tanzimat* (1836-1876), provincial administration was revamped along the French pattern of departments and directors; new legal codes affecting land tenure, commerce, finance, and justice were introduced; and the two famous Rescripts of 1839 and 1856, aimed at the regeneration of government, the nation, and the empire, were promulgated. The whole movement for change culminated in the proclamation of the unprecedented but short-lived Constitution of 1876.

An integral part of the general modernization movement was education. Efforts were made to bring education more under the authority or supervision of the state, and new types of schools were established. These included upper primary or lower secondary schools, such as the *rüşdiyes* and *idadis;* special schools such as the School for Justice Education; higher educational establishments such as the College of the Valideh Sultanah; the School for Secular Learning; the Teachers' College; and the two famous schools for the training of civil servants, namely, the *Mülkiye* (1859) and the *Mektebi Sultani,* also known as the Galatasaray Lycée (1868). One must also include the new military schools and training centers, as well as the Translation Bureau as important novel educational institutions.

In all these institutional innovations, the predominant foreign influence was Western Europe, especially France. The reforms were infused with the general Enlightenment idea of progress or improvement through purposeful change; with the post-French revolutionary spirit of secularism, political rights, and government by law, and with a more "worldly" view of education. Also by the third quarter of the nineteenth century, such concepts as freedom (*hürriyet*), fatherland (*vatan*), and constitutionalism were advocated.

The reforms associated with the military institution had far-reaching educational implications. The new military schools (naval, medical, engineering, music, military sciences) established during and after Sultan Selim III's reign (1789-1807), provided a type of education that went beyond mere training in new combat methods, tactics, and techniques. In a society where higher education was dominated by the religious *medreses,* the military schools exemplified a radically novel conception of higher learning. They included Western languages and sciences in their curriculum. Western experts were appointed as instructors. Translations of Western books were used. And in many instances the medium of instruction was French.

As a result of the military reforms a new group of military officers gradually emerged. Being centrally located in the power structure, they were able to challenge the authority of traditional elites (the despotic Sultan Abdül-Hamid, the conservative members of the bureaucracy, and the *ulema*). In the end, many of them formed the activist corps of the leaders of the young Turk and the Atatürk revolutions.

When one turns to other forms of education, the picture is more complex. Traditionally education in the sense of schooling was a religious and communal affair under the control of the *ulema.* Despite some efforts to bring it more under the aegis of the state, "primary" schooling remained communal and religious until the demise of the Empire and the establishment of the Republic. But there were changes in other types or levels of education, and alternative kinds of training were established. "Barracks schools," based on Lancaster's monitorial system (introduced into Turkey via the Greeks, the Armenians, and American missionaries) for the education of soldiers and officers, were initiated under Mahmud II's reign. More significant perhaps were the new types of schools referred to earlier. These institutions were either completely or in part secular. In addition to such traditional subjects as Arabic, Persian, and religion, in varying degrees they taught such subjects as French, political science (economics), geometry, algebra, physics, natural history, Ottoman literature, drawing, and music.

The lycée at Galatasaray provides one of the clearest illustrations of the ramifications of culture contacts and the transfer of an educational institution into the Ottoman Islamic society from the West. The idea of establishing a Western-modelled *lycée* was conceived by Abdül-Aziz, the first Sultan ever to visit France and for that matter Western Europe, and by a cosmopolitan group of high officials headed by Ali Pasha and Fuad Pasha. All three were impressed by the French system of education and were intimately acquainted with French culture. Like the other new schools, the establishment of Galatasaray in 1868 was closely linked with the reforms in the government and the bureaucracy. Its main purpose was to prepare young men for the new positions in all the branches of the public (civil) service.

The Galatasaray was the most secular and Western of all novel educational establishments. M. Bourée, the French Minister of Public Instruction, helped in planning the curriculum. Subjects included French, the elements of Latin needed for the study of law, European and Ottoman geography, mathematics, cosmography, elements of jurisprudence, physics, chemistry, elements of political economy, rhetoric, geometric drawing, ethics, practical mechanics, medicine and pharmacy, Turkish, and Greek. During the first years of the school's operation, French was the language of instruction; and Frenchmen, including the director, were imported as teachers.

Implicit in the general orientation of the curriculum of the lycée and of other new schools, was a new Western conception of learning. In the traditional schools learning entailed the acquisition of knowledge of God and of man's duties to God. It was designated by the word *'ilm;* and its sole guardians and transmitters were the Ulema. The new type of education, designated by the word *maarif,* entailed "a process of becoming acquainted with things unknown." The word *fen* ("science," art, practical skill) entered the educational vocabulary. And together with French and other modern subjects, it also opened up new careers and new avenues for social mobility.

Underlying the establishment of the Galatasaray lycée was the belief, shared by many Ottoman modernizers, that the "re-formation" and salvation of the Empire rested on the creation of a multi-racial and multi-religious polity which would grant equal rights to all. The social composition of the school was cosmopolitan. It included Greeks, Armenians, Moslem Turks, Roman Catholics, Bulgarians, and Jews. Its first directors were non-Turks. This policy of pan-Ottomanism, which allowed, among other things, the emergence of several foreign-run schools, including the American Robert College, was of tremendous importance in the movement toward change and modernity. On the one hand, it reinforced the emergence of a new type of élite. In the opinion of some Turcologists, the internal struggle for modernization was won when the balance of power was tipped in favor of such élites. Some have gone even farther and have credited the new Western-oriented schools with a determining role in this victory and in the emergence of modern Turkey. On the other hand, pan-Ottomanism allowed separatist movements which operated against the realization of a cohesive polity. The Greeks and the Armenians, for example, identified themselves with their own national and ethnic entities, not with Ottoman cosmopolitanism, and this was reflected and reinforced in their schools. The notion of a *Turkish* nationalism or of a Turkish national culture was as yet absent from the concept of pan-Ottomanism. It was not until Atatürk and the proclamation of the Republic (1923) that the more circumscribed concept of Turkish nationalism became a motivating and determining influence in the building of present-day Turkey.

Despite initial criticisms and mixed reactions, the lycée at Galatasaray quickly became a favored institution for the upper strata of the Ottoman society. By the end of the nineteenth century, in its character, content, and function, the Galatasaray epitomized the Ottoman emerging concept of secondary education and culture. Other schools known as *sultanis* were patterned after it, having as their primary function the education of an intellectual élite who would ultimately be the leaders of the society. In content, a lycée or *sultani* education was based on the concept of general culture (*genel kültur*), similar to the French *culture générale,* and largely defined in terms of humanistic studies. Moreover, in the minds of articulate Ottoman ideologists like Ziya Gökalp and Ismail Hakki Baltacioğlu *sultanis* were perceived as contributing to national and nationalistic goals.

The educational functions of the *sultani* and its role in the training of an élite imbued with a national Turkish consciousness were carried over and reinforced during the republican period. In the educational reconstruction that followed the Atatürk revolution, the *sultanis* were renamed lycées (*lises*) and have since formed the upper cycle of secondary education (grades 9-11).

Ambivalences and Bifurcations. The impact of Westernization and secularization created conflicts, ambivalences, and bifurcations. Opposition to innovation was most solidly evident among the Ulema, the guardians of religion, education, and the ideological and cultural foundations of the society. By and large, the Ulema reacted against all attempts to Westernize or secularize the government, the bureaucracy, the legal codes, learning, and the schools. Most of them clung to the religious conception of schooling and learning. The reformers did not intervene in the Ulema's control of primary education, and the *mekteb* remained basically unchanged until the republican period. Innovation and secularization in formal education were centered around the post-primary level. As a result, an educational bifurcation developed: the new state-regulated or state-supervised schools referred to above, and the traditional Ulema-controlled *medreses.*

In the main, the *medreses* were not affected by the reform movement that spearheaded the establishment of other schools; like the *mektebs* they maintained their traditional religious orientation and functions until the Atatürk revolution. Up to this transfer of power, the *medreses* continued to educate a large number of students—larger in fact than the other schools—who either could not gain access into the more secular establishments, or preferred the education provided in the *medreses.* In the face of clearly perceived differences in the social and economic rewards that accrued from the two types of institutions—the occupational and living expectations of the *medrese* graduate were bleak compared to the graduate of a *sultani* or an *idadi*—many *medrese* graduates became dissatisfied and joined the ranks of deracinated "intellectuals." Nevertheless, despite exceptions, the products of the *medreses,* the so-called *softas,* largely represented tradition, conservatism, anti-Westernism, and reaction. In contrast, the graduates of the civil schools [e.g., the *Mülkiye* (the civil service school), the Galatasaray lycée, the *sultanis*, and the *idadis*] were exposed to Westernism, secularism, and in time constitutionalism, and even Turkish nationalism. Some of them became activist leaders in the overthrow of the reactionary despotism of Abdül-Hamid (1876-1908). The majority, by joining the civil bureaucracy, the professions, and similar "middle class" strata, helped in the creation of an important lower élite group which sanctioned change.

This educational bifurcation, which was both an effect and a cause of a split among élites, affected a very small portion of the population of the Empire. Indeed it should be stressed that the entire Westernization-modernization movement hardly touched the masses. This overwhelming proportion of Ottoman Turks remained illiterate, mostly isolated in rural villages, pristine in modes of thinking and earning a living, politically non-participant, and religiously tied to superstition and a folk type of Islam. "Élite-mass" and "urban-rural" divisions signified momentous dichotomies in the Ottoman society and culture.

Even among the "modernizing" élites, there were variations in ideology and in the perception of what shape a reformed Ottoman polity and society should take. We have already referred to Pan-Ottomanism. Other "pan-movements" included Pan-Turanianism, Pan-Turkism, and Pan-Islamism. Pan-Turanianism envisaged the cultural unity of all Moslem Turks and Christians who claimed their descent from the land of Turan; and Pan-Turkism of all Moslem Turks inside and outside the Empire. Pan-Islamism was the antithesis of the other movements and in essence called for the strengthening of traditional ideas and institutions; change, according to this doctrine, should come from within rather than from without. Thus there was also a bifurcation in ideology: modernist-positivistic vs. traditional, conservative-Islamic. Further, whatever the ideological hue, reformers, modernizers, revisionists, or conservatives did not envisage a radical break with traditional institutions, values, and beliefs. Even the Young Turk revolutionaries, who in 1908 forced upon the Sultan the restoration of the Constitution, conceived of a reformed Empire that would still be Islamic and possess a Sultan and a caliph. The total break awaited further turmoil, a devastating and humiliating war, and the Atatürk revolution.

Education in the New Turkish State. The birth of Turkey as a nation-state is inextricably bound up with Mustapha Kemal Atatürk, a military revolutionary, an uncompromising nationalist, and a Westernist. Atatürk's goal was to build an ethnically and culturally homogeneous modern Turkish nation-state; his motivating ideal was Westernization, entailing such concepts as secularism, nationalism, republicanism, populism, and reformism.

In the attempted metamorphosis there was hardly an area that was not affected. Organized Islam, the warp and woof of the Ottoman tradition, was dealt a death blow through disestablishment and a series of other changes—the abolition of the caliphate, the religious courts, the Tarikat (religious brotherhoods), the fez, the Arabic lunar and solar calendars, and the Ministry of the Şeriat and the Evkaf. Equally devastating to the influence of religion in the society were some of the reforms in education. The Law of Unification of Instruction (1924) placed "all educational institutions" under the control of the Ministry of Education; all *medreses* were closed; the teaching of religion, Arabic, and Persian was proscribed; and the language was reformed (a Latin alphabet replaced the Arabic script and Turkish was "purified" from Arabic and Persian elements). In the political organization of the new state, sovereignty was placed in the hands of the people, exercised through a national assembly, and a republic with a president replaced the Sultanate. Concurrently, a mono-party system was established. New codes patterned after Swiss and Italian models were introduced. Other reforms affected the land tenure system, agriculture, and the economic structure.

Atatürk and his followers perceived the creation of a new Turkey as resting on the transformation of people's attitudes, beliefs, and values as well. In a sense, therefore, the entire modernization movement was a grand experiment in educational reform entailing not only schools but all social and cultural institutions. Here, in some respects, Atatürk systematized and consummated what had been adumbrated before; in others, he demolished inconsistencies and pushed vigorously for innovation. The consolidation of the new state necessitated a national and secular system of schools. This was established, on paper at least, swiftly after the proclamation of the republic. In addition to the educational reforms mentioned above, the first Turkish constitution reaffirmed the previous principle of obligatory and gratuitous primary education and made all types of schooling the concern of the central government; a graded system of schools (primary, middle, secondary, and technical), together with teacher training institutions, was organized; and a new administrative structure centering in the Ministry of Education was set up. In line with the cardinal Kemalist principles of secularism and nationalism, the curriculum was reoriented and revamped. Religion was expunged, and the Turkish cultural content—part of it manufactured—in language, literature, and history was strengthened. In higher education, the University of Istanbul was reorganized, and schools of law, political science, language, history, and geography were set up in Ankara.

"Kemalism" or "Atatürkism" was in the main based on Western models; but its concrete expression and development were also conditioned by the peculiar Turkish traditions and environment. This was exemplified in education, a pivotal area in the new Turkish policy of unconditional Westernization-modernization.

The first and basic educational policy guideline stemming from the revolutionary ideology was to substitute what Atatürk called "national education" for "religious education." By national education Atatürk meant "an education that will be free from all traditional superstitions as well as from all foreign influences, Eastern or Western, that are incompatible with our national character." In practice, this involved the elimination of religious instruction and religious schools, the Turkicization of the language and the content of cultural subjects, and the use of education as an instrument of Turkish nationalism. Further, it implied unification of all educational agencies, especially schools, and the consolidation of policy-making. The revolutionary principle of statism was nowhere more rigidly applied than in education. In short, national education meant a state-directed and centrally controlled, unified, secular system of schools looked on as an important instrument of national consolidation and integration.

The idea of a national system of education with nationalistic overtones may be traced to Western influences. But centralization and bureaucratization were not alien to the Ottoman tradition. The rigidly centralized pattern that has characterized the Turkish educational system since the revolution may also be viewed as the natural consequence of the centralized bureaucratic set-up of the Ottoman system of civil administration.

The educational program required for national and social integration encompassed more than the formal school system. Atatürk and his followers emphasized adult literacy programs, the wider diffusion of mass media of communication, and programs connected with the army as necessary means to bridge the wide cultural gaps between educated and illiterate, urban and rural, élite and masses. Many of these programs were an integral part of the ideology of "villagism," which in simplified terms meant the modernization of the Turkish villages, one of the most intractable problems in the Turkish transformation. To build a viable polity and a new nation the more than 90 percent of the population living in isolated small villages had to be transformed, politically, economically, and culturally. Schools, literacy programs, mass media, and the like were to eradicate ignorance, superstition and lethargy, break down village isolationism, and change the peasant's personal and social perspectives.

Closely associated with the revolutionary social ideology and more directly related to Westernization was the emphasis placed upon scientific knowledge, particularly the application of science to the practical affairs of man. Science and its technological application were viewed as reasons for the superiority of Western civilization and indispensable for the general modernization of the country. According to Atatürk, "Our guide in political, social, and educational life will be science. . . . Progress is too difficult or even impossible for nations that insist on preserving their traditions and beliefs lacking in rational basis."

Atatürkism has remained a pervasive ideology in Turkish development. After World War II, the United States has been a major influence. The large-scale American military, economic, and technical aid aimed at improving virtually every aspect of Turkish society—the army, agriculture, communication, administration, and education. As previously, the modernization of the army had important educational implications. Technical schools and military training programs, established for the purpose of creating a more efficient military force, provided avenues for technical and literacy training for thousands of Turkish youth, as well as opportunities for social and geographical mobility. The military establishment became an important agency of social change and national integration. In the field of education proper, American advisers and American-trained teachers, administrators, and professors introduced an American pedagogical bias into the curriculum of the schools and the teacher training institutions. Educators and policy-makers discussed the ideas of comprehensive schools; education according to the needs, interests, and abilities of the students; vocational and educational guidance; and the like. English supplanted French as the major foreign language. A technical university, the Middle East Technical University (M.E.T.U.) patterned after the Massachusetts Institute of Technology and the California Institute of Technology, was set up in Ankara. A science lycée, supported by Ford money, was also established as a feeder school to the M.E.T.U., and science teachers were sent to the United States for appropriate training. Six colleges (*kolej*) were set up in various cities with English as the medium of instruction.

Atatürk's view of education as basic to the development of the country was carried further by his successors. In 1960, the principle of development through planning was incorporated in the revised constitution, and a State Planning Organization (SPO), under the control of the Prime Minister, was established. Relying heavily on American experts, two five-year development plans were subsequently launched. In both cases educational planning was viewed as an integral part of overall economic and social planning. A distinctive feature of the two plans was that Turkish education, while not sacrificing its historical, cultural, and social mission, was geared to the current and future manpower needs dictated by the goals of economic planning and development. From this it was concluded that major emphasis should be placed upon technical and vocational education and that steps should be taken to control access into the hitherto popular general academic lycées. Here also Turkish educational thinking was influenced by American and European views on the relationship between education and economic development.

COMPARATIVE MODERNIZATION

Since the end of the eighteenth century, both Greece and Turkey have been exposed to outside influences, particularly from Western Europe. In certain respects they have followed parallel lines of social and political development. They have emerged as nation-states with centralized and clearly defined forms of government. Organs of government have assumed functions previously performed by a variety of agencies—the church, the family, and the village. A "feudal" pattern of land ownership gradually gave way to a wider and more equitable distribution of property, and a landed aristocracy to predominantly small farm owners. A primarily agricultural subsistence economy developed into a "mixed" economy with industrial entrepreneurship, application of technology to production processes, and commercial activity. Urbanization broke down the overwhelmingly rural character of both societies and their circumscribed agrarian mode of life. Expansion of communications broke down geographical and cultural isolation and created different world outlooks. An intense nationalism inspired by the French revolutionary ideology became an activating force for political independence, national identity, social cohesion, and socio-cultural development. Opportunities for social advancement were determined less by ascriptive and more by achievement factors.

Related to the above, both societies became more literate and educated. A graded system of elementary, secondary, and higher schools, with teacher training institutions and technical and vocational establishments, took shape. Decision-making was centered in a Ministry and filtered to local authorities through a well-defined bureaucracy. Opportunities for schooling expanded and a different type of education (either completely or partly modeled on Western European patterns) became a means of national integration, social selection, and social mobility.

This pattern of change does not mean that the two societies have reached identical points of modernization, nor that the process of cultural transformation has been uniform. Differences in traditions, in ideologies, in the perception of Western civilization, in resources, in the general institutional structure, and the like have contributed to variations in the tempo, intensity, and general character of social and cultural change.

THE NINETEENTH CENTURY

The process of modernization, due partly to contacts with other cultures, started earlier in Greece than in Turkey. And throughout the nineteenth century it moved faster in the former country. By the opening years of the twentieth century, Greece had established itself as a relatively cohesive national state. The literacy rate was about 60 percent for men and 20 percent for women. Over 60 percent of the elementary school age children and about 10 percent of the secondary school age children attended schools, and a university in the contemporary European tradition flourished in Athens. Turkey, on the other hand, was still in the throes of establishing a national identity. On such rough educational indicators as literacy and school attendance, she was far behind Greece. In these respects, Greece in 1900 was ahead of Turkey in 1960. Turkey did not possess anything resembling a national system of education until after the Atatürk Revolution. Likewise, Turkey lagged behind Greece on such other indicators as urbanization, industrialization, and the size of their commercial middle class.

How can one account for Greece's early start and faster pace of social and cultural change? What is offered below by way of explanation should be taken more as hypotheses for further investigation than as fully documented conclusions.

Clearly, the nature of key social institutions allowed for variations in the perception of Western civilization and in the impetus to change. An outstanding example is religion, which played an important role in both societies. It is true that in one respect, the relationship of Church and State, both Islam and Orthodoxy appear to have had the same traditional foundations (the Sultan-Caliph combination in the former, and Caesaropapism in the latter). In essence this meant no strict separation of the spiritual and the political realms. Also, unlike Western Protestantism, neither Orthodoxy nor Islam gave rise to any "social gospel" theories of social amelioration or change. Further, both Islam and Orthodoxy "regulated" much of a person's social relationships and perception of himself and the world. But compared to Islam, Orthodoxy was characterized by dualities, paradoxes, flexibility, and "tolerance." The implications of this for our purposes here were well stated by a student of Greek Orthodox theology when he wrote:

> . . . The Orthodox have no social systems and no fixed Christian theories regarding social relationships, no theological doctrine of work and profession or sexual ethics, no closed chapter on birth control, no guiding principles of industrialization, no theological appreciation of the modern secularization. The church is not here to suggest norms which would be applicable everywhere and which would give rise to a single form of technical civilization or culture. Another reason is the fact that for the Orthodox, the Bible is not a code of guiding principles for social action. . . . Orthodoxy is, of its essence, continually open to new developments in every situation in the modern world.[3]

No such flexibility, "passive tolerance," or "friendly co-existence" regarding forces of social change were characteristic of Islam. Consequently, with the advent of modernity, while Greek modernizers generally found grounds of agreement, compromise, and cooperation, their Ottoman counterparts met with stiff and irreconcilable opposition. Despite inroads in the traditional structure and a challenge to the power of the *ulema,* the religious institution maintained a strong grip on the society right up to the Kemalist revolution. Ottoman modernizers themselves, despite the impact which Western culture had upon them, were ambivalent about the place of Islam. The élites were split, and so were the schools and the society at large.

In accounting for the variations in the nature and tempo of the beginning stages of modernization, certain qualities in the two societies must be considered. It could be argued that geography played a part. Greece was more clearly demarcated and closer to Western Europe than the Ottoman Empire, whose ill-defined boundaries stretched over parts of three continents. More important than location were differences in traditions and geopolitical circumstances. Compared to Turkey in the nineteenth century, Greece was more homogeneous in race, religion, and language. Moreover, to the Greeks the new nation-state signified the "re-birth" of what they believed was a common cultural heritage. In this respect there were no sharp conflicts in loyalty or in ideological identification. The Turkish problem is well described by Ward and Rustow as follows:

> Nineteenth century Turkey . . . was an empire stretching over parts of three continents; lacking racial, linguistic, and religious homogeneity; precariously compounded of a motley of peoples with separate and competitive traditions and aspirations; and possessed of few natural boundaries. *A more refractory set of ingredients for a modern nation-state is difficult to conceive.*[4] (Italics inserted by the writer.)

Greek modernization was facilitated further by the existence of and the active part played by Greek communities outside the Greek mainland. The opening of the lines of communication between the Greeks of the mainland and those of the diaspora allowed for Western influences to infiltrate and invigorate local movements. Such influences helped strengthen the task of nation-building by encouraging nationalism, patriotism, self-sacrifice, and discipline. No similar circumstances are evident in the Ottoman Empire. The Ottomans were frequently at odds with Western powers and the object of exploitation. The impact of the West as well as the Ottoman perception of Western civilization was different in Turkey from that in Greece. Ward and Rustow describe the Ottoman situation as follows:

> During the Ottoman period it was politically disintegrative in the highest degree, and the process of defensive modernization to which it gave rise was weak, intermittent, and inadequate to the country's needs.[5]

Another differentiating characteristic of the two societies was the level of economic and educational activity. In the period prior to political independence, there was a noticeable commercial and economic vitality among the Greeks. Mercantile activity was fostered, cities grew, and villages, unheard of before, emerged as important commercial and industrial centers. Such economic upsurge was accompanied by the promotion of education. Numerous schools were established and several cultural societies sprang up. By the time of the revolution, Greece already had a large number of schools, doctors, and literate priests.

The educational awakening received an even greater impetus after the revolution. By 1870, compared to other Western European nations, Greece was a "well-educated" nation. C. K. Tuckerman, who once served as U.S. Minister resident in Athens, commented:

> In Greece . . . it may be safely asserted that no man, woman or child born in the kingdom since the organization of free institutions, is so deficient in elementary knowledge as not to be able to read and write. The cost of public instruction constitutes 0.053 of the total expenditure of the State, a larger percentage than is paid for these objects by

either France, Italy, Austria or Germany, and in proportion to her resources, years and population, she stands undeniably first in the rank of nations—not excepting the United States—as a self-educated people.[6]

The commercial and the educational vitality fostered nationalistic sentiments and contributed to national integration. Through commerce there was an exchange of ideas as well, while schools sought to develop the sense of cultural continuity and national identity.

Socio-economic and educational circumstances during the Ottoman period of Turkish modernization were quite different. Villages were isolated communities engaged in subsistence activities. The economic and commercial enterprises in the cities were mostly in the hands of non-Turks or foreigners, increasingly identifying themselves with the interests of their own ethnic groups. There was no sense of national homogeneity among the Ottoman subjects or among the dominant Moslem Turks. Western influences in education did not reinforce indigenous movements; instead, they created cultural and ideological bifurcations.

THE TWENTIETH CENTURY

Both societies experienced dramatic changes in the twentieth century. Turkey underwent two internal revolutions culminating in the demise of the Ottoman Empire and the creation of the modern Turkish Republic. Greece went through four devastating wars. Both countries have been marked by political instability and by extra-legal means of attaining political power. In the 1960's military coups shook the foundations of democratic government. Both societies have sought to build viable polities and economies along the lines of Western European countries. Although significant social, economic, and cultural changes have been characteristic of both, the Turkish course of modernization after 1923 has been the more arresting and all-encompassing. An example of the dramatic pace of change is education.

In 1923, the numbers of children enrolled in Turkish schools were: 336,000 in elementary schools, 5,900 in middle schools, and 1,241 in the *lycées*. About 40 years later, there were over 3 million children in elementary schools, about 318,000 in middle schools, and over 100,000 in *lycées*. Greece has also registered substantial increases in enrollments, but not to the same extent as Turkey. And on most quantitative indicators, including literacy, Greece today is ahead of Turkey. Such comparisons, of course, belie the fact that Turkey started from scratch, so to speak, while Greece already had a well-developed system of schools.

Yet it is doubtful whether educational change in Turkey would have been so marked if her institutional structure and general outlook had not been radically transformed. The Turkish revolution eliminated most of the factors that previously constrained the process of modernization.

For example, the power of organized Islam was crushed and a secular state was established. A strong nationalism centering in a more ethnically homogeneous population replaced the ambivalent concept of Ottomanism. The boundaries of the new state were clearly demarcated. Language was reformed so that it became a more integrative element. Conflicts over Westernization lost their previous salience, and ideas and institutions from the West now reinforced rather than disrupted the process of nation-building. The goal was national consolidation and development along entirely Western lines. In the 1960's Turkey readily accepted the idea of educational planning in accordance with economic development policies.

In Greece we notice an interesting variation. Since no radical change of the Turkish type occurred, the institutions as evolved since independence in the nineteenth century carried the burden of promoting the change demanded by new socio-economic and intellectual conditions as well as by the goals of development. Here Greece was at a disadvantage compared to Turkey. The institutional structure and the attitudes, which in the nineteenth century facilitated nation-building and pushed Greece ahead of Turkey in modernization, became so entrenched that they acted as constraining forces against further change. The institutionalization of classicism and of a strong ideological attachment to the past, according to some, slowed economic change, and indeed contributed to economic backwardness. It stultified the growth of scientific and technical education, it created imbalances in the supply of other types of skills, and perpetuated an arid intellectualism. Certainly in the postwar period, Greece was more ambivalent than Turkey in accepting the idea of adjusting education to economic development policies and contemporary social and cultural demands. In the latest coup d'etat (April, 1967) the new military leaders vowed that they would expunge "foreign ideologies," and "restore" the purity of the Greek tradition. Ostensibly the Turkish military coup of 1960 was to push further the ideas of Atatürkism. It was felt that in the 1950's there were deviations from this basic ideology of modernization and that traditional constraining factors began to appear. Both Greece and Turkey are still grappling with the problems of establishing viable modern polities and economies and of modernizing their educational systems accordingly. What the future course is to be is difficult to predict.

FOOTNOTES

1. Quoted from J. K. Kordatos, *Historia tou Glōssikou mas Zētēmatos* (G. Loukatos, 1943), p. 117.

2. Kingdom of Greece, Ministry of National Education and Religions, *On the Organization and Administration of General Education (Elementary and Secondary): Legislative Decree 4379/1964* (Athens: National Printing Office, 1964), p. 17.

3. J. C. Bennett, ed., *Christian Social Ethics in a Changing World: An Ecumenical Theological Inquiry* (New York: Association Press, 1966), p. 81.

4. R. E. Ward and D. A. Rustow, eds., *Political Modernization in Japan and Turkey* (Princeton, N.J.: Princeton University Press, 1964), p. 438. The writer is indebted to this source for the approach and some of the ideas of this section.

5. *Ibid.*, p. 440.

6. C. K. Tuckerman, *The Greeks of Today* (New York: G. Putnam and Sons, 1872), pp. 179–180.

A Truce Between Two Cultures: Educational Transfer in the Americas

ERWIN H. EPSTEIN

ALL THREE Spanish-speaking Caribbean countries have been occupied by the United States in the twentieth century. Yet Puerto Rico differs from the two other countries, Cuba and the Dominican Republic, in having been occupied the longest and in borrowing most heavily from North American social and political institutions. The relative economic and political stability enjoyed by Puerto Rico can be traced in part to the transfer of institutions and practices from the North American mainland. In this paper we shall examine the transfer of one institution, the system of formal education, and the reception given North American-style instruction by the Puerto Ricans.

THE SPANISH LEGACY

In 1898, Spain ceded Puerto Rico to the United States as a consequence of the Spanish-American War. Upon landing on the shores of the newly won possession, Major General Nelson A. Miles set the stage for the future relations between the Caribbean island and the "Colossus of the North."

> The people of the United States in the cause of liberty, justice, and humanity . . . come bearing the banner of freedom, inspired by a noble purpose . . . [*to*] bring to you the fostering arm of a nation of free people, whose greatest power is in justice and humanity to all those living within its fold . . . not to make war upon a people of a country that for centuries has been oppressed but, on the contrary, to bring you protection, not only to yourselves, but to your property, to promote your prosperity, and to bestow upon you the immunities and blessings of the liberal institutions of our government . . . to give to all within the control of its military and naval forces the advantages of enlightened civilization.[1]

The statement by General Miles can be evaluated best in terms of the political legacy left to Puerto Rico by Spain. Of all the nations of Spanish America few had remained for so long a time under the sovereignty of

Spain as Puerto Rico.[2] Spanish colonization of the island began August 12, 1508 under the direction of Ponce de Leon and lasted, except for a few months in 1598, for 390 years until October 18, 1898.

In the nineteenth century Spain allowed Puerto Rico a degree of self-rule and representation in the Cortes (Spanish legislature). Once permitted a voice in government the island progressed toward a state of almost complete autonomy. In fact, during the thirty-year period before the cession of the island to the United States, Puerto Rico experienced the formation of political parties, the abolition of slavery, the adoption of freedom of assembly and freedom of the press, and universal suffrage. Prior to the American occupation, Puerto Rico was almost a completely independent state, enjoying a status not unlike that of the modern-day English dominions.[3]

The movement toward autonomy was reflected in the Spanish school laws beginning in 1857. These laws allowed for a relatively high degree of decision-making at the local level. The municipalities were given license to share with the insular government in the exercise of authority and in the meeting of expenses. For each municipality there was a board of education comprised of local citizens. The municipal boards of education were extended rather wide latitude, although they were obligated to secure the approval of the insular authority before exercising their functions.[4]

The school laws reflected the relative progressiveness of the law-makers. School attendance was made compulsory for children between ages six and nine. Rural primary schools were to be built, and high schools as well as elementary schools were to be provided in the towns. The procedures for teacher appointment and promotion and other regulations for administration of the school system suggest that the school laws of Puerto Rico compared favorably with laws operating in the United States at the time.[5]

Before education in Puerto Rico became recognized as a state function, it was almost exclusively the task of the Catholic Church. Little public education existed. Some poor children received instruction as charity, but education remained generally for the privileged classes. The school laws of the mid-nineteenth century deprived religious groups of their exclusive hold over the schools. Yet the farsightedness of these laws did not result in an appreciable extension of education to the poorer classes nor in a substantial improvement in the quality of instruction. Despite the good intentions of the law-makers, the administrative machinery for executing the laws was grossly inadequate. The system remained centralized in the hands of the governor, who frequently used education as a tool to carry out political aims.[6]

To be sure, under the Spanish Crown there existed a large discrepancy between the statutes and what was actually done to establish a school system. Nevertheless, constructive laws prepared the way for improved conditions so that, with regard to education as well as affairs of government, Puerto Ricans were less than in desperate need of liberation and the "enlightened civilization" that North Americans were so eager to confer upon them in 1898.

THE ESTABLISHMENT OF AN AMERICAN SCHOOL SYSTEM

When they landed in Puerto Rico, the Americans found an educational system with no schoolhouses and a lack of proper materials. Instruction was typically carried on in the homes of teachers, who often worked at other occupations while performing simultaneously their teaching functions.[7] Teachers were frequently not paid and received little respect and encouragement for their work. They were dismissed from their duties if they expressed heretical, political or religious ideas, and their appointment and dismissal were in the hands of a governor with practically absolute authority over the entire system.[8] And, as was true of most school legislation, the compulsory attendance law was ignored.[9]

The Americans sought to improve these conditions by injecting their own educational program. In most respects they were eminently successful.[10] Statistics on schools and enrollments display dramatic results. Just prior to the American occupation in 1898, there were 525 public schools with an enrollment of 25,615 pupils.[11] By June, 1901, there were 733 public schools with an enrollment of 33,802 pupils. The number of teachers increased from 582 (June, 1899) to 768.[12] By June, 1902, public schools numbered 874 and had an enrollment of 40,933, and the number of teachers grew to 923.[13] In short, the proportion of the school-age population (ages 6 to 18) enrolled grew from 8 percent to 19 percent during the first four years of American influence. By 1910 the proportion of enrollees grew to 26 percent and by 1920 it reached 41 percent.[14] Thus, during the first twenty years or so under the United States flag, the proportion of children enrolled in public schools multiplied five times.

Clearly, however, school statistics yield only a partial view of developments in Puerto Rican education. In addition to improving conditions generally, attempts were made to inculcate North American values and foster patriotic sentiments among the rapidly growing school population. Puerto Rican children were supposed to be educated in much the same way as mainland children. The position of the North American authorities was that "the rule of this people by Spain was one both of suppression and oppression. Whatever aspirations were permitted were toward Spain. . . . The future must be better than the past. The steady pressure in all directions of our American methods toward American ends, gaining in a degree the confidence and cooperation of the great majority of all concerned, was constantly uppermost, meantime using all sources of information to aid in revising the entire scheme of education." [15]

Among the first classroom innovations were the display and saluting of the United States flag and the teaching of patriotic songs in English (although few teachers, let alone students, knew English).[16] Apparently the attempt to inculcate American patriotism and ideals was not merely to prepare Puerto Ricans for being absorbed in the mainstream of North American culture. It was meant also as an experiment in extending North American institutions and values to Spanish America. The success of an American school system in demonstrating the superiority of American ways, it was argued, would invite emulation from other Latin countries. To quote Education Commissioner Lindsay:

> . . . [I]f the Federal Government does come to the aid of Puerto Rico in the establishment of an adequate and efficient system of public schools the time will come when Puerto Rico will reflect greater glory upon the American nation than perhaps any other community within the sphere of American influence.[17]

> Five hundred thousand dollars for one year, or even that sum for a series of years, would not support a very extensive military campaign; but that sum spent on education would work such a change in Porto Rico as to put beyond the question of a doubt the ultimate and splendid success of the ingrafting of American institutions in Spanish America.[18]

One report suggests that by 1900 the average Puerto Rican school child knew more about Washington, Lincoln, and the history of the American flag than the average school child in the United States.[19] To be sure, Americanization was one of the major goals of the education system. Yet indoctrination in American beliefs and the imposition of a North American system were not carried out without hesitation. Teachers and supervisors were exhorted not to disparage the language and customs of the people. There was initially to be no preconceived plan of instruction imposed on the island. The school system was to be developed according to the dictates of experience. According to John Eaton, who was appointed Director of Education for Puerto Rico in 1899,

> Theories will be vain if not fitted to the situation. The origin and race peculiarities of the people must be taken into account, as well as present customs, ideas, and aspirations.[20]

> A great ruler reveals his greatness by his cultivation of the aspirations of his people.[21]

In spite of the professed desire to adjust instruction to the physical and cultural setting of the island, a distinctively North American public school system was imposed. Many changes, including some for which Puerto Ricans were ill-prepared, were rapidly instituted. Not only was an attempt made to instill an appreciation for things North American, but the system was decentralized, coeducation was introduced, and English was made the favored language of instruction.

Coeducation and English instruction were given particularly heavy emphasis. The North American authorities regarded coeducation as a natural condition. If children were to grow up in a world which the two sexes shared as intellectual equals, they had to be educated together.[22] As for English, school authorities believed that the absence of that language furnished the greatest difficulty in the way of Puerto Ricans becoming Americans in thought, belief, and loyalty.[23] The Americans felt that English would be learned rapidly by the children, and Americanization would follow spontaneously. In fact, it was believed that the children would learn English "fast enough to be ready to use English text-books before their teachers in all cases are able to be ready to teach either in the English language or from English text-books." [24] Yet in the imposing of a second language, as was generally true of the foisting of a foreign system of education, policy was executed with ambivalence.[25]

REACTION TO NORTH AMERICAN EDUCATION

The reports of the early commissioners of education for Puerto Rico suggest that the new school program had a generally favorable reception. The Puerto Ricans were reported as being appreciative of efforts to improve education, and it was thought that the building of schoolhouses provided "the most tangible and forceful guaranty of the good faith of our government." [26] Language instruction was a principal topic of discussion and the provision for English was almost universally commended.[27] Indeed, the North American authorities believed that the main object of parents in sending their children to school was to have them learn English.[28] Oliver B. Kern, principal of the San Juan High School, reported in 1903 that "it was even pitiful to see the parents struggling for precedence in the waiting line, so eager were they to place their children in a school where they would learn English." [29]

Not all reaction to English instruction, however, was favorable. The early authorities viewed English as a major instrument of Americanization and thought that a second language would be absorbed readily by the school population. Yet school officials were not unaware of the potential consequences of imposing English, such as the development of strong class feelings. The upper class might use English to their own advantage and exclude the lower classes from access to it. The lower classes might regard English as an attempt to establish class rule.[30] Puerto Ricans generally might fear that Americans were trying to deprive them of their mother tongue.

In accordance with the avowed objective of not disregarding popular sentiment, a policy of having English and Spanish as media of instruction was quickly adopted.[31] Nevertheless, as early as 1903, impatience with the lack of measurable achievements in English induced the American school authorities to make that language the sole medium of instruction throughout the school system, with Spanish taught as a special subject. To provide ample practice, since opportunities for learning a second language were not available outside the classroom, all instruction was made secondary to mastering English. This action prompted bitter opposition from Puerto Ricans, which in turn led to recurrent vacillation in the establishment of a language policy. However, in spite of experiments in using Spanish at different school levels, English remained as the principal language of instruction until after the Second World War.

As long as English persisted as an instructional medium, the major objection of Puerto Ricans to the imposed school system was that the educational needs of children were being sacrificed to the ends of assimilative colonialism.[32] Partisans critical of the language policy pointed out that language changes could come about only with great difficulty. They argued that Americans falsely presumed the island to be analogous linguistically to the Philippines; that American authorities treated Puerto Ricans as if they were a people without a common culture and without a language spoken uniformly by all classes.[33] However much this argument appears to have arisen out of an emotional attachment to the mother tongue, it tended to be borne out by an obvious failure to imbue Puerto Ricans with English. At the time of a major change in the school-language policy following World War II, after fifty years of having English as a language of instruction, few Puerto Ricans had a mastery of that language.[34]

Opposition to the new system was encountered also in other areas. The empty reception given to the school laws of 1899 suggests an early lack of enthusiasm for North American ways. Among other things, these laws authorized the establishment of school districts, urged the districts to organize and establish public schools, defined the relation of the municipalities to the public schools, and granted powers to municipal school trustees to appoint teachers. In short, the laws were directed at establishing a system of school districts whose boards would hold extensive autonomous powers; it was to be a system patterned after those on the mainland, one aimed at stimulating local initiative. Attempts to promote decentralization, however, soon had to be abandoned. It was apparent that the local boards failed to perform their duties and that their activities hinged more on politics than pedagogy.[35] Moreover, local authorities were reported as "being in sympathy with the Spanish system and hostile to the education of the masses." [36] According to Osuna, "the local boards were complete failures; they would not administer the schools efficiently, showing that centralization in school administration and a great deal of it was absolutely necessary for the success of public instruction." [37]

Old educational patterns did not pass away easily. William H. Armstrong, an early supervisor of the San Juan school district, observed in 1902 that the Catholic Church refused to sanction free public school education. He reported that North American ways were not fully understood and that a conservatism prevailed that would not yield readily to innovations. As an example, he cited the difficulty of removing incompetent personnel who were appointed originally because they were friends or relatives of local politicians.[38]

A more serious problem, one which continues to apply today, was the complaint that the educational system laid more stress on Americanization than on educating Puerto Ricans to earn a living and make them, as a people, self-supporting. Puerto Rican nationalists argued that education should be aimed chiefly at eliminating illiteracy and preparing for future occupational roles rather than at promoting patriotic sentiment for the United States.[39]

Of the changes instituted by North Americans, the act which most offended mores was the imposition of coeducation. The move was resented bitterly, due doubtlessly in part to the forceful and almost indifferent manner by which it was carried out. In view of the frequently stated determination of the school authorities to consider popular sentiment and custom in the making and administering of school policy, and of the early awareness concerning the strong feelings against bringing the sexes together,[40] the imposition of coeducation serves dramatically to illustrate the ambivalence of American actions. The handling of coeducation in San Juan by Armstrong is illuminating.

> Until the present year [1902] coeducation has been entirely contrary to the old Spanish customs; in fact, it was regarded as a means to the ruination of the people. To place boys and girls together in the same room without a guardian was an unpardonable crime.
>
> At the beginning of the school year I had determined if possible not only to completely reorganize the system, but to break up this objectionable custom at once, regardless of public sentiment; and after laying my plans before the honorable commissioner of education, Dr. M. G. Brumbaugh, I proceeded to carry them out to the best of my ability. . . .
>
> The plan was publicly announced in the newspapers, but objections at once arose from all sides. It became necessary to close my office to all except teachers. Attacks were made upon me in every Spanish newspaper. The halls of the school building were crowded daily with parents and servants who went to protect the innocent ones during school hours. This was very objectionable at first and greatly impeded the work of the classes. In view, however, of the fact that the guardians themselves might learn something of our methods as well as our good intentions, and that they might see our equipments so utterly strange to them, I considered that little harm and perhaps some good might be the result of permitting them to remain in the schools; indeed, a general invitation to visit the schools was sent to all parents. It required but a short time for these parents to learn that the American school was a great institution, where their children could get not only a good free education, but be under good moral influences at the same time. At present, sad to relate, it is difficult to get parents to visit the schools at any time.[41]

In short, educational transfer in Puerto Rico was initiated and had its greatest impetus at the turn of the century. Since then, policy makers have striven to adapt a characteristically North American educational structure to a Latin culture.

The early attempts to forge an instructional system characteristic of mainland schools met with partial success. Schools were built; enrollments grew; administrative procedures were streamlined; coeducation was introduced, though reluctantly accepted; and English was taught extensively. Yet resentment against North American methods often frustrated the efforts of educational authorities. School policy emerged as a compromise between cultures, and concessions made by the early officials to Latin customs endure today. Hence, the Puerto Rican school system enrolls the highest proportion of school-age children in Latin America, but has a lower proportional enrollment of school-age children than any state in the Union. Coeducation is a feature of the public schools, yet the system is centralized and practices are standardized to the extent that public-school children throughout the island wear uniforms and uniformly learn the same lessons. And, while allegiance to the United States flag is promoted, classes are taught predominantly in Spanish, and an appreciation for Puerto Rican culture and tradition is encouraged.

POLITICAL STATUS AND THE SCHOOL: A SEQUEL

The present Puerto Rican school system was designed in the years between American occupation and the establishment of the Commonwealth government in 1952.[42] During those years, the island developed its unique brand of education from a blend of Latin and North American elements. Though the basic issues of language instruction, coeducation, and the seating of administrative authority have been resolved, they have been so tenuously. Ambivalence continues to characterize school policy; the source of uncertainty is identical to that which plagued authorities during the formative period of Puerto Rican public education. As in the early years, school policy is affected by a political status that is ambiguous and oriented to no permanent arrangement.

Problems of education in Puerto Rico have been as much political as pedagogical. Regardless of how much the mixture is resented, politics is a fact of life in school affairs and will remain so as long as the question of political status lies unresolved. United States leaders traditionally have envisaged a Puerto Rican education that conformed to the needs and customs of Puerto Ricans; yet they have demanded that schools Americanize the population. Consequently, school administrators are placed in an untenable position. Should they require classroom exercises in patriotism to the United States when there is a prospect that the island may become independent? Should not English be the medium of instruction as long as Puerto Rico is associated with the United States? Should the insular school authorities allow local districts as much autonomy in administering school affairs as is given by state officials on the mainland.

Central to considerations of political status is whether Puerto Ricans would lose their customary way of life should the island become a state. Concomitantly, there is a concern as to why Puerto Ricans have not become more Americanized. The school is caught between these concerns. Yet the alignment of political camps infers that the school's role would cease to be a principal political issue once Puerto Ricans are certain of their final status. *Estadistas* (statehooders) claim that Puerto Ricans would learn English and become more Americanized (though they would not lose their customs and traditions) were they to be assured that the island would *eventually* become a state.[43] *Independentistas* (separatists) believe that Puerto Ricans could be instilled with a coherent sense of nationality, though the island need not renounce its close relationship with the United States, were they to be assured of *ultimate* independence.[44] Both groups argue that not to decide definitively on the island's status at a time when Puerto Rico is economically well off and exhibits considerable ability at self-government amounts to colonialism. Congress, however, has been reluctant to decide the status issue, because it is uncertain whether the island can be absorbed successfully into the fabric of North American culture.

The United States cannot avoid the prospect of grappling with an alien culture within its immediate borders. Congress recognizes that not to allow Puerto Ricans to decide upon the status question would be imperialistic. Yet it fears the outcome of a plebiscite in which the islanders would be truly free to vote on their status. Congress intends to hold a plebiscite,[45] but it will not suffice to give Puerto Ricans freedom to decide their destiny. To permit such freedom the federal government would need also to make eminently clear its intention to abide unconditionally by whatever course Puerto Ricans choose.[46] Not to do so could bias Puerto Rican voters by leaving them with the impression that the United States will set their status regardless of how they vote.[47] After all, the federal government has not always exhibited tolerance of the island's Hispanic culture, and United States leaders have occasionally suggested that Puerto Rico could never become a state of the Union.[48] Whatever doubts Puerto Ricans have had in the past that Congress would allow them to conform to statehood in their own way were reinforced by the recent report of the Congressionally appointed United States-Puerto Rico Status Commission that "statehood would necessarily involve a cultural and language accommodation to the rest of the federated states of the Union." [49]

Clearly the political status question poses a dilemma for education. As long as Puerto Ricans doubt that Congress will unconditionally allow the island to become a state, the insular schools will not be able to effectively prepare children for full American citizenship. As long as it appears to Congressmen that Puerto Ricans are not being prepared adequately for American culture and citizenship, they are not apt to allow the islanders a free option for statehood.[50] The apprehension of United States leaders over the prospects of assimilating unconditionally a foreign people is aggravated by the persuasive *estadista* argument that if Puerto Rico were to achieve statehood, nothing would keep the island from retaining as predominant its Latin culture.[51] Regarding education, to be sure, the states and local boards have been allowed traditionally to make and execute school policy. With the Tenth Amendment to the Constitution reserving unspecified powers (including the power to administer schools) to the states, who then could require that Puerto Rico teach school subjects in English and that the islanders be imbued generally with North American values?

The present commonwealth mirrors this ambiguity. It is unlikely that Puerto Rico will either move soon from its commonwealth status or promptly resolve the problem of how to ideologically orient its schools. As long as they are uncertain as to what a vote of statehood or independence might bring *vis-à-vis* Congress, Puerto Ricans are not apt to abandon their present course. As long as this is the case, the schools will be incapable of faithfully serving "national" interests.

CONCLUSION

Americans came to Puerto Rico in 1898 intending to establish democratic institutions and improve the standard of living. Their approach was to impose North American ways and values on a culture that was predominantly Latin. As reflected by the school system they established, American efforts were met with dramatic successes as well as blatant failures. School enrollments multiplied, corruption and favoritism in educational administration largely disappeared, schools were built, materials were supplied, and conditions for learning improved vastly. Yet the tactics of the American authorities were often heavy-handed; coeducation was imposed willfully on a culture in which bringing the sexes together was almost anathema, and English was made a medium of instruction among Spanish-speaking people.

The often unyielding attitude of the early American school officials was anomalous in view of their avowed desire not to threaten the traditional Puerto Rican way of life. The two intentions of North Americans, to Americanize Puerto Ricans and to fit the school system to the culture of the people, led to ambivalence in educational policy-making. Ambivalence in turn resulted in much resentment against North American policies.

Ambivalence was a result ultimately of the difficulty in deciding upon political status. If Puerto Rico were to become a state, then Puerto Ricans were to be given an education directed at assimilating them into North American culture. If Puerto Ricans were to be independent, then an emphasis was to be placed on the merits of their own culture and on educating them to be autonomous. As long as the political status was indeterminate, school policy remained an unstable compromise.

The political ambiguity of the early years persists. Congress resists allowing Puerto Ricans to unconditionally decide the status issue, and educators are uncertain as to how the schools should be run. Exacerbating the problem is a belief among separatists and a fear among statehooders that Congress may not be willing to allow Puerto Rico to become a state. Influential Congressmen have argued that Puerto Ricans have not achieved a common ground with North Americans and should therefore not be granted statehood. Puerto Ricans, on the other hand, have argued that the reason they have not adopted North American ways is because they have not been given reasonable assurance of being allowed statehood.

The school system is caught in the controversy. It cannot orient itself to statehood or independence. It cannot freely promote Americanism nor can it concentrate on instilling an indigenous sense of nationality. Indecision and ambivalence are likely to persist as long as Congress defers in taking definitive action on the status issue. Educational transfer in Puerto Rico has taken the form of a truce between two cultures. And, as truces tend to be, this one is unsteady and waits impatiently for a final solution.

REFERENCES

1. Quoted in Juan José Osuna, *A History of Education in Puerto Rico* (Rio Piedras: University of Puerto Rico, 1949), pp. 259–260.

2. See the statement of Juan Augosto Perea and Felix Benitez Rexach addressed to the Chavez Subcommittee of the U.S. Senate, January 8, 1944.

3. Address by A. Fernós-Isern, *U.S. Congressional Record,* April 22, 1947, A1864.

4. U.S. Bureau of Education, *Report of the Commissioner,* 1899–1900, Vol. 1, p. 226.

5. *Ibid.*

6. For a description of school conditions, see Osuna, *op. cit.*, Chaps. 2–4.

7. U.S. Bureau of Education, *Report of the Commissioner,* 1899–1900, Vol. 2, p. 1651.

8. Osuna, *op. cit.,* pp. 94–96.

9. *Ibid.,* p. 80.

10. Samuel McCune Lindsay, an early Commissioner of Education for Puerto Rico, found that upon his arrival to the island early in 1902, there was already "a good American system of schools of primary, secondary, and grammar grades in every municipality on the island." U.S. Bureau of Education, *Report of the Commissioner,* 1902, Vol. 2, p. 1177.

11. U.S. Bureau of Education, *Report of the Commissioner,* 1899–1900, Vol. 1, p. 240.

12. U.S. Bureau of Education, *Report of the Commissioner,* 1901, Vol. 1, p. LXIII.

13. U.S. Bureau of Education, *Report of the Commissioner,* 1902, Vol. 2, pp. 1177–79.

14. Osuna, *op. cit.,* p. 626.

15. U.S. Bureau of Education, *Report of the Commissioner,* 1899–1900, Vol. 1, p. 234.

16. *Ibid.,* p. 237.

17. U.S. Bureau of Education, *Report of the Commissioner,* 1902, Vol. 2, p. 1202.

18. *Ibid.,* p. 1204.

19. Osuna, *op. cit.,* p. 135.

20. U.S. Bureau of Education, *Report of the Commissioner,* 1899–1900, Vol. 1, p. 230.

21. *Ibid.*, p. 234.

22. U.S. Bureau of Education, *Report of the Commissioner*, 1900–1901, Vol. 2, p. 1228.

23. U.S. Bureau of Education, *Report of the Commissioner*, 1899–1900, Vol. 1, p. 236.

24. U.S. Bureau of Education, *Report of the Commissioner*, 1902, Vol. 2, p. 1183. See also p. 1198.

25. Ambivalence is exemplified by Commissioner Lindsay's remark, "we do not desire to force English upon the people, but we want them to recognize their aspirations in the direction of acquiring a knowledge of English." *Ibid.*, p. 1194.

26. U.S. Bureau of Education, *Report of the Commissioner*, 1902, Vol. 2, p. 1202.

27. U.S. Bureau of Education, *Report of the Commissioner*, 1899–1900, Vol. 1, p. 227.

28. *Ibid.*, p. 1209.

29. *Ibid.*, pp. 1221–22.

30. In a letter to General John Eaton of March 14, 1899, Victor Clark, Subdirector of Public Instruction, observed that "there might be a tendency upon the part of the wealthy people to monopolize English in their own ranks, and to use it to keep political and commercial control, and as an additional instrument for the oppression of the lower classes."

31. U.S. Bureau of Education, *Report of the Commissioner*, 1899–1900, Vol. 1, pp. 236–237.

32. José Padín, Commissioner of Education from 1930 to 1937, commented that "it does not seem to have occurred to those responsible . . . that under normal circumstances only a negligible minority of our people need English as a medium of verbal intercourse while the entire population has need of an education which should be acquired as early and expeditiously as possible." José Padín, "English in Puerto Rico," *La Revista Escolar de Puerto Rico*, XIX, No. 7 (March, 1935), 6.

33. See the testimony by Antonio Ayuso, publisher of *El Imparcial*, before the U.S. 79th Congress, Senate Committee on Territories and Insular Affairs, April 24, 1945, pp. 136–137.

34. See the testimony of Juan Augusto Perea before the U.S. 79th Congress, Senate Committee on Territories and Insular Affairs, April 5, 1945, p. 16.

35. Osuna, *op. cit.*, pp. 130–132.

36. U.S. Bureau of Education, *Report of the Commissioner*, 1899–1900, Vol. 1, p. 224.

37. Osuna, *op. cit.*, p. 133.

38. U.S. Bureau of Education, *Report of the Commissioner*, 1902, Vol. 2, p. 1206, 1208.

39. See the testimony of Antonio Ayuso, *op. cit.*

40. See U.S. Bureau of Education, *Report of the Commissioner*, 1899–1900, Vol. 1, p. 227.

41. U.S. Bureau of Education, *Report of the Commissioner*, 1902, Vol. 2, pp. 1206–07.

42. Among its most significant aspects, the Commonwealth arrangement permits Puerto Rican Supreme Court Justices to be chosen by the elected Governor instead of the President and gives the Governor control over members of the executive branch.

43. See the testimony of Jorge Luis Cordova, representing the Puerto Rico Statehood Association, at the hearing before the U.S. 79th Congress, Senate Committee on Territories and Insular Affairs, April 24, 1945, pp. 149–52.

44. See the testimony of Salvador Perea at the hearing before the U.S. 79th Congress, *ibid.*, April 23, 1945, p. 131.

45. On July 23, 1967, a plebiscite was held in Puerto Rico. This article was written before that date.

46. One way by which Congress could display its good faith would be to renounce sovereignty over the island before sponsoring a plebiscite. Were it to do so and Puerto Ricans were to opt for statehood, Congress could not then stipulate conditions for achieving statehood without risking universal condemnation for frustrating the islanders' aspirations. See the testimony of Noel Colón Martínez, representing the Puerto Rico Bar Association, at the hearing before the United States-Puerto Rico Commission on the Status of Puerto Rico, May 14, 1965, pp. 2–10.

47. Several Puerto Rican members of the United States-Puerto Rico Status Commission were left convinced that Congress would not admit a state into the Union until satisfied that certain conditions were met, namely, "that English [become] the predominant language of its people." Supplemental views of Commissioners Luís Muñoz Marín, Luis Negron Lopez, and Teodoro Moscoso, *Report of the United States-Puerto Rico Commission on the Status of Puerto Rico,* August, 1966, p. 23.

48. See, for example, statements by Senators Ellender and Tydings at the hearings before the 79th Congress, Senate Committee on Territories and Insular Affairs, March 5 and April 27, 1945, pp. 18 and 310–11.

49. *Report of the United States-Puerto Rico Commission on the Status of Puerto Rico,* August, 1966, p. 15.

50. *Estadistas* and their sympathizers are disturbed that no persuasive assurances have been made by Congress that it holds open the prospect of statehood. See, for example, the letter of the Christian Action Party of Puerto Rico, a group that is avowedly noncommittal on the status question, to the U.S. Senate Committee on Interior and Insular Affairs, November 6, 1963. Also see the pronouncement of the *Congreso Puertorriqueño Anticolonialista* in the *New York Times,* October 24, 1965, p. E5.

Independentistas, meanwhile, remain convinced that the federal government would never be willing to grant statehood unconditionally. See the testimony of J. A. Gonzalez-Gonzalez before the U.S. 88th Congress, Senate Subcommittee on Territories and Insular Affairs, November 7, 1963, pp. 18–19.

51. Consider also the implications of the Fourteenth Amendment in protecting Latin customs in Puerto Rico. In a recent ruling of the Supreme Court (*Katzenbach* v. *Morgan,* June 13, 1966) New York State was denied the power to require literacy in English for voting purposes. The Voting Rights Act of 1965 provided that no person having successfully completed the sixth grade in a school under the American flag shall be deprived of the right to vote. The Court ruled that New York could not restrict the voting right to persons having received a sixth grade education in a school that used English as the predominant language of instruction; Puerto Ricans educated in Spanish must also be allowed to vote. Similarly, should Puerto Rico become a state, attempts to induce Puerto Ricans to learn English and adopt new customs by threatening to deprive them of certain privileges extended to other citizens may be construed by the courts as violating the equal protection clause of the Fourteenth Amendment.

A Uganda Secondary School as a Field of Culture Change[1]

F. MUSGROVE

I PROPOSE to examine the Uganda secondary boys' boarding-school, in which I teach, as an institution in culture contact; to consider how far its function must be interpreted in terms of its own dynamism and how far in terms of the parent cultures of the Black and White members of the community. The interpretation I make from data gained chiefly within the school is necessarily incomplete, and a complementary study by a field anthropologist, looking at the school from the point of view of outside society, is desirable. But within the limits of the data available to a schoolmaster I here offer a description and an analysis.

The school is situated in the Western Province of Uganda and serves the entire Protectorate. The school's hundred boys come from 11 of Uganda's tribes: the 5 tribes which contribute more than 90 per cent. of the pupils are the Batoro, Baganda, Banyoro, Banyankole, and Lango. Other tribes, such as the Lugbara and the Etesot, have one or two representatives. The Batoro (46 per cent.), the Baganda (18 per cent.) and the Banyoro (13 per cent.) form the largest tribal groups. The majority of the boys are Christians, though a small percentage (about 5 per cent.) are Moslems. The age-range is considerable, from approximately 11 to, as far as can be ascertained, 24 or so. Within any of the 6 classes the age-range is greater than would be considered normal in an English Grammar School; for example, in Secondary 2, from 12 to 18. The boys are taught in English by European and African staff (4 of the former and 6 of the latter); they are pursuing a 6-year course of studies which leads to the Cambridge School Certificate examination in English, Mathematics, History, Geography, a vernacular language, General Science, and Religious (Christian) Knowledge. The content of the curriculum is substantially that of an English Grammar School: it varies only in giving rather more emphasis to the African continent in Geography, and to African developments since effective European penetration in History. Christian Religious Knowledge is taught as a school subject to all Christian pupils; there are two short Chapel services each day, and on Sunday a full-length Anglican Church

Reprinted, with permission of the author and the International African Institute, from AFRICA, Vol. 22 (1952), pp. 234–249.

service with a preacher who is either a member of the staff, of the C.M.S., or a visiting lay Christian either African or European.

The school thus provides a field of culture contact, and the problem for investigation is the extent and nature of culture change brought about by its activities.

THE SCHOOL AS AN INSTITUTION IN CULTURE CONTACT

The school operates upon the life of Uganda not only through the new ideas and habits carried away by its pupils in their three months holiday each year and when they finally leave, but as an institution which affects in a variety of ways the customs and pursuits of the people. The school, with its European staff, European curriculum, and European standards of conduct, is an integral part of the tribal situation. It is not intelligible when regarded—as Malinowski regarded institutions which involved colour co-operation—as a single social body, a separate cultural entity explicable not in terms of the two parent cultures, but only in terms of its own determinism. It is necessary to ask: How far is the school like a school in any other society? How far are the character and quality of its work shaped by tribal influences? How far by European influences? How far by inter-tribal contact within the school?

The school develops patterns of behaviour which are probably common to schools everywhere. The distinction between the new boy and the boy of senior status is sharp. New boys are initiated into the community in a manner which has more similarity with the ragging of juniors which takes place in an English Public School than with tribal initiation ceremonies. It is customary in the dormitories for new boys to be made to drink successively and rapidly glasses of cold water and to endure similar hardships at the hands of seniors. There is no evidence of direct or even indirect influence of English example, whether through contact with English schoolboys or even schoolboy literature. The school spontaneously develops a group life with its own autonomy, and the distinction between the newcomer and the senior emerges, with its own ritual, as in many other groups.

Other groups within the school are to be explained rather in terms of European than of tribal influences. Age-groups are obliterated by class groups: disparity in the ages of class-mates seems to be less felt than in an English school: a boy of 17 appears to feel no self-consciousness or loss of face from sitting in class with boys of 13, and will usually make his friends among them. I have discovered no school organization or society based upon tribal or religious divisions: a voluntarily formed literary society has a Moslem Muganda president, and the members are Batoro, Banyoro, and Banyankole, all Christians. A school dramatic society, also spontaneously formed, is similarly mixed in composition. A football or cricket captain or a scout patrol leader, when choosing a team for a game, appears to base his choice upon merit—or possibly personal friendliness—but not upon tribal origin. The natural leaders of informal groups are frequently from a different tribe from that of their followers. A boy from the West Nile district, a member of the Lugbara tribe, is a recognized leader in a variety of activities: he is called upon by his schoolfellows to organize and prepare musical entertainments; in a climbing expedition or in schoolboy exploration he is looked to for leadership. Yet he is the sole representative of his tribe in the school and, in a predominantly Bantu school, is very much a foreigner. His authority is often greater than that of boys who enjoy official position and power. Loyalties unknown outside the school are now felt—to the class, the team, the informal group, the House (which stirs strong feelings of rivalry in the inter-house sports and games), and to the school.

Distinctions which were of importance in the home environment fade before a system of European-inspired groupings. The aristocratic Babito, of the clan which supplies the Bakama of Toro and Bunyoro, although respected as people of high station in the villages, live in apparent harmony and equality with commoners in the school: the superior person is now the school prefect, who is respected for his personal qualities and official status rather than for his family background. The distinction between Babito and other Batoro and Banyoro is not always entirely obliterated; occasionally a prefect will complain of the insubordination of a Mubito and explain that "he is beginning to be conscious of his position"; but this is infrequent. A new hierarchy has been formed and receives recognition, which does not reflect social grades outside the school. Thus the distinction between the children of the cattle-owning Bahima and those of the more lowly agricultural Bairu of Ankole is not a deeply felt distinction in the school. Neither are inter-tribal jealousies apparent. Most boys would agree that the most important, progressive, and civilized tribes in western Uganda are the Baganda, Banyoro, and Banyankole or Batoro, in that order. The B'amba are universally regarded as the most primitive. The Batoro will rag the few boys from Bwamba for their primitive home-life, and a M'amba will often try to pass himself off as a Mutoro; but this situation seems to give rise to no bitter feuds or overt tensions, and cliques are not formed along tribal lines. Throughout Uganda the Baganda are often regarded as "exploiters": for example, in Ankolẹ there is feeling among the Banyankole against the exploitation of minerals by the Baganda; but I have found no militant tribal feeling among the boys. In reply to an essay question: "Why I am proud to be a Mutoro/Muganda/Munyoro, &c." I found boys as ready to criticize as to extol their tribes, particularly boys of strong Christian conviction. A number of boys measured their tribes by the Christian yardstick, for dishonesty and drunkenness, as well as on more general grounds, such as laziness or unwillingness of parents to send their children to school. The proportion of boys offering critical comment on their own people did not vary significantly between the tribes—although the strongest criticism of his people was made by a Munyoro (of deep Christian faith). My general conclusion is that groupings within the school are created by the school's own determinism; by the English-type structure of school organization and, negatively, in hindering groupings along pre-school lines, by the influence of European ideas, particularly Christianity, in providing a solvent of criticism for tribal loyalties. It is probable that the boys' behaviour is to some extent situational, and a follow-up of schoolboys in their home environment is urgently needed from field anthropologists.

Although the pattern of organization within the school is little influenced by the structure of African society outside, there is, in fact, a complex interaction between the school and the tribes of Uganda. It is true that, unlike the best village schools, the role of the school is compensatory for, rather than complementary to, society's activities—just as boarding-schools in England in the nineteenth century arose to compensate for defects in the traditional organs of education: the family plus private tutor at the professional and administrative level, the master craftsman plus apprentices at the technological level. These two institutions, partly because of decay within themselves and partly because of the greater demands being made upon them, could no longer meet the requirements of the age. Similarly, the boarding-school in Uganda has the task of compensating for the inability of the family's or native craftsman's instruction to meet modern demands. And yet the school must be regarded as an integral part of Uganda's major tribes in a general sociological sense. It is related to them economically in drawing from them school fees. Fees are approximately 250s. per annum: many boys gain some support from Native Authority bursaries, but the majority need support in whole or in part from private sources. If there is insufficient opportunity for wage-employment in a boy's home district, his brother or other mobile member of the family may have to move to an area, probably urban, where he can earn the money from which the fees may be paid. One boy in the school, whose home is in western Uganda, is maintained by a brother who has moved to Nairobi to obtain sufficiently remunerative employment. A major factor determining a schoolboy's choice of employment after school is whether it will enable him to support at school his brothers and sisters.

A more direct influence of the school on tribal society is through the pupils themselves. The boy at school becomes accustomed to new amenities and a new routine of life, and he carries his new standards of conduct and comfort with him during the vacations, and when he leaves school. He becomes accustomed to wearing shorts and a shirt, stockings and shoes, to putting on a raincoat in a storm instead of carrying over his head a banana-leaf. His diet is changed and, with the exception of the Bahima who eat a great deal of beef at home, he gets into the habit of eating far more meat than his parents do. And he acquires the expensive taste for milk in his tea. After the constant availability of school transport, he no longer assumes, as does the typical villager, that almost any journey must be made on foot. His standards of cleanliness in clothes, houses, and his own person are raised; his personal habits are modified by the school routine, the insistence on working even when it is raining, upon being at a particular place at a particular time. He protests against all these changes in his behaviour—except the enforcement of cleanliness which he pretends is superfluous. Without exception the boys contrast the school unfavourably with conditions at home on the three counts of clothing, diet, and routine. They complain that the school issue of clothing, which is compulsory dress, is irksome and far inferior to their private wardrobes; they complain that they are ill fed; and in particular they lament the regularity, routine, and comprehensiveness of the school time-table. These three complaints are expressed vocally to people who have their confidence, and all three occur in over 90 per cent. of the essays written on "The Difficulties of my Life at School." I have been out on a day's excursion with parties of boys who have refused to eat at particular times because "the bell is sounding now for lunch at school. We are away from all that." This happens not only with junior boys but with pupils who have attended the school for six years. The boys themselves give no indication that they are growing out of harmony with their homes: they profess an earnest desire to return to its superior comforts and more humane parental discipline. It is only after a boy's confidence has been fully gained that he may admit: "The rigid routine here means that I know when I shall get my lunch. At home I never know, and I have no right to expect it at a particular time. Here I can make an official complaint if the food is ill cooked or insufficient, or if there is no tea. At home if there is no tea I am simply told that there is none and have to be satisfied." Similarly in matters of dress. In confidential conversation a boy may confess how, in his younger days, the possession of a pair of shorts[2]—such as those provided by the school—was the very limit of earthly ambition. And although boys profess to be clean without the need for school regulation—and will make the customary charge of uncleanliness against any tribe they judge to be their inferior—in fact they are learning at school new standards. I know of no instance of a Mutoro boy—and the homes of the Batoro cannot be more than a few miles from the school—taking home during half-term or other free time a schoolfellow from a different tribe: he is aware that his home will be judged by the new school standards and is afraid to risk the comparison.

From a survey of schoolboys it is impossible to say with any certainty how far these new standards and attitudes are influencing the behaviour of other people with whom the schoolboy has contact. All that can be said with certainty is that new habits are being formed at school: at home the boy may modify them, he may exercise them with approval and be imitated, or he may exercise them in defiance of reproof and so cause tensions. It seems probable that a schoolboy, at least in the junior classes, retains enough of his parents' outlook and attitudes to remain and feel in harmony with them. In the first three forms of the school the following traditional beliefs appear, from conversations and discussions, school essays and questionnaires (after making full allowance for test resistance), to gain about 40 per cent. acceptance: (1) Some stones can talk and some trees both talk and bleed. (Two trees and one large stone in Toro, within a few miles of the school, are supposed by local people to have objected to the attempts of road-makers to remove them, to have bled and cried out, and to have caused the death of workmen. The road now circumvents these obstacles.) (2) The earth is flat. (3) That a Moslem can charm a thief or evildoer and so secure his detection, and can cause physical injury to befall an offender. (This is a widespread belief to which 90 per cent. subscribe.) (4) A cook can put something into his employer's food to make him increase his wages. (5) There are fairies in the forests which bring (chiefly) bad luck. (Boys are full of instances of alleged encounters with fairies, and two compositions about exciting adventures have claimed personal and unpleasant experience of them.) (6) A witchdoctor can give a man a medicine which will make the girl he wants come to him. (7) Some people can change into animals.[3]

There is evidence that these beliefs still have considerable effect, at least on the behaviour of younger boys. I know a junior boy who has asked a witchdoctor for a medicine to ensure his safe journey to school; another, with a scarred forehead, who believes that by burning him a witchdoctor prevented him from going blind. There is a sharp decline in such beliefs in the top two forms, and senior boys ridicule them; but there is probably some relapse in the holidays. In an article in the school magazine of Busoga College (June 1951) a fifth-form boy wrote:

> When I go about the villages I meet all sorts of temples made for heathen gods, with many people who daily give homage to them. Worse still, many of the so-called Christians go and worship such gods in time of great trouble, and when they somehow get over that trouble they declare that they were saved by one of those gods or other.

Unfortunately the writer makes no comment on the educational status of those who thus revert to pagan practices.

The ideas contained in Western culture as presented to schoolboys often cause less tension than might be expected, since some are largely restatements, with a new terminology, of beliefs already held. The Hebrew cosmology, which most boys believe to be an integral part of the Christian religion, corresponds closely to their own cosmology. The members of all the tribes represented in the school see the earth as flat and the sky as an inverted bowl; the Bantu tribes suppose a region under the earth where there is a large lake. For the Batoro the heaven (*Iguru*) is ruled by Ngwarwa) by Nyakakaikuru, a little woman who holds up the skies, for the Banyankole); *Iguru* is peopled with beings who are tall, have tails and long hair. (The Batoro will ridicule a person with long and unkempt hair by saying: "Your hair is like that of the Children of Heaven.") The Batoro imagine the subterranean region to be ruled by Okuzimukwanyabuyongo and to be inhabited by the Bachwezi. The Bachwezi may appear on the earth's surface at night (they are often identified with the "fairies"): they are tall people with long spears and are to be avoided. The spiritual geography of the older Christian religion—heaven and hell, God and Satan, angels and devils—fits easily into this pattern. Thus it becomes possible for a second-form boy, writing for me an essay on what he wished to do when he left school, to say that he wanted to be an air pilot so that he could fly to the sky in order to see if there was a way through into heaven. This seemed to be a humorous sally, but on questioning the boy his proposal seemed to have been made in all seriousness.

Other aspects of Christianity (as often taught in Uganda) require little adjustment of mental habits on the part of the people. Minds habituated to accepting witchcraft as a theory of causes (as illustrated by Evans-Pritchard in *Witchcraft, Oracles and Magic among the Azande*) have no difficulty in attributing misfortune and illness to the displeasure of an angry Christian God. They are also accustomed to the process of thought by which the failure of Christian prayer is taken by Christians as an added proof of God's existence and benign intentions: there was no response to the prayer because it was God's will that something contrary should happen. In the same way, the African who enlists the aid of a witchdoctor to find a thief but meets with no success, simply argues that the witchdoctor was bad and the medicines poor. His faith in the system is unbroken. My pupils, in some instances, are fully alive to the fact that they have been told to reject certain beliefs for others which have no more evidence or only the same sort of evidence, and a small percentage of boys say frankly that they see no superiority in the new faith and, while remaining technically Christians, do not in fact embrace the faith.

Within the school, and particularly with the more advanced pupils, the tensions arise not so much between the new Western and the old indigenous cultures, but between the two apparently contradictory elements introduced from the West, the religious and the scientific. School "Brains Trusts" have a flavour of a meeting between Mr. Gladstone and T. H. Huxley: the questions are those which were asked of the divines of the late nineteenth century: How can we square evolution with Genesis? How can we reconcile a scientific account of historical change with the intervention of God in human affairs?

The evidence both implicit and explicit of boys at all levels in the school is that their education causes little disharmony at home. The boys themselves are always anxious to return home; when they write essays about important events in their lives they frequently deal with some happy family occasion; they view with distaste the possibility of obtaining employment away from home, and look on Englishmen in Uganda as callous and unfeeling for leaving their homes and relatives in England. They assert that their parents wish them to be educated and, far from expecting trouble or insubordination to result, expect to receive advice and informed help from their educated sons. The schoolboy at home on holiday is usually treated as an honoured guest: no work is expected of him—though he may work in his own coffee garden, the profits accruing being used towards school fees—and he is welcomed home as a decoration to the family entourage. This picture I have formed mainly from the talk and writing of schoolboys, but it is supported by Lucy Mair's observations in a village in Buganda in the mid nineteen-thirties: "The parents themselves are anxious to have their children go to school; there is no question of the children being taken from their influence against their will. . . . The parents do not themselves feel that European education is likely to make their children disrespectful. Indeed I remember one father declaring that children were better kept in order at school than at home . . . when at home they (the schoolboys) seem to spend a good deal of their time paying calls in their smart school uniforms." I too have found that many parents regard the school as an active ally and request the school to punish a boy for some misdemeanour at home. An important chief in Toro recently asked that his schoolboy son should be dealt with by the school for defying his orders; another father asked the school to punish (and arrange for the cure of) his son who had contracted venereal disease in the holidays. In the case of this Uganda secondary school it is a very doubtful proposition indeed, and one to be treated with the greatest caution, that higher education is creating tensions and cleavages between its products and the relatively uneducated villagers.

On the other hand it is true that the school causes social stresses in other ways. Even if it is doubtful how far new attitudes and values are carried directly from the school into wider society, it is clear that the school's indirect consequence for social habits is considerable. Senior boys are persuaded that it would be foolish and indeed impracticable to marry until they are over thirty. (A high proportion of school leavers are already over twenty, although this age is tending to fall.) Many realize that they may have to move to a town to obtain employment, and that, unlike the majority of their fathers, they will be entirely dependent on a money income. A post in commerce, industry, or a Government department, taken after a secondary-school course and without further training, is unlikely to be worth more than 120*s.* per month. (This, for example, is the salary of an Assistant Labour Officer on first appointment.) Accommodation for a married man in Kampala will usually be in the region of 50 to 70*s.* a month. If a boy trains as a teacher at a two-year training centre he will earn 170*s.* per month; if he goes through Makerere College, 255*s.* In the country, the wife of a professional man (e.g., police sub-inspector or assistant agricultural officer) would normally, unless she herself had received a higher education, make a substantial contribution to the family income by cultivation; her husband would build his house at negligible cost from local materials, and rent for 5 or 6 acres would probably be no more than 5*s.* a year. Children would also be an economic asset in helping on the land. In the town, a wife and children are economic liabilities. Moreover, the educated African has acquired new tastes which need satisfying from his income—for European dress, a more varied diet, a bicycle, a gramophone, visits to the cinema. Potential wives face serious competition from these diversions. Many boys, particularly those from the Lango and northern tribes, are in favour of polygynous marriage: almost 50 per cent. of the boys have stated that ideally they would prefer polygyny to monogyny, but they realize that, as the educated class, they may not find the economic basis even for monogyny.

THE SCHOOL AS A NEED-SATISFYING INSTITUTION

The school is in contact with Native society and, by direct and indirect influences, is modifying behaviour at many points. But it is not merely a superimposed agency of change; it is a response to society and satisfies deep needs.

If Malinowski's analysis of the functions of institutions, as elaborated in *The Dynamics of Culture Change,* is correct, the school could be effective only by operating on its indigenous counterpart, by providing for the same basic needs but more effectively than the indigenous institution or complex of institutions. In so far as family instruction, for example, in house-building and agriculture, may be regarded as a counterpart, the school is not so much a substitute as a supplement. It is true that education of whatever kind—even of the most purely academic variety—provided it is given in a school, is regarded as nurturing ability in all departments of life: schoolboys have an implicit faith in the "transfer of training." A School Certificate in academic subjects is taken as an indication of ability in commerce, agriculture, or crafts, and parents expect this versatility from academically trained sons. If the commercial success of a local Indian is discussed with schoolboys, their diagnosis is: "He is helped by two sons who have School Certificates," and the comparative prosperity of Indians in Uganda is attributed to their allegedly superior educational facilities. In this general sense, the school is regarded as improving on all indigenous forms of education, whatever their nature.

But the dynamism of the school cannot receive a complete explanation in terms of old needs now more effectively met. The school is satisfying new needs which have arisen from the European contact itself. Although we must count among these needs the acquired taste for European-type material comforts, this does not seem to bulk large in a schoolboy's—or his parents'—calculations. The following type of reason for desiring education is, indeed, given in some cases: A senior boy explained that it was his mother's wish that he should become a doctor: without schooling he would, like most of his family, spend his life cutting reeds from a swamp; with a higher education he might become a doctor, enjoy a higher standard of life and, in particular, possess a motor-car. (A doctor is one of the few African Government servants who can expect to be provided with a car almost immediately after qualifying.) But the great majority of boys and, it appears, their parents, have not made such calculations. Even when they have been made, they have not necessarily demonstrated the material advantages resulting from a school education. Boys at school are fully aware that without education it is possible to obtain a good employment even as a semi-skilled worker. A bricklayer may earn 7s. a day, a possible 100s. a month—more than a boy with a School Certificate is likely to earn as a clerk in a Government department. Moreover, as a semi-skilled artisan he would be paid daily and could live the episodic life which is dear to him. An African shoemaker, working for an Indian in a town, might earn over 13s. a day; and tailors might gain even more remunerative work. But the boy at school, in possession of this knowledge, will still persevere through his six-year course, provided he can continue to raise the fees, with the likelihood of a vocational course to follow lasting from two to five years, before he receives his first salary of between 150 and 200s. a month.

The literate skills of a boy will, of course, be welcome for their practical value in the home: he will keep his father's coffee or cotton accounts, he can write to buyers, he is valuable in the market when transactions are being made. The boys accept an obligation of service, at least within their clans, as a corollary to education. Boys seem to feel deeply this sense of service, and there is little indication, at school at least, of marked individual self-seeking. The majority of boys have thought little about their careers after school: it is one of the problems with senior boys to persuade them to think about their prospects and decide on a suitable field of employment.

The above are incidental reasons for wanting education. After eliciting the boys' ambitions, I have been struck by the desire for employment in which school training will have little direct value. "European-type" employment in offices and Government departments has no allurement for them—it is bondage, slavery to a routine and to a hierarchy, distasteful even though it involves European dress and other desirable features of European life. The majority of boys want to own land and be farmers, or to own and run their own small businesses: they don't want a boss, particularly European or Asian, and they don't want to be dependent on a salary. They envisage a period of employment, even those who aspire to the higher professional ranks, of from five to ten years as a prelude to individual enterprise, in which they can save the money necessary for establishing their own concerns. They are not primarily concerned to find employment in which they can "put their education to good use."

The school, far from flourishing in response to "indigenous" needs, appears to flourish in despite of them. Thus before the English contact, family instruction placed great emphasis on correct speech, clear articulation, and respectful address. The modern secondary school, partly by removing the child from home influences and partly by its comparative neglect of the vernacular and emphasis on English, starves this need which was felt by the earlier society. A recent African writer says:

> In most ancient African societies (the Baganda for example), great importance was attached to how children should speak and how they should not speak. . . .
> But the schools have upset all the old systems of society. The children no longer spend enough time with their parents. . . . The schools

> do not as yet pay much attention to how the children speak their mother tongue, and there is therefore no longer that speech training which was once one of the refinements of society.[5]

Many teachers feel that the school is not satisfying needs which were met effectively in the old order. Miss Constance Aitken discusses this problem in an article on secondary education for African girls:

> The girls' needs for physical activity, for self-expression through craft-work or art and music . . . are all met in African tribal life. . . . Initiation ceremonies, weddings, and other festive occasions also provide an outlet for self-expression in singing and dancing.
>
> The desire for all these things must still be strong in girls in secondary schools, yet they are to a very large extent cut off from all the old ways of satisfying these desires, and it is an important part of our responsibility as secondary schoolteachers to discover the best ways of providing outlets for these desires.[6]

And yet the school enjoys a widespread popularity in spite of these apparent defects: after experience of schoolboys' demands for the most arid treatment of academic knowledge, for the bare bones of English grammar and the complexities of a remote historical period, I am tempted to say because of them. My pupils seem to feel little need for the new knowledge to be related to the concrete situations of their homelives, and regard such treatment with suspicion, as a frivolous evasion of the real work of the school.

The school is a response to needs not felt in pre-contact times: it is an institution in which a new ideal type of man can be shaped—the "educated man." It may be that this ideal had a counterpart in the ideal of the great hunter or the great warrior of former days and, if so, the new ideal has effectively replaced it. The most cogent criticism of a boy and encouragement to different behaviour is to point out that his present conduct is not that of an educated man. The exhortation to be "good," manly, loyal, Christian, or even courageous meets with far less response. The boys judge Europeans by their educational status: they count a man's degrees and diplomas and by them measure his worth; his military record and decorations, on the contrary, are of no account and may even be damaging in their sight. Graduate status is the ideal—regardless of social or economic benefits which may attend it. Race antagonism decreases in proportion to the number of university graduates in the White ranks. The boys have no objection to positions of power and wealth being held in their localities by educated Englishmen; they are deeply resentful when such positions are held by men of obviously inferior culture and education. It is by appreciating the force of this ideal that a teacher can do his best work, for it affords the most powerful solvent of old irrational attitudes and beliefs. Thus a boy in the junior school will still cling to many old beliefs: that the earth is like a bowl, that a chicken is in some sense the cause of thunder, that in Toro the Bachwezi made the crater lakes to water their cattle and, as spirits, are today the cause of earth tremors. Already, after six years in the primary school and one or two in the secondary, they have sufficient scientific knowledge to discount these beliefs. But it is only the senior boys, after a further four or five years at school, who clearly reject them; yet these boys have no more logical evidence or weight of knowledge to the contrary than they had five years previously. It is not additional knowledge and its logical application which has convinced them that the earth is a sphere; they have come to accept this proposition as one held by all truly educated men.

It is one of the weaknesses of Christian teaching that it is often undertaken by enthusiastic but uneducated men, and the boys' scepticism is in accordance with the preacher's low educational status. A. T. Culwick observed in *Good out of Africa*[7]: ". . . however modern and abreast of the times the leaders of Christian thought at home may be, it is most unfortunately true that very few 'advanced' Christians seem to find their way into the African mission field, and by far the greater part of the teaching given to the Bantu peoples is in fact the dogma of a bygone age. Both Christianity and the African are the losers" (p. 16). My pupils are quick to appreciate that many Christian preachers are not 'advanced' and judge the content of their teaching accordingly. The schoolboy magazine article already quoted, speaking of the Balokole sect of Christians, goes on to observe that "The movement is an excellent one, but most of them having only the rudiments of education, cannot express their ideas properly, hence they make but a poor impression on the people."

The nature and potency of the "educated man" ideal is fundamental to an understanding of education in Uganda. The European missionaries who first came to Uganda seemed to Africans to have a power not possessed by Native kings: the converts of Ashe and Mackay were known as "readers," and it was the power conferred by literacy which Mwanga, Kabaka of Buganda, feared. Knowledge of books was the significant attribute of the White man and the apparent source of his superiority, as Mackay had early appreciated. "Mackay, with great foresight, had, on first coming to Africa, brought out a printing press with him." [8] The fear of this power gained through reading, which was felt by those in authority, and its attraction for the people, are clear from the account given by Ashe:

> And then we heard the terrible news that the Christian readers had been seized and many of them put to death. Nyonyi Entono, my friend [a Roman Catholic reader] . . . was cruelly and shamefully mutilated by the order of the king [Mwanga]. He recovered, and afterwards actually became *katikiro,* or chief judge, in place of the haughty chancellor. That functionary killed two of his pages who had been seen reading. The same day Kagwa (Apolo) was called to the king's presence with another youth; a stormy scene ensued. . . . Then the king turned to Apolo: "Are you a reader?" he cried, trembling with passion. "I read, my Lord," was the brave reply. "Then I'll teach you to read!" shouted the angry king, and gashed him too with a spear, and then took the wooden handle and broke it over his back.[9]

In the villages of Western Uganda "reader" and "Christian" are still convertible terms. Literacy is sought now as in the 1880s as the essentially valuable contribution of the white man to Uganda.

The other attribute and apparent source of white power today is Western technology, and the ideal of many African schoolboys is changing slightly in its content to include not only the man who knows the meaning of books but also the one who knows how to handle machines. Engineering machinery now operating in Uganda, as well as its emphasis in many films and publications presented, for example, by the British Council, are encouraging this remodelling of the ideal. Many boys have now accepted a new ideal of "the technical man" and wish to become motor mechanics (carpentry has not the same appeal). A. N. Whitehead has pointed out in the *Aims of Education* that for English boys, in the rhythm of their development between 12 and 15 years of age, science is a thing of romance, making an appeal to the imagination rather than to the intellect. My African pupils who have accepted the technical ideal seem to remain at this stage: their ambition is not necessarily or even frequently an indication of mechanical aptitude, and it would probably be a grave mistake to develop education in response to this romantic urge alone.

The school offers the means for fashioning an ideal type of self. This, I believe, is its main function in Uganda society. The pupil demands much of the school and of his teachers, whose work he makes exacting. His attitude to the school is that it should give much—including a high standard of material amenities—to which, with few exceptions, he was never accustomed at home. The school should be the great provider and, if it falls short, the boys are inclined to sulk. J. F. Ritchie, in his psycho-analytical study,[10] attributes this to the child's search for stability and equilibrium, for the perfection of the nursing situation:

> Unfortunately the pupil demands of it [academic education] more than it can give, for he wants a system of perfect order and he wants it ready-made. He does not understand that he cannot gain psychically from education unless he makes personal efforts, nor that he is unable to assimilate order from without unless he can make contact with the rudiments of order in his own mind.

This analysis is in keeping with my own experience in Uganda. The African pupil is seeking subtler satisfactions than are credited in the familiar stereotype of the educated African seeking European-type employment, dress, and living-conditions, and discarding his uneducated family as now beneath his station.

The school is an institution which satisfies certain needs not only of Uganda but also of English society. Its nature can be fully understood only in its role as a field of co-operation between Black and White. Englishmen enter the school to teach from a sense of service, a sense of romance, an opportunity for travel, or as an escape from difficult emotional or material circumstances at home. Schoolboys, without significant exception, allege that their teachers have come to positions which are far better, offering higher salaries and other material inducements, than they could have obtained in England. In some cases this is at least part of the truth. The school provides opportunities for professional employment, and its sociological role within the context of England and Uganda considered as a single field, is to maintain the traditional role of Empire in providing a comprehensive form of poor relief for a margin of all classes of English society. The sociological consequences for English society are the loosening of family ties and the modification of English attitudes to "the Native" brought about by the letters, publications, and conversations when on leave, of members of the staff. The contribution of the school to English ideas about African people cannot be generalized. In some cases experience in the school merely confirms the race stereotype already in the teacher's mind; in other cases it gives a vision of Africans as real and individual people, sharing the same humanity but moulded by a different culture.

The school as a co-operative enterprise between Black and White does not serve a single idea, and the larger society of which it forms a part varies in extent according to the particular need which the school satisfies.

THE SCHOOL AS A FIELD OF CULTURE CONFLICT

It is one of the limitations of those who have sought the identity of institutions in a unifying principle that they have overlooked the possibilities of institutions as fields of conflict. Malinowski, making a scientific approach, looked for the integrality of institutions; his scientific concept of integrality has the same consequence as Rousseau's philosophical concept of the General Will which is indivisible: both lead to a denial of the reality of conflict within a living community and of the fact that an institution may be a centre of conflict for constituent groups as well as of their interdependence. Bosanquet, making a philosophical approach although enlisting the support of psychology and sociology, maintained that the reality of institutions "lies in the fact that certain living minds are connected in a living way"; but the connexion must be harmonious: the institution expresses an ethical idea and not a number of warring ideas; by definition there is no possible form of conflict while the institution remains an institution.

No sociological survey of the school in which I teach could be complete without an account of the process of conflict as well as of co-operation. Black and White cooperate to achieve their respective satisfactions, but tensions arise in the act of co-operation. There is no smooth transfer of culture, but a complex pattern of acceptance and rejection. From the culture tensions a new synthesis emerges which is different from both parent cultures.

This is most clearly so in the field of religious practices and beliefs. Although, as I maintained above, some of the mental processes required by Christianity correspond closely to those required by Native religion, and are received with little protest or modification, others receive less ready accommodation. Some boys reject the Christian teaching of meekness and allege that this is taught by Europeans, at such blatant variance with modern European practice, in order to emasculate the African and condition him to a role of tame subordination. Others, and particularly those under the influence of the Balokole, accept the Christian virtue of meekness as a central tenet: it provides them with a strong defence mechanism in the culture conflict. For them, the necessary consequence of meekness and repentance is forgiveness: it is usual for them to claim exemption from school punishments on the grounds that they have repented and are filled with humility, and it is the master's Christian duty to forgive. The influence of the Balokole movement is itself an expression of culture tension: the sect is essentially separatist; it is also salvationist, and its members can relegate all Europeans who are not within its ranks to an inferior standing on earth and eternal torment in Hell.

It is difficult to predict the final outcome of our teaching and, in the case of Christian teaching, to be sure whether the resultant attitudes and beliefs can be meaningfully labelled "Christian" at all. The warning and suggestions which Professor Karl Mannheim[11] made to Christian thinkers in England in view of transitional social forms, applies with even greater force to missionaries and preachers in transitional Africa: "A rule may sound very Christian in the abstract; in the concrete it may produce opposite results." . . . He would solve the dilemma by making the theologians little more than annotators of the process of social change, waiting for new behaviour patterns to emerge, and labelling them Christian or non-Christian as the case might be. Mannheim is "inclined to think that a redirection of habits and codes will have to be made in future in consultation with sociologists and other experts. Their information will bring home to us how rules work in practice; the final recasting of norms will still be left to the theologian and philosopher." . . . Christianity thus ceases to be prescriptive or to claim to know what is a Christian rule until its function in a particular social context has been observed.

But the teacher cannot stand as an aloof commentator; he is part of the process of culture change; but with sociological insight he can see how the culture he is transmitting is in fact received, and the mutations it undergoes in the act of reception. To this end he can plot the course of cultural obstruction to the new attitudes, values, and explanations which he offers.

The deepest and most general cultural obstacle I have found in my pupils is their assumption about the nature of causation, whether in the world of nature or of men. Causation in terms of the slow and spontaneous action of nature they find difficult to appreciate. In Geography they are sceptical about the method of the formation of mountains, the age-long work of glaciers, the action of rivers in changing the earth's configuration over the centuries. They want the more dramatic, immediately observable results of human action, or of an agency acting with the more easily understood motive and purpose of, and in the same time scale as, an individual man. Of the long natural process which results in a "river capture," or the formation of a delta or fiord, they say: "But I cannot imagine it." They draw the diagram and make the notes but remain only partially convinced. In History teaching I have found a similar problem. An event caused by a single man is intelligible; an event which results from a complex of interacting forces, economic, geographical, cultural, operating over periods longer than the human life-span, is seldom appreciated. Invariably in answer to a History question which asks why something happened, even the most senior and intelligent boys will give a catalogue of preceding events without attempt to establish causal connexions, and will usually see the solution to the problem in the action of an individual man just prior to the event.

But there are more concrete expressions of the conflict between the two cultures represented in the school. The boys tend to be stereotype-minded and to see Europeans in a preconceived mould. Junior boys make no distinction between Europeans; they are unaware of the differences between the various European nationalities or the wide variety of groups within England and their dissimilar attitudes. (The main distinction they make is between educated and less educated.) Their stereotype is formed chiefly from reports of European behaviour towards the Native in Kenya and South Africa. Any member of staff who has lived or worked in Kenya is suspect. This stereotyped European has quite definite characteristics, and boys claim to be able to recognize the man from Kenya by the way he drives his car—recklessly, and to the danger of Native life. But all Europeans share these characteristics and use cars as lethal weapons. Contrasting personalities and differences among Englishmen on the staff help to break down this stereotype, and the fact of living with them in a community—for the great majority of boys have never spoken to an Englishman before coming to the secondary school. The teaching of History in which distinction is made between English and European groups illustrates the wide variety of outlook and attitudes among Europeans and has a similar effect.

There is other evidence that the suspicions with which a boy comes to school are, at least in some respects, reduced by his experience there. Thus most of my pupils bring to school the suspicion that white men are cannibals. They share the belief with the people in the villages that a red vehicle on which a bell is rung and which carries red buckets is used for predatory raids. (This description is given by boys in western Uganda who have never seen a fire-engine and have no conception of its purpose. The whole notion presumably comes from up-country visitors to Kampala who have seen red buckets outside the fire station and assumed that they contained human blood.) However strongly this belief may have been held in pre-school days, and although some junior boys still profess to believe it, I know of no schoolboy action apparently taken upon such a belief: no boy, for instance, has ever refused or appeared afraid to visit a European member of staff after dark.

But the boys are usually ready to impute unworthy motives to White activities. Thus they approach the very fact of education itself with an ambivalent attitude, for in one of its aspects it means to them a measure to consolidate White ascendancy. For this reason they resent manual work —they do not wish to be trained as slaves; but they also suspect the literary education they so earnestly desire: boys have told me that they are taught English so that they can more easily understand and readily obey the orders of Englishmen. They suspect any book written specifically for African pupils, or any form of teaching which takes their particular needs into account; they allege, without any evidence, that they are given a brand of education inferior to that given to boys in England, a special sub-scale variety designed for them. This charge is made particularly by the more senior boys. They ask suspiciously whether boys in England do gardening. And why cannot they take the Higher School Certificate as well as the School Certificate? But the conflict which is probably the most deeply felt arises, as I illustrated above, in the matter of school routine. After six years at the school boys are still fretful against the orderly pattern of daily life which they never knew at home.

The English schoolmaster is not in a good position to judge in what manner this aspect of his industrial culture, the methodical routine of work, is transmitted by his pupils to the wider society of which they are members. In the school it appears to be completely rejected and borne only from necessity. There is urgently needed the dispassionate outside commentator on the schoolboy in his home environment, whose information will help us to understand more fully how the school is operating in the wider social context of which it is an integral part.

FOOTNOTES

1. The opinions expressed in this article are the personal ones of the author and should not be regarded as stating the views of the Government of Uganda.

2. A poem written by a junior boy on the subject of shoes goes as follows:

> Lovely things, I thought much about you in childhood.
> Before I had you I wanted you dearly
> For you are so beautiful and have all my love.
> Oh! how beautiful you are and perfectly shaped,
> How clean you are and well kept,
> I marvel you shine with such brightness.
> I would never have thought you could cause so much pain.

3. It is, perhaps, of interest that, by a curious coincidence, on the morning when I had planned to make inquiries about belief in metamorphosis, at the routine chapel service the following portion of the Scriptures was read:

> "And the Lord said unto him, What is that in thine hand? And he said, A rod.
>
> And he said, Cast it on the ground. And he cast it on the ground, and it became a serpent; and Moses fled from before it.
>
> And the Lord said unto Moses, Put forth thine hand and take it by the tail. And he put forth his hand, and caught it, and it became a rod in his hand." (Exodus, ch. 4)

4. L. P. Mair, *An African People in the Twentieth Century,* 1934, pp. 68–69.
5. E. M. K. Mulira, *The Vernacular in African Education,* pp. 36–37.
6. *Oversea Education,* vol. xix, No. 3, April 1948, pp. 705–6.
7. Rhodes Livingstone Paper No. 8, 1942.
8. R. P. Ashe, *Two Kings of Uganda,* 1889, p. 149.
9. *Ibid.,* pp. 218–19.
10. J. F. Ritchie, *The African as Suckling and as Adult,* Rhodes-Livingstone Paper No. 9.
11. Karl Mannheim, *Diagnosis of our Time,* 1943.

The English Approach to Educational Reorientation in Postwar Germany

ROBERT F. LAWSON

THE ONLY REAL GUIDE LINES for the educational efforts of the Allied Occupation in Germany were those set down at Potsdam, the elimination of National-Socialist ideology and the introduction of democracy in Germany.[1] The latter point is broad enough to allow a fully planned program to opererate under its heading, but in fact, no such positive plan was ever made. Thus, the occupying powers were able to proceed generally in accordance with their own national approaches to the formation of an educational system, and could differ considerably in their beliefs regarding educational needs in Germany. Because of their aversion to externally imposed schemes and with the conviction that re-education could only succeed through independent German efforts, the British even more than the American program appeared to lack clearly specified goals.

Certain principles were mutually understood as applicable to German education, of course, especially after Control Council Directive 54, for the "Democratization of Education in Germany," was issued.[2] Equality of educational opportunity in a democratic society required qualitatively equal training for elementary and secondary school teachers, free public schools for all children, a longer period of common and compulsory schooling, and more accessibility to higher education for lower-class youth. In spite of the inexplicit nature of the principles of Directive 54, there was general agreement between the two Anglo-Saxon powers as to what they meant. There were, however, even between these powers, differences in approach significant of larger differences in conceptions of educational administration, organization, and theory.

During the early war years the British maintained a distinction between "good" Germans and the Nazi governing power, but for Britons as well as for Americans, German and Nazi tended to become merged into a collective evil as the war continued and bitterness increased. As the view that Nazism had grown out of German traditions, especially Prussian militarism, replaced the sympathy for a German people whose ideals of

Reprinted, with permission of the author and publisher, from the COMPARATIVE EDUCATION REVIEW, Vol. 8, No. 1 (June, 1964), pp. 58–64.

freedom and morality were being destroyed by Nazi oppressors, foreign observers looked to German historical traditions and social institutions for the deeper causes of Hitler's rise to power. As is often the case when causes of national ills are sought, education is a prime suspect, whether or not a causal relationship can be justified and regardless of the dependence of education on other social or political institutions. Thus, it was a simple step to relate the world crisis to the alleged failure of German schools to build character and to educate the masses to political responsibility. Re-education was therefore intended to encompass social and political reform.

Although there was more respect for German academic traditions in England than in the United States generally, it was part of the reform effort to persuade the Germans to ease away from so preponderant an academic program, particularly in the secondary schools. If the German people were to understand concepts of political responsibility, social justice, and international good will, and apply these concepts in their national life, all schools had to give more attention to them, and *Gymnasien* and universities had to produce leaders with learned democratic attitudes. The universities, considered by the British to be centers of reactionary thought, were the object of much of the re-education effort, which was not altogether consistent with the policy of working from the bottom up, but was perhaps indicative of the importance attached to educational provisions for training leaders in Europe.

University reforms were intended, among other things, to broaden the base of recruitment by establishing scholarship and loan fund programs, to make the universities more responsive to the society as a whole by creating university advisory councils representative of diversified interests, to direct responsibility for and participation in university affairs downward, to include younger staff members, and to divorce university teachers from the officialdom, yet encourage in them a sense of civic obligation. The attempt at first to determine necessary reforms on the basis of recommendations made by a delegation of British university teachers in 1947, coming after attempts to denazify university faculties and to restrict admission by a *numerus clausus*, brought bitter complaints from Germans who resented the direct interference with their academic traditions. The complaints were not ignored by the British, however, and in 1948 a German commission was formed, whose recommendations could be received without criticism of outside interference and which did stimulate progress in independent efforts toward university reform.[3]

Communication and education media were devoted to the task of propagating democratic ideas, as defined however vaguely by national custom of the occupying power and the interpretation of the assigned personnel. The belief that the attitudes and information necessary to a people's government could be transmitted as rapidly and effectively as totalitarian doctrines had been is not entirely fallacious, but the essential differences between democracy and totalitarianism make it much more difficult to effect the changes in individual and social behavior required by the former.

Moreover, the belief in the efficacy of education alone to change the nature of society suggests that the power of the school is great enough to accomplish ends opposed to its own supporting structure.

Even though the general objective of "democratic re-education" was accepted, the implementation procedures were only vaguely defined and not unified even in the British and American zones. The British approached the task of reconstruction primarily on the local levels of German administration. In practice, this meant there was a certain looseness and informality about British efforts, which possibly prolonged the re-establishment of stable, systematic governmental functioning, but this loss was more than compensated for by the ease with which the transition to German control was able to be made in the British zone. British military government avoided an attempt to structure or administer strictly either the educational system or the state.

The initial postwar educational efforts were, as in the American zone, confined to satisfying the immediate needs of schools and children so that the schools could begin to operate again. This required a great effort under the circumstances and was still the primary educational concern in Germany when control was handed back to the German *Länder* in the British zone under Military Government Ordinance 57 at the close of 1946.[4]

With this Ordinance, German authorities returned to almost full power in school administration. British Military Government kept the reviewing authority in personnel questions, required reports, and continued to make school inspections. However, there is no evidence to indicate resentment against these reserved powers. Actually, the ability of British education officers to win German confidence and their skill in reorienting attitudes without aggressive imposition of their own ideas led to constructive cooperation in educational reform after 1947.

Although not as persistent as the Americans in personnel screening, the British concentrated on teachers and books more than on organizational change. In accordance with British policy, the work was done largely at local levels, with a considerable degree of personal contact and persuasion, and a consequent minimum of misunderstanding or resentment.[5] Education officers met with teachers and presented them with information and assistance. The approach was not entirely satisfactory from the standpoint of total social reform, but it was practical and personal. The aim was to get the schools started in the right direction as soon as possible, but also to start a process of attitudinal reorientation which would bear fruit in future years. The attitudes of teachers were considered decisive in the longer period of time required for permanent educational change.

Besides the continuous personal influence of education officers on teachers, the textbook supervision,[6] and the attempted university reforms, the British relied on information centers, exchange visits, jointly-sponsored courses, cooperation with other international agencies, and encouragement of progressive activity among German authorities to further intellectual and social changes in education. The program was only loosely organized, but the participants understood the aims and functioned quite effectively with this understanding.[7]

The British officers were occasionally criticised for a "colonial attitude" of tolerance, efficiency, superiority, and aloofness.[8] But this criticism, like that against American formalism and proselytizing, was not strong enough to negate a high general respect among Germans for the methods of both powers, due at least in some measure to the usually good relationships between individual education officers and the Germans they worked with.

The British apparently never attempted and were careful not to suggest an imitation of their own system. Nevertheless, British influence was overtly or subtly manifest in many education proposals made by the Germans. This can be seen immediately, for example, in the Hamburg school reorganization of 1949, which patterned secondary school branches after those of the English 1944 Act. In some ways, the British achieved better results than the United States Occupation authorities, but there are a number of reasons other than the effectiveness of their approach to account for it. The geographical and historical proximity of England to North Germany and the existence of some similar academic traditions made for easier communication. Moreover, both countries had a similar need to update their educational systems, and had to do it in face of serious economic and social problems left in wake of the war.

The fact that few educational reforms were realized by the end of the Occupation has little to do with differences in program or method. In both the American and British zones, where little forceful imposition was applied, there were simply too many immediate problems and the situation of military occupation, in whatever form, was too unfavorable for German educators to find their way to large-scale school reforms. However, the ideas promoted during the period returned in German educational planning later, which indicates a greater effectiveness than probably would have been the case under a rigid program.

There was inevitably some anti-Occupation feeling among Germans and there were, of course, harmful as well as constructive aspects of the Occupation effort. German educators as a group cannot be identified as fully in support of British and American aims for reeducation, nor were they severely critical. One reason for this is the deep division between German educators who favored the kind of progress in education advocated by the Anglo-Saxon powers, and those conservative educators who adhered to tradition and rejected outside interference as an attempt to undermine German standards. This division was not new in Germany nor is it peculiar to Germany, but German educators were in the unique position, having had their entire system compromised to the point of destruction, of having to begin again philosophically as well as materially. The pressures of time and convenience favored re-establishing traditional patterns, but pressures from the Occupation and recognition of the need for social fulfillment encouraged educational change. Educators had to make a stand in terms of these two basic directions. For many, the choice had already been made during the Weimar years, but the acuteness of the problems of total reconstruction made the stand a much more general and crucial issue for education than would normally be required. The resultant conflicts, manifest in such questions as school fees, comprehensive schools, and secondary school selection, were to carry beyond the Occupation period into independent German educational actions.

The Germans faced numerous obstacles in their own efforts to reconstruct education in the early postwar years. The change from Nazi power and ideology to the governing power and cultural pressure of a foreign power was confusing at best, especially for the youth, and introduced a general wave of nihilistic thinking. The tug-of-war between East and West, centered in Germany, led many Germans to despair of their role as a pawn in the struggle. Further, the attempt to introduce democracy involved hardships, indecision, and conflict reminiscent of the Weimar period, and not more promising in outlook. In this atmosphere, it is remarkable that so much enthusiasm for future progress was aroused, and part of the credit must be given to the Occupation personnel who, in spite of faults and mistakes, ran a "benevolent despotism" ultimately designed to help Germany.

When the Occupation effort is harshly criticized by German outside observers, it must be remembered that four or five years is a short time to accomplish any kind of meaningful cultural change. Moreover, there was little special training provided officers for the tasks they had to perform, and only vague policy directions to guide them. They simultaneously acted in such conflicting roles as conquering authority and counseling friend. They had the task of defining democracy for a foreign people, and explaining methods whereby its essence could be instilled in public life. And they had finally the formidable assignment, only gradually realized, of attempting to distinguish absolute political or educational values from our own national bias. It is not surprising then, that the best remembered and universally acclaimed effort at reeducation in the British zone was not part of the official program.

The German Educational Reconstruction (commonly called G.E.R.) was initially organized in England by German emigrants and interested English citizens before the end of the war. It reflected English faith in voluntary educational effort, and has been evaluated as the most positive contribution to the reorientation of the German school system after the war.[9]

The initiative for the effort came from S. H. Wood, director of teacher training in the British Ministry of Education, in 1942. The organization was founded in February, 1943, by a small group which included Fritz Borinski, secretary from 1943 to 1945 and Minna Specht, both of whom continued to be active leaders individually in German and international education after the war.[10] From this beginning of direct, independent action by a small number of German and English participants, G.E.R. was to expand to an international organization and engineer a large scale exchange of German and English visits in the late forties.

The guiding principle for this organization was general reorientation of German social attitudes and intellectual dogmas. It included in its goals disseminating information on Germany to the English people, and later, on other nations to Germans; working out suggested plans for reconstruction of the educational system; gathering together German emigrants to assist in the program, and making contacts with educational and youth leaders who would be able to help Germany later.[11]

All during the later war years, the G.E.R. members in England followed these plans. They made lectures, prepared and distributed materials, and gathered people together in an effort to break down the distorted view of Germany, and bring back the distinction between "Nazi" and "German." They made individual contacts, informed the general public, and represented German education at international conferences. Perhaps most important, they rallied despairing German emigrants to a positive cause, and kept some kind of cultural contact between Germans and a foreign democratic nation.

In the summer of 1945, G.E.R. members gained access to prisoner-of-war camps in England, and began their direct efforts at German reconstruction. Many German emigrant members of G.E.R. returned to Germany to continue the work actively, and arrangements were begun to start bringing German educators to England for information visits. Through this organization alone, 345 or more Germans were brought to England between 1945 and 1950.[12] The list includes such well-known educational names as Professors Blättner (Kiel), Nöhl (Göttingen), Weinger (Göttingen), Becker (Bonn) and Flitner (Hamburg), Dr. Minna Specht of the Odenwaldschule, Dr. Koelle of UNESCO's Hamburg Institute, and the Hamburg and Munich school ministers, Landahl and Hundhammer. G.E.R. guests came from all over Germany and from educational positions in the broadest sense: youth officials (including those serving in juvenile courts and reform schools), teachers of different levels and from private as well as public schools, labor union representatives, social workers, political and administrative officials, pastors, and university and technical higher-school professors.

By 1949, G.E.R. *Land*-groups were formed in Germany and plans were underway to invite English guests to Germany. A letter from G.E.R., London, in February, 1949, recommended cooperation with the Education Branch of military government in the common enterprise of reconstruction, but it is impossible to say whether this recommendation was prompted by previous lack of cooperation, or whether this was merely a restatement of general G.E.R. policy of cooperation with other similar efforts. It is likely that there was some governmental pressure at this time to consolidate the various efforts for more effectiveness.

The *Times Educational Supplement,* on June 10, 1949, reported representation from Wales, Scotland, France, Sweden, Switzerland, and the

U.S.A. as well as from Germany and England at a G.E.R. conference held at the Odenwaldschule in Hesse. Addresses were given and discussion took place on the social and political bases of education. But the most interesting aspect of this conference was that, being held in a school, the delegates could actually meet and talk to German children. To bring this realistic aspect of an educational conference into sharper focus, the two top classes of the school participated in the meetings. Undoubtedly it was easier to do this in the free, progressive atmosphere of the Odenwaldschule than it would have been elsewhere, and it is probable that Minna Specht, head of the school and early member of G.E.R., had a great deal to do with the success and realism of the conference.

In 1950, a German headquarters was established at Bonn to assist and advise the regional groups. In July, this became the central office of G.E.R. for work in both England and Germany. Plans were initiated for 600 students from German *Hochschulen* to work on the English harvest. The student harvest scheme was repeated every year until 1955 and proved to be one of the most successful of the later major undertakings of the organization. The students lived in camps or with English families, worked two months and had one month free to travel. Favorable reports from both sides indicated that much was accomplished in good will and information exchange. G.E.R. had no ready source of funds and communications constantly expressed a need for financial support. This particular effort was covered by grants from ministries of education in the German *Länder,* from the German foreign office, and interestingly, from the Office of the High Commissioner for Germany.[13]

Between 1950 and 1951, the letterhead of the organization changed from German Educational Reconstruction to G.E.R., A Society for Promoting Anglo-German Education Relations, indicating a need for more subtlety in contacts with Germany and a regained position of equality for Germany in foreign relations. The organization leadership and activity was increasingly being taken over by the German office and plans were initiated to organize as a German corporation under the name, *Deutsch-Englische Austauschstelle G.E.R.*, e. V. That the organization was never independently strong, however, is shown by the continual requests for contributions and the frequent suggestions for coordination with other exchange groups and educational, cultural, and social agencies.[14]

In 1951, 441 young people participated in youth-group exchanges, conferences were held in London on Political Behavior in England and Germany and on Industrial Relations, and an adult-education group from Oxford and a group of English hospital workers visited Germany under G.E.R. auspices.[15]

The founding assembly of the *Deutsch-Englische Austauschstelle G.E.R.* met in January, 1952, and set its goal in the first article of the charter as deepening the cultural and educational connections between Germany and England, and furthering any exchange serving this purpose.[16] Significant during this year also was the G.E.R. conference on youth exchanges. The initiative for this aspect of the exchange program had come primarily from the German side, and they worked to build up this emphasis. The conference report stressed the importance of bringing youth together, and insisted the critical point in the connection must be the personal relationships and human understanding. The bringing together of youth from different nations was to be the organization's unique contribution to peaceful cooperation of the peoples. Plans were made for choosing "partner" groups, financing, and handling accommodations.[17]

But the problems became greater, while the need of and support for G.E.R. became smaller in subsequent years. A continual stream of exchange activities was coordinated through the group, including a conference with English visitors on the German vocational school system, a meeting of German philologists from England and one of the English philologists from Germany, a tour of the *Ruhrgebiet* by English coal-miners, visits by English teacher trainers to Germany and German police officials to England. However, 1955 was the last really active year from the standpoint of initial goals, and even by this time the exchanges had lost much of their early significance. The youth-group exchange was dying out because the group requests were growing smaller, while individual requests, more difficult for G.E.R. to handle, were overwhelming and heavy on the German side.[18]

In the minutes of the G.E.R. meeting of March 16, 1956 the question was first recorded, which had doubtless long been present among G.E.R. friends and members: "Every Organization must continually ask itself, whether it still has a legitimate task." Evidently, enough members answered the question affirmatively for a decision to continue functioning, but active support dropped off rapidly. In 1958, G.E.R. in London was dissolved, ostensibly because of financial reasons.[19]

After 1958, some of the English G.E.R. work was taken over by the Educational Interchange Council in London under H. J. Walker. But a real sister organization in England for the *Deutsch-Englische Austauschstelle,* which now was located in Frankfurt and connected with the *Europäischer Austauschdienst* was lacking. The exchange of librarians, housewives, and gymnasts between 1958 and 1960, though possibly beneficial to the groups involved, were a far cry from the zealous, vital service performed by G.E.R. in the early post-war years.

The reports of the 1960 and 1961 meetings show the bureaucratic character of the new organization. Little individual, direct accomplishment of the G.E.R. group is reflected, as opposed to the earlier period, when G.E.R. was characterized by close, personal contacts and a direct approach to rebuilding international relations. There is a dramatic difference between the personal tone of the farewell letter from Eric Hirsch, longtime secretary in London, in 1958 and the formalism so prevalent in the 1960 *Niederschrift.*

Probably few people in the two countries were even aware that G.E.R., in some form, was still functioning in 1961. But a great many

German educators in the British zone remembered the early activities of the group, and credit it with a large role in the transition to outward-oriented thinking in Germany, which is a key part of a program of re-education from totalitarianism.

The immediate postwar period in Germany has particular significance for the educator in that the entire Occupation program, from the British and American points of view at least, was a re-education effort involving the reorientation not only of political but also of social and intellectual attitudes. This inevitably caused a comparison and sometimes conflict of national aims and values and it is to the credit of the two forementioned powers that Germany accepted the reorientation basically, rapidly developed a functioning democracy, and allied herself strongly with her former conquerors in the West.

Inasmuch as the points of Control Council Directive 54 and other suggestions of the western occupying powers reintroduced earlier German school reform ideas or responded to social-educational needs of post-war Germany, they had an effect on German education. Where an Occupation aim represented a particularly national characteristic, there was little residual effect after outside controls were removed, unless the corollary practices were perceived as profitable to Germany for meeting the needs of youth in a changing society. In the latter case, there is only a connection between national school practices, not necessarily between German adoptions and Occupation school reform attempts.

It is only in the sense that the program for the re-education of Germany provided for a flow of information from the outside world, stimulated the reawakening of pre-war liberalism and the rediscovery of earlier progressive German trends, proposed new ideas for consideration, or even called for an educational *Auseinandersetzung* among German teachers, that this program contributed to the reformation of German education.

REFERENCES

1. "Report on the Tripartite Conference of Berlin (Potsdam), 17 July–2 August 1945," Section III. A. 7, in Beate Ruhm von Oppen (ed.), *Documents on Germany under Occupation, 1945–1954.* (London: Oxford University Press, 1955), p. 43.
2. *Ibid.*, p. 233.
3. See Robert Birley, "Education in the British Zone of Germany," *International Affairs*, Vol. 26, No. 1, January, 1950; "Germany: The British Zone of Occupation," in *The Yearbook of Education* (London: Evans Bros., 1948), p. 520; and British Foreign Office, *University Reform in Germany: Report by a German Commission* (London: H.M.S.O., 1949).
4. Ruhm von Oppen, *op. cit.*, p. 192.
5. Interviews with German educators and officials in Hamburg, 1961.
6. The Textbook Section at Bünde seems to have been an exception to the flexible British administration. In their zeal to confirm the belief that Nazism reflected ideas already present in German culture, the censors condemned even Grimm's Fairy Tales. Kurt Zeidler, retired school inspector in Hamburg and co-author of post-

war English language texts, complained to the writer in 1961 that the textbook policy was so directed to minutiae and so destructive of German traditions that it was difficult for writers to contribute anything of educational value.

7. Letter from W. R. C. Chapman, former British Foreign Office lecturer, March 20, 1962.

8. Helen Liddell, *Education in Occupied Germany* (Paris: Librairie Marcel Riviere et Cie, 1949), p. 128.

9. Dorothea Blattner, "Britische Einwirkungen auf das deutsche Erziehungs und Bildungswesen von 1945 bis 1949," unpublished thesis, Kiel University, 1960, p. 27.

10. For a complete account of the founding membership, see Fritz Borinski, "German Educational Reconstruction," in *Erziehung und Politik: Festschrift für Minna Specht* (Frankfurt, 1960), p. 77.

11. "Die Geschichte von G.E.R.," *Die Sammlung,* III (1948), p. 51.

12. "Deutsche Gäste der G.E.R. bis Jan. 1950," mimeographed. This document as well as the G.E.R. letters and reports cited on following pages were made available by Dr. W. Koelle in Hamburg from his private files.

13. Letters from G.E.R., London, February 8, 1949 and July 26, 1950. Letter from G.E.R., Geschäftsstelle, Bonn, April 15, 1950. *Annual Report, G.E.R.,* 1951.

14. Letters from G.E.R., Bonn, December 20, 1950, and March 1, 1951.

15. *Annual Report, G.E.R.,* 1951.

16. *Satzung der Deutsch-Englischen Austauschstelle G.E.R.,* approved by *Gründungsversammlung,* Wiesbaden, January 20, 1952.

17. *Bericht über die Konferenz über internationalen Jugendaustausch,* Frankfurt, November 29/30, 1952.

18. *Protokoll der Mitgliederversammlung der Deutsch-Englischen Austauschstelle G.E.R.* e. V., March 12, 1955.

19. *Protokoll der Mitgliederversammlung der Deutsch-Englischen Austauschstelle G.E.R.* e. V., June 27, 1958.

Part Two

Education and the Polity

An area of concern among social thinkers, statesmen, educators, and policy makers through the ages has been citizenship training or, more technically, political socialization. It has been assumed that the operation of a political system rests upon norms, values, orientations, or states of mind shared by the members of society. Political socialization, or simply "politicization," is the process by which the individual is inducted into his political culture. How, where, when, and by whom is citizenship developed?

Since Plato and Aristotle, training in citizenship has been regarded as one of the main tasks of education in general and more particularly of schools. Education as public policy has often been justified on the need to institutionalize goals and norms to create national consensus, integration, and solidarity. This has been true of the movement toward public education in the United States, and of state education in the European countries and in the new nations. The political significance of schooling, from the politicization standpoint, is manifested in all countries, be they activated by nationalist, communist, or democratic ideologies.

Recent approaches to problems of education and political socialization have been less concerned, if at all, with normative questions—such as, What should the attributes of a good citizen be?—and a logico-deductive type of reasoning, and more with empirical analyses. The questions raised have been of the following variety: What knowledge, values, or attitudes does the school deliberately seek to impart or develop concerning the nation and its political system? How is this deliberate instruction (or indoctrination) organized and carried out, and by whom? What knowledge does the pupil possess of his nation's history, the rights and obligations of the citizen, the system of government, decision making, and so on? What are the pupils' attitudes toward and perceptions of political institutions, political authority figures, and the like? How does the pupil perceive his role in the political system and its parts? What is the actual role of deliberate instruction in the politicization of the youth relative to other agencies like the family, the church, and his peers? At what level of the individual's development and schooling are various political attitudes developed?

Prompted by concern with citizenship training, an increasing volume of research in the United States has concentrated on children's attitudes toward or images of the political world. The empirical studies of Robert Hess, David Easton, and Fred Greenstein, to name but a few of the better-known political socialization scholars in this country, have explored various aspects of the relationship of children and politics. Among the areas examined are children's attitudes toward political authority figures, such as the President or Governor; the roles of sex and social class in influencing political awareness; the relationship between the child's images of political authority figures and of the father or other adults; party awareness among children, and the role of the school vis-à-vis other social institutions in the development of politically relevant attitudes. The reader is urged to consult some of these studies, which are cited in the bibliography. Although they deal with the socialization of political attitudes in the United States, their method, concepts, and techniques could be applied to other countries.

The first article in this section exemplifies another line of research into the politicization of youth. Richard H. Solomon concentrates on the cultural content of elementary school readers and compares attitudes and values abstracted from them at two different periods in Chinese history, the Republican and the Communist. He examines the efforts made by the Communist regime to redefine the traditional basis of "social authority" by analyzing images and attitudes on loyalty toward family, party, and nation, on authority figures such as Mao, on social responsibility, women, work, and education. From such sources as children's stories, Solomon shows how cultural change is being purposely induced to conform to new goals and norms, in this case to those of the Chinese Communist ideology.

A second major area of concern in the study of the relationship between education and the political system has been the political leadership or elite. Studies of political elites have assumed that in every society it is possible to identify a group of people who are at the top of the power hierarchy and who are characterized by some degree of exclusiveness and corporateness. Although they are a part of the total political culture of a society, elites are assumed to possess a separate group character.

Recent inquiries into the educational aspects of political elites have often sought to establish the role of schooling in elite recruitment, formation, and maintenance or change. This has usually entailed study of the educational characteristics of political leaders in terms of amount, level, and type of schooling, the role of particular types of schools in the training of potential elites, and the institutional or other mechanisms linking education to attainment and maintenance of elite status. Rupert H. Wilkinson examines some of these interconnections by focusing on the gentleman ideal in classical China and late Victorian England. The classical content and the general orientation of Confucian and Victorian Public School education sought to promote skills, attributes, and values such as manners, accent, the sense of privilege and duty, respect for tradition, a spirit of public service, self-assurance and discipline, aesthetic sensibility, scholarship, and a general versatility of mind, that were accepted as hallmarks of the governing elite. The gentleman elite was largely recruited from the "gentlemanly class," the landed gentry who had the means—hence the leisure—and the upbringing to cultivate the amateur spirit of public service. Wilkinson also brings out some of the differences between the two cultures. Both societies stressed "group spirit." But while Chinese etiquette focused loyalties on the family, the Victorian Public School emphasized the school community and the "House." Further, while Public School education resembled "military service," gentlemanly virtue was sought in the Chinese clan through "scholarship." Wilkinson's study raises the important question of the extent to which such elitist education and leadership sacrifices intelligence, productivity, and scientific advancement for the sake of loyalty and national cohesion.

The interrelationships of education and elites is constantly invoked in discussions of the problems of the "developing" nations and of their push for modernization. The three remaining articles deal in one way or another with aspects of this political-educational linkage. Munir Bashshur analyzes data on the political role of one institution, the American University of Beirut (AUB), in terms of politically relevant careers of its alumni and the social stratification system of Lebanon. The University, "an elite-perpetuating institution," does not generate mobility from a lower to a higher stratum. Yet, Bashshur observes, there are occupational shifts among the alumni in the upper strata. The AUB graduates constitute a cadre of "professionals" and "administrators" with potential power to enable them gradually to build a new political structure.

David Abernethy and Trevor Coombe note that, in the ex-colonial territories of Africa, Western-educated individuals became nationalist leaders and currently constitute the modernizing cadres. The educational policy is largely influenced by the political orientations of these new leaders. The political significance of the recruitment patterns of schools and universities (who gets what) and of the careers of school leavers is also stressed by Joseph Fischer in his essay on modernization in Burma and Indonesia.

The essays by Bashshur, Abernethy and Coombe, and Fischer deal with other questions relating to education and the polity. Schools function as integrative agencies in the society. Yet in some respects education, particularly in transitional and sharply divided societies, may actually be "malintegrative." This is clearly brought out in Bashshur's study of the American University of Beirut; that institution seems to reinforce the already existing religious, ethnic, and elite-mass bifurcations of the Lebanese society. Likewise, Fischer points out, the religious, ethnic, and linguistic orientations of education among the minorities of Burma, coupled with the local pattern of recruitment, exacerbate ethnic divisions and conflict. According to Abernethy and Coombe, expansion of education in the developing societies of Africa may indirectly "strengthen tribalism or regionalism and retard the government's campaign to create a national society."

The double-sided aspect of the political role of education, namely, its capacity to foster both stability and instability, is explored in greater detail in the Abernethy and Coombe essay.

This section does not deal with all of the aspects of education and politics. It does not look at the school system as a political organization seeking to promote its own interests and vying for political power with other organizations. Nor does it examine education as a political issue involving parties, religious organizations, teachers' unions, voluntary associations, and similar "interest groups." By and large it is limited to the political significance of schools as socializing, training, and selective institutions.

Educational Themes in China's Changing Culture

RICHARD H. SOLOMON

One of the striking contrasts between a Communist revolution and one of the "nationalist" variety lies in the differing attitudes held by the revolutionary elites towards the traditional culture. Nationalist leaders tend to come to power with a vague commitment to restore the values of the traditional society in a modern context; yet a good deal of their energy in the early years of nation-building is expended trying to relate cherished cultural doctrines to the often incompatible demands of modernisation.[1]

The Communists, in contrast, take power with a relatively well-developed image of the new social roles and structures required of a nation "building socialism." They make no bones about their intention to demolish much of the old tradition, and encourage the development of a new socialist culture to guide the people along the road to Communism. The following characterisation of socialist education by a member of the Chinese Communist Politburo suggests the conscious Communist dedication to Party controlled cultural change:

> Socialist education is one of the powerful weapons for transforming the old and building the new society. The purpose of the socialist revolution and socialist construction is to do away with all exploiting classes and all systems of exploitation including their remnants and to bring into being a Communist society . . . Such education can be led only by the political party of the working class, the Communist Party.
>
> . . . to carry the combination of education with productive labour into effect means a fight with the old traditions that have persisted for thousands of years. Without the Communist style of toppling down the old idols, burying doctrinairism, and daring to think, speak and do, without the creative spirit of combining the universal truths of Marxism with the concrete realities of our country, we cannot succeed. Today, in our educational work, vigorous efforts are being made to pull down the out-dated and set up the new.[2]

Reprinted with permission from THE CHINA QUARTERLY, Vol. 22 (April–June, 1965), pp. 154–170.

This assault on the traditional culture is at once a source of strength to the Communists, and a source of much opposition. Because the transition to Socialism, in the Party's eyes, requires the destruction of competing sources of social power and the deprecation of "unprogressive" cultural values, the Communists tend to alienate much of the old ruling elite, the non-Communist intellectuals, and older carriers of the traditional culture. On the other hand, by destroying a cultural tradition that contains blocks to modernisation, *and by presenting one specified and all-inclusive alternative,* they tend to reinforce the coercive basis of their control through ideological commitment of the younger generations to the roles and goals of the modernisation process. And at least in their image of the new society, they give the "new" youth a vested interest in the responsibilities and rewards of nation-building.

A great deal of the initial tension between a Communist elite and the "masses" they attempt to lead can thus be viewed as a clash of values, goals and methods between the apostles of a new culture and the bearers of the old. Consequently, it is no accident that all Communist régimes put an enormous amount of energy into educating the younger generations, for it is through fostering the inculcation of a "socialist" culture by the "masses" that the Party can stabilise its rule, extend its control, and concentrate popular energy in the tasks of economic development.

This viewpoint of a Communist régime's early years of control as an effort at forced cultural change is the basis for the present comparison of certain cultural themes found in early Republican and Communist Chinese educational materials. It also is the basis for posing several questions, in the conclusion, about the relation of the new "Communist" culture to the goals of the modernisation process, and to problems of social integration where an elite holds value priorities and goals that may not be shared widely by the general population.

CHINESE CHILDREN'S READERS: ONE VIEW OF CULTURAL CHANGE

A number of articles published since 1950 have dealt with such aspects of Communist Chinese education as its new institutions and techniques, its ideological rationale, and the general content of the courses given and the materials used.[3] Our purpose here is to look in considerable detail at the themes of certain educational materials—second, third, and fourth grade children's readers—with a view to abstracting from them an image of the kinds of cultural changes being fostered by the Communist elite on the mainland today.[4]

This analysis is based on two sets of Chinese children's texts. The first set of twenty-one stories, containing seven selected at random from readers of the second, third, and fourth grades, comes from texts published in Shanghai by either the China Book Company or the Commercial

Book Company during the period 1922 to 1929. The texts were approved by the Ministry of Education of the Republic of China in Peking. The second set of twenty-one stories, again seven tales selected at random from each of the three grades, was published in Peking in 1960, and, of course, under the control of the Communist Ministry of Education. The samples for analysis of the Republican and Communist eras are thus matched for size and grade level. Random selection eliminated bias in the choice of stories for analysis.

The contemporary stories should certainly give us a clear view of the Communist themes of education, and hence an image of the major outlines of the new culture they are trying to promote. But what do the stories from Shanghai in the early Republican period tell us about either the traditional culture or its change in the early years of the national revolution? In this brief article it can only be asserted that the stories, overall, seem to reflect the cultural quandary of Chinese intellectuals in the decade following the May 4 Incident. On the one hand the ferment of the times had succeeded in undermining the authority of the formal intellectual and cultural tradition, but on the other no doctrine or viewpoint had succeeded in rising above the many contending points of view to acquire the status of a replacement. The readers from the 1920s reflect this in that they include tales and themes both ancient and modern, Chinese and Western. Stories of George Washington and the Scottish hero Robert Bruce are juxtaposed against legendary Chinese tales and heroes. The impact of the early Republican era texts reflects neither the assertive call of a new and appealing life-style nor the full dignity of respected ancient tradition.

NEW ASPECTS OF SOCIAL AUTHORITY

How does a history- and culture-conscious elite attempt to direct a forced cultural change?[5] These educational materials indicate that a major aspect of the Communist educational effort is being directed towards redefining the traditional basis of social authority. The redefinition, not unexpectedly, is in favour of the Party and state, and would seem to be the base from which the Communists hope to direct a more thorough-going reorganisation of social activity in creating a new world. (Certain dimensions of this new world are also revealed in the reader analysis, and will be discussed briefly in the next section.)

A New Status for the Family. The traditional Chinese social structure was distinguished by the strength of the family. The individual's social identity was largely determined by where his family stood in the social hierarchy, and by his own position within the family. Ultimate social loyalty was accorded to parents by virtue of the Confucian stress on "filial piety." The political system was even viewed as a structural extension of the family; the proper official was a "father and mother" to the people under his jurisdiction and the Emperor was "The Son of Heaven."

The Communists have tried to shift the primary social loyalty that had been vested in the family to the Party and the Nation. This shift is initially suggested in the children's readers by the decreased emphasis placed on activity within the family. Nine of the 21 older stories are focused around family interaction, whereas only five of the Communist stories take place in a family setting. The content of the stories, however, states clearly the identification of the Party with that of a nurturant parent. One story, entitled "To Follow the Communist Party Forever!" describes the poor and brutal life before "Liberation" and the happy life that followed punishment of the wicked landlords. The story concludes: "I often think that the Communist Party is my 'mother.' Without the Communist Party, how could I enjoy a happy life such as today?" Another tale, in which a blind woman describes a young child leading her to work every day, ends: "I want to write a happy song to praise our children and their great 'mother' who educates them to grow up—our Communist Party."

Now the great acts of filial piety are reserved for the tasks of the Party and Nation. In the tradition of the Confucian tales of sons and daughters who sacrificed themselves for their parents' comfort and safety, the story of Hsiang Hsiu-Li describes the complete giving of oneself to the safety of the factory:

> Realising that an extremely severe accident was undoubtedly going to happen, at the critical moment Hsiang Hsiu-Li rushed to the fierce fire and with her body attempted to keep the alcohol from flowing to the sodium. The fire burned her hands and clothes. But there was only one idea dominating her mind: that no matter what might happen, she was determined to prevent the explosion of the sodium and therefore to keep the factory property from being damaged.

The family system is never directly attacked in the Communist texts; rather, it is made clear that in cases of conflicting social loyalty, allegiance goes to the larger social collectivity—just as in the preceding incident it was stressed that there is greater valuation of *society's* productive mechanism than *individual* safety. "The Story of Ma Hsiao-tsui" is a tale of a young girl forced to choose between support of an Uncle's antisocial activities and the security of the state. On a visit to her relative's house, she "saw her uncle talking with . . . two crooks." She thought, "My uncle is a wealthy farmer; his thinking is backward. These two people are talking so sneakily to him; they must be crooks." After the two men left, she confronted her relative: "Uncle, there is a lot of talk about you. My mother has been asking me to tell you that you have been associating with the crooks. The day before yesterday the government declared a policy. If you resist you will be severely punished. If you turn in the counter-revolutionaries and declare yourself you will not be punished so severely." The county government arrested her uncle the same night. "After her persuasion her uncle turned in the two crooks and the other land-owner . . . Ma Hsiao-tsui removed a threat to the people, and they were all very grateful to her."

It is interesting to note that the Communist stories make a clear distinction between the Party and the Government. The Party is characterised as the good provider, the "liberator" from the horrible, pre-1949 life. The Party is warm and personal, usually being represented by an energetic and helpful local Party cadre. The Government, by contrast, is rather impersonal and, as in the last story, primarily a punitive institution. The Communists have evidently attempted to split these two aspects of social authority, reserving for the Party the positive allegiance due to a "kind father," while deflecting onto the "apolitical" state bureaucracy the frustration and resentments which come from the administrative application of Party policies.

From Family to Party. An adjunct to the reduced emotional position of the family in Communist China is a shift in the primary source of guidance in calculating social action. Riesman has noted change in the Western cultural tradition from guidance by the stable pattern of group relations, *tradition direction,* through self-guidance by an abstract but early internalised set of moral principles, *inner direction,* to calculation in terms of the norms and values of the peer group, *other direction.*[6] The Chinese seem to have attempted to alter this pattern of social guidance both by skipping over the phase of inner direction and localising the source of other direction. The traditional family and educational system helped the member to delimit acceptable behavioural patterns. This is reflected in the old set of stories where teachers and family members are portrayed as the major source of guidance.

The Communist stories, in contrast, describe individuals acting under the influence of such superiors as production foremen or Party cadres—rather than family members or teachers. The ultimate source of social guidance, the Party, is indicated in several of the stories. A diligent worker, who studied to improve himself even as he went to political meetings, concludes his tale with:

> I want to study harder to *accomplish the duties assigned to me by the Communist Party*—to complete my education and serve my country.

These are the words of a youngster whose parents had been killed by the hard life of the old society:

> I often think that the Communist Party is my "mother." Without the Communist Party how could I enjoy a happy life such as today's. I must work hard and get educated and *follow the Communist Party forever!*

And the poem "Why Has Everything Changed" concludes, not with a reference to the hard work and the initiative of the people, but with the lines:

> Why has everything changed?
> Because we have Chairman Mao.
> Because we have the Communist Party.

This "Party directedness," however, is not without qualification. The readers suggest in an ambivalent way that while ultimate guidance comes from official superiors, individual initiative is a desirable characteristic. Consider the words of a mother who worked on a cotton farm. Her daughter asks her if she will pick cotton on the morrow. " 'Oh yes,' said the mother, '*the boss* said this is good weather for picking cotton, so *I think* I will work longer tomorrow.' " This tension between the "boss said" and the "I think" is a major contradiction for a totalitarian régime that wants ultimate social control and at the same time an ambitious, hard-working population that will take its own initiative in approved areas of activity.

Father Mao. One of the most interesting cultural redefinitions illustrated by the children's texts is the changed characterisation of figures of authority. The old readers describe authority as both harmful and irrational, something to be avoided by keeping to oneself. The 1920s story of "The Clam and the Sea Gull" recounts how these two creatures started fighting on the beach one day when the seagull tried to eat the clam. The story concludes with a fisherman coming along and, euphemistically enough, "harvesting" the two squabblers. Even more revealing of the harshness of traditional authority is the story of "The Ducks and the Frog." Miss Golden Eye, a frog, tries to warn three ducks playing in her pond that they might be caught and made into duck stew:

> Three ducks, three ducks
> Listen to me.
> If you return today,
> Tomorrow's dinner you will be.

The ducks are enraged at the frog's impudent admonition and they gobble her down. But sure enough, the ducks are caught and cooked up for stew. The tale concludes:

> The one who interfered was killed
> Also killed, they who had no sense.
> Could this be coincidence?
> Could this be coincidence?

Powerful and authoritative figures are thus portrayed as harsh even to those who, meaning well, interfere in other people's business. Staying in your own place, and minding your own business are the safest ways to avoid involvement with powerful "others" who are heartless and potentially destructive.

How different is the Communist *image* of authority! The Party is the great liberator of the people from the oppressive old society. It provides a rich new life and opportunity for education. "The Story of Chairman Mao's Visit to a Play" clearly identifies the great leader as a kind and humble father. Mao comes to see a play in a small town and arrives late. At first he quietly sits down in a seat in the back of the auditorium; but the people recognise his presence and all rise to offer him their seats:

> Chairman Mao walked to the front, after seeing that no one wanted to sit down, and sat in a chair occupied by a young boy. Chairman Mao held the young boy and let him sit on his lap. The curtain went up, and Chairman Mao and the young boy watched the play together.

Another tale describes a woman giving Mao a basket of eggs during a campaign of the civil war. Mao refuses the gift, but the woman insists. Then, rather than keep the eggs for himself, Mao gives them to some of his wounded soldiers. Another war-time incident describes Mao giving his own coat to a cold sentry, and in disregard of his own comfort, arranging for comfortable accommodation for his troops. This side of Communist authority is kind, generous and humble—the image of a nurturant and helpful father.

The harsh and vengeful aspects of Communist authority, however, are not neglected in the readers. The reactionary classes of the old society and their contemporary supporters are the objects of the kind of treatment indiscriminately applied by powerful individuals in pre-revolutionary days. The hatred of the anti-revolutionary forces is described in this characterisation of "Li Tzu-ch'eng—A Great Leader":

> He suffered all the oppressions, and a cut-down of wages from the landlord. Once he was even arrested and beaten by the magistrate. Finally he was punished and made to stand with a rope around his neck under the hot sun. Therefore, his enmity for the bureaucratic class and landlords was very deep.

The fate of those who become the objects of this rage and enmity is swift and unyielding. The previously mentioned tale of Ma Hsaio-tsui concludes with the following account of the end of the "crooks" who had been with her uncle before his arrest:

> [The two crooks and the landowner] were under the counter-revolutionist Lee Tai-ping who acted as marshal. Lee Tai-ping grouped some crooks together and wanted to be "king." This whole group of counter-revolutionists was wiped out completely and quickly.

Thus, while the image of Communist authority is kind and helpful to those who work with the revolution, it remains ready and willing to "wipe out completely and quickly" those who do not follow the Party's guidance.

ASPECTS OF A NEW WORLD

In addition to the altered characterisation of authority relationships, the readers indicate a number of aspects of the traditional Chinese social culture which the Communists are attempting to modify.

A Sense of Social Responsibility. The other aspect of the overriding authority of the traditional Chinese family was a rather low level of integration of the larger society, of a propensity to make decisions for the welfare of the bloodline rather than larger social collectives, and a limited concern for social problems outside the family. This aspect of the old culture is illustrated by the 1920s story of a poor man who asks a friend to lend him some grain. The friend replies that if he will wait until the harvest is in he will lend him three hundred dollars. The poor man replies with a fable about a fish trapped on a dusty inland road who asks a passer-by for some water. The passer-by tells the fish to wait a while and he will bring him all the water from a distant river. "The fish answered, 'I only need a spoonful to keep me alive. When you return from bringing all the water of the river to me, you'll find me in the market with all the other dead fish.' " Here social responsibility outside the family is avoided with useless promises of "pie in the sky," even in a case of life and death. In contrast, seven of the twenty-one Communist stories describe people successfully asking aid of unrelated others, or carrying out some nurturant social act, as in Mao giving his coat to a soldier, or a student helping another pupil to learn a lesson.

A New Status for Women. A number of social analysts have suggested that emancipating women from their traditional social role in the home is a key element in accelerating the pace of social change; this is because women are by inclination conservative, and retard the education of "modern" children through their dominant influence in the child's early life.[7] The set of stories from the Republican era lays no great stress on women taking active and exciting social roles, whereas seven of the Communist stories in the sample of 21 contain women as major actors. Three of these model young females could easily be described as heroines, such as the brave Hsiang Hsiu-li who lost her life in trying to save the factory from destruction, and Ma Hsiao-tsui who saved the village from counterrevolutionaries by reporting them to the government. "The Story of Li Chun-hua" seems to embody the model of feminine behaviour in New China:

> Liberation! Down with the landlord and those who oppressed the farmers. Now I can have books to read; how happy I am!
>
> After I finished primary school I worked in the Peasants' Association. Then the commune was founded. Father worked in the steel mill,

mother worked in a cafeteria, brother went to kindergarten, and I learned to drive a truck. I really thank the Party and Chairman Mao. I must produce enthusiastically!

The Excitement of Education. One of the major attributes of a modern culture is a view of the world as a rational natural system, open to understanding through human intelligence, not dominated by whimsical supernatural forces or a vague, implacable "fate." While the readers do not delve into the subtleties of epistemology, their differing views toward education are indicative of a major cultural shift in a view of the natural world and man's place in it.

The set of readers from the 1920s views education not as the inculcation of instrumental or task-oriented techniques, but as the acquisition of a social skill useful for impressing others. In "The Little Pig Wants to Study," some little children on their way to school encounter a pig sitting on a stump. He asks them where they are going; they reply that they are going to school to study. "What is the use of studying?" asks the little pig. The children reply, "By studying one will become clever."

The other side of the coin of admiration for cleverness is ridicule for those who are stupid. The tale "Marking the Boat to Find the Sword," describes a poor uneducated old man riding on a crowded boat down the river. While showing off his sword to the passengers he accidentally drops the valuable heirloom over the side, and quickly borrows a knife to notch the boat at the place where the sword fell over.

> Someone asked him why he was carving the boat, and the passenger replied, "When the boat stops, I'll know where to look for the sword."
>
> So now, whenever someone does something stupid, we say "He is marking the boat to find the lost sword."

Whereas only one of the old stories contains a tale whose major theme concerns education, five of the twenty-one Communist tales concentrate on the excitement of learning and the value of education in increasing productive capacity. This passage from "The Words of Li Chun-hua" conveys the general attitude towards learning:

> The Communist Party came, and we poor people rose up. Now there is no worry about food and clothing, and the living conditions improve every day.
>
> Then one day mother said she would send me to school. I was so happy I jumped. I thought of before, when I would see the landlord's children attending school, but I couldn't. I could only collect a few branches for the landlord as fuel. I felt that I was treated unfairly. Freedom! Down with the landlords and those who oppressed the farmers. Now I can have books to read. How happy I am.

Work! Work! Work! The type of cultural shift just described in the characterisation of education is paralleled by the changed attitude towards labour. In the 1920s story "Waiting by the Tree for Rabbits," a lazy farmer is described as astounded to see a rabbit, in great confusion, run headlong into a nearby tree and kill itself. "The farmer decided that if rabbits did this, he would give up farming and live off the rabbits which ran into the tree. Every day he would sit by the tree and wait, but no more rabbits came, and his farm became overgrown with weeds."

This implicit ridicule of the foolishness of the lazy farmer is in great contrast to the seriousness with which work themes are presented in the contemporary tales. The Communist children's stories do not bear an over-romanticised attitude towards work. Rather, they stress a variety of more complex themes: The tale of heroic Hsiang Hsiu-li places a higher value on productive capital than human life. "Every Morning" stresses diligence. Young children daily lead a blind woman to a factory from her bus stop. When a snowstorm prevents her from taking the usual bus trip they go to her home "to see if something is the matter," and to help her get to the factory in spite of the storm. "The Words of a Worker" stress the importance of education and skill for productivity. Pride of craftsmanship and patience are conveyed in "A Small Patch." Perhaps the most consistent theme throughout these stories is the identification of productive labour with the new and happy life which the Communist Party has given the people with their "liberation."

The high valuation placed on education and practical toil in these readers is indicative of a more general change of cultural attitude. In new China man is both capable of and encouraged to manipulate his natural environment by virtue of intelligence and acquired skills. In Florence Kluckhohn's terms, the cultural shift has been from the Taoist and Buddhist view of man *in* nature, to man *over* nature. Similarly, the model of the Communist man is no longer defined in terms of his *being*—as part of a stable cultural tradition—but in the *becoming,* through learning and toil, which will produce the eventual Communist utopia. And finally, this new world view suggests that the Communists have reversed the time perspective of the traditional culture from concern with the *past* traditions of the Confucian family system, with its ancestor worship, to the tasks required to reach the *future* goal of a Communist society.

MOTIVATION AND SOCIAL CHANGE

Thus far this analysis has concentrated on the cognitive aspects of cultural change, on the new Communist view of man's relation to his social, physical and temporal environments. Examination of the children's books according to methods developed by David McClelland and others[8] for assessing the *motivational orientations* of their authors, however, suggests that the Communists are attempting to both redirect and intensify the motivations of the Chinese under their control.

The Increase in Achievement Orientation: A Striving Communist Elite. Is the desire to be creative, to meet high standards of performance, and to have a successful career the motive of modernisation? McClelland has tested this hypothesis by scoring sets of twenty-one children's stories from a sample of more than fifty nations according to his *need achievement* assessment procedure.[9] He found a positive correlation of about +0.5 between this *need* score and indices of subsequent successful performance in economic development.[10] In interpreting this relationship, McClelland suggests that, "the readers . . . appear to reflect more the motivational level of the adults at the time they are published . . . than the motivational level that the children will have ultimately when they grow up."[11] The actual process of inculcating this psychic need in the individual personality is grounded in a child-rearing environment including a non-domineering father, a nurturant and stimulating mother, and continuous exposure of the child to standards of excellence that he is capable of reaching with reasonable effort.

Scoring of our two sets of Chinese stories reveals the *need achievement* level for the readers from the 1920s to be considerably below the mean score of McClelland's sample of nations for that period; below by —0.9 standard deviations. The score for the set of Communist stories is above the mean for the 1950 sample of nations by +0.32 standard deviations.[12]

In the light of the previous analysis of the themes of the children's readers, and McClelland's analysis of the meaning of this motive score, what interpretation should be given to this result? First, it is clear that there has been a significant increase in the saliency of achievement oriented activities; this associated with the change in political leadership on the mainland. The Communists have set high standards for the people, and their educational materials stress individuals actively working to meet and exceed these standards. Secondly, the readers indicate a focusing of the area in which achievement is valued. The old set of stories do not stress achievement in any particular setting. The primary area for social achievement in the traditional culture, competition in the Imperial examination system (and in subsequent access to the political arena) is expressed in the 1920s as a desire to be clever. The Communists have emphasised education as a means to building a better material life rather than as an end in itself.[13]

Need Power and Need Affiliation: Motivation and Social Control. Social scientists are only beginning to investigate in a formal way the psychological dimensions of leader-follower relations in different cultures, and the motivational basis of social controls. One start to development of standardised measuring instruments for such analysis is found in two additional scoring categories that McClelland has developed. His *need affiliation* scoring system is designed to measure the need for warm and friendly-interpersonal relations, and the *need power* category attempts to measure the need to control other people's behaviour or to control the means of such control. Analysis of a sample of children's readers from more than fifty countries according to these two scoring systems reveals that the combined motive pattern of high *need power* and *low affiliation* is characteristic of stable dictatorships, such as Hitler's Germany, Soviet Russia and Franco's Spain.[14] Evidently a need to control other people's behaviour or opinions, and a low desire for positive emotional response, finds cultural expression in a political system that does not hesitate to use coercive measures to maintain control, and a passive acquiescence, or apolitical withdrawal, on the part of the general population.

Scoring of the two sets of Chinese children's stories finds that *need affiliation* was quite low in the stories from the early Republican era (—2.02 standard deviations below the average score for the sample of nations of that era) and —0.55 below the 1950 mean for the Communist stories. The rise in *need affiliation* is related to the descriptions of comradely relations in the stories of Communist activity during the civil war years; yet the score remains considerably below the mean for the entire sample of countries that McClelland has analysed.

The *need power* score, high in the old set of stories (+1.53 standard deviations above the mean) is phenomenally high in the Communist set (+3.27). The increase in concern with control is found in the hate and violence directed at "counter-revolutionaries," as would be expected in a Communist régime.

With its combined motive pattern of high *need power* and low *need affiliation* Communist China thus compares with other stable dictatorships. As well, there has not been a major change in this motive pattern from the 1920s to 1960; rather, an alteration of the symbols towards which control and affection are directed, and an increase in intensity. The Communists appear to use these traditional motives of social relations both to increase the negative sanctions applied to those who do not follow the will of the leadership, and to increase the emotional rewards to those who give themselves to co-operation with the régime by acquiring the behavioural patterns the Communists value most highly. The stability of this motive pattern in China increases our belief that in some psychic sense a society supports a political system which "fits" its cultural emotional needs. It also reinforces the expectation that those now in power in China will not hesitate to use whatever coercion is necessary to maintain control.

Emotionalism and Nation-Building. Many observers of mainland politics have been struck by the extreme emotionalism of Communist China's mass campaigns.[15] The Peking leaders' willingness to manipulate emotions to a high pitch is expressed in a more formal way here by the great increases in motivational concerns analysed through the children's readers. *Need achievement, need power,* and *need affiliation* have increased over the early Nationalist era by +1.22, +1.74 and +1.47 standard deviations respectively. The intriguing question that remains to be answered is why the Communist leaders apparently feel that intense population motivation is an effective substitute (at least in the short run) for both human skills and material resources in building a new nation.

CONCLUSION

An overall view of this analysis of Chinese educational materials suggests that the major thrusts of the Communist-induced cultural change are in the directions of a redefined attitude towards the natural environment and man's place in it, and a reorganisation of the system of social relations. Loyalties are being transferred to the larger social collectives of Party and Nation, and people are being encouraged to manipulate their natural and social environments in order to work towards a better life in the future.

In the less malleable domain of psychic motives affecting behaviour, the Communists have relied on traditional emotional bases of social relations and control (analysed here in terms of McClelland's categories of *need affiliation* and *need power*) to increase the rewards for effective co-operation and the sanctions against defection. *Achievement motivation* has been expanded from its traditional limited basis in competitive scholarship to mass popular mobilisation for task-oriented learning and productive labour. The extreme emotionalism of the Communist efforts at nation-building is suggested by the large increases in scores for both *need achievement, need power* and *need affiliation.*

In retrospect one is impressed with the central relevance of the themes expressed in the readers to the major goals the Communists have laid down for the society, national unity and development of the economy. The reduced role of the family, development of a sense of social responsibility, and the emotion attached to Mao and the Party all help to break down the particularistic emotional attachments that limited social integration in traditional China. The expanded range of task-oriented social contacts and the guidance provided by the Party create the image of a mobilised yet disciplined nation working towards the goals of a better material and intellectual life. The new cultural elements of a rational view of the world and valuation of hard work and education, combined with emotional concerns of meeting high standards, a desire to be creative, and the development of a successful career provide the human energy and skills for economic development. Thus, at least in the *image* of the new life they seek to promote, the Communists have spelled out elements of a new culture that should aid in the implementation of their political goals.

This is in strong contrast to the values, goals and world-view disclosed in the readers from the early Republican era. The educational elite in the 1920s appear to have rather mechanically juxtaposed certain Western cultural themes with those of the traditional Chinese culture, producing a sense of cultural diffuseness characteristic of an ongoing, unresolved attempt to combine tradition with modernity. But while the Nationalist educational leaders lacked a well-formed image of where they were going in the modernisation process—an image which they could convey to the younger generation—they were also not politically hostile to the traditional culture, and hence less likely than the Communists to alienate certain large segments of the population still committed to much of the old culture.

Lest we obliterate the distinction between the *image* of Socialist China and the realities involved in inculcating a new and in many ways radically different way of life, three particular problems that face the Communists in "selling" this new life should be pointed out:

1. The problem of *mobilisation:* The readers convey an image of a society activated in learning, working, and building a new life. This total social mobilisation, while providing the elite with enormous quantities of human labour, can, however, become a liability as well as an asset. If through economic failures, limited educational opportunity, and inability to provide enough places for work in the modern sector of the economy this activated population is given no constructive social role consonant with its expectations, real problems of absorption are posed. Thus, in deliberately stimulating popular participation the Communists have exposed themselves to the risks of either apathetic and cynical disappointment and withdrawal, or active opposition should they fail to provide for such high expectations.

That the problems of dealing with an unabsorbable mobilised population have already faced the Peking leaders is suggested not only by the economic failures of the Great Leap Forward and the turning back of students to the farms, but even more dramatically in the sudden influx of refugees into Hong Kong in the summer of 1962.

2. The problem of *credibility:* The Communists have based their claim to political legitimacy on their infinite wisdom and ability to unify and develop the nation. The exclusiveness of their control is based on possession of all that is true and on their ability to effectively implement the truth. While simple trust may make the image of Father Mao an effective basis for total authority over the generation in childhood, those of the age of reason require more convincing grounds for faith. To them wisdom, truth and implementive skills must be continually reaffirmed, or else authority must revert to more elemental and gross methods of coercion for its legitimation.

The "Hundred Flowers" period of open criticism in 1957 was revealing in this regard for it exposed student disaffection with Party leadership, among other reasons, for its "managing" of communications. Students felt manipulated by the suppression of information, as was the case with Khrushchev's secret speech of 1956 denouncing Stalin, and censorship of the news.[16] It is as yet unknown to what extent the admitted failures of the "Great Leap Forward" period have produced disaffection and cynicism about Party claims to dominant control because of their sole possession of the skills of leadership.

3. A third problem facing the Communists is embodied in *the paradox of total Party control combined with individual initiative,* as was suggested earlier in the analysis. Normal human needs of personal integrity and initiative, when encouraged to take the form of creativity as they have been in these readers, come face to face with restrictive Party demands for detailed leadership and control. The 1957 incidents again are instructive, for students complained that "the main shortcoming [of life in new China] was 'excessive restrictions' upon youth. . . ." that they had been "turned into 'robots' and educated into 'yes-men' who did not dare to express their aspirations." [17]

FOOTNOTES

1. For a description of this process in the case of China's early nationalistic revolution see Mary C. Wright, *The Last Stand of Chinese Conservatism* (Palo Alto: Stanford University Press; 1957), pp. 300–312.

2. Lu Ting-yi, "Education Must Be Combined with Productive Labour," *Red Flac.* July 1, 1958. Quoted in Bowie and Fairbank, eds., *Communist China, 1955–1959* (Cambridge: Harvard University Press, 1962), pp. 440, 449.

3. Theodore Hsi-en Chen: "Red Education in Communist China," *Current History,* July 1950; "New China: New Texts," *ibid.* December 1950; "New Schools for China," *ibid.* June 1952; "Education for the Chinese Revolution," *ibid.* January 1957; "Education and Indoctrination in Red China," *ibid.* September 1961; "Elementary Education in Communist China," *The China Quarterly,* No. 10, April–June 1962; C. T. Hu, "Communist Education: Theory and Practice," *ibid.;* I. C. Y. Hsu, "The Reorganisation of Higher Education in Communist China, 1949–61," *ibid.,* No. 19, July–September, 1964.

4. Why use stories from children's grammar school texts as an aid to understanding the complexities of cultural change? David McClelland, who has used readers as the basis for cross-cultural analysis of national "motive" patterns, suggests several reasons: The texts are relatively standardised cultural products, and thus facilitate cross-cultural comparisons, or, as in the present case, the analysis of change over time in a given culture. "The stories are 'projective' and tend to reflect the motives and values of the culture in the way they are told or in their themes or plots. [They] are also less subtle, more direct in their 'message' than many other forms of literature." David C. McClelland, *The Achieving Society* (Princeton: Van Nostrand, 1961), p. 71. While we would not look to the readers for a detailed view of a culture, they do seem useful for revealing a distilled image of the values, motives and points of view which are perceived by the educational elite as being most important for training the younger generation. Their value lies more in the insights they may give into the mind and value-system of the contemporary social leadership than for predicting the future behaviour of the younger generation.

5. A major problem facing analysts of culture or "national character" is the absence of a commonly accepted set of categories for the analysis of empirical materials—categories which are related to a general theoretical conception of human behaviour. Thus, to some extent, each analyst has to go it alone, making the best use he can of his own wits and a variety of unintegrated theoretical conceptions. This is true in the present case, although the following analysis bears the particular influence of the writings of David McClelland, *ibid.,* and Florence Kluckhohn,

"Dominant and Varient Value Orientations," in Kluckhohn, Murray and Schneider, eds., *Personality in Nature, Society, and Culture* (New York: Knopf, 1956), pp. 342–357.

McClelland's detailed study, *The Achieving Society,* provides not only a useful summary of what many Western sociologists have had to say about the relation of motives, values and perceptions to economic and social change, but it also is a major theoretical and methodological statement in its own right. The insights discussed in *The Achieving Society* were useful in interpreting the themes that the first part of the present analysis disclosed in the Chinese children's readers, although the analysis itself was carried out in an open, unstructured manner, not bound to any preconceived set of analytical categories.

The second part of the analysis, in contrast, makes direct use of McClelland's methods for scoring *need* or motive themes in imaginative cultural materials or individual written protocols, and interprets the scoring of the readers in the light of his large-sample analysis of the relation of psychological motives to economic development and cultural change.

6. David Riesman, *et al., The Lonely Crowd* (New Haven: Yale University Press, 1961), especially pp. 9–25.

7. See McClelland, *op. cit.,* pp. 399–400.

8. For a full description of the development and technique of these scoring categories, see: J. W. Atkinson, ed., *Motives in Fantasy, Action, and Society* (Princeton: Van Nostrand, 1958).

9. The procedure is based on a content analysis scoring system with three basic coding categories: expressed concern with meeting culturally defined standards of excellence; concern with development of a successful occupation; and expressed desire to make some useful social or scientific innovation.

10. For a full description of McClelland's analysis of the relation of need achievement to economic growth, see: McClelland, *op. cit.,* Ch. 3.

11. *Ibid.,* p. 102.

12. I am indebted to Mrs. Ai-li Chin for selecting and translating the sets of stories upon which this analysis is based, and to Dr. McClelland for carrying through to completion the very rough scoring of the stories which I first attempted. He has reported the results of his scoring in an article, "Motivational Patterns in Southeast Asia, with special reference to the Chinese case," *The Journal of Social Issues,* 1963.

13. A further intriguing problem, one which can only receive speculative consideration here, is whether the Party has also sought to provide a child-rearing environment likely to produce ambitious and creative individuals who will bear the future burdens of social leadership. Emphasis on active social roles for women, a decline in the authority of the family and father implied in the transfer of loyalty to the Party and Mao, and the emphasis on high standards, as revealed in the readers, suggests that the Communists have at least tried to meet key elements of McClelland's model of the *achievement-orientation* producing social environment.

But has the warm and encouraging family been destroyed in China, as so many Western accounts of the "People's Commune" system have stressed? A recent psychiatric investigation of a small number of Chinese children by a Canadian doctor, during a visit to the mainland, suggests that at least in certain locations in the late 1950s the family remained an effective socialising unit. See: Dr. Denis Lazure, M.D., "The Family and Youth in New China: Psychiatric Observations," *Journal of the Canadian Medical Association,* January 27, 1962, pp. 179–183. Dr. Lazure notes that while the Communist leaders "have effectively accomplished the revolution of transferring the emotional investment formerly reserved for the family to society as a whole and to the role which the individual will play in building his society," they have not destroyed the family, just reduced its importance. Through systematic use of "persuasion," they have "managed to present Party leaders not as obstacles between the child and his parents, but rather as infinitely wise and generous beings who stand above the family and who only naturally must take precedence in the child's mind." He found that although "liberation" of the mother from the home for productive labour had reduced the frequency of parental contact, "now that she is freed from the tasks of cooking meals and running the house, the mother is able to devote her time entirely to her children when she arrives home from work."

In sum, then, it seems likely that ambitious and creative individuals will not be found lacking among future generations of Chinese. The significant questions for further research, however, are how large a segment of the population will be highly motivated to participate in *achievement oriented* activities, what the most highly valued achievement activities will be, and the political relations between the most highly motivated segment of the population and the larger numbers who are followers, not leaders.

14. See McClelland, *op. cit.*, pp. 167–170.

15. For a particularly provocative analysis of this problem see: Lucian W. Pye, "The Dynamics of Hostility and Hate in Chinese Political Culture," MIT, Center for International Studies, C/64–23, June, 1964.

16. See Roderick MacFarquhar, *The Hundred Flowers Campaign and the Chinese Intellectuals* (New York: Praeger, 1960), p. 134, and *passim* Ch. 8.

17. *Ibid.*, p. 173.

The Gentleman Ideal and the Maintenance of a Political Elite

RUPERT H. WILKINSON

> The stock exchange is a poor substitute for the Holy Grail. . . .
>
> The bourgeoisie produced individuals who made a success at political leadership upon entering a political class of non-bourgeois origin, but it did not produce a successful political stratum of its own although, so one should think, the third generations of the industrial families had all the opportunity to form one.
>
> Joseph Schumpeter[1]

LEADERS ARE NOT ALL GOVERNORS, for government survives by magic as well as by reason, by dignity as well as by its decisions. "Rationalist and unheroic," the bourgeois lacks "the mystical glamor and the lordly attitude" which made the mediaeval lord respected as a ruler of men.

So runs Schumpeter's argument. It is an argument that stresses *aptitude*—political aptitude—rather more heavily than it does *motivation*. The bourgeois, contends Schumpeter, often "wants to be left alone and to leave politics alone" for the very reason that he senses his inadequacies in the political sphere.[2] What Schumpeter does not really detail are the positive factors—the attitudes and motivations—that directed the landed classes, rather than the bourgeoisie, towards public service. The purpose of this paper is to examine these factors, and to suggest that they were all part and parcel of a "gentleman ideal." I am going to argue that this ideal was a sort of controlling link in a two-way relationship between government and a political elite. On the one hand, it aided government recruitment by making public service a gentlemanly obligation. On the other hand, it defended the identity, the political power and the social prestige of an elite group by inspiring that group to retain their grip on public affairs.

In both Imperial China and Victorian England, the gentleman ideal was promoted by education systems whose values were those of the landlord rather than those of the urban businessman. As with values, so with power: Confucian education and the Victorian Public School both conferred career advantages on the gentry, on the group whose living came from rents—and from certain professional but non-entrepreneurial func-

Reprinted with permission of the author and The American Sociological Association, from SOCIOLOGY OF EDUCATION, Vol. 37, No. 1, pp. 9–26.

tions.[3] Through education the gentry retained prime access to high positions in government.[4] Not only did the classical curriculum—tailored to civil service examinations—favor the cultural background of the landed family, but the whole education system actually made gentlemen by the same indoctrination that made rulers. Students from non-gentry origins were stamped with the gentry's traditional outlook. It was, as one English historian described it, the manufacture of "synthetic gentility." [5]

THE DEFINITION OF A GENTLEMAN

At this point, we should define the word "gentleman," and establish more clearly the relation between the gentleman ideal and a way of life connected with land. In *The Concise Oxford Dictionary*, a gentleman is defined as (1) a man "entitled to bear arms" but not of the nobility, (2) a man with "chivalrous instincts, fine feelings and good breeding," (3) "a man of good social position, a man of wealth and leisure." [6] Let us for the moment, ignore the first part of this definition: the "entitled to bear arms" phrase stems from feudal concerns with soldiering—a subject beyond the scope of this essay. What should first be noted is the overtone of moral superiority that the definition carries. The very word "gentleman," in fact, displays the same character, and Reinhold Niebuhr points out that this is also true of both "gentleman" and "nobleman" in other European tongues.[7] In China, likewise, the nearest equivalent to "gentleman," *juin-tze,* meant literally "superior man"; the superiority it referred to was first and foremost moral.

Now, there are two secondary characteristics of the gentleman concept that are particularly important for our study. The first is classical learning and the second is the possession of leisure.[8] Both were concerned with an aesthetic ideal of elegant ease—or at least a *posture* of ease.[9] In China, as in 18th and 19th Century England, this ideal was defended by families who possessed or wanted to possess landed wealth; and it supported a moral premium on moderation, self-restraint and social harmony.

To the gentleman, and those who respected him, classical culture was supposed to confer moral advantage by providing select access to past wisdoms. Confucian doctrine stated quite explicitly that great virtue could only come through learning. In England, the moral claims of the classicist —to be truly "civilised," etc.—were fainter, but in tacit form they existed.

Both societies, however, made familiarity with a classical body of knowledge a matter of aesthetic, as well as moral, advantage. "Puns, euphemisms, allusions to classical quotations, and a refined and purely literary intellectuality were considered the conversational ideal of the genteel man," commented Max Weber on gentlemanly society in Imperial China.[10] To a lesser extent, the power of the apt and witty classical allusion carried advantage in England. Certainly it did in the (old-style) Houses of Parliament.

Classical culture, in short, contributed to the differentiated style that gave the gentleman elite its magical aura. In both societies, respect for classical education was linked with the agrarian traditions of the ruling group. Gentry classes, compared with urban and business classes, seem to venerate tradition above the uncertain promises of change. In "classic" literature and art, the gentleman finds his preferences fulfilled. For, by definition, a classic only becomes a classic when it gains a measure of antiquity; when it appears to conform to a well-ordered structure; and when it follows absolute and unquestionable rules.[11]

Despite this common theme, the connection between classics and leisure, and the relation of both to public service, was not precisely the same for Confucian China as it was for Public School England. In each case, it is true, classical knowledge was a prerequisite for passing civil service examinations. (Although Latin and Greek by no means monopolised British Civil Service examinations, they dominated Public School entrance tests, and the Public Schools in turn provided the best access to high government office.) In England, however, the factor of leisure counted for more than it did in China.[12] The gentlemanly figure was one who didn't have to work too exclusively or too obviously for a living; he had leisure and means both to pursue culture and to seek relatively unremunerative public office. This, at any rate, was the image that the British gentleman elite presented. It linked an amateur ideal to the spirit of public service. I do not here imply that English gentlemen did not seek culture for its own sake. By the end of the Nineteenth Century, indeed, the moral propagandist Samuel Smiles had convinced even gentlemen that Work was good in itself. Be that as it may, public service and classical attainment were useful adornments for the man who wished to feel himself a leisured gentleman, free of the need to view work solely for the bread it won.

In China, economic factors dictated a somewhat different role for the concept of leisure. According to Chang Chungi-li's estimate, the largest source of income for the Ch'ing Dynasty's *literati* elite was official, professional and "gentry" services (including local government and teaching). This accounted for 46% of the elite's income, compared with 32% from land rents and 22% from commercial activity.[13] Since the official, both at local and Imperial level, commonly made a comfortable living, he did not depend on private means as did the British M.P. and the unpaid Justice of the Peace. Consequently, it is doubtful whether the Chinese *literati* sought public office as a symbol of gentlemanly leisure. In China, the factor of leisure operated more as an attitude of mind: both in government policy and in gentlemanly manners, it was leisurel*iness* that counted. On the personal plane, leisureliness went with the *juin-tze's* attention to gracefulness, formal dignity and etiquette. On the official plane, it appeared from time to time in a *wu-wei* (do-nothing) policy of governing. Just as Sir William Gilbert's aristocracy "did nothing in particular and did it very well," so many Imperial bureaucracies followed a course of elegant inaction. Such a course Confucian wisdom had appeared to sanction by claiming that rulers could induce a measure of social harmony through the sheer weight of personal, moral example.

If the Chinese did not really seek office as a symbol of leisure, he did seek it as a symbol of classical culture. This was true at least, Levenson argues, by the late *Ming* dynasty. Chinese educators used both amateurism and a brand of careerism to produce a public service elite. It was careerist in the sense that schools and tutors concentrated mainly on preparing their students for government examinations that would qualify them for public office. Yet, the system was amateurist in the sense that the classical curriculum was itself "non-vocational" and that office was sought as the highest symbol of a generally cultured man.[14]

Susceptibility to appeal by symbol—that is the key link between the gentleman ideal and the formation of a public service elite. On the one hand, duty symbolised privilege: public service certified membership in a social elite.[15] On the other hand, and conversely, the education system made privilege a reminder of moral duty.

This mutual interaction of privilege and duty, of group status and group service, was the way by which gentlemanly education wrought cohesion out of man's egoism. True, the school of Confucian ethics, like that of Thomas Arnold, made direct appeals to altruism. But, tacitly at any rate, both systems recognise that appeals to altruism were not enough. As Reinhold Niebuhr wrote in *Moral Man and Immoral Society,* egoism, especially "group egoism," is too strong a force to be combated simply by educational appeals to seflessness. Niebuhr's prescription was to use moral restraints to reduce egoism, but also to rely on coercion, balancing group power against group power.[16]

The two education systems under review had a somewhat different approach to the problem of egoism. What they in fact did was to couch appeals to egoism *within* an appeal to altruistic public service. They posed public service as a moral status-symbol, as a credential of membership in an elite which enjoyed moral prestige as well as political power. To implement the beliefs that this involved, two factors were necessary. First, the social climate had to be such that the notion of an elite group setting a moral example to the non-elite could win general acceptance throughout the society as a whole. This factor obtained in Confucian China as it did in the subsiding Evangelicanism of Late Victorian England. Both societies displayed clearcut class differences; and in both the ruling class could enhance its authority by appearing an Institute of Good Works, a moral elect.

The second factor applied to attitudes within the elite itself. To perpetuate the elite, gentlemanly education[17] had to see to it that the student perceived self-interest largely in terms of moral prestige, and that he identified himself closely with the public service elite. It had, in short, to make him see privilege and duty as two faces of the same thing. The way that the education system instilled such an attitude was to play on *aesthetic* emotion. It made the individual seek public leadership because to do so was tasteful, beautiful. This tendency to confuse beauty and virtue, manners and morals, is a major characteristic of the gentleman. "Manners makyth man" said the Fourteenth Century founder of a famous Public School,[18] and over the course of years, "manners" came to mean a host of aesthetic devices that moulded the gentleman to his political role. The same pattern of devices also emerged in China, where it was a strong tenet that outer propriety could affect inner virtue. The way in which these devices worked should be examined in some detail.

THE MECHANISM

Both education systems transmitted values through etiquette, a code of behavior sanctioned by mystical tradition and group standards of good taste. It was a code, therefore, whose enforcement depended less on coercion than on the subtle pressures of majority opinion. Most important, the same body of etiquette which instilled intense communal loyalties also created the differentiated style of the elite: it inculcated distinctive manners and bearing, and it accustomed the individual to colorful privileges of status. In other words, etiquette mirrored perfectly the role of the gentleman ideal that we referred to at the beginning—the ideal's function as a two-way link between duty and status, between the spirit of public service and the identity of an elite.

The etiquette of Confucian education was called *li,* and it is significant that originally this word referred only to rules of religious worship. As such, *li* ordered the rituals which fanned communal loyalties. Not only did it govern ancestor-veneration and other ceremonies exalting the clan, but it was applied to Imperial court ritual as well. The symbolic message of ceremonial *li* was that the individual should subordinate himself to the community, be it the family or the nation, whose historic continuity denoted a group immortality.

It was perhaps inevitable that *li* should also come to confer privilege on those who headed the community. Family elders and government officials alike were marked out by *li* for special acts of deference, modes of address, etc., by others. At one end, indeed, the ethical sanctions of *li* merged with the sumptuary laws that enforced privileges of degree-holders and officials. Even these exclusive legal privileges, however, included many that were aesthetic rather than utilitarian, perquisites of dress and ornamentation.

Unlike Public School etiquette, much of *li* existed in writing and was taught as an academic subject. The more learned a man was, the more propriety he was expected to show.[19]

> He'd a lordly look and natural dignity. A man like that, if not a god, must be at least a high official or a ruler of men.[20]

So wrote a story-teller of the Tang dynasty. In fact, "natural dignity" was supposed to be acquired through learning, for not only did Confucian thought blur the distinction between manners and morals, but it declared that scholarship was a prerequisite for moral superiority.[21] And since a degree—or kinship with a degree-holder—was the main qualification for membership in the gentleman elite (*shin-shih*), it followed that scholarship awarded social status at the same time that it conferred moral prestige.

Whereas Chinese etiquette focused loyalties first and foremost on the family, Public School etiquette focused on the school community and its sub-unit, the House. Both systems, therefore, confronted the individual with a community small and immediate enough to appear as a vivid entity. And in each case, the community dwarfed the individual against an awe-inspiring array of historical tradition. Public School etiquette, like its Chinese counterpart, constantly invoked "School tradition" to demand group-directed behavior. Tradition was the silent arbiter of "good form," endorsing "House spirit" and "teamwork," decreeing what habits were "done" and what were "not done." [22] At many Public Schools, unwritten rules set out initiation rites which made the entering "new boy" perform exercises of deference to the school community and its proud traditions.[23] Other rules inspired deference to the school community by ordaining a student hierarchy of rank and privilege. Many of the privileges were aesthetic in value, referring to details of dress; and naturally the most prized emblems were reserved for the community leader—the prefect, the football captain. In addition, a myriad train of sartorial "colours" went out to the athletic heroes who won public victory for their house or school.

From the above it can be seen that the same etiquette which accustomed the student to style-differences based on rank-differences also enlisted hierarchy as a creator of deference to the community. It wasn't simply that the system awarded most prestige to those who performed distinguished public functions for the community as a whole. It was also that the whole ethos of Public School hierarchy, like that of the Chinese clan, tended to keep the individual, especially the more junior individual, "in his place." Conceit above one's station seems to have been counted a prime offence at many Public Schools. At Harrow, for instance, it was "swagger" for a junior boy to roll up his umbrella out of doors, or to enter another house than his own uninvited. And at Haileybury, a junior who showed hair under his cap would be told by prefects or others "to take *side* off." [24] (Note that words like "swagger" and "side" all carry pejorative connotations of aggressive, individualist behavior.) Aesthetic requirements, indeed, demanded some moderation from the prefect himself. Public School notions of leadership emphasised a style that Cyril Connolly called "prettiness": an effortless grace, a casual assurance, the light touch in command.[25]

At this point some general reflections should be made on the style that dignified and differentiated the gentleman elite. First, it could claim to be the only national style, and this enhanced its magical aura. In both societies, most of the non-elite had mannerisms and speech which varied sharply between geographic regions. By contrast with these differences, the style of the gentleman had a cosmopolitan flavor. In Nineteenth Century England, the development of transport facilities increased the number of Public Schools which could boast a national clientele. (Most Public Schools, it will be remembered, were boarding schools.) A Public School accent and manner sprang up, cutting across regional differences. In China, likewise, a central, mandarin dialect and bearing existed, but the most important national feature of the elite style was the ability to write—and write elegantly. The Imperial examinations, drawing candidates from all over the Empire, maintained the unifying influence of Chinese writing and calligraphy. If and when he became an official, the Confucian scholar was expected to be able to write government memorials in a beautiful style that betrayed no trace of his regional origins.

The national style of the elite was well-suited to the amateur ideal, the gentlemanly concept of the whole man. The gentleman was taught to consider himself above specialization, whether in the sense of regional style or that of technical know-how. Both of the latter were reserved for his social inferiors, since specialization in any form was deemed narrowing. With regard to technical specialization, furthermore, such expertise was the mark of one who had to use knowledge to earn a living and not for the leisured pursuit of wisdom and beauty. In any event, thought the gentleman, effective leadership depended on general qualities of mind, on moral stature and on mannerly self-assurance: endowments like these far outweighed any amount of specialised skill. Such a non-technical bias was well in tune with the credentials and aptitudes of those who presided over gentlemanly education. In Public School England, the archetype educator was the classically trained Churchman; his counterpart in Confucian China was the scholar who, very often, had failed to win a government post and had turned to teaching as the nearest substitute. Neither sort of educator was likely to give much place to technical expertise in his overall concern for moral education.

The second major point about the style of the elite was the psychological effect it had on the elitist individual. A prime assumption of the gentleman was the notion that outer actions could strengthen inner faith. It was an assumption that seems to have contained some truth; by all accounts the style of effortlessness did bolster self-assurance, and attention to prescribed courtesies did enhance moral self-esteem. What is more, the following of a set etiquette, ordained not by the individual but by community tradition and group standards of good taste, gave the individual a sense of social belonging. As Erich Fromm has pointed out, the lone Englishman in the jungle who still "dressed for dinner" could, by so doing, feel at one with his home community.[26] And when the etiquette followed was that of a traditionally superior class—in this case, the gentry—so much the better for the individual's self-assurance.

Related to the above was another psychological effect of gentlemanly style. It was an effect described by the reporter, James Morris, who applied it to the entire English character. "In their *private affairs*," wrote Morris, "the English try to be *undemonstrative* but in *public manners they do what the drill sergeant says*. They march down the years to the twirl of the band-master's silver stick and with bags and bags of swank." [27] Morris was referring mainly to the British love of pomp and pageantry, but his observation is equally applicable to the gentleman's concern for elegant and courteous manners. For like public ceremonial, manners tend to substitute formal channels of expression for spontaneous demonstrativeness.[28] Equally like public ceremonial, manners encourage the individual to seek emotional outlet in an elaboration of aesthetic form. It can be seen, therefore, that manners tend to collectivise feeling. Not only is it their role to harmonise individual egoisms, but the criteria of good manners depend, almost by definition, on group standards of good taste.

The whole tenor, in short, of gentlemanly manners was to stress social harmony and co-operation by the same token that it inhibited private demonstrations. The courtesies that the gentleman performed were courtesies of duty and command; in the final analysis they were not courtesies of intimate friendliness and emotional warmth. If the gentleman's behavior was group-directed, class-directed, community-directed, his motivation was not "outer-directed" (to use David Riesman's term). The gentleman practised manners less to win the approval of others than because his manners were both the obligation and the distinction of the public service elite.

This brings us to a third point about gentlemanly style—the social significance of the word "harmony." In that word lies one of the reasons why the gentleman tended to identify beautiful manners with superior moral character. For "harmony" has a moral as well as aesthetic connotation, and to the gentleman it represented a prime value in itself. On the personal plane, it meant gentle-ness, or what the Chinese calld *ching*: the curbing of base and selfish passions. It was a quality very much bound up with the amateur ideal of the well-rounded man, for it sought to secure moderation by *balancing* virtues and aptitudes against one another. Behind the value of personal harmony there rests a certain belief that faults are but virtues pushed too far, to the exclusion of other virtues. "Respectfulness, without the rules of propriety, becomes laborious bustle," wrote a Chinese sage, ". . . carefulness (becomes) timidity; straightforwardness (becomes) rudeness." [29]

On the social plane, the gentleman's concern with harmony led to an emphasis on moderation and compromise. This was partcularly true of Public School England where the sportsman's ethic of the "good loser" reigned. But it also characterised Imperial China. If Confucian morality added an ideological note of bitterness to bureaucratic faction fights, it also induced the losing party to promote its views by mere advice-giving or by protest resignations rather than by violence. Applied to political thought, the gentlemanly ideal of social harmony befitted best a minimal concept of government, an outlook which saw the ruler as guardian rather than innovator. New ideas and methods nearly always appear to disrupt, however much they may serve the long-run interests of social harmony. In Chinese society, moreover, we have already seen that classical precepts supported the *wu-wei* (minimal) notion of central government by declaring that a ruler could induce social harmony purely through personal, moral example. It is also likely that an executive authority will be tempted into a relatively passive role whenever it lays great stress on the magical properties of government. Pre-occupation with a style of graceful ease, a style betokening mastery of life's struggles, may encourage the ruler to avoid those struggles in the first place. The more a ruler enters into the day-to-day affairs of his subjects, the less easy he will find it to maintain that mysterious aura of different-ness and infallibility which gives a government magic dignity. As studies of primitive societies seem to indicate, there is a certain relationship between mystic ritual and requirements of physical cleanliness.[30] On the political level, accordingly, the ritual aspect of government may demand "cleanliness" from human squalor and strife.

THE CONTEXT

As I have constantly suggested, gentlemanly values were nurtured by a landed way of life. The premium on social harmony, after all, was best suited to a relatively stable agrarian society, especially one cushioned by geography from the disruptive effects of outside influences. In both societies under review, a rentier group had found the leisure in which to elaborate an elegant style and to pursue classical learning for reasons not directly utilitarian. Above all, they had been able to develop the political uses of etiquette, securing social harmony by ethical obligation and by manners as much as by legal coercion. For the elite, duty and responsibility were matters more of class honor and obligation than of individual, rational decision. Similarly, the gentleman commanded deference from his social inferiors not for what he did but rather for what he was—a member of a certain class.

From this it follows that the value of social harmony included the conservative notion that social inequality, tempered by inter-class obligation, was in accord with the laws of nature.

> The rich man in his castle,
> The poor man at his gate,
> God made them, high or lowly,
> And ordered their estate.[31]

So wrote Mrs. Alexander, that most prolific of Victorian hymn-writers, and it is significant that the above verse comes in a much-loved children's hymn praising the divine beauties of nature. (Equally significantly, the verse has now been dropped from most hymn-books.) The same assumption, that a natural hierarchy characterised society and universe alike, marked the dominant Confucian tradition during our period of review, the *Chu Hsi school.*

It is widely recognised, of course, that in both societies a structure of well-defined classes did not preclude social mobility. And it was here that education had a major part to play, reconciling social mobility with clearly marked class distinctions. Both Confucian education and the Victorian Public Schools absorbed into the gentleman elite individuals from families below the elite. By perpetuating an attractive gentry style and manners, and by associating such style with moral status, the education systems played on the ambitions of the social climber. They gave him gentlemanly status, and by the same process indoctrinated him with gentlemanly attitudes.

High among these attitudes, as we have already stated, was a strong leaning towards the public service professions. The whole ethos of both education systems was far better suited to government leadership than it was to the pursuit of business profit. In the first place, government—and in England, the Church—had far more need of the gentleman's magic style than did the textile mill or the trading firm. Not until the Twentieth Century and the development of Public Relations, have business firms rivalled governments in their systematic attempts to win power by emotional appeal, by magic display of a group image as well as by rational persuasion.[32] Compared with the commercial expansion and enterprise that characterised both Imperial China and Victorian England, government was a *relatively* static affair.[33] The ruler's main task, like that of the Public School prefect, was to consolidate rather than innovate, to harmonise different interests and to keep order. Where change was required it was a matter of gradual adjustment rather than of dynamic invention. Under these conditions of leadership, a respect-incurring *manner* of command was indispensable.

What I have just stated is really the corollary to Schumpeter's description of the apolitical bourgeois. If the bourgeois felt a greater aptitude for the world of business, the gentleman felt a corresponding confidence in the world of government, whether as a local magistrate or as a national bureaucrat. Accordingly, one effect of the gentleman's going into public service was to sharpen the distinctive appearance of the gentleman elite; by emphasising the value of dignity and magical style, political experience strengthened those qualities in the class that possessed them.

The second way in which the education systems oriented their members toward government occupations was to make the educational community—the Chinese clan, the Public School—a symbol for other communities which would later claim the individual's loyalty. When the educational community played on aesthetic emotion, it was really forging a *nationalism;* through the pressures of etiquette and tradition, the community induced the individual to identify himself with it "voluntarily." What concerns us here, however, is that the individual was expected to relate to other groups as he related to his educational community. In China, this principle, the inculcation of loyalty by analogy, was reflected in the terms *fu ma kuan*, "parent officials," and *tzu min* "children people." [34]

It could be argued, of course, that the ethos of gentlemanly education should have promoted loyalty to any group, including the private business firm. Assuming the gentleman went into business in the first place, such an argument might possibly be true. A Far Eastern businessman once told me that in his experience British executives were far more apt than Americans to remain with one "House" during their entire careers. But gentlemanly education encouraged its youth to identify most readily with those groups which, like the educational community itself, enjoyed hallowed traditions, a strong *esprit de corps*, and a magic sort of personality. These traits characterised a formally-organised civil service and the nation as a whole far more than they did the rationalist business firm. Certainly this was, for the most part, the case in an individualist, entrepreneurial stage of economic activity, before the "professionalization" of management, the growth of giant corporations, and the rise of the "organization man."

In Public School England, the traits of the educational community, with its monastic barrack-room living, were also those of the military regiment. The same resemblance between education and military service did not obtain in Confucian China. There virtue was sought through scholarship rather than athleticism; and moral suasion was preferred to muscular evangelism. Not surprisingly, the Chinese held professional soldiering in low regard, and Imperial defense suffered accordingly.[35]

The third way in which the education systems directed their members toward government service was to act as a sounding-board for the landed gentry's traditional prejudices about careers. This was particularly true of China, where merchants were officially excluded from degree-examinations, and Confucian thought identified private profit-seeking with *li*—roughly defined as selfish greed. To a lesser extent, anti-trade prejudices marked Public School opinion in the Victorian era, despite the constant intermarrying between Money and Birth. Ideally, the gentleman viewed money as a mere *provider*, a guarantor of leisure and culture. He could not view money as a *score*, the measure of industrial creativity, because he was brought up to seek honor in community leadership rather than in private enterprise-building. Behind these attitudes there probably lay a fear, the fear of rising commercial power and its threat to the traditional order of a gentry-dominated world. Economic factors aside, the gentleman could not help but distrust the businessman. Where the latter was individualist in his striving, the other respected public service as the duty of a close-knit class. Where the businessman hailed energy and efficiency before all else, the gentleman placed equal weight on dignity and custom. Where one, in short, was mainly rationalist, the other was traditionalist.

The position, in Victorian England, of the private "professions" affords a further perspective on gentlemanly attitudes towards public service. By and large, the Church, the Law, Teaching ("at the right place") and to a lesser extent Medicine seem to have occupied a middle ground of prestige between government occupations and most forms of commercial activity. There is some evidence, though inconclusive, to suggest that the more famous Public Schools admitted with complete readiness the sons of professional men at an earlier date than they generally did the sons of businessmen.[36]

Reflection about the comparative prestige of the professions is instructive, because it reveals further the relationship between attitudes toward employment and the maintenance of a political elite. Within the hierarchy of professions themselves, T.H.S. Escott, the Victorian commentator, observed that G.P.'s and solicitors had lower occupational status than had barristers and clergy. This phenomenon Escott traced to two factors which fit fairly well into our description of the gentlemanly outlook. In the first place, Escott argued, the lower professions appeared to have a narrow *expertise,* whereas the activity of the barrister and the bishop could make a *general* impact on the public mind. Secondly, doctors and solicitors had to undergo the vulgar commercial process of receiving money directly from their clients.[37] Hypothetical as these arguments are, the fact that a distinguished Victorian could write them is significant in itself.

Taking all the major professions together, one characteristic they held in common was an outward contempt for aggressive salesmanship. As T. H. Pear points out, a private profession has clients, whereas a trade has customers. What is healthy competition to the second is client-stealing for the first.[38] In other words, a profession possesses a group spirit which mutes any competitive individualism that occurs within it.

If the profession has a group spirit, it also has an elite spirit. To cite Pear again—the professions have often been described by their critics as "conspiracies against the public."[39] Like a bureaucratic civil service, a profession derives some of its elitist *esprit de corps* from formal methods of recruitment. These, in fact, form an integral part of what constitutes a profession. Thus, quite recently, the editor of the *Princeton Alumni Bulletin* could define the professions as:

> those vocations which rest upon a systematic body of knowledge of substantial intellectual content and which are entered by advanced degrees, i.e. examinations demonstrating minimum standards of education and competence.[40]

Now, to the extent that this definition stresses specialised and theoretical expertise, it is unfriendly to the amateur ideal of the gentleman. On the other hand, the professional examination, like its civil service counterpart and like the various Public School initiation rites, invests a group with a mystique. By confronting new members with a traditional body of knowledge to be rigorously learned, the profession acquires the aura of historic continuity; it appears as a group which is more than the sum of present members. Recruitment by formal examination, moreover, gives the profession the image of a community not lightly entered nor easily understood by the outsider. It should also be noted that, until the rise of the American business school, this professional mystique was largely withheld from the businessman who learned his job more by individual experience than from a clearly-recognised, communal body of knowledge.[41]

From the foregoing it can be seen that the ideals and requirements of the private profession were fairly similar to those of the political elite. Both groups appeared to imbue their members with properties that did not originate with the individual but belonged to the group as a whole. Among such properties, in the case of the private profession, was the possession of esoteric knowledge; like the classical culture of the Chinese degree-holders, professional knowledge bore the image of an immortal entity conferred upon the individual by the elite group, whose trust that knowledge was.[42] On a somewhat vaguer note, the Public School treated wisdom in the same way—as the property of a status-group and external to the individual. It was on just this point that in 1924 Sir James Barrie made a speech twitting the schools. Apparently, he said, they claimed to possess a "mysterious something" that "oozes out of the historic old walls." By way of reply the *Times* claimed solemnly that the "something" came from outside the individual; it was "non-analysable" and non-intellectual, and it induced boys to distrust their individual intellects and do an unselfish job.[43]

SOCIAL MOBILITY AND HEREDITARY PRIVILEGE

The *Times*-Barrie exchange, however comic its tone, has a meaning which is central to our understanding of the gentleman elite. For the gentleman's distinctive aura depended, at least in part, on a tacit claim to qualities derived mystically from outside the individual. From this point of view a hereditary ruling class enjoys advantages of prestige over a purely merit-selected ruling class. The latter must base its leadership qualifications on an aggregate of individuals still alive, on the character they have shown, the efforts they have made, and the training they have received during their own lifetimes. By contrast, an aristocracy can attribute its leadership qualities to a long line of ancestors,including famous men whose glory is intimately linked with that of the historic community. Moreover, the person who claims that he is *born* to rule bases his claim on a far more mysterious process than the person who claims that he has tangibly proved himself worthy to rule.[44]

Biologically, of course, the above is nonsense. There is little evidence to suppose that leadership qualities, even qualities of style and manner, can be inherited. When men claim that the aristocrat is born to rule, they really mean that he is brought up to rule. Family traditions and home influence are just another form of education.

This does not alter the fact that a political elite with a hereditary core can claim a glamor that a "meritocracy" will find it hard to equal. Mythical as the basis of that glamor may be, it will nonetheless exist in the eyes of the non-elite, provided social values are not actively hostile to the notion of hereditary privilege. And if the hereditary ruling class can match its aristocratic aura with claims to reward merit, it will have unusual power to inspire deference in the non-elite and attract new blood into its ranks. Against the material inducements of private profit-making, the political elite will be able to offer its *nouveau* recruits the honor of association with the aristocrat—and with the latter's public service tradition.

It was on these lines that the social composition of the gentleman elite in both societies was formed. On one hand, the education system conferred prime advantages on well-to-do families, especially among the landed, and this group formed the nucleus of the political elite. By adjusting its curriculum to the requirements of civil service examinations, the education system harnessed the public service traditions of the gentry to the recruitment needs of bureaucracy. On the other hand, the political elite absorbed a limited number of the non-elite. Furthermore, government recruitment stressed merit criteria in selection; although it must be said that the very criteria themselves, emphasizing classical knowledge and a certain set style, favored the gentry individual.

What the political elite really did was to compromise between hereditary privilege and the reward of merit. Confucius himself appears to have supported this ambivalence; he favored government recruitment based on merit, but he would have allowed the nobility certain ritual privileges.[45] The same compromise appears in the British honors system, where hereditary titles co-exist with a hierarchy of earned knighthoods and orders. Behind the compromise lay a rationale, however unarticulated, that every critic of elitist education should consider. In terms of effective leadership, the gentleman elite stands or falls on the assumption that before one talks of selecting political ability one must talk of producing political motivation, of inducing men to take on public responsibility in the first place. And the most potent way to produce political motivation—so runs the elitist argument—is to secure "a social stratum . . . that takes to politics as a matter of course." [46]

CONCLUSION

By its very nature, the gentleman elite paid an intellectual price for its self-perpetuation. Social mobility or no, to the extent that it indulged hereditary privilege, it inevitably lost some "village Hampden" his opportunity.[47] The very process, moreover, of making political gentlemen displayed weaknesses: loyalty-indoctrination by aesthetic device inhibited rigorous questioning; and the amateur figure showed little sympathy for technological innovation and expert method. Gentlemanly education, like society itself, faced an age-old dilemma: the fact that loyalty-training and intelligence are not easy companions.

In judging the productivity of gentlemanly education, however, one should not simply ask how much national intelligence it produced and whether a less elitist system could have produced a greater aggregate of skills and ability. These questions are important, but to meet the champions of the political elite one must meet them on their own ground. And to do this one must ask other questions. Did gentlemanly education make up for its intellectual deficiencies by supporting a spirit of public service, by ensuring that enough men of some raw ability and integrity preferred government responsibility to private profit? Could a more democratic system of education have poured the same flow of talent into relatively unremunerative government posts? On the other hand, at what point does such a flow defeat its own ends by starving industry, science and other key occupations that nourish the state? These questions are barely within the scope of this paper but they are worth the asking.

FOOTNOTES

1. Joseph Schumpeter, *Capitalism, Socialism & Democracy,* Harper, New York, 1942, pp. 137, 298.

2. Joseph Schumpeter, *ibid.*, pp. 137–8.

3. The Chinese gentry were perhaps subject to more social mobility than the English gentry; their social status depended directly on membership in, or kinship with, the degree-holder group. *Shen-shih,* the Chinese word commonly translated as "gentry" literally means "degree-holders." When I talk of the Chinese gentry, I mean those families enjoying social prestige and a respected standard of culture, non-commercial but not necessarily large landowners. They shared status and values in common rather than great wealth.

4. W. L. Guttsman, "Aristocracy and the Middle Class in the British Political Elite, 1886–1916," *British Journal of Sociology,* London, March 1954. Robert Marsh, *The Mandarins: The Circulation of Elites in China,* Free Press, Glencoe, (U.S.A.), 1961, pp. 78–82.

5. E. Wingfield-Stratford, *The Squire and His Relations,* Cassells, London, 1956, p. 389.

6. *Concise Oxford Dictionary,* Oxford University Press, 1953.

7. Reinhold Niebuhr, *Moral Man and Immoral Society,* Scribners, New York, 1932, p. 126.

8. It is interesting here to note that in the Oxford Dictionary the subsidiary *legal* definition of the gentleman contains the factor of leisure: a man "who has no occupation."

9. ". . . moderate in his words but ardent in his actions." Confucius, *Lun Yu,* Part XIV, Ch. 29.

10. From *Max Weber: Essays,* translated by H. Gerth & C. W. Mills, Kegan Paul, London, 1947.

11. *Concise Oxford Dictionary, op. cit.,* see under "classic," "classical," and, by contrast, "romantic."

12. The Chinese official, it is true, enjoyed leisure in which to pursue prestige-conferring cultural pastimes. But his public post made leisure possible, not *vice versa.* cf. Jacques Gernet, *Daily Life in China on the Eve of the Mongol Invasion,* Allen & Unwin, London, 1962, p. 183.

13. Robert Marsh, *op. cit.,* p. 65.

14. John K. Fairbank, ed., *Chinese Thought & Institutions,* p. 321 (chap. by Levenson).

15. Robert Marsh shows how local leadership *functions,* rather than *wealth,*

gave the Chinese landowner and even merchant the most prestige, *op. cit.*, p. 38.

In Victorian England, similarly, the *nouveau riche* industrialist raised his social prestige by taking on the style and duties of the country squire.

16. Reinhold Niebuhr, *op. cit.*, espec., pp. 20–21.

17. Here I include family upbringing under gentlemanly education. In China, of course, Confucian education was closely linked to family upbringing: there was no dominant system of private boarding schools. It should also be noted that clan rules (codes of behavior for family members) were most elaborate, by and large, in gentry families.

18. William of Wykeham, Bishop of Winchester, who founded the sister institutions, Winchester College (the Public School) and New College, Oxford.

19. Again it is here relevant that clan rules of propriety were most elaborate in the families of the *shen-shih*—degree-holding genty. Cf. D. S. Nivison & M. Wright, *Confucianism in Action*. Stanford University Press, 1959.

20. "Foxes' Revenge," a *T'ang* story in *The Courtesan's Jewel Box,* Foreign Language Press, Peking, 1957, p. 96, quoted by Robert Marsh, *op. cit.*, p. 2.

21. "No virtue can remain untainted without learning"—Confucius, *Li Ki* (Book of Rituals), Sect. I. But, of course, careerism affected many scholars' pursuit of culture. cf. "The Bookworm," a satirical short story of the *Ching* dynasty, by P'u Sungling, in *Famous Chinese Short Stories,* retold by Lin Yutang, Pocket Library, New York, 1954.

22. Vivian Ogilvie, *The English Public School, Batsford,* London, 1957, pp. 181–3. Cf. C. E. Pasco, *Everyday Life in Our Public Schools,* Griffith & Farran, London, 1881.

23. Ogilvie, *ibid.*, pp. 181–3 and G. F. Lamb, *The Happiest Days,* Joseph, London, 1959, pp. 19–26.

24. E. H. Pitcairn, *Unwritten Laws & Ideals of Active Careers,* Smith Elder, London, 1899, pp. 286–9.

25. Cyril Connolly, *Enemies of Promise,* Macmillan, New York, 1948, pp. 174, 214.

26. Erich Fromm, *Fear of Freedom,* Routledge & Kegan Paul, London, 1960, p. 15.

27. James Morris, in *New York Times Magazine,* Nov. 13, 1960. Italics added.

28. In China, the prominence awarded writing as a gentleman's means of expression itself tended to dampen spontaneity. "Phantasy and ardor fled from the formalistic intellectualism of the spoken word into the quiet beauty of the written symbol."—Max Weber, *op. cit.*, p. 430.

29. *Lun Yu,* Part XIV, Chap. 29.

30. Lucy Mair, *Primitive Government,* Penguin, London, 1962, p. 225.

31. "All Things Bright & Beautiful," *Hymns Ancient & Modern,* London, Clowes and Son.

32. Admittedly, the Chinese central government entered into many industrial pursuits, e.g. the salt and iron monopolies. But civil servants were not recruited as potential entrepreneurs.

33. It is my private hypothesis that the rising fashionability of the advertising and public relations occupations in Britain is due to this very fact. For what are advertising and public relations but the professionalised practice of manners, far from the greasy wheels of technology. Further, the commercial exploitation of hostmanship introduces a note of leisure—or the posture of leisure—into office hours.

In connection with my discussion of the *professions* and *elitism,* (see below) one should note the steady attempt of advertising to make itself into a profession, with formal examinations and such titles as "Practitioners in Advertising."

Before advertising, however, could become fashionable, the gentleman had to say goodbye to his disdain for the commercial middleman. Long before this, though, another commercial occupation had attained some gentlemanly acceptance: namely, banking.

34. C. K. Yang, *The Chinese Family in the Communist Revolution,* M.I.T., Cambridge, Mass., pp. 5–6.

35. Cf. J. K. Fairbank & Edwin Reischauer, *East Asia—The Great Tradition,* Vol. I, *A History of East Asian Civilization,* Houghton-Mifflin, Boston, 1960, pp. 189–91.

36. T. C. Worsley, *Barbarians & Philistines,* Hale, London, 1940, pp. 97–8. T. W. Bamford, "Public Schools & Social Class, 1801–1850," *British Journal of Sociology,* September, 1961. This article indicates that in the period preceeding that under review, the most famous Public Schools admitted considerably more boys from professional families than they did from business families.

37. T. H. S. Escott, *England: Its People, Polity, & Pursuits,* Chapman & Hall, London, 1885, pp. 355–6.

T. H. Pear points out that the practice of selling medicine for profit around 1800 lowered the prestige of G.P.'s—*English Social Differences,* Allen & Unwin, London, 1955. It was ungentlemanly, perhaps, to make a great deal of money very obviously from a humane service.

38. T. H. Pear, *ibid.* 22.

39. T. H. Pear, *ibid.* 37–8.

40. John P. Davies, writing in the *Harvard Alumni Bulletin,* Cambridge, Mass., March 17, 1962.

41. Elitism in the professions suggests that, ironically enough, democracy may encourage the growth of its own brand of elitism, by demanding formal criteria for the entering of many occupations. In the same way, the Chinese bureaucracy set tests which increased the exclusivist aura of government, although the tests were designed to call forth talent and reduce family influence in recruitment.

42. This is not to deny a great difference between the Confucian concept of knowledge and the Victorian professional one. Unlike the latter, Confucian knowledge was absolutist, discouraging further additions, to a known body of principles, and accordingly opposed to inductive thinking. It might be said, however, that one characteristic of professional examinations is their tendency to stress memory-work, the learning of fact and generally accepted principles.

43. Edward Mack, *Public Schools & British Opinion Since 1860,* Methuen, London, 1938, p. 401.

44. Lucy Mair, *op. cit.,* p. 218.

45. *Analects,* Books III, Chap. 22.

46. Joseph Schumpeter, *op. cit.,* p. 298.

47. "Full many a gem of purest ray serene
The dark unfathom'd caves of ocean bear;
Full many a flower is born to blush unseen,
And waste its sweetness on the desert air.
Some village Hampden that with dauntless breast,
The little tyrant of his fields withstood;
Some mute inglorious here may rest,
Some Cromwell guiltless of his country's blood."

—Thomas Gray, "Elegy Written in a Country Churchyard"

Political Recruitment and Integration in Lebanon: The American University of Beirut

MUNIR A. BASHSHUR

On December 3, 1966 the American University of Beirut (AUB) celebrated the completion of its first hundred years. It has been a century of great changes and great tensions both within the university and in the area that it serves. In no other place outside the Western hemisphere can one find an example of transfusion of American culture as successfully performed. Unlike the British or French education in Africa, interest in the work of AUB is heightened by the fact that it was not an extended arm of the state or part of an overall scheme for the colonies, but rather a private agency working under private initiative. Furthermore, from its inception AUB has functioned as a college, not a secondary or a primary school, and as such it has acted as an important source for the elite of the country.

The role of such an institution can be investigated along several lines: as a transmitter of foreign culture and a bridgehead for foreign influence, as a center for learning and discovery, and as an agent of social mobility or a source of elite recruitment. In a country like Lebanon, characterized by sectarian divisions and by strong pressures from outside, it would be of value to explore the ways in which this university contributed to political and social integration, and the kind of leadership it provided for the country.

Many of the peculiar characteristics of Lebanon stem from the manner in which the country attained statehood. While Lebanon is a name that goes back to Biblical times, the present state of Lebanon is only forty years old, and it received its independence a little less than a quarter of a century ago. The nineteenth century witnessed two particularly significant developments that left their imprint on its present character: 1) the religious wars between the Christian Maronites and the Moslem Druze;[1] and 2) the advent of the religious-educational missionaries.

RELIGIOUS WARS

The first religious clashes took place in 1841, after which the Ottomans established a constitution giving the Maronites the upper hand in the north, and the Druze a similar position in the south. This arrangement did not settle the problem, and finally in 1861 a major war broke out. Immediately afterwards an international commission of six countries (Great Britain, Austria, Russia, Prussia, France, and Turkey) was set up to investigate the disturbances, and in 1864 it promulgated a new constitution formalizing and defining the autonomy of Mount Lebanon.[2] Under the terms of this constitution Lebanon was to be administered by a Christian Ottoman governor to be chosen from outside. But the government was to be appointed by the Ottoman government with the consent of the Powers and to be assisted by a Central Administrative Council, on which the more important religious communities were to be equally represented.[3] This constitution was the first legal framework for the distribution of public offices among the various religious sects. Lebanon was ruled according to its provisions until World War I.

After World War I the Sykes-Picot Anglo-French agreement defined the spheres of influence in the territories which were under the Ottoman Empire. In 1922, the council of the League of Nations placed Syria and Lebanon under the French Mandate. To the pre-war Mount Lebanon were added the coastal towns of Beirut, Tripoli, Sidon, Tyre, and the district of Biqa' in the east, and Jebel Amel in the south to form what was called "Grand Liban." In 1926 this state was given the official name by which it is now known, the Republic of Lebanon.

This post-war rearrangement brought into one state a religiously heterogeneous population far more complex in its composition and connections with the neighboring Arab countries than the simple bi-polar religious composition of the original Mount Lebanon. In the newly added coastal towns the population was largely Muslim Sunni, and in the Biqa' and Jebel Amel largely Muslim Shii. The geographical unity which distinguished Mount Lebanon was also disrupted by extending the boundaries of the new state to the hinterland where no geographical limits stood between Lebanon and its neighbors. In the words of Hitti, "What the country gained in area, it lost in cohesion. It lost its internal equilibrium. . . . The Christian overwhelming majority was seriously reduced." [4]

The French Mandate lasted from 1922 till 1943. In September, 1943, Lebanon as we know it today was recognized as an independent sovereign state.

RELIGIOUS EDUCATIONAL MISSIONARIES

The second most significant development of the ninteenth century was the missionary activity and the greater exposure of Lebanon to the West. Roman Catholic missionaries arrived in the country early in the seventeenth century. Those who received their education in the mission schools and the Maronite College of Rome, established in 1584, spearheaded a new social order based on religious ties and sentiments rather than on feudal ties. Thus, the emerging social pattern gradually evolved along Christian-Druze lines rather than around the relationship between landowner and peasant.[5] This new realignment of positions set the stage for the religious wars which erupted in the 1860's.

The activities of the Catholic missions in the field of education culminated in 1875 in the establishment of the Jesuit University in Beirut which continues to operate at the present time.

The American missionaries arrived in the country in the 1820's, and the first American school was in operation in 1824. By 1827 there were thirteen schools with about six hundred pupils.[6] The work of these schools progressed at an irregular rate until the middle of the nineteenth century, when their numbers started to increase steadily. Their aim was decidedly religious.[7]

The natives of Lebanon, however, were far from passive agents playing into the hands of the missionaries; their great demand and zeal for education superseded all other considerations. One of the early missionaries reported that, "while the people of a given village would not receive a missionary as simply a preacher of the gospel, they would accept a school from his hands and welcome him on every visit to the school as a benefactor." [8]

The religious wars of the 1860's are generally viewed negatively as events that formalized the sectarian structure of Lebanon. While this is true to a large extent, they also accelerated social and economic changes. According to Henry Jessup:

> Some of the power of the old feudal families and tribes was broken, as was the power of the native religious hierarchy; the ruling Muslim mobility of Damascus was destroyed, and tens of thousands of people were forced out of their villages and into Beirut and other cities because of fear and privation. There they encountered new influences. . . . New economic structures requiring new skills and knowledge emerged, resulting in a surging demand for education.[9]

Thus in the aftermath of the 1860 war a new society was being born. This climate, plus the failure of the mission Board to meet a growing demand for higher education "other than to train native clergy . . . sparked the birth of AUB and determined its nature." [10] The purpose of the college was stated as follows:

> The pupils should be educated with reference to the business which they propose to follow. . . . Thus avoiding the reproach of sending forth helpless drones upon society. . . . [C]are should be exercised to prevent the students from becoming denationalized. . . . [I]n the interests of the independence and self-support of the student body the principle of self-support should be fostered as far as possible.[11]

In 1862, Daniel Bliss, who was to become the first president of the college, expressed his belief that the new school, "Should cast in just as much good seed as possible and thus prepare material for constructing good government and good society," when the Ottoman despotism passed away.[12]

Although the religious purpose of AUB was strong, it was broader in its scope and more cognizant of the local needs than the Mission Board. The present catalogue of AUB defines its aim in the following words: "The University emphasizes true scholarship which teaches students to think for themselves. It stresses high academic standards and high principles of character. It aims to produce men and women who are not only technically competent in their professional fields, but who also have breadth of vision, a sense of civic and moral responsibility, and devotion to the fundamental values of human life." [13]

AUB AND POLITICAL RECRUITMENT

Confessionalism in Lebanon is the basis of recruitment to public offices. From the presidency of the Republic down to the office clerk, positions are allotted to the various religious sects according to their proportion in the population of the country. This arrangement has frequently been decried as wasteful, inefficient, and detrimental to the unity of the country.[14] But some regard it as a "working political framework," as a fundamental "prop" for system maintenance and for avoidance of injury, or as the most appropriate arrangement until a better substitute is found.[15] What is of concern to us here is that under such an arrangement, the role of the university as an agency of political recruitment becomes seriously impaired. Three factors may be said to help sustain the role of the university despite this fact: first, political power in Lebanon is not heavily concentrated in political offices; second, employment in the public sector does not dominate employment in the private sector; and third, there is a tendency to employ educated persons in the public sector without subverting the confessional balance.

Following Lasswell,[16] one can say that the influential are not always located in political offices, although those who occupy such offices do possess influence. This becomes clearer as one descends the political and administrative scale. Even at the upper echelons, political involvement is really tangible only at times of appointments or in certain times of crisis when the confessional or communal balance is at stake. One gets the feeling that the formal political structure is only loosely related to the real power structure in the country. Arnold Hottinger put it as follows:

> Politics in Lebanon seems to evolve on two different planes: an onstage of official government and parliamentary political life and a backstage of personal, confessional, regional group, family and interest group politics. Such [a] statement could be made for any country. But what singles out Lebanon is the fact that the onstage has remarkably little connection with the backstage, and needless to say, that the backstage decisions invisible as they are are the ones that really count.[17]

This dichotomy is reinforced by lack of congruence between Lebanon as a state and Lebanon as a nation. Lebanon as a state has remained stable not by virtue of internal cohesion and commitment to a national identity, but "from the willingness of a majority of Lebanese to put up with a regime which is not legitimate in order to prevent it from assuming a legitimacy which is disapproved." [18]

In the absence of commitment to Lebanon as a national entity, the Lebanese government is more of a dispenser of benefits than a power center. As such, it finds itself one of the many agencies in the society which share the function of dispensing benefits. Because more educated people become alienated from the public sector for lack of sectarian credentials and obtain jobs in the private sector, which is less scrupulous of such credentials, the sectarian set-up has worked to the advantage of the private sector.[19]

In spite of the foregoing remarks, some information on the number of AUB alumni in public employment will be useful. Of 154 Lebanese alumni who graduated between 1922 and 1960, the writer has found that only 21 (13.6%) were government employees, while 75 (45.6%) were employed by private, national, or foreign agencies and 45 (29.2%) were self-employed. One reason that accounts for this, is the absence of a law school at AUB, which deprives it of direct access into governmental offices. In a study of the members of the 1960-64 parliament, it was reported that 37 out of 99 members held law degrees, while ten held M.D.'s and M.A.'s, five, B.A.'s, three, engineering degrees, and two, Ph.D.'s.[20]

Further, direct recruitment of AUB graduates into governmental offices is rendered more difficult by the fact that the Lebanese government and civil service were largely patterned after the French. Out of the 99 members of the 1960-64 parliament it was found that 53 studied in French institutions while only 19 studied in American or English institutions.[21]

The political role of AUB, therefore, should be investigated not in terms of the number of alumni who find their way into governmental offices, but rather in terms of the broader spectrum of the power structure of the Lebanese society. For as Coleman has remarked, "Any discussion of the relationship of education to the recruitment of political elites in a particular society inevitably focuses on its social stratification system and on the degree of upward mobility within that system." [22] In other words, the role of education in political recruitment should be explored in terms of the upward mobility that it generates among its recipients.

The most salient characteristic of AUB is that it is an elite-perpetuating institution. It not only places its alumni in high level jobs, but it also draws its students from high level backgrounds.

In a study conducted by the present writer in 1962 on a sample of AUB students and alumni the results shown in Table I were obtained. Here data on the Lebanese subjects only are presented to allow for a comparison with the Lebanese labor force. The table shows that while 41% of the active labor force in the country pursue semi-skilled, unskilled, and farming jobs, only 8.5% of the students come from such backgrounds, and none of the alumni enter such jobs.

TABLE I. PATERNAL OCCUPATIONS OF STUDENTS AND OCCUPATIONS OF ALUMNI COMPARED WITH THE OCCUPATIONAL PURSUITS OF THE ACTIVE LABOR FORCE IN LEBANON (PERCENTAGES)

Occupation	*Active* Labor Force*	*Paternal Occupations of Students*	*Occupations of Alumni*
Managerial	0.9	7.0	6.1
Large-scale businessmen and landowners	1.8	26.9	9.5
Professional	1.3	16.0	39.8
Administrative and clerical	10.8	18.4	35.8
Middle and small-scale businessmen and landowners	39.9	19.9	3.4
Semi-skilled, unskilled workers and farmers	41.1	8.5	0.0
No occupation	4.2	3.3	5.4
Total	100.0	100.0 (N = 331)	100.0 (N = 148)

* For the manner of obtaining this distribution, see Munir A. Bashshur, "The Role of Two Western Universities in the National Life of Lebanon and the Middle East," (unpublished Ph.D. Dissertation, the University of Chicago, 1964).

These data indicate another phenomenon, perhaps more significant relative to AUB's role in modernization. While about 30% of the students come from the category "large-scale businessmen and landowners," only about one-third of the alumni enter this occupational category. On the other hand, while about 40% of them enter the "professional" category, only 16% of the students come from professional backgrounds. It should be noted that the two categories, "large-scale businessmen and landowners" and "professional," are in the "upper" social stratum of Lebanon. (Only 4% of the total active labor force is in these two categories.) What is happening here is not mobility from a lower social stratum to a higher one, but a change in the kind of occupancy within the same stratum—from an elite rooted in the prestige of landownership and money to a skilled and trained elite. The same conclusion can be drawn from a comparison of paternal occupations of students and the occupations of alumni in the two categories: "administrative and clerical" and "middle and small-scale businessmen and landowners," the first being more dependent on education than the second.

What we are witnessing is not exactly political recruitment in the proper sense of the word, but political transformation. The three-quarters of all the alumni who enter "professional" and "administrative and clerical" jobs would not have the kind of influence that would unlock for them the doors of the traditional Lebanese political structure; it is the kind of power that would enable them to build gradually a new political structure. Their power is, on the whole, not the inherited kind, but the achieved, and as such they are contributing significantly to the modernization of Lebanon. As Geertz reminds us, "the growth of a modern state within a traditional social context represents, not merely the shifting or transfer of a fixed quantity of power between groups in such a manner that aggregatively the gain of certain groups or individuals matches the losses of others, but rather the creation of a new and more efficient machine for the production of power itself, and thus an increase in the general political capacity of the society." [23]

The mobility pattern illustrated in Table I could be reinforced by income analysis. Table II presents comparative data on the income of fathers of students, of alumni, and of the Lebanese population.

The high selectivity of AUB students is demonstrated by a comparison between the incomes of their fathers and the general income pattern of the Lebanese population. However, a comparison of incomes of

TABLE II. PATERNAL INCOME OF LEBANESE STUDENTS COMPARED WITH THE INCOME OF THE ALUMNI AND THE POPULATION

Income bracket (in L.L.)	*Paternal Income of Students %*	*Income of Graduates %*	*Lebanese Population* Income Bracket*	*%*
Below 8000	27.2	24.3		
8000–12,999	14.7	26.4	below 5000	50.0
13,000–29,999	24.8	28.4	5000–15,000	32.0
30,000–99,999	13.7	12.8	over 15,000	18.0
100,000 and over	5.3	2.7	total	100.0
N.A.	14.3	5.4		
Total	100.0 (N = 331)	100.0 (N = 148)		

* Mission I.R.F.E.D.—Liban, *Besoin et Possibilités de Developpement Du Liban,* 1960–61, Vol. I, p. 24.

graduates with incomes of fathers of students shows that the graduates are not at all superior to fathers of students; the reverse could very well be true. The similarity in income patterns corroborates the conclusion made earlier, namely, that the mobility affected by the alumni of AUB takes the form of a shift in kind of occupation rather than in terms of traditional prestige (income) reflected.

AUB AND POLITICAL INTEGRATION

The American University of Beirut is far from being a meeting ground for the various social strata of the country. The fact that it is a tuition-charging institution places a heavy barrier in front of low income groups. In the first year of the Faculty of Arts and Sciences the tuition fee is L.L.1650; for the boarder, costs rise to a minimum of L.L.3500. Students in the professional schools pay more. Scholarships are too few for the solution of the problem.

In a country where the family income of one half of the population is below L.L.5000, AUB cannot expect to act as a bridge between the rich and the poor. However, it may be argued that discrimination on financial grounds takes place much earlier in the educational careers of the students. Of the 331 Lebanese students covered in the 1962 study, 308 (93%) received their previous education in fee-charging private national or foreign schools.

Another important discriminating factor is the medium of instruction. English, the chief language at AUB, is not the national language of the country; as a medium of communication it contributes adversely to the creation of an integrated political community. Although English remains the second language for most AUB students, through this medium students develop certain modes of thinking and values that are not shared by the rest of their countrymen.[24]

Vertical integration (elite-mass) is interlocked with horizontal integration at more than one point. This is due to the fact that the elite are members of various sub-systems; from what sub-systems they are recruited and in what proportions affect the degree and extent of horizontal integration.

It should be noted that along with the integrative function an educational system performs a differentiating or sorting function. The differentiating function refers to the process of sorting the students into different levels, or more important, into different fields of study. This process is particularly evident at the university level.

RELIGION

As religion is the most important sub-system in the Lebanese society, a comparison of the religious composition of the student body with that of the

TABLE III. COMPARISON OF THE RELIGIOUS COMPOSITION OF AUB STUDENT BODY AND THE LEBANESE POPULATION

	*Lebanese Population (1956)** %	*Lebanese AUB Students (1966–67)*** %
Sunni	20.2	17.8
Shii	17.7	4.3
Druze	6.2	6.2
Total Muslim	44.1	28.3
Greek Orthodox	10.6	23.7
Armenians	5.8	16.4
Maronites	30.0	8.7
Catholics	6.4	10.3
Protestants	1.0	11.3
Other Christians	1.2	—
Total Christians	55.0	70.4
Other	0.9	1.3
Grand Total	100.0	100.0(N = 1381)

* Figures released by the Bureau of Vital Statistics. [See *al-Nahar* (Beirut) No. 6249, April 26, 1956.] The last official census was taken in 1932. Since then, all population figures have been estimates.

** Student figures presented in this paper were obtained from the official authorities of the University (the Registrar, and the Bursary Students' Office).

total Lebanese population is necessary. This is presented in Table III.

Clearly, there is a marked bias in favor of the Christian as compared to the Muslim segment of the population of Lebanon. Only 28.3% of the students are Muslims against 44.1% of the population; on the other hand, 70.4% of the students are Christians against 55.0% of the population.

Among the Christians, the Maronites, the original inhabitants of Mount Lebanon, constitute the largest single sect in the population (30%). Yet only 8.7% of the students are Maronites. The Protestants, on the other hand, who represent 1.0% of the population, account for 11.3% of AUB students. Similarly, the Greek Orthodox and the Armenians are represented by more than twice their share of the population.

Among the Muslims, the Shii, who constitute 17.7% of the population, represent 4.3% of the total student body. The Shii are the most deprived religious group in the country, educationally, socially, and economically, and they and the Maronites are the least represented groups on the student body. But while the Maronites stay away from AUB by choice (the majority enter the Jesuit French University), the Shii fail to gain access into AUB, or any other university, by necessity.[25]

Religiously speaking, therefore, AUB is far from being an integrative agency; in fact the evidence shows that it is acting in the opposite direction, namely as a differentiating agency. This is not the result of discriminating policies on the part of the university. The low proportion of Muslims in general and Shii in particular in the student body is an example of an educational process fortifying what Coleman calls "the self-perpetuative propensity among preexisting inequalities." [26]

Additional evidence on the pattern of religious distribution was obtained by looking into the representation of each of the sects in the various branches of study (see Table IV). This table indicates the following:

1. About an equal proportion of each religious sect is in the fields of Arts and Sciences and Business Administration. However, only a small proportion of Maronites pursue graduate work. In contrast, Protestants are least represented at the undergraduate level; the majority pursue graduate studies.

2. The Protestants and Armenians, who are represented in AUB in larger proportions than any other sects, concentrate in the professional fields of medicine, pharmacy, nursing, public health, and engineering.

3. The Shii and Maronites, who, relative to their distribution in the population, are least represented in the university, concentrate in engineering more than any other sect. The Shii have the smallest proportion in the field of medicine.

4. Agriculture attracts the smallest proportion of students, particularly among the Maronites and the Protestants.

The religious diversity of the Lebanese population and its acceptance as the basic framework for public employment render the task of national integration difficult if not impossible. Binder describes the Lebanese process as one of "Countervalence," which represents "that which is opposed to modernity and democracy." He continues:

> The lack of uniformity [in religious composition] is of great political consequence, for it indicates that time will cause the people of Lebanon to grow further apart rather than become more closely integrated unless some force breaks the boundaries of existing power structure.[27]

The question is whether in time Lebanon can develop into a modern integrated society overriding these divisional forces. Short of open revolt, Lebanon's only hope seems to reside in an educational system that cross-cuts these forces and gradually "breaks the boundaries of the existing power structure." Education may accomplish this by responding more equitably

TABLE IV. DIFFERENTIATION OF THE LEBANESE STUDENTS AT AUB BY FIELD OF STUDY AND RELIGION—1966–1967 (%)

	Arts and Sciences and Business Administration	*Arts and Sciences (Graduate)*	*Medicine*	*Pharmacy, Nursing, and Public Health*	*Engineering*	*Agriculture*	*Other, Special, and U.O.P.*	*Total*
Sunni	54.3	8.1	7.8	2.0	21.2	4.1	2.5	(245) 100.0
Shii	49.1	10.2	1.7	8.5	23.7	5.1	1.7	(59) 100.0
Druze	44.2	10.4	12.8	2.3	17.4	4.7	8.1	(86) 100.0
Greek Orthodox	46.9	7.0	10.0	6.7	22.9	2.1	4.1	(328) 100.0
Armenian	41.8	5.0	7.9	25.5	15.4	2.6	1.8	(227) 100.0
Maronite	55.0	3.3	5.8	5.9	29.2	0.0	0.8	(120) 100.0
Catholic	48.4	8.3	6.2	8.4	24.6	2.1	2.1	(142) 100.0
Protestant	36.9	9.5	12.8	19.8	17.2	0.6	3.2	(157) 100.0
Other	41.2	0.0	5.9	0.0	35.3	5.9	11.8	(17) 100.0
Total	(648) 46.9	(100) 7.3	(119) 8.6	(142) 10.3	(294) 21.3	(35) 2.6	(43) 3.1	(1381) 100.0

to the social and religious spectrum and by turning out an increasing number of persons set upon building a new social order. What is disappointing is that the educational system in the country is still dominated by private schools, particularly at the secondary level (only 28 secondary schools in the country are government schools),[28] which, by and large, are also differentiated along religious and commercial ilnes.

NATIONAL ORIGIN

Another factor of great importance regarding horizontal integration is the national origin of the student body. The data for 1966-67 show that out of a total of 3246 students, the Lebanese constituted the largest single group (42.4%). The Lebanese were followed by the Jordanians and Palestinians (16.1%), and Syrians (8.7%). Eighteen Arab countries accounted for 78.7% of the student body. Non-Arab Asian and African students (from Iran, Pakistan, Afghanistan, Kenya, and Ethiopia), accounted for 12.7%, and Western countries for 8.6%. The United States accounted for 5.4% of the student body.

National diversity has been a tradition and a source of pride for university authorities. The university catalogue includes the following statement:

> The American University of Beirut represents a venture in international education that is almost unique among the universities of the world. . . . The cosmopolitan campus and classrooms of AUB provide a living laboratory where students from many lands, many of whom will become leaders of tomorrow, meet at a formative period in their lives to learn how to work together in a spirit of mutual understanding. This is vitally important today when the many old and new states of the world must adjust themselves to the realities of living together in a rapidly shrinking world, if they are to survive in peace.[29]

The implications of this atmosphere for political integration may be approached from two levels: intra-state and inter-state. AUB draws its students from a circle stretching beyond the boundaries of the country in which it is located. The tensions it experiences, reflecting Lebanese forces, are, in a sense, diluted by this outward extension. On the other hand, the tensions of the outside (particularly the Arab) are brought to bear on its campus. Thus AUB, more than any other institution in Lebanon, is a microcosm for all the tensions that beset the Arab region as a whole.

This seems to fit into the Lebanese pattern perfectly; for it should be remembered that Lebanon is an Arab country whose attraction to the outer Arab world fluctuates in strength from time to time. It is neither independent enough to go its own way nor committed enough to be an Arab entity. Thus the same policy of compromise at the level of internal affairs guides the country in its inter-Arab affairs. Both policies are intertwined, and the stability of one depends to no small degree on the stability of the other.

In a major sense, then, in the national composition of its student body AUB reflects the same compromising attitude as Lebanon toward its Arab neighbors.[30] If Lebanon should join a larger Arab union, then AUB would have acted as an inter-Arab integrative agency; in the meantime, it keeps the bridges open.

But AUB's "bridges" stretch to the non-Arab regions of Asia and Africa as well. In 1951, several Asian and African countries (including some Arab countries) and AUB signed a contract to provide scholarships at AUB for students from these countries. Since then, 7594 students from 21 countries received training at AUB. Forty percent came from four countries (Iran, Pakistan, Ethiopia, and Afghanistan). Of all the non-Arab students from Asia and Africa enrolled in 1966-67, 67% are recipients of AID scholarships, compared to 13.3% of the Arab students. The majority of the students who come from such Arab countries as Sudan, Morocco, Yemen, and Libya are AID scholarship holders. These countries are "off-center" from the traditional Arab sphere of AUB.

It can perhaps be argued that AID policy works toward the integration of the people in these countries in the sense that it helps the less advanced to catch up with the more advanced. However, the impact of this policy on the Arab students who come from AUB's most immediate surroundings (Lebanon, Syria, Jordan, and Iraq) is less than certain. When President Penrose signed the contract in 1951, he must have foreseen the implications of this move and the ensuing controversy. In his yearly report he answered his critics in the following words:

> To those who may think that an agreement between the United States government and a private institution is unusual it may be said that the institution itself is unusual in that it is there possible to offer to students from a number of different countries training programs which would have to be established in sextuplicate if they were to be supported by Point IV funds allocated to individual countries.[31]

To many the problem had more than one angle, and the one chosen by Penrose was the least disturbing. The effect that the contract had on the national composition of the student body, on the fees charged to the non-aided students, and on the attitudes of the Arabs towards the University, was far from negligible. It is not an exaggeration to say that many Arabs felt neglected.[32]

CONCLUDING REMARKS

The role of the American University of Beirut in Lebanon and the Middle East is remarkable. The university has successfully weathered the impact of three major political changes in the history of the region, none of which was especially congenial to it. After one hundred years AUB is still going on. Its impact on the political process has been quite imperceptible as far as number of AUB graduates entering political positions in Lebanon is concerned. Yet, in another sense AUB's impact has been quite tangible. The university has infused the leading strata of the society with new knowledge, skills, and values. As such, AUB has contributed to the gradual movement of Lebanon towards modernity.

In connection with Lebanese national integration, AUB may be said to have been "dysfunctional." This is illustrated by the social and religious origin of the students and by its language of instruction. However, considering the unique nature of Lebanon in the Arab and international context, AUB may also be said to have been "functional." Lebanon is an independent country (even before independence it had a large degree of autonomy). Yet it is part of a larger Arab region, neither completely Christian nor completely Moslem, neither completely Western nor completely Eastern. It is in this accord between Lebanon and AUB that the reasons for the successful continuation of the institution are to be found.

NOTES AND REFERENCES

1. The *Maronites* are members of the Roman Catholic Church and acknowledge the supremacy of the Pope. They are distinguished from the rest of the Roman Catholics in that they retain their autonomy under their own patriarch and exercise oriental rites in their religious services. Almost all the Maronites east of the Mediterranean are concentrated in the mountain regions of Lebanon. The *Druze* are a distant offshoot of Islamic religion. Though officially they are considered as Muslims, yet they maintain a tight communal solidarity and are disassociated from the rest of the Muslims. For the origin and beliefs of these communities see Albert Hourani, *Minorities in the Arab World* (London: Oxford University Press, 1947).

2. Mount Lebanon did not include Beirut or the seashore towns but simply the mountain regions rising to the east of Beirut; Beirut itself was kept as a Turkish province and in 1888 became the seat of a Turkish administrative district.

3. Albert H. Hourani, *Syria and Lebanon* (London: Oxford University Press, 1946), p. 33.

4. Philip Hitti, *Lebanon in History* (London: Macmillan Co., 1957), p. 490.

5. Iliya Harik, "The Maronite Church and Political Change in Lebanon," in Leonard Binder, ed., *Politics in Lebanon* (New York: John Wiley, 1966), pp. 46–47.

6. Rao H. Lindsay, *Nineteenth Century American Schools in the Levant: A Study of Purpose* (The University of Michigan, School of Education, Comparative Education Dissertation Series, Number 5, 1965), pp. 89–90.

7. *Ibid.*, p. 106.

8. *Ibid.*, p. 109.

9. *Ibid.*, p. 172.

10. *Ibid.*, p. 181.

11. Frederick Bliss, *The Reminiscences of Daniel Bliss* (New York: Fleming H. Revell Co., 1929), p. 168.

12. Lindsay, *op. cit.*, p. 184.

13. The American University of Beirut, *General Catalogue*, 1965–66, p. 10.

14. Raymond Edde, a noted Lebanese parliamentarian, called for the "removal of the sectarian divisions in Lebanon by three means: religiously mixed schools, military service and civil marriage." See *al-Safa'* (Beirut), No. 1110, November 12, 1965.

15. See Clifford Geertz (ed.) *Old Societies and New States* (Glencoe: The

Free Press, 1963), pp. 145, 214; Binder, *op. cit.*, pp. 41, 323; and *al-Safa'* (Beirut), No. 1108, Nov. 10, 1965.

16. Harold Lasswell, *Politics: Who Gets What, When, How,* (New York: Meridian Books, 1958), p. 13.

17. Arnold Hottinger, "Zu'ama and Political Parties in the Lebanese Crisis of 1958," *Middle East Journal,* Vol. XV, 1961.

18. Binder, "Political Change in Lebanon," *op. cit.*, p. 309.

19. There are no available data on the proportion of people in the public sector as compared with the private sector. The following information might, however, be revealing: of a total active labor force of 616,000 in 1964 it was estimated that 425,000 (59%) were dependent (salaried) persons, and the rest independent. Yet of the dependent persons only 30,000 were in civil service, while 220,000 were in agriculture, 98,000 in industry, artisans and construction, 82,000 in transport, commerce and finance, 56,000 in "other services," and 130,000 in occasional employment. See Republique Libanaise, Ministere du Plan, *Liban: previsions sur les Besoins en main c'oeuvre et les Besoins en Formation,* Document prepare pour le Seminaire OCDE-INAD, Beyrouth, 1966, p. 35. Obviously a large proportion of the dependent persons in agriculture, industry, etc., are employed by private individuals or agencies.

20. Mary-Ann Gebara, *The Social Background of the Lebanese Parliamentary Elite (1960–64).* (Unpublished Master's thesis, American University of Beirut, 1964.)

21. *Ibid.*

22. James B. Coleman, ed., *Education and Political Development* (Princeton, New Jersey: Princeton University Press, 1965), p. 25.

23. Geertz, "The Integrative Revolution," *op. cit.*, p. 121 (footnote).

24. Albert Hourani, *Syria and Lebanon, op. cit.*, p. 84. It should be remembered that when AUB was founded Arabic and not English was the chief medium of instruction. This continued until 1880, when English replaced Arabic. Equally important was "the increased prevalence of British influence" as a result of the British occupation of Cyprus and the Anglo-Turkish treaty. See Rao Lindsay, *op. cit.*, p. 189.

25. In 1962, the Maronites constituted 42% of all the Lebanese students at the French Jesuit University, while the Shii, together with the Druze, constituted only 8.4%. See Munir A. Bashshur, *The Role of Two Western Universities in the National Life of Lebanon and the Middle East.* (Unpublished Ph.D. dissertation, the University of Chicago, Chicago, 1964.)

26. Coleman, *op. cit.*, p. 31.

27. Leonard Binder, "Political Change in Lebanon," *loc. cit.*, pp. 303–305.

28. In 1964–65, of a total of 77,677 students at the intermediate and secondary level, 26,499 (34.2%) were in government schools and the rest were in private schools (national and foreign). Many of the private schools are religious in nature or draw the majority of their students from one religious group or another.

29. The American University of Beirut, *General Catalogue, op. cit.*, p. 10. The same statement appears in the back issues of the catalogue starting with 1963–64, but not before.

30. By coincidence it is found that the total student body of AUB is divided between Christians and Muslims in almost the exact proportions of the Lebanese population (54.6% Christian and 45.4% Muslim for AUB against an official figure of 55.0% and 44.1% respectively for Lebanon).

31. American University of Beirut, *Annual Report of the President,* 1950–51.

32. The proportion of students coming from Lebanon, Syria, Jordan, Palestine, and Iraq dropped from 85.8% in 1952 to 83.0% in 1955 to 80.3% in 1956 to 67.8% in 1960 and leveled off to 69.9% in 1963–64, 70.3% in 1964–65, and 69.1% in 1966–67. The proportion of the Lebanese in the same years remained, in fact about constant, ranging from 40% to 42%.

Education and Politics in Developing Countries

DAVID ABERNETHY

TREVOR COOMBE

EDUCATION AND POLITICS are inextricably linked. A government's education policy reflects, and sometimes betrays, its view of society or political creed. The formulation of policy, being a function of government, is essentially part of the political process, as are the demands made on government by the public for its revision. And the implementation of education policy has political consequences by affecting, among other things, types and levels of employment, social mobility, and the ideas and attitudes of the population.

Such links seem obvious when they are stated. They exist universally but tend to be obscured in societies which are both well-educated and politically stable, especially if education is locally controlled and ostensibly non-partisan. In general, the political significance of education in contemporary societies increases with the degree of change a society is undergoing. The massive changes which developing countries have already experienced and those, whether induced or not, which are in process, render all the more conspicuous the reciprocal relationship between politics and education in these areas.

Impressive evidence of this relationship may be found in the progress of colonies towards independence. The contribution of Western education to the eclipse of Western colonialism is now fairly well understood, at least schematically. The crux of the matter is that the successive generations of men who became nationalist leaders had attended colonial schools and metropolitan universities. The values, the vocabulary, and the organizational methods they derived from the political traditions of the West were employed, successfully in the long run, in combating colonial rule.

This revolutionary role of education was neither intended nor foreseen by the colonial educators of the nineteenth and early twentieth

---

Reprinted, with permission of the authors and publishers, from the HARVARD EDUCATIONAL REVIEW, Vol. 35 (Summer, 1965), pp. 287–302.

centuries from whom the nationalists had received their schooling: missionaries who taught primarily in order to proselytize, and government officials who generally believed they were training indigenous subalterns for the colonial administration. Yet the unintended consequences of their educational labors have been, from a political point of view, the most important ones.

This lesson, learnt reluctantly and sometimes too late by the colonial powers, may yet apply equally to the newly-independent countries. Most nationalist leaders, once in power, have employed mass education in their campaigns to eradicate ancient antagonisms of tribe, religion, and class, and in general they regard schools and colleges as primary means of building their new nations. Constructing schools is one way in which the leaders may commend themselves to their constituents; indeed, for many rural communities, a school is the only sign that government is doing anything at all. But the stresses and tensions of the pre-independence period may be aggravated by the programs of educational development carried out, often with the best of intentions, by independent governments. Burgeoning educational opportunities may produce new challengers for positions of power or rebels against social order, and by accentuating old rifts or opening new ones impair the attainment of national unity. Having helped to unseat the empire-builders, the spread of education may well conspire against their nation-building successors.

Whether or not education has all the disruptive consequences of which it is capable depends upon those who shape policy: the planners, advisers, civil servants, and politicians—not to speak of the parents of school-children, teachers' organizations, religious and student bodies, and others whose influence on policy is seldom negligible and sometimes decisive. Such groups do not necessarily conceive their interests in terms identical to the government's, and policy must be formulated by discussion and compromise, sometimes by the exertion of governmental authority and sometimes by capitulation to public or sectional demand. In this process the long term political consequences of policy may be lost sight of or evaded. It should be a responsibility of planners and advisers to acquaint themselves with the political ends the government intends the education system to serve, and to point out to government the effects, for good or ill, which may be expected to follow from alternative courses of action.

The ensuing discussion will proceed by generalizations which may not apply universally but which do indicate a wide range of relationships. The effect of education upon political behavior, the political role of teachers, and educational issues of political importance will be considered in turn. "Education" will refer to the school and university system under government control or supervision. "Politics" will be taken to mean: 1. activities focused on the acquisition and use of power through control of institutions of government, 2. activities in which public issues are discussed and demands upon government expressed, through parties, interest groups, mobs, or solitary individuals, 3. actions of the formal institutions of government, which make laws, interpret them, and attempt to carry them out through a bureaucracy.

EDUCATION AND POLITICAL BEHAVIOR

Three aspects of this question will be considered in detail: group attitudes, unemployment, and the political role of the intelligentsia.

Group Attitudes. Significant differences between population groups in educational opportunity and attainment are often reflected in the distribution of political and economic power and employment, particularly in the civil service. These inequalities have various causes. The former colonial powers in different situations favored both minority (or suppressed) groups and dominant groups when to do so enabled them to consolidate their power. Superior educational opportunities have thus enabled some formerly subordinate groups to leapfrog over their rulers or oppressors and gain prominence within modern political parties and the civil service, while elsewhere they have merely reinforced in the modern sector the power relationships of the pre-colonial order. In some societies culture and religion have predisposed certain groups towards Western education and alienated others from it. Invariably the latter groups have suffered a relative disadvantage on this account. The problem of group relations is particularly acute in such countries as Sierra Leone, Uganda, and Malaysia, where the adoption of universal suffrage has elevated the majority group in a population to political power, while minority communities retain their educational and economic superiority.

In all these cases, the power relationships among groups have been affected, often crucially, by the number of school-places respectively available to them and the intensity of their response to Western education. Certain groups, feeling themselves to be deprived of decent schools or to be the victims of cultural imperialism within the classroom, have pressed strongly for separate school systems, if only to preserve their group identity. Faced with threats of violence from linguistic or religious minorities, some governments have complied with their demands, while others have insisted upon a uniform educational system in the hope of overcoming latent or actual social schisms.

The value of single school systems in plural societies is generally defended on two grounds: that they promote equality of opportunity for all groups, and that young people discover by studying together that their differences are less consequential than their common membership in society. The second argument is supported by circumstantial and scholarly evidence (though there is also evidence to the contrary). It is strikingly borne out by the histories of nationalist movements throughout the developing world, whose leaders, though drawn from different regions, religions, or tribes, have often been alumni of the same schools and colleges, and frequently became acquainted first as fellow students. Opportunities of this kind tend to diminish, however, as school systems expand, since the more they expand the more homogeneous are their units likely to be. It is becoming increasingly possible for a young person to proceed from junior primary school through college without leaving his home province or tribal area. As the civil administration and commercial enterprises expand in keeping with the country's development, it is likely that he will as often as not find employment in that region as well. In some countries this might be of no significance, but where parochial values and loyalties tend to be paramount, the expansion of education may indirectly strengthen tribalism or regionalism and retard the government's campaign to create a national society.

The schools, however, are valuable in other ways to a country's leaders in achieving this goal. It will be readily apparent to them that the school population is a large and vulnerable audience of considerable political importance. Half the total population may be under the age of twenty. Sending a large proportion of these young people to school directly promotes national unity, since it ensures that a significant sector of a diverse population is endowed with some common modern skills, attitudes, values, and tastes. In particular, the larger the school population the more people are brought within reach of government propaganda. Curricula may be designed which describe what ought to be believed about the country's leaders, the colonial past, the constitution, the dangers of sectionalism, the national culture, the need for development, and the students' own civic responsibilities.

Few developing countries thus far, however, have made a comprehensive and sustained effort to remake the curriculum, though key sectors such as history and civics have frequently been attended to. Even where the government favors it, the inertia of the previous system must first be overcome. This implies at least producing new text-books and indoctrinating the teaching force.

Most young people receiving an education do not advance beyond the primary schools, which are generally poorly staffed and parochial in atmosphere; these children receive, therefore, a confused idea of the nation and their place in it. Propaganda or civic instruction is likely to be more effective in secondary and higher institutions, which only a small proportion of eligible children attend. Even here, however, nationalist propaganda may be so crude or so dull that it calls forth little sense of commitment from the students, though they may pay lip-service to the current slogans. Whether the nationalist message is imparted or not depends largely upon the attitude of the teachers, among whom many may not support the regime. Such teachers are unlikely to use their classrooms, except under compulsion, to teach political ideas with which they disagree. Instead they may well communicate their own discontents to their students.

Regardless of the difficulties, as their resources increase and perhaps also in response to political unrest and disaffection, more governments may be expected to mount a campaign through the schools to attach young people to their views about the nation and the duties of citizens.

Unemployment. The relation between education and unemployment is complex. It hinges mainly on the fact that in societies where most adults have been subsistence farmers for generations, education makes young men disinclined to follow their fathers' occupation, and also on the anxiety of parents to ensure that their children have a better lot in life. The inculcation of personal ambition is one of the most radical innovations for which education is responsible. Nevertheless, if there were enough satisfying alternatives to subsistence farming, the ambitions of rural school-leavers would not necessarily precipitate a serious unemployment problem; but in few developing countries do these alternatives exist. For instance, the obstacles confronting a young school-leaver who wishes to farm for cash are formidable. They may include overcrowding of the land, traditional systems of tenure which give no scope to youthful entrepreneurs, a lack of private or public loan capital, and rudimentary transport and marketing facilities, any one of which is a sufficient deterrent. Other alternatives to subsistence cultivating are farm laboring and commercial or industrial employment. The wages of a farm laborer are, however, seldom satisfactory to a school-leaver (nor is the work generally congenial to him), and trade and industry in the rural areas can usually absorb only a small fraction of those who leave school there and want paid work.

The result is that a very large number of them sooner or later make their way to the towns, to escape the dead-end and dullness of subsistence cultivation and to claim the kind of employment they regard as their due. On the latter score most are bound to be disappointed. Few of them have completed the primary school course, and fewer know a trade or have mastered a marketable skill. With bare literacy their only qualification, most are compelled to seek unskilled labor or none at all. Since it is becoming customary to enter school at an early age, increasing numbers of young people are disqualified from any position because of their youth. The same circumstances are true of town-bred school-leavers, except that their standard of educational attainment is generally superior to that of their contemporaries from rural areas. Of the thousands who cannot find work in town or country, most become loafers, dependent upon the hospitality of friends or relatives who are often the very people to whom they owe their schooling.

Some school-leavers are attracted to the political party youth brigades and serve as minor party activists, selling membership cards, collecting funds, spreading political news or instructions, and controlling crowds at mass rallies. For some of these duties their schooling is useful. By performing them they are able to achieve a sense of station and self-esteem which otherwise is denied them.

It is frequently suggested that unemployed school-leavers are "political dynamite," the stuff of which revolutionaries are made. This may be so, but certainly not as a matter of course. Disgruntled and restless though they are, these school-leavers stand not at the center but on the perimeter of significant political events. The characteristic forms of political disturbance for which they are responsible are not revolutions but acts of arson, assault, and intimidation directed against political opponents. Disrespect for law, property, and the person may have been encouraged by their political leaders before independence, and paid political dividends then, but in the post-independence period of reconstruction and development such behavior is generally regarded by the leaders as a liability. It is, however, the actions of such young criminals and disturbers of the peace which emphasize to the public and the government the gravity of the problem of unemployment, not the more numerous and equally unfortunate unemployed who simply vegetate in town and country, return reluctantly to their farms, or, as some do, withdraw pathologically from the struggle.

Unemployment sets a crucial test for the governments of developing countries, as the very success of the education system in turning out literate young people directs attention to the necessity of using them productively. Many governments have responded imaginatively, introducing jobs-for-the-jobless schemes inspired by their commitment to development and their anxiety to channel the national enthusiasm of their young people. These schemes go under such names as "Pioneer Brigade" (in Ghana) or "Youth Service" (in Zambia); they may even be sponsored by a Ministry of Youth. They operate in part as extensions of the education system by providing further education, training in a trade, or literacy instruction; they advance the development program through construction and agrarian projects; and they discipline an otherwise irresponsible section of the population.

Schemes of this kind are unlikely to absorb all the educated unemployed and may in any case simply postpone unemployment. Another possibility is that the civil service may swell noticeably in its lower ranks, posts being created in accord with "Parkinson's Law." Bureaucracies in developing countries are generally handicapped by having far too few people in their middle ranks (because the output of secondary schools is too small) and an excess in the lower ranks. Enlarging the latter category is bound to make administration more cumbersome and inefficient. The inability of bureaucracy to meet the demands made upon it by political leaders is likely ultimately to have serious effects upon the political process itself, as citizens are tempted to act extra-legally to achieve what the government appears to have promised them but not delivered.

A more subtle and promising response to unemployment is one which attempts to check it by matching the output of skilled persons from educational and training institutions with the long-term manpower demands of the economy. Obstacles in the path of this attempt are chronic shortages of artisans, technicians, and skilled modern farmers and the legendary reluctance of educated people in developing countries to engage in what are usually called manual occupations. This has unquestionably been the case in the past, partly because of a lack of facilities for vocational education, but mainly because people made a realistic assessment of the road along which social, economic, and political advancement lay. It is possible that the legend is now in danger of being overtaken by events. There is evidence that secondary-schoolboys in some African countries (and university students in Latin America) tend to rate technical occupations more highly than before and that these occupations are eagerly sought after. The reasons for this very significant shift in attitude are perhaps the universal prestige and mystique of modern technology, the sophisticated facilities for technical training which are now in operation or being planned, and the increasing opportunities for well-paid skilled work as color barriers fall and industry expands. But what has probably been indispensable is the success governments have had in propagating the idea of development as the keystone of their ideologies. Without the fervor of a national campaign in which elements of national pride and national service are involved it is unlikely that matters would have proceeded very much further than during the colonial era.[1]

The Intelligentsia. Unemployment among the educated classes is not confined to school-leavers, though in the developing world as a whole the problem is most acute among them. Several countries, particularly in Asia and the Middle East, have a vast and unrationalized system of higher education which produces a large proportion of graduates who are unable to find suitable employment. This situation is partly a function of economic capacity, but more importantly it is a result of their being taught in inferior institutions by poorly qualified instructors, according to curricula which bear little relevance to the needs of the countries and the kinds of work which are available. Like the other kind of jobless, these hapless graduates are of concern to governments, and similar methods of rehabilitating them are attempted. Inflating the civil service is one; retraining is another. Preventive measures are also afoot: compulsorily raising admission standards at colleges, increasing lecturers' salaries, reforming curricula, and—most significantly—expanding facilities for scientific and technological education and employment.

Meanwhile the students in these countries are often a political force of some consequence. Their working conditions are deplorable enough to cause chronic dissatisfaction and resentment, aggravated by the dispiriting knowledge that their ambitions are unlikely to be realized. They tend to blame their plight on the government in power and the privileged classes in general, especially since the students are themselves increasingly representative of all classes of the population. They are thus amenable to the persuasions of radical political organizations and can be readily organized for demonstrations, strikes, and mob action. This problem of "student indiscipline," both in and out of the classroom, has frequently disquieted national authorities and been a spur to educational reform.

In African countries, where there are fewer institutions of higher education and fewer high school graduates to fill them, such problems are unlikely to be as serious. The issue there is not whether college and university graduates with local or foreign training will be employed, but rather how their employment *en masse* in the upper ranks of the public service affects political life, especially in those states where the civil service and the national party are closely linked. A civil service composed largely of young nationalistic technicians may develop an extreme distaste for the older men who, though not specialists, hold important government posts. This sentiment will probably be reciprocated by the politicians, who view the new generation of technocrats as inexperienced and lacking real roots among the people. The situation is complicated by the fact that the "older" political generation is itself relatively young. Leaders in their late 30's or 40's foresee many years in power and are quite unwilling to turn over the reins to a generation which, even though better trained, did not share their struggle for freedom.

The danger in this situation is that the government will deteriorate as cooperation diminishes between the makers and implementers of law. On the one hand, the leaders in power form an increasingly entrenched and defensive elite, concerned more with preventing *coups d'etat* from below than with grappling with the substantive problems of development. On the other hand, the bureaucracy may become preoccupied with political intrigues within its own ranks. Numbers of ambitious young men compete with each other not only for top civil service posts but also for ministerial positions, basing their claims on professional competence rather than on popularity with the masses, with whom they have had little contact. The future may belong to the new generation. The question is whether it can attain power legitimately, and whether once in power it can govern with the masses' interests at heart.

Incumbent rulers may perceive a threat to their positions in another group of specially qualified intellectuals: professional men outside the civil service. These men—notably lawyers, religious leaders, journalists, and academics—may protest actions which appear to violate the civil liberties of the population and their own professional codes, and may become nuclei of opposition within or outside the dominant party. Depending upon how beleaguered the government feels, these criticisms may be tolerated—even heeded—or rejected as injurious to national unity and based on anachronistic notions of civic morality. The most effective sanction a government may level at professional men is to subvert them, by taking over or closely supervising their training, controlling their appointments, and censoring what they write, teach, or preach. Erring professions may thus be turned into branches of the civil service or the party.

THE POLITICAL ROLE OF TEACHERS

Teachers, and ex-teachers, have played a disproportionately important part in the politics of developing countries; in most African legislatures, for example, they constitute the largest vocational bloc. Because in earlier years the variety of jobs open to a man with some schooling was not great, especially where a color bar was enforced, and the educational qualifications required of prospective teachers were fairly modest, the proportion of white-collar workers who were members of the teaching profession was considerable. Consequently teachers were conspicuous among those who became eligible for membership of legislatures as these were made increasingly representative, particularly when precise educational qualifications were demanded of aspirant legislators. Thus, a teacher's chances of becoming a legislator were statistically more favorable than the chances of those in most other occupations. In addition, as one of the few literate persons in a village or rural district, he tended to receive the respect of the local people because of the knowledge he possessed and because he was articulate and could defend their interests most convincingly before the authorities. In the towns, teachers frequently interested themselves in mutual aid and welfare societies, and became versed in methods of organization, committee procedure, and administration; these societies were in turn often the forerunners of nationalist political parties. A teacher could secure a local power base, located not least among his former students, gain experience in public affairs, and put both to good use when he entered politics. The teaching profession was a springboard for the potential politician, much as the legal profession is in some developed countries.

The teacher is politically significant not only as a direct participant in politics but as a crucial communications link between the modern elite and the mass of the people. As a group, teachers tend to occupy a middle position between the two. Their education raises them above the common man, yet they are too numerous, too geographically dispersed, and too disparate in educational accomplishment and sophistication, for all of them to be considered members of the elite. Between the small, urban, westernized group holding political power and other positions of authority and influence, and the mass of rural peasants and cultivators, there is frequently very little communication. The teacher straddles two ways of life. Through him ideas of nationalism may be transmitted from the political leaders and the press. He is often—whether or not this is legally permissible—a party activist involved in proselytizing, political organizing, and political education. And it may be that through him some of the less articulated needs of the rural people are made known to the leadership.

It is not always the case, however, that a teacher is able to establish this sort of close connection with the people. It is no doubt very rare for a teacher not to be used as a source of information about the world beyond, and especially as the interpreter of news from the mass media. But he is often acutely uncomfortable in his rural environment (which might not be the one in which he was raised), a stranger by birth or preference to local customs, and painfully aware of his isolation from other educated people. As the tutor of the young in admittedly necessary but unwelcome ways and ideas, he might encounter resentment and opposition from the elders of the society. If his own political persuasion is different from that of his community, his alienation from that community is likely to be nearly complete.

In other ways the teacher's special status is a key to the malaise which currently affects the teaching profession in developing countries. With the introduction of mass education, the teacher's status tends to suffer a relative decline, because he is imparting to others the very skills which used to raise him above them. Moreover a rapid increase in school capacity requires a rapid increase in teaching personnel, and as minimum standards of entry are lowered to bring in many new teachers, the prestige of all teachers is apt to fall, not least in their own eyes. If large numbers of new teachers are not recruited, the chances are that class sizes will expand appreciably, or that the number of double session schools will be increased. Either way the teachers will be overworked. With the growth of local government, responsible for financing at least the primary stages of public schooling, the teachers may come to be regarded by the community merely as local employees and treated as such. And, following independence, as localization programs and a surge of development projects provide opportunities for new and lucrative posts in the civil and foreign services, industry, and commerce, many of the most competent teachers are attracted to them and leave the profession. This drainage is both a cause and an effect of the decline of the teacher's status relative to the administrator or the entrepreneur.

Although it is difficult to generalize about the political consequences of this decline, it is reasonable to suppose that if teachers are unhappy in their vocations, if they are not receiving from their government and the public the salaries, working conditions, and recognition they feel are their due, they are more likely to leave the profession, or devote their energies to raising its status, than "build a nation" through classroom precept and example. Teachers may be constrained from actively opposing the government, particularly if they are civil servants, but they can sabotage its long-run objectives by not conveying to their students in an enthusiastic manner those values which the politicians wish to instill in youth. The strike of their teachers' union for higher pay, better pensions, more adequate housing, and easier work loads, is a more direct expression of disaffection which has been and will continue to be resorted to.

Thus the teaching profession presents a paradox. Teachers are indispensable to the nation-to-be. Their primary function is to instruct the young, and they are also a vital link between rulers and ruled. However, the very forces of mass education and democracy which are expected to advance the growth of national consciousness stimulate the alienation of the teachers from their government and seriously inhibit their role as mediators to the masses of national values.

EDUCATIONAL ISSUES OF POLITICAL IMPORTANCE

Education is a matter of fundamental public policy which represents more accurately than any other the conception a government has of society.

This is especially true of the developing countries, where education policy must plot the most effective route by which traditional society becomes transformed. The issues which this policy thrusts into public discussion embrace some of the assumptions upon which the transformation rests and by which it is justified. Among these issues, and by no means exhausting them, are the questions of language medium, curriculum, religious schools, and post-primary education.

Language Medium. Few of the many possible solutions to the problem of the language of school instruction are satisfactory. In almost every developing country the population is linguistically diverse. Establishing any one of the vernaculars as a universal educational medium is likely to be greeted with indignation and resentment by speakers of the other vernaculars. Establishing each of them as the educational medium in its respective area, while satisfying many sensibilities, may invite difficult pedagogical problems in areas (especially cities) of mixed populations, and it will almost certainly perpetuate group insularity and hostility. Most indigenous languages, however glorious their classical past, have not made organic, spontaneous adaptations to the linguistic requirements of the modern world. New lexicons of technical and scientific terms and professional jargon must be contrived and teachers trained in their use, and these are drawbacks which are potentially crippling to a struggling education system. Nevertheless it is sometimes politically impossible for a country's leaders to dismiss the indigenous language from the schools, especially if (as with Arabic) the language is closely tied to the national religion and has achieved symbolic value in the anti-colonial conflict. Countries which do not possess local languages with developed written literatures have perhaps the easiest choice; this is the case in most of Africa, where the colonial language has become the official language and is retained as the medium of instruction in schools from the beginning of or from some point during the primary grades. But where indigenous literary languages have powerful support, as they do in India, Ceylon, and Malaysia, the retention of the language of the alien ruler for use at least temporarily in the higher levels of education, or the imposition of an indigenous but not universally known "official" language, are bound to provoke ardent opposition from cultural nationalists.

Though the language issue continues to excite political dissension in many countries, the spread of a single language through the schools can be of immense value in promoting a national society and in facilitating the spread of political ideas and efficient administration.

Curriculum. Curriculum policy is a live public issue because it intimately involves the complex psychological relationship of the people in developing societies with Western culture. Schools and universities generally adapted from the metropolitan country curricula whose relevance to the indigenous society was often negligible, or when modified by expatriates for local use, unconvincing. Despite their inadequacies, the curricula achieved a symbolic value for the modern elites of developing countries, who had been instructed in them, and by mastering them had demonstrated their ability to match the Westerner on his own grounds.

Nevertheless there is a strong feeling among the leaders and leading educators that their societies can no longer afford irrelevance in school and university curricula. Where energies are directed towards the development of the country and the growth of a self-conscious and self-esteeming national community, the curricula must be de-colonized and nationalized, created by local experts to suit local circumstances and needs.

In this process attitudes have changed in interesting and subtle ways. In the colonial period, attempts to lend an indigenous and utilitarian color to the conventional curriculum were fiercely resisted by nationalist leaders on the grounds that special treatment implied their inferiority. Now that these leaders are in control of education the trend is toward change in this very direction, colonial curricula being regarded as a denial of nationality and insufficiently geared to the needs of development. But it is not surprising if the change has been too sudden to satisfy some of the intelligentsia who have a deep commitment to the alien culture and who fear for a decline in local standards. Often members of the public are likely also to resist, feeling that their children should not be deprived of the kind of education which has so obviously benefited their leaders.

Religious Schools. The existence of a Christian mission school system, which very often sponsors considerably more schools than the government, is a reminder to political leaders in developing countries of their colonial past. Church-State relations have been a lively issue in Western education, but they assume a new dimension in non-Western countries where mission schools, although part of the state system, may be directed and partly financed by foreigners. The future of the missionary contribution will largely depend upon the solvency of the government, the degree to which the people associate missions with the colonial enterprise, the readiness of the missions to accept new curricula and official inspection, and their willingness progressively to relinquish control if the government favors the nationalization of schools in the long run. If the missions succeed in establishing their identity as a national institution, and if an indigenous religion is not bound up with the expression of nationalism, the Christian educational sector may find the government anxious to cooperate with it, rather than to eliminate it.

Paradoxically, though Christian schools may be tolerated or even welcomed, there is proceeding in several countries, notably in North Africa, a significant confrontation between the leaders of indigenous religious bodies who also control an extensive traditional education system, and the modern leaders in government. The latter cannot afford to permit a considerable proportion of their youth to be educated out of modern society. Nor can they afford to alienate entirely the religious leadership among whom a great deal of power over large sectors of the population still resides. It is rare for a ban on traditional religious schools to be declared; it is more usual for the government to suggest or sponsor some means by which the traditional system may be integrated in the modern system without detriment to religious values. The issue is not yet resolved, and its political implications are considerable.

Post-Primary Education. The planning of secondary and higher education is of vital significance for the efficient functioning of government and the maintenance of public order, since it relates closely to the problem of replacing expatriates in responsible positions in the public service and security forces with local men and women. It has repeatedly been made clear in a great many countries that localization is an issue of capital importance, capable of inflaming public feelings and driving governments into precipitate action in order to satisfy their constituents and their administrative officers. Dissatisfied junior civil servants may effectively express their anxiety for promotion by going on strike. Serious enough though this may be, junior officers and other ranks in the security forces are capable of far more radical and significant action. Being in possession of the only organized instruments of force in the country, the police and army are able to present their demands persuasively. Thus the government's staffing policy may provoke a breakdown in administration, martial law unlawfully imposed, or the overthrow of government.

In deciding the pace of localization the government is faced with a number of difficult alternatives. A gradualist policy would probably ensure that services were maintained at least at the level to which the country, under colonial rule, had become accustomed. But such a policy invites frustration and rebellious protest and is moreover a severe challenge to the self-respect of an independent government. There is in addition the real possibility that popularly elected local Ministers might meet with less than enthusiastic cooperation from the senior and sometimes more conservative expatriate officials of their departments.

On the other hand, rapid localization (especially if it takes place under duress) is likely to cause dislocation and require the promotion of obviously unqualified people to executive positions. This could jeopardize the reliability of development projects, which, in turn, would be sure to disappoint and anger the public. It could mean, also, that public safety and the integrity of the state would be endangered if the security forces were reduced to incompetence. It requires a fine sense of timing and sensitivity to the moods of both civil servants and the public, to carry through successfully an entire program of localization.

The success of this program—both its speed and its effectiveness in maintaining efficiency and good order—depends ultimately upon the existing stock of secondary school and college graduates and the capacity of the country's education system to supply them at the right time with the right qualifications. Three issues are involved here: breaking the most pressing bottlenecks, reducing wastage, and improving the scope of the system so as to supply the most urgent needs of a developing country: for competent administrators, security force officers, civil engineers, technicians, artisans, public health experts, agricultural extension workers, and the like.

CONCLUSION

This discussion of the complex relationship between education and politics may have given the impression that education policy derives from various forms of political disorder, and that its consequence is the intensification of disorder rather than its elimination. This is only partially accurate, since any one country will seldom be afflicted by all the ills to which developing countries in general are susceptible. In any case the mainspring of education policy in most countries is less a calculation of political costs and benefits than the conviction that education *per se* is an inalienable human right.

The kinds of social problems which influence educational policy, or which are indirectly produced by it, are, however, regrettably real. The magnitude of the social change with which developing countries are contending ensures that their characteristic condition is one of political instability. The expansion of education contributes directly towards instability because it generates demands upon the political system which that system is unable to meet. On the other hand the adequate provision of education at all levels is a necessary condition of political stability: only with trained manpower can public demands be satisfied by the government and its bureaucracy, and only a public educated to its responsibilities can participate with understanding in the task of nation-building.

No overall education policy in a developing country lacks political hazards, and wise decisions of policy do not always entail the least risk. A government may have to take chances on unpopular measures which are designed to achieve long term ends. On the other hand, some immediate public demands may have to be satisfied in order to avoid the loss of crucial popular support, even if conceding such demands invites political difficulties in the long run. A considered choice of policy, however, is impossible unless those who advise governments on the making of policy appreciate the dual political role of education in promoting both public order and unrest, and especially the potentially conflicting political consequences of any policy decision. With this understanding, the contribution they may make to education, and education in turn to the growth of stable and viable nation-states, will be enhanced.

FOOTNOTE

1. It is doubtful in any event that a similar occupational revolution has begun in agriculture, which provides a livelihood for most people but retains very few who are educated and mechanically skilled. This revolution may have to await some form of compulsory national service program, as well as radical changes in systems of land tenure and rural social organization, the pricing of commodities, and the provision of credit.

Education and Political Modernization in Burma and Indonesia[1]

JOSEPH FISCHER

OF ALL THE MAJOR modern developmental institutions in Southeast Asia (and in most underdeveloped countries) the least studied, the least evaluated and the least planned has been education. This is most noticeable in those two countries of the Southeast Asian region which appear to exhibit the greatest amount of centralization—Burma and Indonesia. Such educational control that exists in both countries has been limited to financial and personnel manipulation (with indifferent success) or, in the case of Burma, to commandeering universities. This lack is indeed surprising in countries apparently so committed to socialism, to reliance upon military authority, and to strict regulation of most political activities and all mass media. In Burma and Indonesia the contrast between the relatively great amount of planning and control of formal political and economic organizations and the comparative *laissez-faire*-ism that is permitted in their educational systems is remarkable. Some of the major reasons for this may be attributed to the following:

1. the assumption among most elites (as well as in UNESCO and among many economists) that education is inherently functional to rapid economic growth; and that the chief national problem is merely quantitative—providing more schools, equipment, teachers, and graduating more and more students;
2. the complex and unwieldy structure of educational systems in terms of size, breadth and diversity which make them far less amenable to planning and control than other sectors of development;
3. the enormously increasing and extraordinarily self-generating demand of the general population for more and more educational opportunities with resultant conflict between the desires of the individual and the resources and the goals of the state with respect to the uses of education;
4. the general world-wide paucity of social science research on educational systems from which emerging nations might draw for the purpose of planning and evaluation.[2]

The first assumption has recently been questioned in Burma and to a somewhat lesser extent in Indonesia. It has been triggered by the apparent

Reprinted, with permission of the author and publisher, from the COMPARATIVE EDUCATION REVIEW, Vol. 9, No. 3 (June, 1964), pp. 282–287.

failure of secondary schools to meet manpower needs and by university over- or under-production of professionals. Concern and heated reaction among some Southeast Asian leaders has been generated by the supposed general unresponsiveness of schools to national demands and in particular to the continuing lack of discipline among university students. In Indonesia a Department of Higher Education was created in 1962 primarily to control the size of faculty enrollments and to diminish university conservatism and inertia. However, so little research has been undertaken by education officials, and politicians show so little imagination in dealing with teachers and students, that the "reforms" of Djakarta have had very little effect. The military government of Burma has been almost exclusively consumed with the pacification of its universities through such questionable acts as blowing up the Rangoon Students' Union Building, closing Mandalay and Rangoon Universities, and transferring control of university administration from academicians to the officer corps. The misunderstandings of the functions and effects of schools by both governments have adversely influenced national development. What Indonesia and Burma intend with education reforms and what the two countries believe ought to be or is the developmental contribution of education, are seldom consonant with actual realities. The largely unanticipated consequences[3] of educational expansion particularly upon the political process and upon the pace and character of industrialization further frustrate countries torn by lack of consensus, limited by resources and threatened by external forces. The fact that both Burma and Indonesia appear to be relying heavily upon mass education in their drive for rapid modernization underscores the need for a hard look at the entire educational process. In this paper a few of the considerations about which such a "hard look" might be centered are presented. These will be expressed through the exposition of selected propositions related to education and political change by reference to Burmese and Indonesian experiences. These propositions are not presented necessarily as hypotheses, though some could be tested as such. Rather the chief focus here is upon suggesting fruitful lines of research and upon illustrating the potentialities of educational data and materials for the study of political modernization in underdeveloped countries.

> *Proposition I:* It is in the environmental, often informal elements of the school situation that one is often likely to find many of the crucial and most effective aspects of the relationships of education to the political process.

For example, with regard to political values, data from two large high schools in Burma (in Rangoon and Mandalay) obtained three years ago indicated that political propaganda is more likely to be transmitted outside than inside the classroom. In these two cases the curriculum was found to be singularly lacking in treating, for example, imperialism, Chinese-Burmese relations, *Pyidawtha* and other welfare plans, and the "Burmese Way to Socialism." Student interviews further indicated that the major sources of effective political transmission appeared to be as follows: youth associations, the movies, and contacts with politicians. It was surprising to find so few students who had read government tracts or local newspapers and so many who were familiar with small circulation "intellectual" magazines and ephemeral pamphlets. It was expected but nevertheless noteworthy to find so little factual or propagandistic material on domestic affairs and international realities in the entire instructional secondary school program. The same may be said of both Burmese universities, the major difference here being the greater importance of student on-campus political activities and off-campus contacts.[4]

In Indonesia, the Government's extraordinary drive for consensus has resulted in the transmission of a barrage of political slogans and ideologies. The uses of mass media and the effective rural net of Communist Party activities have perhaps been in part responsible for the relative success of such a program. Again it is to be noted that with the exception of *sekolah rakjat* (primary schools) most of this is taking place outside of schools and universities or in the general educational environment rather than in classrooms.[5]

In Indonesia and Burma in both high schools and universities some of the most rewarding areas for those seeking to study the acquisition of political knowledge and political values among youth are as follows:

1. peer group relations among students including the languages used by them for social and educational activities, residential patterns (ethnic dormitories, etc.);
2. non-school community activities including such things as contacts with political elites, intellectuals, foreigners, and attendance at movies;
3. participation in national youth associations and on-campus political organizations.

Among the formal school experiences the following appear to be of importance in accounting for the politicization of youth and in political change:

1. lack of meaningful contact and discourse among teachers, administrators and students resulting among other things in a distinctive, relatively autonomous, more increasingly powerful youth sub-culture;
2. student subject-matter specialization or occupational preference;
3. educational barriers or limitations including unwieldy academic requirements and examination systems, material shortages of books, classrooms and study places.

Although in the foregoing the non-school elements are emphasized, it was attendance at school that largely created their importance. In this sense, the school is the locus for investigations of political values and knowledge among educated youth. As such it is possibly a much more rewarding starting point for research on political modernization than Gallup-like surveys of the general population or intensive studies of formal adult political organizations.

Proposition II: The changes and trends in school and university enrollments are likely to be adumbrations of major shifts in the general social, political and economic structure.

Perhaps the most important question to ask here is who is going to school—and in particular then who are the potential elites? What are the ethnic, religious, racial, regional and social class backgrounds particularly of those entering, leaving and graduating from what types of high schools, colleges and universities? [6] In this context a number of factors appear significant:

1. the extent to which educational systems diminish, increase or otherwise significantly affect cultural diversity;
2. the political consequences of the part played by schools in stratification and changing social structure;
3. the general and specific relationships of school leavers and graduates to patterns of political recruitment and national economic needs.

The above factors are especially relevant in countries such as Burma and Indonesia which are rapidly expanding their educational systems. Expansion, of course, is predicated on their belief that mass education is overwhelmingly beneficial to national development; however, serious dysfunctionalities can be observed.

In Burma minorities such as the Shans, Karens and Arakanese view new educational opportunities in ethnic, linguistic or religious terms. These groups tend to look at schools as providing outlets for their own cultures. Since the lower schools recruit locally, their student populations are relatively homogeneous thereby diminishing acculturative possibilities and contributing to ethnic separation and conflict which often flourishes later when these students enter high-prestige urban high schools and universities. Evidence of this was reflected in the degree to which interviewed high school and university students were unresponsive to symbols of Burma as a nation; and in their responses to a number of questions which reflected primarily local rather than national loyalties. It was further revealed in the marked extent to which extra-curricular activities at Rangoon University among minorities were centered in ethnic, regional, and religious associations.

In Indonesia, the existence in public schools of an official *lingua franca* which is not the native language of the country's largest ethnic group, the complete secularism in education (in particular to the exclusion of Islam), and the unequal distribution of population (mainly in Java) and natural resources (mainly in the Outer Islands) have so far removed schools from much cultural conflict. The entire system of education and particularly its higher levels tends to be viewed primarily in national terms and has become perhaps the major symbol of Indonesia's motto, "Unity out of Diversity." Thus the contrast with Burma was striking. The author's sample of Indonesian students showed them to be much more conscious of nation, much more committed to central goals and much more affected by national ideologies and slogans. Burmese students were found to be much more anomic, politically ambivalent, and dissatisfied with both civilian and military leadership.

Shifts in occupational preferences reflected in school enrollments among certain cultural groups in Burma and Indonesia are also noteworthy. High school students from majority ethnic groups whose parents have had at least a high school education indicate occupational preferences which are much more consonant with present political realities and economic opportunities. The Javanese and Burmese are likely to opt more and more for careers in the applied sciences, economics, teaching, and the military while minority students (particularly those whose parents are illiterate or semi-literate) tend to follow the traditional academic paths to law, medicine, and administration. These would include in Burma the Buddhist Karens, Shans, and Kachins and in Indonesia the Minangkabau, Atjehnese and groups from Kalimantan and the lesser Sundas. On the other hand, certain minorities that are politically vulnerable such as the Chinese, Arakanese, Ambonese, Eurasians and Lampong groups are turning to business, local politics or are emigrating. These trends are reflected particularly in current enrollments by faculty at Rangoon University, University of Indonesia and Gadjah Mada University as compared to the enrollments of a decade ago.

> *Proposition III:* In a burgeoning mass system of education in transitional societies the frustrations and alienation of students to familial adults and to power elites are enormously intensified to an extent unknown heretofore.

In Burma and Indonesia getting a six-year elementary school education is no longer a novelty; present enrollments are about 1,600,000 and 9,700,000 respectively.[7] The popular demand for education in these countries is thus indeed great, the average dropout rate in lower schools of about 25 per cent notwithstanding. A high school diploma is fast becoming a minimal requirement for social mobility and economic success. If the schools have any holding power and any real influence upon young people it is in generating new desires. Social scientists are fond of speaking of the "revolution of rising expectations" but its magnitude, causes, and character have seldom been investigated. As more and more Burmese and Indonesian students advance through higher and higher educational levels the greater their individual dissidence becomes. As the desires and expectations of these more and more highly "educated" multiply commensurate political and economic opportunities and rewards for them in the first decade of their adulthood rapidly diminish. The prospects of students coming from formerly disadvantaged families for acquiring higher social status through traditional educational means are dim; the number of bureaucratic positions available grows smaller and government employ becomes less secure. Students from advantaged backgrounds are often forced to severely alter traditional occupational preferences or become members of the growing numbers of the "educated unemployed" which include in Burma some 30,000 high school leavers and 1500 graduates while the figures for Indonesia are about 45,000 and 2,000 respectively.[8]

Survey data from sample university student populations indicate that despite their apparent support of the nation and dominant political parties they are as a group the most critical and the least supportative of the political status quo. It is true that there is much less dissent among students pursuing careers in the applied sciences, but now in Burma there is a relative oversupply of such persons which is causing dissatisfaction. In addition it is these recent science graduates (particularly those with foreign degrees) that are most critical and intolerant of conditions under which they are compelled to work.

Another major source of political unrest stems from the fact that high school education is regarded as incomplete and not terminal with the resultant low market value of the secondary school leaving diploma.

> *Proposition IV:* Future changes in national social structure, in the political culture and in power elites are likely to be reflected first in characteristics of student populations in certain schools and universities in underdeveloped countries.

Under certain circumstances units of the educational system may be microcosms of the power elements in the larger society with respect to social class and cultural representation in student enrollments. Such units may also reflect power shifts and microcosms of future changes. In these cases, studies of political attitudes, of the impact of political participation, of political knowledge, and of the political preferences and commitments of potential elites are likely to be more feasible and fruitful if centered upon the composition, behavior and values of students in selected high schools, colleges and universities. In Burma no more than two universities and six high schools would be involved in such research; in Indonesia no more than three universities and fifteen high schools.

High school and particularly university enrollments in Indonesia clearly indicate the magnitude of social change with respect to future elites. About 30 per cent of the present enrollments at the three major Indonesian universities have been recruited from the lower classes and from rural regions. This figure represents a doubling over the last five years. The domination of urban and *prijaji* class elements in Indonesian politics thus may be well on its way toward decline. On the other hand, in Burma recruitment at high prestige secondary schools and Rangoon University still reflect urban and civil-servant class dominance.

Also significant particularly in Indonesia is the extraordinary increase of female students in universities where figures are now approaching 40 per cent of total enrollment. The rise of rural and female representation coupled with the previously mentioned increasing numbers of non-Java and of nominally Islamic or non-Islamic youth in higher education presage considerable political redirection. The holding power and coverage of elementary schools will further serve to make visible in national and regional politics groups and types of individuals that heretofore have been absent or dormant. The extent to which students indicate commitments to nation rather than locality or language, to occupation and profession rather than mere degree acquisition or government employ, and to economic rewards rather than social prestige are major indices of the political functionality of contemporary Southeast Asian educational systems. These will equally be an important measure of the stage of nation-building in the countries of this region, particularly in Burma and Indonesia. It may well be that the most basic test of the commitment of such countries to planning and political modernization is to be seen in the uses, control and evaluation of their educational systems in relation to needs and realities of human and national development. With respect to such outcomes the following general observations are offered. These are presented merely to indicate the range of possibilities for research and programing and are not meant as educational dicta.

In so far as formal education goes the following modernizing elements among others may be found in its institutional framework:

1. selection, promotion and later recruitment based on relatively universalistic criteria.
2. generally standard, objective measures of achievement.
3. merit and criticism based mainly on individual performance.
4. increase of specialization and specification resulting in greater rationalization and economy in the use of knowledge and skills.
5. increased professionalization with commitments to occupation, standards of work, research and the like.
6. the great and perhaps only systematic exposure to the world pool of developing ideas and technology.
7. socialization experiences for students which may prepare them for future roles in highly politicized, economically insecure and rapidly changing societies.
8. acculturation experiences which may result in developing common cultural values and thus in creating more of a consensus in otherwise extraordinarily diverse societies.

The extent to which these elements are operative and/or result in constructive contributions to political modernization in societies like Burma and Indonesia appear to depend upon the following:

1. partial displacement of motivations of social status and prestige with those based upon economic rewards and ends.
2. altering the relatively conservative nature of existing schools (especially universities) as reflected in the traditional behavior of teachers, professors and administrators towards students as disciples, towards examination systems viewed as barriers rather than means of evaluation and communication, and towards the restricted availability of books, study facilities and equipment.

3. quality and seriousness of efforts in rationalizing not only educational in-put but out-put as well.
4. making adequate provisions for the new, mass-like character of secondary and higher education through improving teaching conditions, and functionally differentiating levels and types of schools and educational alternatives.
5. maintaining relatively open access to the educational system in terms of providing like but regulated opportunities for mobility for diverse elements of the population.
6. some intelligent manipulation of educational environments with respect to functional socialization and acculturation of students.
7. realistic knowledge among elites of on-going educational environments, of differences among each generation of highly schooled youth, and some perception and anticipation of inherent educational discontinuities.

REFERENCES

1. This is a revised version of a paper read at the April 1965 Association of Asian Studies meeting. The writer is grateful to Professors Lauristan Sharpe and Robert O. Tilman for organizing a panel on modernization and to Professor Michael Moehrman and Mr. James Dalton for constructive comments.

2. For an excellent albeit preliminary survey see Seymour M. Lipset, "University Students and Politics in Underdeveloped Countries," Minerva, III (Autumn 1964), pp. 15–56.

3. For example, the hostility of Burmese and Indonesian military leaders to civilian higher education; the intensive recruitment of *Partai Kommunist Indonesia* of primary school teachers in rural areas; the continuing oversupply of humanities and law graduates; the diminishing prestige and utility of vocational schooling despite strong governmental support and foreign aid.

4. This survey was undertaken in the field in mid-1962; additional data was obtained via correspondence in early 1964.

For a view of the complexities of student activism and a correction of student stereotypes with regard to indiscipline and the like see Josef Silverstein and Julian Wohl, "University Students and Politics in Burma," *Pacific Affairs,* xxxvii (Spring 1964), pp. 50–65.

5. Donald Hindley (*The Communist Party of Indonesia 1951–1963*, pp. 196–198) rightly cites the comparative disinterest of university students for the PKI and leftist youth associations. However, during the period 1949–1961 most Indonesian students were a-political due to their *prijaji,* Islamic, and middle class backgrounds and more significantly to the availability of high status government positions. Student dissent and Communist influence have become quite marked since 1962 with the rise of students from "rural" backgrounds and diminishing prestige employment opportunities.

6. Such data has hardly been collected but for some examples see Silverstein and Wohl, *op. cit.,* pp. 56–57; and this writer's, "The Student Population of a Southeast Asian University: an Indonesian Example," *International Journal of Comparative Sociology,* II (September 1961), pp. 224–233; and his *Universities in Southeast Asia* (Columbus: Ohio State University Press for Kappa Delta Pi, 1964), pp. 105–121.

7. A convenient recent summary of educational statistics may be found in *Education in Asia* (Tokyo: Ministry of Education, 1964).

8. These estimates were obtained in 1962 from the Indonesian Department of

Higher Education and the National Planning Commission of Burma. The figures are indicative but not entirely reliable; if criteria of disguised unemployment were to be applied or if the number of graduates holding positions totally unrelated to their schooling were to be considered these figures would be higher and much more alarming. Such data, however, are for the present almost impossible to obtain.

Part Three

Equity, Efficiency, and Educational Planning

Leaders of nations usually wish to advance national welfare, and often view schooling as an agent in national social and economic advancement. But other agents are also available among which leaders must choose in advancing national goals. Decisions must be made to invest resources in schools or in hospitals, roads, telephones, or other facilities.

Policy makers are concerned with advancing welfare, but also with doing so at the lowest cost in resources. Hence, efficiency, or increasing the contribution of agents of economic growth at the minimum expenditure in resources, is a principal focus. Economists have been increasingly called upon not only to ascertain how much of a nation's resources should be allocated to alternative modes of development, but also how each mode can increase its contribution to economic growth. Their task ordinarily requires computing present and projected costs and benefits of alternative potential investments.

On the one hand, economists weigh education against other alternatives. On the other hand, they also weigh the relative costs and benefits of different levels and types of education. For example, they might examine the relative efficiency of primary, secondary, and higher education. They might contrast the value of special or technical education to the value of general education. They might critically view a variety of academic fields. Or they might evaluate the contributions of teachers versus materials.

Once relative costs and benefits are calculated, economists are often requested to formulate plans for resource investment and development. We refer to the application of cost-benefit analyses in designing programs to increase the efficiency of schools as "educational planning."

This section presents economists' views of the role of education in economic development. It offers also views of other social scientists concerning that role, with attention given especially to how formulas for increasing economic efficiency may conflict with national aims of achieving social equity among individuals.

Education contributes to economic growth by providing for a more skilled labor force and by producing workers who can more easily adapt to change. To be sure, economic success is not guaranteed by a high output of educated people: much depends on the use made of education. Yet by increasing individuals' productive potential economic advancement is facilitated.

The costs of enhancing human capital are high. Education is expensive both for the public generally and for individuals. Ken Kehrer shows that costs are not merely direct expenditures; they include also income or production foregone, because productive people are in school instead of working. Since it is difficult to estimate the potential income of people not engaged in productive labor, assessing the costs of education can be complicated.

Likewise, estimating the benefits of education is not simple. Kehrer is quick to point out that a purely monetary value cannot be put on the benefits from schooling. Education enriches lives culturally and aesthetically. It is intrinsically a source of pleasure and not simply a means of increasing one's earning potential. Moreover, how can a financial estimate be made of skills which are never marketed? Surely the education of women represents an investment in the potential of future generations, regardless of whether or not women enter the labor market.

In addition, Kehrer suggests that social, or indirect, benefits from education represent more than the aggregate benefits to individuals. Individual benefits "spill over" into the economy as a whole. Because of the advanced schooling of some, others (e.g., employers and relatives) may earn higher incomes. Education contributes also to the advance of knowledge generally. Because of these broad social benefits, society is a beneficiary of each individual's added schooling.

Effective planning for education cannot be confined to a narrow financial framework. Because schooling is functionally interlocked with the socio-economic environment, plans must be socially as well as economically oriented. Educational planning, the process of designing a pattern of action by which schools are made to achieve national ends, deals with people and not commodities; it cannot be assumed that people act passively. The projected stock of needed skills in the economy must be considered, but so must incentives and other social-psychological factors.

Simple planning formulas which neglect these factors can result in calamity. C. A. Anderson notes that some writers favor nonliterary, or "practical," education to foster economic development in the new nations. These writers believe that schooling should be localized and adapted to the particular needs of societies; that schools should produce individuals with skills appropriate to the demands of the job market. Yet accounting for market needs alone fails to heed important societal demands. Schools may be functionally appropriate for serving the requirements of the job market, but not for facilitating political consensus. Goals of national integration might be better accomplished by a general education that stresses history, tradition, and language than by "pragmatic" schooling. More important, practical education does not necessarily produce individuals who find employment suitable to their training. Plans calling for extensive vocational education to provide needed skills might fail because the job aspirations of would-be workers are influenced more by the prestige of jobs than by the kind of instruction provided in the schools.

Archibald Callaway points out one very important danger of improper planning. He notes that although most African nations do not contain completely literate populations, a majority of people do receive elementary schooling. Universal primary education is most often revealed as an opportunity; less often is it viewed as a dilemma. As their economies grow, underdeveloped nations tend to extend primary schooling greatly. In contrast, the number of jobs to which primary school leavers are likely to aspire and which they may be trained for does not increase correspondingly. Mass unemployment of school leavers results in wastage of human resources and in a potentially explosive cadre of discontent job-seekers. To plan for more secondary schooling at the expense of primary levels might be less equitable by its limiting of opportunities underneath. But to plan for more elementary schooling at the expense of post-primary levels is to encourage training for work that is not really necessary. Callaway, like Anderson, suggests that solutions should be outlined in terms of school leavers' views of their life goals, determined largely by what happens outside the school, in the society and the economy.

In the final two articles of the section, the dilemma of equity versus efficiency is made most explicit. Chaim Adler views the Israeli school as embodying the modern tendency of societies to diminish ascriptive and encourage achievement role orientations in elite selection. This tendency toward democratization might inevitably conflict with purely economic development goals. Extending primary schooling to all sub-populations and channeling the highest proportion of lower class students into potentially prestigious types of post-primary education satisfies goals of democratization. However, these measures are compatible with modernization only as long as they do not diminish the general scholastic level of the schools. Adler suggests that the Israeli school, through a series of stages, has progressed toward modernity. Yet he feels that the schools will not fully achieve their goals unless education begins well before the first grade, and progress to the highest educational levels is increasingly facilitated for children of disadvantaged sub-groups.

Anthony Crosland similarly views movement toward modernity as proceeding in stages. He deplores the British failure to move from a tripartite system and further modernize its schools. The ends of an avowed egalitarianism as displayed by the establishment of universal primary schooling are seen as being far from realized. Crosland advocates comprehensive secondary education and abolition of the divisive 11-plus examination as a necessary next step toward achieving equity. To be sure, the school alone cannot bring about equality of opportunity. Yet education can do much to facilitate social mobility and diminish the inequities that otherwise exist in British society. Moreover, Crosland views democratization as not being necessarily incompatible with efficiency. A system that allows only students from "better" backgrounds to receive more and better schooling is wasteful of the resources embodied in those who are not chosen to advance. We need only to see that less selective school systems exhibit greater efficiency than the British system.

Crosland concludes with a point that is central to considerations of equity versus efficiency. Educational research can tell us how better to achieve a given objective, but it cannot tell us what the objective ought to be. As an addendum, one could say that however efficient or equitable a school system becomes depends ultimately on a value component. Discussions of the effectiveness of schooling are pointless when government leaders do not make national goals explicit. Development and democratization cannot be fruitfully pursued by the schools unless these goals have been fully accepted by those in positions of power.

*Human Resources Development Planning**

KENNETH C. KEHRER

THE PURPOSE OF THIS PAPER is to summarize research which has recently begun to develop techniques for deciding how much of a developing society's scarce resources should be allocated to education and training, as well as for determining the relative emphasis to be placed on different levels and kinds of education.

THE RATE OF RETURN TO EDUCATION

(i) *The Question.* What is the net value (expected benefits minus costs) to an individual or the economy of different kinds and levels of education and training?

This is essentially two questions: one focuses on the decision of an individual, while the other concerns choices by society. Both the personal profit and the national productivity orientations seek to weigh alternative uses of resources; the alternative which maximizes the difference between expected gain and loss, expressed as an average annual rate of return on the cost, is regarded as the best investment.

(ii) *The Research Technique.* Much of the research conducted to date has consisted of attempts to identify the costs and benefits of kinds and levels of education; dollar value has been taken as the yardstick in most cases.

When the question focuses on the individual, the future stream of gains attributable to an extra period of education can be compared with the costs incurred in obtaining that increment. Since a dollar received in the future is less valuable than a dollar received today, the future gains must be discounted by an appropriate factor, analogous to an interest rate. The rate which equates the costs incurred in a given year with the discounted benefits is the "internal" rate of return. The person making the

* This investigation was undertaken as part of the 1966 Summer Research Project of the Office of Program Coordination, Agency for International Development. For a more complete survey of the literature, see the author's *A.I.D. Discussion Paper No. 15*. The helpful comments of Andreas M. Kazamias, T. W. Schultz, and Barbara Kehrer are gratefully acknowledged.

decision can then compare various internal rates of return on different courses of education and training. He may also weigh an extra year's schooling against an investment in real or financial assets. The rates of return will presumably provide guidelines toward rational economic action.

For the individual, the discounted future earnings attributable to education is frequently taken to be the relevant concept of benefit. But these extra earnings may understate the benefits of an increment in education. Education may lead to benefits which exceed the extra money earned by the educated. Jobs which require relatively more education may be the "preferred" jobs. If this is true, the analyst should add a dollar sum which approximates this nonmonetary attraction to the total benefits. Part of the value of an extra period of education may be the option it gives one to continue still further up the education ladder. The value of this option will vary with the rate of return on higher educational stages and the probability that the option will in fact be used. Viewing education as a series of related steps, Weisbrod [40] demonstrated that the expected rate of return on primary education in 1939 would rise from 35 percent to 52 percent in the U.S.

In arriving at a measure of benefit, the analyst generally compares lifetime after-tax earnings of people who have had relatively more education with those who have had relatively less. But this may attribute increases in earnings to education which may actually have been caused by systematic differences in intelligence, ambition, family connections, mortality rates, or unemployment experience. Becker [3] has demonstrated that adjusting U.S. data for differential ability reduces his estimate of the rate of return on college education from 11 to 9 percent. Denison [13] reduced the observed earnings differentials by two-fifths as an arbitrary attempt to correct for the possible overstatement of the benefits of education.

Identifying the costs of education can also be a major problem. For studies of the private rate of return, only the costs incurred by the individual (or his family) appear to be relevant to his decision to obtain more or less education. A large part of the costs borne by the individual are "opportunity costs"—costs which are approximated by the income that he could have earned if he had been working instead of being in school. Schultz [31] has found opportunity costs to be about 60 percent of the total costs of high school and college education in 1956.

Education is also a source of present and future pleasure. Treating expenditures on education as an investment neglects the consumption aspects of the educational experience, reflected in the evidence that many people thoroughly enjoy schooling. The impact of education on consumption also appears to endure beyond the period of schooling, extending the range of leisure activity. Schultz has suggested elsewhere [33] that the value of these consumption components should be identified and subtracted from total costs in any study of the rate of return to education as an *investment*. This approach has been criticized by Bowen [5] on the grounds that it is difficult to estimate the consumption element of educational costs. Even if the consumption costs could be conceptually separated from the investment costs, he argues, the information would be of little use since one could not decrease the consumption expenditures without at the same time cutting back on the investment expenditures on education. Bowen suggests, alternatively, that the worth of these consumer experiences be estimated in money terms, and that they be added to the benefits in the cost-benefit calculation. This method encounters difficulties too, for the evaluation of the consumption part of education depends upon the preferences of individuals and society as a whole, with respect to both education and other kinds of consumable experiences. Lewis [22] has asserted that a developing country cannot afford the luxury of the consumption components of education.

A set of similar studies has questioned whether *society as a whole* is investing the proper share of its resources in education. These studies assume that earnings reflect productivity in a market economy, and look at differentials in earnings as an index of the impact of education on economic development. Along with other types of cost-benefit studies, analysis of the social rate of return to education shares many of the problems pertaining to the private rate, discussed above.

The relevant concept of cost here clearly appears to be all costs, including public subsidies. Problems arise on the benefit side, however, due to the existence of "external economies" and the nonmonetary attractions of educationally heavy occupations.

External economies (often called indirect benefits or social benefits) consist of those benefits which are not confined to the individuals receiving education; rather, they spill over to the economy as a whole. Society may gain more from the education of ten more college students than the simple sum of their discounted future increases in income. For example, some other persons may earn higher incomes because of the further education of these ten. Possibilities include their employers, subordinates, or families. Education may move individuals to perform acts which give pleasure to others. Failure to allow for these kinds of external consequences of education would distort any attempt to assess its relative costs and benefits.

Then too, education is inextricably associated with advances in knowledge, which have important economic effects. The social and political external benefits which society as a whole receives may also have certain economic effects. Weisbrod [40] has suggested that these savings might be estimated by means of "avoidance costs." If it were not for education, society might have to pay more for police protection, traffic control, and medical care (as opposed to prevention).

As society becomes more affluent, people tend to place more and more weight on the nonmonetary attractions of a job or career. Since a disproportionate share of these attractive jobs are open only to college graduates, the social rate of return should take the value of this benefit of education into account. Villard [39] has suggested adopting an upward revision of the benefits, as in the individual rate of return calculations. Bowen [5] disagrees, arguing that the important consideration is whether or not the nonmonetary attraction to the employee is a cost to the employer. No revision of the benefits is called for if attractions like "prestige" only change the willingness of people to enter different occupations at fixed pay scales. But if the employer offers subsidized housing, travel, lush offices, generous paid vacations, or other fringe benefits which increase his costs, the rate of return should be adjusted upward.

Bowen's arguments neglect the possibility that the nonmonetary attractions of certain jobs may be detrimental to the income or rate of growth of income of a society. Others [5, 30], including Balogh [2] and Lewis [22], have asserted that the attractions of white-collar jobs in underdeveloped countries have diverted workers away from preparation for the technical and mechanical occupations which are so necessary for development.

These controversies ultimately hinge on whether the benefits under review are those which enter into a standard measure of economic well-being like GNP, or a less narrow concept like social welfare. Nonmonetary attractions of educationally heavy jobs would raise the rate of return on education expressed in terms of social benefits, but not always in terms of GNP.

(iii) *The Limitations.* The limitations of the rate of return approach concern two aspects of the use of current earnings data in the calculation of benefits. On the one hand, present differences in the earnings of one occupation relative to another may not persist into the future. On the other, current earnings may not be an adequate measure of the productivity of a worker.

The structure of relative earnings among occupations is expected to change over time as relative scarcities change. Suppose high schools had to pay higher salaries to attract and keep relatively scarce science teachers than to hire abundant history teachers. The observed rate of return on a specialization in science would be greater than the return on a history concentration. Drawing a policy prescription from this evidence, it would appear that more science teachers should be trained on the margin. Individuals who opt for this training might be surprised later in life to discover that abundant science teachers were then earning less than the scarce history teachers.

The existence of divergent rates of return on preparation costs for alternative professions may set into operation market forces which will tend to destroy those differences. In the course of development, the income structure of occupations changes substantially and rapidly. It is not clear how accurately current or historical rates of return predict future rates. Renshaw [30] and Machlup [24] expect future rates of return to be lower than present ones, due to the phenomenon of diminishing returns.

The evidence, however, supports the proponents of the rate of return approach. Miller [26] has found that the returns on increments of education do not fall over time as an increasing proportion of the population obtains education. Becker [3] has also discovered nearly constant rates of return on college education between 1940 and 1950. Renshaw admitted that factors like dynamic technological progress could produce such results. It thus may be plausible to predict future rates of return on the basis of current ones.

Whereas the existence of such constant rates of return may be adequate justification for a personal decision to obtain more of a specific kind of education, it may not be a correct indicator for social or government expansion of education expenditure. This is because earnings may not measure productivity. High rates of return on a medical education or the study of probate or tax law reflect the high earnings of the practitioners, rather than the social productivity of these professions. The high incomes are the result of barriers to entry into the profession, or confusing laws and arrangements which necessitate the services of duly licensed specialists or "insiders." Society could instead choose to remove restrictions on entrance into medical school, or change the laws that create economic advantages for a few.

This question is further muddled by the realization that all education gives the recipient some monopoly power over a non-recipient. An economist can earn a relatively high income because he has worked at understanding a set of problems; if the answers to those problems were common knowledge, it is doubtful that the rate of return on a Ph.D. in economics would be as high.

The criticism of the rate of return approach on the grounds that current earnings are poor guidelines to future social productivity is especially telling in the context of the less developed countries. There the wage structure is particularly distorted. Hollister [17] has emphasized the misallocations of labor resources that occur when wages do not provide employers and employees with cues for decision-making.

Also damaging to the rate of return approach is the failure to account adequately for the interaction between the education of one person and the benefits others receive from it. Certain kinds of education may be complementary (e.g., that of doctors, nurses, and laboratory technicians). Educating one group but not the others may be fruitless. In cognizance of these complex interactions, it is widely held that society's return on education expenditures is greater than the sum total of individual returns on the same expenditures. Attempts to investigate these relationships border on (1) studies of the residual in economic growth on the one hand, and (2) correlations between levels of education and economic development on the other.

THE RESIDUAL IN ECONOMIC GROWTH

(i) *The Question.* How much has improvement in the quality of labor contributed to economic growth in the past?

The quality of the labor force is expected to rise as its members receive more and better education and training. This approach seeks to isolate the impact of education and training on the historical growth rate of GNP. The procedure used, however, is indirect; the contribution of improvements in the quality of labor is generally found as a residual.

(ii) *The Research Technique.* Economists traditionally identify two kinds of physical inputs in the production process: capital and labor. The analyst asks what the contribution of these identifiable factors of production has been to the historical rate of growth of output. Given the latter, he calculates constant price indices of the amounts of capital and labor actually used in production during the period in question.

Since he is interested in the contribution to output growth of both capital and labor, the analyst wishes to combine these two indices into one overall arithmetic index of inputs. To do so, he takes a weighted average of the original indices, using the share of output earned by the owners of capital as the capital weight, and weighting the labor input index by labor's share of the output.

The composite input index is then compared with a constant price output index. Simply subtracting the rate of growth of the inputs from the rate of growth of output yields the residual.

Although this residual has been attributed to many things, it has most often been identified with improvements in the quality of labor, the impact of education and increases in knowledge, or technical progress. Other possible explanations include improvements in the health of the labor force and in the conditions under which labor works, progressive historical improvements in the quality of machines or management, increase in the size of firms, and new products.

How large is the residual? Kendrick [20] performed the calculations outlined above for the U.S. economy from 1889 to 1957. He found that the output index increased at an average annual rate of about 3.5 percent, compared to the 1.9 percent per annum increase in the combined input index. This left a residual of 1.6 percent, which Kendrick called "total factor productivity." Hence 46 percent of the rate of increase in total output is not attributable to the rate of growth of capital and labor.

Kendrick's study also examined the contribution of the residual to increases in productivity of output per unit of labor input. He attributed only 20 percent of increases in productivity to increases in the amount of capital used by each worker on the average. If only one-fifth of the increases in output per worker are brought about by increases in capital per worker, the remaining 80 percent is the unexplained residual.

The size of the residual and the uncertainty about its components have been a challenge to further research. One method of gaining insight into the puzzle of the residual would be to trace out the implications of specific assumptions about the way inputs are transformed into outputs in the production process. Solow [34] and Massell [25] both assume that productive enterprises are exactly reproducible, and that inventions and technical change proceed in such a way that they do not, in and of themselves, change the relative use of capital and labor.

Although they utilize different data sources and perform slightly different adjustments to allow for unemployed machines, Solow and Massell obtain virtually identical results. Solow's finding was that the residual contributed 87 percent of the increase in output per man hour; Massell found that 90 percent of increases in productivity in the U.S. economy from 1915 to 1955 were attributable to the residual. That is, if doubling the inputs used in production exactly doubles output, and if technical progress has a neutral effect on the relative use of inputs, almost nine-tenths of historical increases in productivity are unexplained by the traditional inputs.

Another approach to the problem posed by the residual would be to attempt to disaggregate it into recognizable elements. Denison [13] identifies inputs other than capital and labor, and subracts the rate of growth attributable to all identifiable inputs from the total rate of growth of output. The resultant small residual is called the effect of advances in knowledge. Denison makes separate estimates of the impact on output of factors like formal education and the growth of the size of firms. Thus he is able to reduce the size of the residual by explicitly considering factors which had been lumped together elsewhere.

In estimating the contribution of schooling, Denison [13, Ch. 7] uses the rate of return approach of the last section. On the basis of 1949 data, he compares the average earnings of males over 25 with the amount of formal schooling they have obtained. The average differences permit calculation of an average rate of return on extra education. This rate of return is then used to relate net changes in the stock of educated people to the influence of improved labor quality on the growth rate. For the period 1929-1957, Denison calculates that the rate of increase in GNP due to the education of the labor force alone was .68 percent. Since GNP grew at the rate of 2.93 percent per annum, education of the labor force accounts for almost one-quarter of output growth. Rising educational attainments of the labor force accounted for more than 40 percent of the increase in per capita income.

Harberger and Selowsky [14] used Denison's approach in the study of an underdeveloped country. Although they considered official investment rate projections for Chile implausibly high, they nevertheless found official projections of growth rates to be attainable. This was because increases in the quality of labor as the result of education were expected to add .93 percent to the Chilean growth rate during each of the years from 1967 to 1970.

As one of the steps toward that conclusion, Harberger and Selowsky calculated rates of return on several stages of education. In Chile, special education beyond the primary level appears to have the highest payoff, 29 percent per annum. Primary education itself was found to return 24 percent on its costs, while the rates of return on secondary and university education were 16.9 and 12.2 percent, respectively. These returns were combined in a weighted average rate of return to education of 21.8 percent, which was called the "marginal efficiency of educational capital." Information about the changing size of the labor force, and the amount of education they had experienced, permitted calculation of the contribution of improvements in labor quality to the growth rate.

(iii) *The Limitations.* Studies of the residual have dramatized the importance of education in the process of economic growth. But this success may also be a weakness. The emphasis on rates of growth of GNP has perhaps occurred at the cost of underemphasis of other social goals. In the economic sphere, a society also has objectives with regard to price stability, full employment of labor, the distribution of income, and the composition of output. The work reviewed in this section has not attempted to analyze the impact of education on these areas of concern.

The research performed by Kendrick, Solow, and Massell fails to take into account the interaction between capital and technical progress. The capital input series essentially reflects the exact duplication of old machines in the manufacture of new ones. In these studies there is no way to allow for the fact that newer machines are usually better than their older counterparts. Thus, estimates of the contribution of capital may be too low, and the size of the residual may be exaggerated.

The work originated by Denison has attempted to sort out these kinds of interrelationships, but the methods of calculation employed have frequently been questioned [15, 8]. Though Denison and Harberger and Solowsky claim to measure improvements in labor quality derived from education, they include only formal education in their analyses; informal education and on-the-job training are neglected. In addition, the returns computed in the course of these studies are private, not social, returns. No effort is made to understand the contribution which education and work experience make to increased mobility and adaptability, and hence to more rapid application of advances in technology.

To the extent that the residual approach uses rates of return and draws policy prescriptions from historical behavior, it is subject to the limitations discussed earlier. Moreover, unless one is willing to assume with Denison that an extra day of education, say at the primary level, has the same effect on GNP as a day spent at any level (even post-graduate), this form of research appears to add little to the policy-making framework. That is, decisions about the allocation of resources to education which were based upon rate of return calculations would not gain substantial insights by also undertaking analysis of the residual. Harberger's work has demonstrated new uses for this technique, however, and it may not yet have been pursued far enough.

The residual has established the relative significance of education in economic growth. Dissatisfaction with the large portion of unexplained phenomena, and a desire to understand the causal relationships prompt an interest in statistical inference. Pursuing Denison's study in a behavioral direction, one would encounter the attempts to correlate indices of education with indices of development.

THE CORRELATION BETWEEN EDUCATION AND DEVELOPMENT

(i) *The Question.* Is there a systematic relationship between a society's educational attainment and the level of its GNP?

Since expenditures on education are expected to increase incomes, questions arise as to what the nature of this relationship is. Will a nation which devotes a relatively large share of its resources to educating its labor force *always* obtain relatively higher levels of GNP? Will it obtain extra income immediately, or only after some delay? Does the same relationship hold among industries, and among firms?

(ii) *The Research Technique.* Perhaps the easiest correlation to envisage is the one expected between education expenditures and GNP over time. Schultz [32] and Harris [16] have attempted correlations of this kind for the United States. Their hypothesis, that levels of expenditures on education are related to (or cause) levels of GNP in the same year, has come under attack by Bowen [5]. He argues that education is a long-lived asset; the recipient of education earns (or contributes) a higher income for most of the rest of his life. Thus the economic effect of an increase in education expenditures should not be sought in the year of its disbursement. GNP may even be lower that year, due to the diversion of labor resources from factories to schools. Education expenditures today should instead be related to future rises in GNP.

The choice of an appropriate time lag for the regression model is a difficult one. Most choices are either arbitrary or designed to obtain the neatest results, after trying a host of alternatives. Rather than adopt these indefensible positions, an alternative is suggested by the nature of the lagged response. The level of GNP ten years from now is seen to depend partly on education expenditures last year, partly on those of this year, partly on next year's expenditure, and so on. In other words, the level of GNP in a given year depends upon the total stock of educated persons in that year. This stock is the result of all past additions to education minus any attrition.

Schultz [31, 32] has attempted to measure the stock of educational capital for the United States. His suggestion to weight younger persons more heavily than older ones when adding up the stock of education has been criticized by Bowen. The weighting procedure is correct if one wishes to know the salable value of education, Bowen asserts, but it is not desirable for the relation of current educational attainments to current GNP. This controversy hinges upon whether educational units are commensurable over time.

Opinions on the intertemporal quality of education vary markedly. Denison [13] concluded that a graduate of eighth grade today is equivalent to a 1910 college graduate. At the other extreme, Machlup [24] contends that the quality of a given grade deteriorates with the dilution of the quality of students brought about by the drive toward universal education. When the length of compulsory education is changed from, say, six to eight years, schools merely stretch the same educational content over two extra years, to cope with the new seventh and eighth graders who have less ability or motivation on the average than their predecessors.

Another way to investigate the education-income relationship is to observe the differences among countries. Svennilson, Edding, and Elvin [35] have attempted inter-country correlations between per capita GNP and enrollment rates. The latter are the number of students enrolled in a particular grade or stage of education expressed as a percentage of all students whose age qualifies them for it. Bowman and Anderson [10] also made international comparisons of income and education levels. They first divided countries into three groups according to their index of energy potentials per capita. This was used as a proxy for productive potentials; energy potentials being considered independent of past capital accumulation, the quality of labor, and socio-economic attitudes and organization. For each group, GNP per capita was correlated in turn with each of the following variables: (1) the percentage of adults who are literate, (2) the percentage of population in post-primary school, and (3) the percentage of population, age 5-14, enrolled in primary school (primary enrollment rate). Their study also tried to correct for agricultural potential on the basis of cultivated hectares per capita. Despite all of this careful work, neither the Bowman and Anderson study, nor the work of Svennilson, Edding, and Elvin produced very strong conclusions. To be sure, GNP per capita was positively related to indices of education, but there was considerable dispersion.

In a recent study, McClelland [23] has attempted to use a dynamic approach to cross-country analysis which allows for the introduction of the time lag. He compares enrollment rates in one period with growth rates in a later period. Grouping the countries studied by an electric power index, in the manner of Bowman and Anderson, he observes that countries with higher university enrollment rates in 1950 achieved greater increases in per capita income during the 1950s. These differences allow him to calculate an annual rate of return on extra university education of 12 percent. McClelland also concludes that countries with higher secondary enrollment rates in 1930 grew more rapidly during the 1950s than countries with lower rates. However, his analysis is severely challenged by

Bowman [8, 10], who found that income in the 1930s explained enrollment rates in the 1950s better than schooling in the 1930s explained income in the 1950s.

Little work has been accomplished in the area of inter-industry or inter-firm analysis. Cross-sectional correlations between the training or education of workers and the profitability of firms or industries await further study.

(iii) *The Limitations.* The correlation analyses are subject to chicken-egg controversies, for while it can be shown that countries that invest relatively more in education reap higher rates of growth of national income, it can also be demonstrated that nations that have high levels or rates of growth of income tend to consume more education.

The cross-country work of Svennilson, *et al.* does serve some useful purposes, however. Planners in a developing nation are able to look at their own educational programs in the perspective of the experience of other countries. The current levels of education in more advanced countries can give planners a general idea about future demands, and the experience of these countries can also be instructive.

There is a danger, however, in regarding the levels of educational activity associated with advanced countries as norms. Many developing countries may have over-invested in education, as Anderson and Bowman [9] and Lewis [22] have suggested. It is also probable that the more complicated levels of technology associated with today and tomorrow will require higher levels of education at every stage of development than have been observed historically. Since the effectiveness of education appears to depend upon the extraschool environment, more education would be required in a primitive rural area than in a city to achieve equal results. In any case, identical education expenditures in two countries would imply equal educational output only if teachers, buildings, and other resources were used with the same efficiency.

Correlation analysis suffers from many of the same problems as the rate of return studies. It is forced into assuming that a great many other things are equal. The external benefits of education are not explicitly considered. For example, in the cross-country correlations, no attempt was made to measure the effect of education in one country on the incomes of other countries. Bowen [5] concludes that simple correlations of this kind cannot give us any information about the quantitative dimensions of the contribution of education to development.

In the face of all of these difficulties, planners have still managed to design and implement programs for human resources development in the past, and they will continue to do so in the future. What methods of analysis have they utilized? One set of studies is designed to assess the demands of the economy for skilled workers. Other kinds of analysis have set their goal to be the supply of these skills.

FORECASTING AND PLANNING FOR MANPOWER REQUIREMENTS

(i) *The Question.* What is the quantity and composition of additional skilled persons needed over the planning period in order to support the desired rate and pattern of economic development?

The production of goods and services requires capital and labor; the production of certain kinds of goods and services requires certain kinds of machines and labor. Labor is differentiated by skill, and skills are usually obtained over the course of time through formal or informal processes of education and training. Given the output goals of an economy, it is necessary to determine how many skilled workers in each skill category will be needed, just as one estimates the requirements for the number and types of machines.

(ii) *The Research Techniques.* There are essentially three methods of forecasting manpower requirements: (1) employer surveys, (2) analysis of the experience of more advanced countries, and (3) use of fixed-coefficient projection techniques.

Surveys of employers' expectations can be restricted to those industries which are expected to expand, and the information may be collected inexpensively. The shortages revealed by employer surveys may, however, be relevant only in the short run. Employers probably possess shorter planning horizons than is suitable for decisions made on behalf of the whole society. The immediate nature of employers' perceived demands is important with regard to skills which require long periods of training. An educational system cannot be asked to give three years of training to a person required next month.

The experience of other countries, whether similar or more advanced, can also yield information about the size and composition of skilled labor pools. Again, planners must be cautioned against relying on the pattern of skills observed in other countries, for most of the same reasons that reliance on the enrollment rates of others may be inappropriate. Substitution can take place between labor and machines, and among labor of different skills. The value of looking at skills used in other countries depends upon the range of substitution permitted by available technology, as does the entire manpower forecasting and planning exercise.

Some production processes are characterized by fixed coefficients—i.e., the amount of labor necessary is determined once the amount of capital to be employed in the operation is known. A good example is the ordinary shovel. It is generally set into operation by one worker. Less than one worker will not do, and more than one worker using a shovel may be almost as bad as none. Other production processes are capable of using a wide variety of combinations of men and machines. The use of fixed-ratio projection techniques thus pertains more to some processes than to others.

The methodology of projecting manpower requirements with fixed ratios has been described exhaustively by Sugg [38] and Parnes [27]. First, it is necessary to obtain an estimate of total employment for the target date. This can be accomplished in several ways. If the planner is fairly confident that he can predict future investment, he can estimate future employment on the basis of fixed incremental capital-labor ratios. Alternatively, the planned investment figures could yield the level of increased output when divided by incremental capital-output ratios. The amount of labor necessary to achieve those increases in output can then be obtained with the use of assumptions about productivity (output-labor ratios). These anticipated levels of employment can be corrected for observed trends or any other relationships the analyst can discover between employment in various industries and other economic indicators.

The projection of employment of undifferentiated labor thus should take into account any anticipated changes in demand, hours worked, or productivity. The level of aggregation chosen usually depends upon the information available, but a detailed analysis of the projections by sector or industry is desirable. By disaggregating, allowance can be made for changes in industrial structure which occur as industries grow at different rates.

It is then necessary to determine the skill composition of the projected employment by industry. This is accomplished by applying existing or anticipated occupational composition patterns for each industry. Data availability will again determine the choice of skill detail, but attention should be addressed to the skills which require long periods of training.

In practice, as in the Mediterranean Regional Project of the OECD [28, 29], fixed-ratio projections are adjusted on the basis of the experience of other countries and surveys of employers.

Once the manpower requirements have been forecast, it is possible to trace their implications for the educational system and training institutions. The requirements can be compared with the expected supply by the target date, and shortages and surpluses of various occupations and skills can be ascertained. On the basis of these projected gaps, the educational planners can expand some activities and curtail others.

An essential link, however, must be forged conceptually before supply can be contrasted with demand. It is necessary to determine the amount of education and training required by each occupation. The translation of the demand for labor differentiated by skills into the composition and duration of education has never been accomplished satisfactorily. Even the detailed job analysis and exhaustive listing of educational qualifications for very specific occupations by the OECD [27] have proven inadequate.

The problem is that very few jobs require a specific combination of ability and training. Most skills fall between two extremes: occupations which require only a short period of observation, as opposed to jobs which require the mastery of precise operations which can only be learned over a considerable time span. Not only must the duration of training be decided upon, but the choice must be made between formal and informal education. There appears to be a wide range of substitution between educational qualification and job experience in many occupations. The problem is further complicated by the observation that general education often enables a person to grasp specific instruction more readily.

(iii) *The Limitations.* Manpower planning implies that the levels of economic activity which have been forecast could not take place without the specified training. This is not completely correct, but it is probable that the activities could not take place *very well* without the required skilled workers. Bruton [11] has argued that since there is evidence that substitution is far from perfect among skills in a less developed country, the manpower forecasting and planning approach may be relevant for its needs. He cautions against always assuming that the education sector will or should respond to the needs of the production sector. Often the latter will initiate an activity in response to the existence of a pool of skilled labor resources.

The record of manpower forecasts, however, has been rather poor; major projections have been substantially inaccurate. Bowen [5] has suggested that they tend to understate the future demand for labor of various skills, due to the rapid pace of scientific developments. Difficulties are also encountered in projecting the employment of people with general training. Even where the notion of fixed coefficients is approximated, as in the case of engineers, the graduates of training programs may thwart the planners by not entering the occupations for which they were trained.

Bowman and Anderson [9] agree with the earlier criticism by Bowen [5] and Hollister [17] that manpower planning is only a partial method of analysis, since it ignores costs. It may be true that employers will need workers of specific skills, but are they willing or able to pay for them? Manpower planners have often been guilty of identifying shortages and proceeding to train the appropriate number of workers regardless of cost. Decisions to train additional workers or to expand educational facilities, under conditions of scarcity, require the balancing of costs and benefits.

Manpower planners frequently assume that formal education in vocational and technical schools is the only source of middle level manpower. This neglect of the possibilities for on-the-job training and skill upgrading has contributed to inaccurate forecasting, and wastefulness, since technical schools are very expensive.

Hollister [18] has criticized the Mediterranean Regional Project of the OECD [27, 28, 29] for concerning itself too narrowly with educational planning, at the expense of programming and implementing activities. With the exception of Bowman and Anderson, who find it totally useless, the critics of manpower forecasting and planning believe that this kind of analysis has a role in decisions about the allocation of resources to and within education and training.

EDUCATION PLANNING MODELS

(i) *The Question.* Education planning models are designed with specific questions in mind. The complex interrelationships of an education system are simulated, in order to provide a framework for testing the consequences of alternative policies and investment patterns over time. A model can be used to discover which alternative best achieves particular objectives. Models may be designed to generate consistent plans, assess the feasibility or costs of a proposed plan, or point out the bottlenecks to further educational development.

(ii) *The Technique.* All education models express the interrelationships of the education system in algebraic form. This means that all important flows of students, teachers and the services of equipment, textbooks, and buildings are explicitly related to each other in quantifiable ways. For example, the enrollment of sixth graders in 1971 equals the number of fifth graders in 1970 times the progression rate (or one minus the wastage rate). The progression rate is thus the sixth grade enrollment in one year divided by the fifth grade enrollment of the previous year, and the wastage rate is the sum of the drop-out and failure rates.

Once the relationships have been stated algebraically it is possible to begin assigning numbers to the various symbols. The purpose of the model will dictate which variables are assigned values, and which will be determined in the solution of the model. Values must be assigned to the parameters, which relate the variables to each other. These numbers may be taken from history, or they may be set by policy. For example, drop-out rates can be those observed historically, or extrapolations of recent trends. Policy decisions could be reflected in, say, pupil-teacher ratios. Solutions to the model can be made subject to constraints on resource use; even social and political constraints can be built into the model, if they can be quantified.

The early educational planning exercises were supply models. Tinbergen, Correa, Bos, and others at the Netherlands School of Economics were in the vanguard of these efforts. Much of the work which was carried out under Tinbergen's [36] direction, however, consisted of the application of pre-existing economic models to the problems of education. In essence, the Tinbergen models investigated the paths followed by key variables in response to changes in assumptions.

The most complete supply model has been developed by UNESCO with the cooperation of ECAFE [37]. It was designed as a tool to aid the Asian member nations in developing educational policy. After specifying, quantifying, and programming the relationships, it became possible to observe the implications of changes in the educational system almost instantaneously. The costs of new programs became readily apparent, in spite of the long time spans they embraced.

However, these models were only looking at half the problem of allocating resources efficiently in the education sector. They dealt solely with the cost or supply side of the problem, in much the same way as the manpower projections dealt only with the demand side. Correa [12] considered both sides of the problem, but even there the first part of his book was devoted to the supply of labor, and demand considerations were postponed until the latter part. The integration of supply and demand into one model had to await quite recent developments.

Linear optimizing models have been applied to human resources development planning by Adelman [1], Bowles [6, 7], and Benard [4]. The models used by Benard and Adelman encompass the entire economy, but they give detailed attention to the education sector. Using data from Argentina, Adelman's model efficiently allocates investment resources to both education and real capital. With respect to the education sector, the model determines the number of graduates from each of the various schools, and allocates these graduates to different sectors of the economy, in response to their labor requirements.

Bowles takes the resource flows from the rest of the economy as given, and attempts to allocate those resources efficiently among educational activities. His study of Northern Nigeria incorporates variations in educational policy, such as the increased use of audio-visual equipment, or the introduction of team teaching. Among the constraints on his solutions are politically determined minimum levels of secondary enrollments, and limits on the pace of expansion of facilities.

In order to make decisions about resource allocation, these models require a criterion. Bowles seeks a solution which will maximize the contribution of the educational system to future (discounted) national income. Adelman similarly attempts to maximize the discounted sum of GNP, but in other trials she experimented with maximizing the growth of GNP between a base year and a target year. In another set of runs, she minimizes the discounted sum of net foreign capital inflows, an approach which is of interest to those concerned with foreign assistance. It is interesting to note that, in the operation of both models, technical and vocational education was a bad investment; the benefits derived from them failed to cover their cost.

Perhaps the most significant aspect of this new approach is its promise as a means of integrating the other techniques of human resources development planning. Not only have demand and supply been brought into the same model, but other approaches have been incorporated.

To arrive at the productivity of various kinds of education, Bowles calculates rates of return, and then proceeds to assume that these rates will remain constant. Dividing the labor force into three skill categories, Adelman borrows from the manpower planners by assuming fixed productivity ratios in each category, and refusing to permit labor in one category to substitute for any other. The output-skilled labor ratios are derived from correlations between education and income. Unlike Bowles, however, her model does not have constant rates of return from each stage of education; the returns are allowed to vary with the relative scarcity of the skills (supply) and the growth of various sectors of the economy (demand).

(iii) *The Limitations.* Models are only as powerful in generating solutions as the knowledge built into them. To the extent that the recently developed models synthesize the various techniques of human resources development planning, criticism of the models is criticism of the state of the entire field.

For example, if one argues that Bowles's assumption of perfect substitutability among different kinds of educated labor is unrealistic, one is actually quarreling with the advocates of a fixed rate of return. Studies conducted to date have assumed either no substitution, or perfect substitution among skills. The truth lies somewhere in between, and studies of the elasticity of substitution between skills are clearly required.

The particular objectives which the models maximize are subject to the same criticism as the rate of return analysis. Since the models use this kind of analysis to determine the desirability of different stages and types of education, they also fail to account adequately for noneconomic social benefits, the consumption aspect of education, external economies, and complementarities. Bowles and Adelman, like the other analysts discussed in this paper, find it easier to deal with formal education, and tend to ignore the economic contribution of on-the-job training, in-service programs, and extension activities.

Adelman's investigation of the relation between output and labor differentiated by skill is a fresh approach to the correlation problem. Efforts like this may yet provide a bridge between rate of return analysis and the manpower requirements approach. Further clues may be provided by inter-firm correlations. More detailed information about the range of possible substitution among skills could be useful as constraints on the perfect substitutability models. Since manpower projections tend to understate the future requirements for skilled workers, they might also be effectively utilized as a constraint, providing a floor on the formation of skills.

Very little is known about the translation of the requirements of producers (labor differentiated by skill) into the composition and number of school graduates. Most studies avoid this problem by specifying labor demanded by the production sector in terms of educational attainments. But just what precisely does an increment of education change in a man? This question is acute enough with respect to how education relates to economically useful skills, let alone how it influences the total man. A greater understanding of the relation between education and development is undoubtedly dependent upon our knowledge of how a person's economic and social activities are transformed by his educational experience.

REFERENCES

1. Adelman, Irma, "A Linear Programming Model of Education Planning—A Case Study of Argentina" (Preliminary Draft, December 20, 1965).

2. Balogh, Thomas, "What Schools for Africa?", *New Statesman and Nation* (March 23, 1962), p. 412.

3. Becker, Gary, "Underinvestment in College Education?" *American Economic Review* (May 1960), pp. 346–354.

4. Benard, Jean, "Analyse des rélations entre production, travail et education a l'aide d'un modèle dynamique d'optimation," mimeo (CRPREL: Arcueil, 1963).

5. Bowen, William G., *Economic Aspects of Education: Three Essays* (Princeton: Industrial Relations Section, Princeton University, 1964).

6. Bowles, Samuel Stebbins, "The Efficient Allocation of Resources in Education: A Planning Model with Applications to Northern Nigeria." (Unpublished doctoral dissertation, Harvard University, September 1965).

7. ———, "A Planning Model for the Efficient Allocation of Resources in Education," revised mimeographed version (Harvard University, April 1, 1966).

8. Bowman, Mary Jean, "The Human Investment Revolution in Economic Thought," draft of a paper for Educational Sociology (January 24, 1966).

9. ———, and C. Arnold Anderson, "Commentary on AID's Education and Manpower Programs in Africa," mimeo (July 4, 1966).

10. ———, "Concerning the Role of Education in Development," in Clifford Geertz (ed.), *Old Societies and New States* (London: The Free Press of Glencoe, 1963), pp. 247–279.

11. Bruton, Henry J., *Principles of Development Economics* (Englewood Cliffs, N.J.: Prentice-Hall, 1963).

12. Correa, Hector, *The Economics of Human Resources* (Amsterdam: North Holland Publishing Company, 1963).

13. Denison, Edward F., *The Sources of Economic Growth and the Alternatives Before Us*. Supplemetary Paper No. 13 (New York: Committee for Economic Development, 1962).

14. Harberger, Arnold C., and Marcelo Selowsky, "Key Factors in the Economic Growth of Chile: An Analysis of the Sources of Past Growth and of Prospects for 1965–70," paper presented at the Next Decade of Latin American Economic Development, a conference at Cornell University (April 20–22, 1966).

15. Harbison, Frederick, and Charles A. Myers, *Education, Manpower, and Economic Growth* (New York: McGraw-Hill Book Company, 1964).

16. Harris, Seymour, *The Market for College Graduates* (Cambridge, Mass.: Harvard University Press, 1949).

17. Hollister, R. G., "On the Economics of Manpower Forecasting," *International Labour Review* (May 1964), pp. 371–397.

18. ———, "A Technical Evaluation of the State of the First Stage of the Mediterranean Project," mimeo (OECD: February 1966), DAD/MRP/66.1.

19. Houthakker, H. S., "Education and Income," *Review of Economics and Statistics* (February 1959), pp. 24–28.

20. Kendrick, John W., *Productivity Trends in the United States,* National Bureau of Economic Research (Princeton: Princeton University Press, 1961).

21. Lewis, W. Arthur, "Economic Problems of Development," in *Restless Nations: A Study of World Tensions and Development,* Council on World Tensions, Inc. (New York: Dodd, Mead & Company, 1962), pp. 68–85.

22. ———, *The Theory of Economic Growth* (Homewood, Ill.: Richard D. Irwin, 1955).

23. McClelland, David C., "Does Education Accelerate Economic Growth?", *Economic Development and Cultural Change* (Vol. XIV, No. 3, April 1966).

24. Machlup, Fritz, *The Production and Distribution of Knowledge in the United States* (Princeton: Princeton University Press, 1962).

25. Massel, B. F., "Capital Formation and Technological Change in United States Manufacturing," *Review of Economics and Statistics* (May 1960), pp. 182–188.

26. Miller, Herman P., "Annual and Lifetime Income in Relation to Education: 1939–59," *American Economic Review* (December 1960), pp. 962–985.

27. Parnes, Herbert S., *Forecasting Educational Needs for Economic and Social Development* (Paris: OECD, Mediterranean Regional Project, October 1962).

28. Organization for Economic Co-operation and Development, *The Mediterranean Regional Project—Spain* (Paris: OECD, 1965).

29. Organization for Economic Co-operation and Development, *The Mediterranean Regional Project—Turkey* (Paris: OECD, 1965).

30. Renshaw, Edward F., "Estimating the Returns to Education," *Review of Economics and Statistics* (August, 1960), pp. 318–324.

31. Schultz, T. W., "Capital Formation by Education," *Journal of Political Economy* (December 1960), pp. 571–583.

32. ———, "Education and Economic Growth," in Nelson B. Henry (ed.), the Sixtieth Yearbook of the National Society for the Study of Education, Part 2, *Social Forces Influencing American Education, 1961* (Chicago: University of Chicago Press, 1961).

33. ———, "Investment in Human Capital," *American Economic Review* (March 1961), pp. 1–17.

34. Solow, Robert, "Technical Change and the Aggregate Production Function," *Review of Economics and Statistics* (August 1957), pp. 312–320.

35. Svennilson, I., F. Edding, and L. Elvin, "Targets for Education in Europe in 1970," in *The Policy Conference on Economic Growth and Investment in Education,* Vol. II (Paris: Organization for Economic Cooperation and Development, 1962).

36. Tinbergen, Jan, "Quantitative Adaptation of Education to Accelerated Growth," in Herbert Parnes (ed.), *Planning Education for Economic and Social Development* (Paris: OECD, 1962), pp. 159–165.

37. United Nations Educational, Scientific and Cultural Organization, "Perspectives of Educational Development in Asia: A Draft Asian Model," Conference of Ministers of Education and Ministers Responsible for Economic Planning of Member States in Asia (Convened by UNESCO in cooperation with ECAFE), mimeo (Bangkok, November 22–29, 1965).

38. United States Department of Labor, Bureau of Labor Statistics, *The Forecasting of Manpower Requirements* (Washington, April 1963).

39. Villard, Henry H., "Comment" on Gary S. Becker, "Underinvestment in College Education?", *American Economic Review* (May 1960), pp. 375–378.

40. Weisbrod, Burton A., "Education and Investment in Human Capital," *Journal of Political Economy* (October 1962), pp. 106–123.

Technical and Vocational Education in the New Nations

C. ARNOLD ANDERSON

INTRODUCTION

THE PRESCRIPTIONS FOR EDUCATIONAL POLICY in developing nations set forth by different experts and international agencies are wildly discrepant. One recommendation may be very persuasive until one reads an opposing one. Some expatriate advisers suggest programs that have been rejected repeatedly in their own country. A specialist may set down clear lines of policy but the methods by which he proposes to implement it can have quite contrary tendencies. Most of the recommendations for vocational education in particular lose their appeal if one traces their ramifications into other parts of the educational system or if other aims for the school system are considered.[1]

Exploration of a few interrelationships between education and indexes of economic development provides clear warning not to rely upon simple formulas (see Table I).

The level of employment of scientists and engineers (the kinds of high-level manpower needed for a technologically progressive society) is high in the high-income countries. Large enrolments in secondary schools and universities undergird that cadre, but primary enrolment and employment of teachers show little correlation with the supply of technologists. An abundant supply does not appear to require high levels of expenditure on schooling relative to national income, nor does it presuppose a bias of higher education toward those specialties, but rather the reverse. One infers that both employment and production of technologists may be as much a reflection as a cause of development. The proportion of university students enrolled in those subjects actually is lower in the countries spending the largest share of national income on schools and is unrelated to per capita income.

Though employment of teachers and enrolments (especially in secondary schools) are fairly closely associated with per capita incomes, the evidence is of a circular or spiral cause-effect sequence as far as levels of income and schooling are concerned,[2] and the percentage of national income spent on schools is unrelated to income level among countries. But while high enrolments in universities are correlated with high levels of

TABLE I. CORRELATIONS AMONG SELECTED EDUCATIONAL AND ECONOMIC VARIABLES

	1	2	3	4	5	6	7	8
1) GNP per capita	—	.67	.82	.74	.76	.83	.02	.10
2) Primary enrollments		—	.48	.16	.74	.10	.30	−.40
3) Secondary enrollments			—	.76	.67	.79	−.01	.38
4) University enrollments				—	.39	.78	−.25	.73
5) Teachers employed per 10,000 population					—	.37	.07*	.14
6) Scientists and engineers employed per 10,000 population						—	−.30	.46
7) % of university students studying science-engineering							—	−.50#
8) % of national income spent on education								—

With % of students studying arts, humanities, and law: *$r = -.07$ and #$r = -.21$

Source: F. Harbison and C. A. Myers, *Education, Manpower, and Economic Growth,* 1964, p. 39. Definitions of variables are given in the source. $N = 75$ countries.

employment of technologists and with heavy expenditure on education, emphasis on science and engineering in university curricula is less marked in the countries having large university enrolments in relation to population.

Some of these relationships are unexpected and several are less definite than one would have expected. No doubt if one had data on male students alone, for example, the relationships would in some respects be altered. But if one reflects upon the conditions that must be met if a country is to have an adequate supply of productive labor, the pattern exemplified by the table of correlations seems to be reasonable. First, there must be opportunities to use skills and those opportunities must be clearly visible. Second, there must be a differentiated structure of incentives so that individuals will prepare themselves for the jobs, and these incentives must be cograduated with the importance of the positions for development. Third, a sufficient amount and variety of schooling and training must be available to turn out the kind and number of skilled men needed. Fourth, the social climate must support the foregoing conditions by stimulating people to make use of their training in more than a routine way. Some writers would add a fifth condition: the government must use coercion to make people work where they are judged to be needed.

Many prescriptions for education prove to be unworkable because they rest on fallacious reasoning and vague assumptions. If poor countries could have a larger proportion of their people at work in skilled jobs, incomes would rise. But projections of supposed needs for workers—or even of their availability—do not supply either the knowledge of how to put men at productive work or the needed complementary factors. Although a technological society must have a work force possessing the proper spectrum of skills, it does not follow that men are most suitably trained in vocational schools. Performance on the job and "skill" taught in school may not be closely related, but even when skills can be effectively "taught," that is not always best done in formal schools. However, less developed countries do not have the resources with which to combine practice and participant observation with classroom instruction, since operating effective training programs presupposes experienced instructors and a core of trained men already employed.

The pleas for agricultural instruction in the regular elementary and secondary school system bring forth the most exaggerated rhetoric; for example:[3]

> The school must provide the nucleus of modern agriculture in the villages. It must become a centre not merely (indeed not even primarily) of a drive for literacy but a drive for better techniques of raising crops, of choosing and preparing food, and eventually even for the establishing of rural industry, processing the crops grown.

Undeniably economic development requires a productive agriculture, which must rest on a considerable spread of new technical ideas among farmers. But small children are not farmers, and for many reasons set down in the following pages it is doubtful whether even secondary schools should "teach agriculture." We should be forewarned about such proposals by our own educational history. Effective secondary-level systems of agricultural or other vocational schools appeared only late in our economic history, and few observers would say that such schools are basic to our technological virtuosity today. It helps to innoculate one against utopian educational plans to remember that the now-developed countries achieved an advanced economy with school systems that would have seemed unbelievably crude, arid, and irrelevant to the tasks of social change.

Certainly there is a positive correlation between schooling and economic development, for a society cannot operate an economy in the absence of the skills presupposed by it. The now-developing countries want an educational system adequate "to the situation in which an underdeveloped country that has to catch up with the rest of the world within a certain space of time finds itself." [4] This is an ambiguous notion, and may conceal an inherent impossibility, leading to waste and frustration.

RATIONALE OF THE DEMAND FOR A "PRACTICAL" EDUCATION

> It is a commonplace of all educational thinking that every school, to be of any real use to a child, should be adapted to its environment.[5]

The obviousness of that assertion is deceptive. No one would favor "unadapted" schools, and such schools would contribute little to development. But the inference that what is called for is a "practical" education lands one in further ambiguities. Thus, some writers would conclude that underdeveloped societies must have non-literary sorts of schooling.[6]

> Educational approach to a people so different in language and customs will obviously be more clear and certain through the concrete and definite processes of industrial training than through reading and writing.

Other writers come to favor vocational training by a misreading of the education prevailing during the colonial period. They assume that "new" nations need a new kind of school.[7]

> In many of these countries, local educational curricula used to be modelled on those used in the West, and bore little relation to local conditions. In such cases, once the country becomes independent, it is found necessary to draw up school curricula which suit its needs and circumstances and the national culture.

Only brief reflection should be needed to decide that the arrival of independence supplies few prescriptions for what is to be taught in a nation's schools. One could argue even that with independence a nation can proceed, unencumbered by the caution or prejudices of colonial officials, to copy the kind of education that was associated historically with Western economic development.

Some commentators give the plea for a "new" education a particular interpretation by concluding that to be practical education must be "localized" in content.[8]

> The leaders of education, speaking of their countries' needs, have stressed . . . the desire to accelerate the reorientation of the educational patterns and systems to the economic and social needs of their individual areas. . . . The education for the future citizen of Africa must be a modern African education.

Numerous corollary and derivative arguments can be found. One reads that lessons should deal with objects, not words. While few teachers would reject this aim, education must instill the ability to conceptualize and to manipulate symbol systems. The opposing of words and objects is not illuminating. A closely related position favors the teaching of science, with less emphasis on languages and literature. One can accept this stipulation readily, yet point out that science courses often are as verbal and non-object-oriented as Latin.

Few proponents of "practical" education would be content with establishing only skills. Pupils should acquire also certain attitudes that will motivate them to be effective workers. One can, then, find various combinations of the arguments for "localizing" education, "adapting" it to the particular life of a nation, establishing its autonomy from metropolitan models, and insuring that it teaches "useful" skills. A particularly common variant is that the village schools should relate their lessons to the local life of farmers.

If one pores over these programmatic statements he becomes convinced that nearly all of them are ambiguous and that they supply few definite guides for operating a school system. Eventually the crucial question arises: how would you determine whether a school system is adapted to the conditions of a particular society? Were, or are, our schools adapted to life in Western countries; in which features; to what degree? If adaptation were so clear a goal, there would be fewer controversies about schools, and the Soviet regime would have made fewer sudden and drastic switches in educational policy.[9]

An educational system could be functionally appropriate for certain sectors of a society but not for others; for example, schools could facilitate political consensus but serve the requirements of the job market poorly or serve only certain job markets well. Education may prove very responsive to the practical needs and personal wishes of certain subpopulations but not of others. It may insure continuity of the nation's literate culture but not prepare pupils for adjusting to social change. A school system (or some part of it) may shift from being seemingly non-adapted to being more functional, not because the schools changed but because the society changed—or people's perceptions of how to use what the school taught them changed. Thus, aspirations for occupational advancement and knowledge of how to utilize schooling for that purpose may spread into new sectors of a society.

Most important of all, to what society are the schools to be adapted? Today one would not propose that curricula be oriented mainly to the society that is passing away as a consequence of development. If technological progress is the aim, few lessons can deal with the society of the pupils' parents. Only to a limited extent can schools organize instruction around the present conditions of pupils' lives with their families. Children are being prepared to live in a society that is not yet born or that can as yet be found only in a few localities. Insofar as teaching is directed toward the society that is to be, it must be unadapted to "the society." [10]

What one may call the "holistic" argument about the adaptation of schools to a society is really untestable.[11] It follows that one can draw few definite prescriptions for curricula from these various broad contentions about improving the utility of education.[12]

In the last analysis, perhaps the concern should be not whether schools are adapted to the society but rather with how various institutions make use of the products of the schools. Unemployment of graduates may be due to political policies that overexpand the school system, to rigid and unrealistic wage structures imposed upon employers, or to ignorance among employers of how to use the better-trained labor force.

Even if policy makers set themselves to prepare pupils for particular occupations in what are judged to be the growth sectors, numerous questions remain to be decided. Agreement must be reached as to which kinds of "practical" instruction will prove useful when pupils become employed. Among these varieties of training, priorities will have to be worked out. But there is a limited part of children's lives that can be committed to preparation for work and for other adult roles. General education can hardly be crowded out of the schools, and the priorities among different sorts of vocational training must be determined within the framework of the whole curriculum.

Finally, all instruction has costs. These costs must be balanced against the estimated returns for different combinations of general and vocational training and for different kinds of the latter. Since teachers, particularly of technical subjects, are the scarcest resources of the educational system, where and for which sorts of courses teachers are used will determine how effectively productive manpower can be turned out. A related question will turn on investments in vocational schools as contrasted with subsidies or other incentives to induce employers to take on a large part of the responsibility for technical education.

VOCATIONAL TRAINING (NON-AGRICULTURAL)

Proposals to inaugurate vocational schools, as have been shown, commonly rest on arguments that education should serve practical ends and be adapted to the needs of the local society. Usually also it is asserted that such courses are more likely than conventional lessons to arouse attitudes of workmanship among pupils. The following quotation represents this point of view.[13]

> Primary education should prepare children who would not go on to secondary education for productive occupations. In that connexion, it was stressed that primary education should be self-contained while being preparatory to secondary education and should have a practical bias. [Secondary schools] would gain by adopting an agricultural or technical bias.

There is also a more subtle corollary debate. Some writers contend that peasants will not be able to fit into modern types of industry unless their whole outlook on life is remolded. Hence, schools should attempt to surround vocational training with lessons designed to create a new outlook on life. An opposing group asserts that a sufficient supply of workers can be drawn out of the subsistence sector and immersed in new ways of living by an active labor market. The first group tend to favor vocational schools; the second group tend to assign responsibility for training to employers and to place more emphasis upon using schools to prepare youth for training rather than to give the training.[14]

A ministry of education can choose among several programs of vocational preparation. (The focus here is mainly on the secondary level.) 1) Schools can give direct training in specific manual skills or in such quasi-vocational subjects as technical drawing and metal working. These courses can be a part of all curricula or provided for only certain sets of pupils. 2) Schools can emphasize science rather than vocational skills on the assumption that the latter will be learned more fully by pupils with a grasp of the fundamentals underlying technology. An unusual and promising variant is to include construction of laboratory equipment in the science course. 3) Some advisers propose that apart from solid courses in science, mechanical toys be supplied from the first years of school, thus making play of the learning of technical fundamentals. 4) Some advisers would recommend restricting the specifically vocational element in schools to the provision of generous amounts of well-prepared information about occupations.[15]

What employers often perceive more clearly than educational planners is that general and vocational education are complements, not substitutes. Even in the developing countries, those individuals with the best general education will qualify for the larger amounts of on-the-job training, and this training is given at the employers' direct expense. The policy implications of this situation are underlined by the endemic complaints of employers that what new employees lack is not so much technical skill as readiness in language and general alertness to assimilate technical instruction.

One of the most basic objections to providing elaborately differentiated vocational training lies in the tendency of workers to enter occupations other than those for which they were trained and to shift in later years to still others. Only in part is this behavior induced by job obsolescence or differing growth rates of occupations.[16] Perhaps the job market is a better judge of what skills are needed and of which individuals can best acquire them than are the curriculum planners. Given the high rate of inter-occupational mobility, until vocational aptitudes can be predicted accurately, vocational choices should be deferred as late as possible —unless officials regard compulsory allocation to jobs as preferable to appropriate allocation. Unless demand—not putative "needs"—for different skills can be predicted accurately, there is little warrant for constructing elaborate technical schools. It is more prudent to plan only broad categories of training and outputs by level of school. This also argues for deferring vocational training when feasible until after employment.

Even under colonial rule, the territories that are now independent nations had craftsmen and large numbers of semi-skilled workers, and many had sizeable stocks of clerks.[17] By the time of independence most countries had transportation and communication systems and often numerous industrial establishments. Those first cohorts of non-farm workers came not from vocational schools but from training programs operated by the railroads, police, ministry of works or agriculture, and by private firms. Those programs had one singular merit that supplies a principle for policy: vocational training was given near the point of employment. By this method it is committed rather than potential workers who are trained. More important, there is an enormous saving in the number of vocational teachers required, and the teachers normally are up to date in technical operations. Under such conditions the numbers trained are likely to correspond fairly closely to the effective demand. Planning offices, by contrast, seldom can build forecasts for skills on solid evidence.[18]

There is a widespread belief that colonial officials in most parts of the world deliberately introduced "bookish" education. To the contrary, in most areas they, as did missionaries, struggled for generations to establish trade schools and practical courses. It was the local peoples who demanded the standard type of school, perceiving that graduates of these schools received better jobs than individuals with trade training.[19] After independence there has been astonishingly little deviation from the colonial pattern of education.[20]

AGRICULTURAL EDUCATION

> Elementary education must strive to impart directly available technical knowledge to the rural youth, enabling them to increase production. Above all, elementary education must cease to alienate pupils from their environment and render them unfit for the purpose to which education ought to be dedicated, namely, the rise in rural welfare.

> The reorganization of elementary education ought to be so conceived as to create prestige and status for agricultural work.[21]

> Since most pupils will not go beyond the village elementary school, subjects should be taught in such a way that they can have practical application in the daily living in rural areas. Fundamental lessons of good agricultural practices are introduced through the school garden and farm animal projects.[22]

Other writers go so far as to argue that rural schools should gear their numbers to the rate at which agriculture is adopting new technologies into which the primary school graduate can fit.[23] Tempting as it seems to envisage adjusting rural enrolments to the presumed capacity of agriculture to use literate individuals, such a policy is unworkable and would be unacceptable politically. Depending upon the country and upon its stage of development, varying proportions of peasants' offspring will be drawn into non-farm jobs. Moreover, the rate of migration out of villages will vary widely among the parts of each country. It is wasteful to teach farming to those who will leave the villages; they need to acquire a capacity to assimilate on-the-job training when they arrive in town. How, then, decide which rural schools should have an agricultural bias in the curriculum? Children who will remain in the villages will benefit little from practicing a poor imitation of their parents' tillage practices. Why should parents tolerate such a waste of their children's time? If the school is to teach an improved agriculture, where will teachers be found who are knowledgeable in the agricultural practices suitable for the specific agronomic area in which they are employed? What peasants' children need is the same training as pupils in towns; namely, "functional literacy, some acquaintance with mechanical principles, adaptability to technical change and progress, and an appreciation of the sources of information." [24]

In the literature on developing countries one finds the same fallacies that once pervaded educational writings in Western nations. For example, migration of farm children to towns is attributed to the "unadapted" lessons in rural schools. Yet surely it is education as such, not some particular kind of education, that increases receptivity to the appeal of non-farm jobs —assuming that it is pull and not push that underlies migration. Proposals to indoctrinate farm youth with appreciation of agriculture and with respect for farm life are not persuasive. Schools "in which agriculture as an occupation is held up to respect" [25] can be imagined, but not schools capable of giving farming sufficient prestige to restrain migration. No doubt "physical work should also be presented in its positive aspects," [26] but no schools in any country have achieved that aim. Indeed, a basic aim of education generally and the principal appeal of schooling to individuals is that it opens the way to escape from physical labor.

It is not true that peasants' children in developing countries categorically reject farming as an occupation. Farming is accorded intermediate prestige, even ahead of some white-collar jobs. Those youth who perceive that they can get hold of land, capital, and credit in areas with good market opportunities view farming favorably.[27] If indoctrination kept "too many" youth in farming areas, those opportunities would be even scarcer than at present.

The educational problem for operating farmers and for mature youth committed to farming is quite different. For the peasant adult, it is mainly the various sorts of extension education that are called for, perhaps supplemented by short-term residential courses in special training centers. For the youth who can plan with confidence to become farmers, there are practicable sorts of secondary agricultural training, although expectations for these kinds of courses should not be set high. For one thing, the number of youth who will be both interested in becoming farmers and assured that they can succeed in doing so will be small at the age when entry to secondary school occurs. Many will make this choice only after they discover that they cannot win entry to a more esteemed secondary course or to a preferred kind of higher education. So we come back to the principle that vocational agricultural training, like other vocational training, should be given near the point of use.

But secondary courses in agriculture have another justification, which is shared by university training in agricultural sciences. Most developing countries will have a large roster of positions of varying levels in their agricultural programs, private and public. Particularly at the secondary level, it will be necessary to train these individuals locally.[28] But to set up training programs (including bursaries for overseas university study in agriculture) will prove wasteful without accompanying policies to enlist the graduates in jobs for which they were trained. Few countries yet have faced up to the need to provide salaries and perquisites for agricultural-service workers as attractive as those for other positions with the same formal qualifications.[29] Since the preponderant drift is out of and seldom into agricultural jobs, the effectiveness of the training programs for these specialists will be determined mainly by the conditions of employment rather than of instruction.

In both elementary and secondary school, then, the appropriate education for the improvement of agriculture is a good general education. Except for a minority of pupils, science should take priority over agricultural courses. Science courses are more likely than work in school gardens to undermine folk beliefs. Moreover, the drudgery of school gardens disenchants more pupils with farming than it encourages.

There is, however, one additional kind of agricultural training that is seldom mentioned: instruction about agriculture for all university students, most of whom will achieve influential positions in their society. In most circles the theory of planning rests on an assumption that industry is important but that agriculture is unimportant except as a source of capital for industry. Most development practitioners and many writers share the socialist disdain for agriculture. Accordingly, solid instruction about the economy of agriculture would be a useful element in university programs for all students. Their decisions will have greater impact upon a country's agriculture than any imaginable curricular materials taught to village children.[30]

CONSTRAINTS ON VOCATIONAL EDUCATION INHERENT IN THE EDUCATIONAL PROCESS

Several inconsistent—and in the writer's belief unwarranted—expectations commonly held with respect to vocational education have been discussed in the previous pages. Pursuing the point, to ask schools to make pupils ready to participate in a new technological pattern of living while at the same time nourishing a renaissance in local traditions is virtually to insure that neither task will be done well. To instruct pupils in farming practices that run counter to their parents' habits is not congruent with efforts to build a part of the curriculum around tribal customs.

But even if these conspicuous incongruities are avoided, the very structure and atmosphere of the school system in most underdeveloped countries create serious obstacles in the road to a varied and useful course of study. Nearly all the proposals to rely upon the schools to provide an exciting preparation for a new society pay too little attention to the problem of finding qualified teachers. Most of the teachers lack more than the ability to convey simple lessons in a routine manner.[31] Given the strangeness for most pupils of even the 3-R's, often combined with teaching in a strange language, departures from the conventional curriculum threaten to overload pupils and curriculum as well as to exceed the capacities of teachers.

Another difficulty arises from the fact that a school system is not unified but is made up of levels and perhaps also sectors and streams among which pupils are expected to flow in orderly routes.[32] Each level of school has a dual task. It is to purvey materials of immediate utility, that will be useful to all citizens in later life—such as literacy and numbers. At the same time pupils must be qualified for the next stage of schooling. Only for the unusually able pupil will this situation cause no strain. The elementary teacher, for example, can try to make her classes appealing and realistic and useful, but it is the teacher who will next have the pupils who will judge how well the former taught the class. A teacher seldom has a voice as to which of her pupils will be admitted into the more advanced classes or school. Naturally she will hesitate to enrich her pupils' lessons at the expense of drill in the conventional program.

Inevitably, given limited resources, there must be some selective device to determine which children can advance. Almost always this is an examination, the content of which reflects the curriculum of the university and is designed essentially to identify those with promise for university study. Perhaps also the ultimate criterion is metropolitan standards in professional and graduate schools.[33] Even if teachers were willing to venture, parents commonly resist any departure from the syllabus that has proved to lead to esteemed schools or certificates. This is a salient reason why vocational schools often have had vacant places, though pupils will desperately seek entry into even vocational schools if they can be used as a backdoor into the respected higher schools.[34]

There is a universal character to science and technology, as well as to the 3-R's. These subjects are believed to be essential both for promoting development and for university study along with the accepted arts subjects. This universality is a barrier to injecting local and "adapted" material into the lower schools. The alternative of ruling in advance that only certain children or only those in certain localities shall have an opportunity to prepare for the preferred schools cannot be defended in many countries today, however much scope such a policy might give for a more "useful" curriculum for the majority of children. Pronouncements favoring "practical" education can be taken seriously only when a country imposes examinations in "practical" subjects on every pupil on a par with examinations in the more bookish subjects. The schools attended by the children of national officials and the salary schedules those officials establish in the civil service for the various specialities tell us how important they think vocational subjects are. Schools as well as courses of study are judged by examination results. Since teachers are judged by the same measures, they will seldom embrace even an admittedly more useful curriculum until they are confident that they will be compensated satisfactorily for bearing the risk.

The particular pleas for orienting village schools to agrarian life run up against all the foregoing dilemmas as well as some special ones. Those advocates try to harmonize what cannot be harmonized; for example:[35]

> In general, countries prefer to adopt the principle that the pattern of education shall be identical for all. That does not preclude giving a special orientation to the schooling provided in rural areas; however, any rural orientation of primary or secondary education must in no way compromise the chances of the recipients who wish to continue their education.
>
> The urban school is not a "better" school than the village school, but both should be better adapted to the community in which they have to play their part. . . .
>
> Even a definite rural bias need not in any way hamper a pupil who later proceeds to higher education of a more academic type: but should rather help him to think in concrete terms. . . .

Village schools cannot be sealed off in order to give them a special curriculum. A dual, urban and rural, structure of education will cease to be tolerated by virtue of the same attitudes that lead parents to accept the worth of schooling itself. By the time village families come to see any point in having their children attend school they will have discerned that certain kinds of schooling lead to more rewarding careers—whether or not they are most useful for national welfare. Even under favorable circumstances the handicaps of rural schools are great. Peasants will protest any additional, formally instituted, barriers to the educational advancement of their children. No doubt rural schools are too bookish and less practical than they might be, though not only in Tanzania or Brazil. Perhaps too many youth seek jobs in cities. Few schools can prepare all pupils for immediate entry to good jobs. But all those conditions will have to be borne so long as nations wish their best-educated men to be the peers of leaders elsewhere and so long as mass education is a prime goal in its own right.

WHAT SCHOOLS ACCOMPLISH IS DETERMINED BY THEIR MILIEU

Predicting the effect of school instruction upon the life of a society a few decades later is hazardous, even if we assume pupils learn what they are taught. In the then different society, will individuals be able to use what they learned in school? Will tradition-minded adults, mass media, and daily life reinforce or negate school lessons? Most important, what supplementary learning from experiences and from agencies outside the school is presupposed if school lessons are to be effective? [36] Skills and ideas contribute little to social change unless individuals perceive why new ways of behaving are called for and unless they embody those new activities in their own lives.

One should not forget how modest has been the place of the school as a source of change in Western societies before the latest generations. There were many channels for social mobility, powerful inducements to accept new ideas, and diverse living models of success for youth to emulate. In most developing countries, outside the capitals, the supply of cultural agencies is impoverished. But in most Western countries even frontier communities had newspapers, a handful of lawyers, physicians, clergy, teachers, and educated mothers, not to mention often lyceums, libraries, workingmen's institutes, and similar institutions. These are almost entirely absent in developing countries. In the West those agencies rested on widespread literacy but they in turn made literacy functional, and they supplied models for careers. In such communities the school had to assume only a modest socialization task, mainly supplementing or embodying influences plentifully available outside the schools. In most of the developing countries the school must carry a larger burden of general education than schools did in our past, and few of the existing auxiliary educational influences highlight the value of pragmatic and enterprising modes of life.

There is a curious ambivalence displayed by national officials in developing countries (and by their foreign advisers) toward youth's reaction to education. Education is held up as a magic key to national progress, but the majority of pupils are implored not to aspire to stay in school many years. Schooling is held to be a political right, but the successful pupils are criticized for developing occupational aspirations modeled on their seniors. National leaders continue to reward the bookish sorts of education while affirming piously the need for practical education.

It is in the counterpoint between children's aspirations and their expectations that we find the heart of the problem of how education is related to vocational life. It is through the self-conceptions represented by these attitudes that education becomes woven into development. As long, then, as white-collar jobs typically pay better and yield more dignity, astute youth usually will turn their backs on other jobs. But youth do not hold stubbornly to vain aspirations, for they are shrewd observers of shifting opportunities. The attractiveness of courses in school will reflect the attractiveness of the jobs to which they normally lead.[37]

If youth do not find work commensurate with their training, surely that disharmony springs from official blundering or utopian predictions of development more than from misguided education—particularly in countries imbued with socialist ideologies. How much a society benefits from its youth's capabilities depends upon how well those who supply jobs can make use of the training received by youth. There is an inconsistency between the demonstrated inaccuracy of manpower forecasts of allegedly needed skills and the reiterated insistence on setting up very specific training programs. This association of planning with the impulse to manage others' lives flies in the face of the demonstrated perceptiveness among school graduates of occupational opportunities.

One may, perhaps, conclude that what is needed is occupational information, but information also has its costs.[38] It costs the individual to identify the most appropriate education or the most suitable position, and an effective system of vocational information cannot be provided cheaply. Investment in supplying occupational information to improve the job-seeking activity of youth presumably would pay off better than building vocational schools to train them for jobs that may not materialize. A flexible, that is a general, education rather than specific training may be the best preparation for what is after all to most men their principal vocational training, the training they receive as participants on the job.[39]

FOOTNOTES

1. The faculty of the Center have discussed these questions so often that one cannot decide where particular ideas originated. My first statements on this topic were included in the study prepared for the World Bank mission to Kenya. See also P. Foster, "The Vocational School Fallacy" in Anderson and Bowman, *Education and Economic Development* (1965), ch. 8 and his *Education and Social Change in Ghana* (1965); and M. J. Bowman, "From Guilds to Infant Training Industries," *Ibid.,* ch. 6. The study of Turkish secondary schools by A. Kazamias was also part of the interchange of ideas.

2. Bowman and I inferred that economic level of countries predicts later edu-

cational levels better than the opposite; see C. Geertz (Ed.), *Old Societies and New States,* 1963, pp. 247–79.

3. T. Balogh, "The Economics of Educational Planning," *Comparative Education,* 1:5, 1964.

4. UNESCO Conference of African States on the Development of Education in Africa, *Final Report,* 1961, Annex IV, p. 55.

5. UNESCO, *Report of the Educational Planning Group on Their First Mission to Somalia,* 1962, p. 175.

6. T. J. Jones, *Education in Africa,* 1924, p. 41.

7. R. Dottrens, *The Primary School Curriculum,* 1962, p. 31.

8. Source cited in n. 3, ch. 1, p. 3. No one, of course, would dispute that arithmetic examples should use local units of measurement and local examples, as could, in large measure, history and literature books.

9. The *Times Educational Supplement* for March 11, 1966 (p. 723) carries the following Moscow item. "A decision made last week by the party central committee and council of ministers has annulled the universal vocational training. . . . The drawback of the system was that it obliged education authorities to provide industrial experience and technical training even in areas where there were no facilities. It distracted children from academic work, moreover, and cut down the time available for classroom work. It often imposed professional specialization quite unsuited to the pupils. In many factories children undergoing production training were simply a nuisance." I predicted these outcomes in detail after my 1958 visit to the Soviet Union.

10. There is danger in the use of local history and folktales; they may exacerbate tribal or regional tensions. In many societies there is a serious question as to what can be considered "local" materials.

11. One can think of clear negative uses of the criterion; for example, if nongraduates of schools obtained better jobs than graduates.

12. That schools rely heavily upon rote learning is no proof that "unrealistic" content is at the root of the problem. Rote learning is prominent in all schools, and, there is a common exaggeration of children's dislike of initially "meaningless" material.

13. Source cited in n. 3, p. 36.

14. Quoted from an unpublished paper by M. Blaug.

15. One strong argument for giving science priority is the widespread inability of peasant children to view the physical world as neutral and manipulable.

16. Many entrants to technical schools took their less preferred opportunity, hoping to use it as a backdoor into preferred schools and non-technical jobs, but many also change their occupational interests over time.

17. Whether colonial officials might have produced a larger supply of these trained men is another question.

18. Presumably also training on the job and work experience produce stronger commitment to occupations than does attitude indoctrination in schools. For certain skills having wide application and low obsolescence a better case can be made for vocational schools; typing and bookkeeping are good examples, as are perhaps also certain trades such as carpentry.

19. In that setting "academic" education was really vocational education as it has been in Western nations for generations. The question of pupils' aspirations is discussed below.

20. See Foster in Anderson and Bowman, 1965, p. 144. The similar situation in Latin America can hardly be attributed to colonial officials.

21. Balogh, *op. cit.,* p. 13.

22. M. Leach, "Working Group on Educational and Cultural Advancement in Latin America," State Department conference report (unpublished), 1961, ch. 11–7, App. 6–1, p. 5.

23. Source cited in n. 3, pp. 11, 41.

24. M. Wolfe, "Some Notes on Rural Educational Policies," in R. F. Lyons (Ed.), *Problems and Strategies of Educational Planning,* 1965, p. 73.

25. UNESCO educational planning mission to Trinidad and Tobago, *Report,* 1964, p. 27.

26. *Ibid.*

27. Evidence on this point is provided by Foster's studies in Ghana.

28. Some men may work in the extension service for years and later become farmers, but that is beside the point.

29. Preliminary study of data for Kenya suggests that employment in the agricultural programs there has more appeal than in most other countries; this may well reflect the excellence and scale of those programs and their demonstrated utility (even though initially established for the benefit of the expatriate settlers).

30. See the various articles of Clifton Wharton, Jr. on this topic.

31. C. E. Beeby, in *The Quality of Education in Developing Countries,* 1966, discusses many of these questions perceptively, especially those revolving around the quality of teachers.

32. What we know as elementary or secondary school may be split into two or more levels each, with corresponding selection mechanisms at each border.

33. Upholding standards by external examinations may not be wholly pointless, given the quality of teachers and the weakness of academic norms in the general population.

34. A forthcoming study by P. Foster and R. Clignet on the Ivory Coast demonstrates that opening university entry to graduates of technical-secondary schools quickly improves the attractiveness of the latter.

35. These quotations are taken, respectively, from FAO, *Seminaire sur l'Enseignement Agricole,* 1963, p. 19; the UNESCO mission report on Somalia, *op. cit.,* p. 177; Nuffield Foundation, *African Education,* 1953, p. 155.

36. "The world of the Amsterdam child is, apart from the people living in it, a world of objects. Everything is man-made. . . . The Papuan child's world is entirely different. . . . It cannot be subjected by simply moulding and remoulding it at will. It is a world with a will and intentions of its own. . . . The teacher of a training course for village teachers in New Guinea . . . propounded the theory that the subject of natural history must be aimed at instilling a love of nature into the pupil. A praiseworthy object if the pupil were a young barbarian from Amsterdam, but senseless and even wrong with regard to young barbarians from New Guinea. Senseless because nature is their worst enemy, wrong because in this way nature again is invested with a subjective meaning (be it this time a benign one). These boys should be taught to regard nature as an object. (J. van Baal, "Education in Non-Western Countries," *International Review of Education* 10: 6, 8, 1964.)

37. These conclusions are documented at length in Foster's Ghana investigation. Aparecida Gouveia has recently shown that acceptance of technical secondary schools by Brazilians has increased in Sao Paulo but not in other parts of the country, and she concludes that the change reflects "the heavy concentration of industrial plants in the Sao Paulo metropolitan area, and the availability of well paid technical jobs in the modern sectors of the economy." (*Sociology of Education,* 39:155, 1966.)

38. G. J. Stigler, "Information in the Labor Market," *Journal of Political Economy,* 70(5, Pt. 2): 94–105, 1962.

39. I began by drawing on data supplied by Harbison and Myers. Their recommendations and mine are on the whole parallel. However, I would question the practicability of massive shifts of subjects studied among students.

Unemployment Among African School Leavers

ARCHIBALD CALLAWAY

THROUGHOUT WEST, EAST, AND CENTRAL AFRICA TODAY—at a time when all these countries want to quicken the pace of development—masses of young people drift from rural areas to the cities in search of work. Mainly primary school leavers with an aversion to traditional farming, they set out hopefully to become first-generation wage-earners. But neither the jobs nor the vocational training exists that could meet their demands. And, as each year passes, the numbers of unemployed in the cities swell.

What steps are being taken to create employment for these school leavers? Are these efforts seen as an integral part of national economic and social development? What further measures can be taken? These questions call for the urgent attention of governments, both of the newly independent African nations and of those approaching self-government.

Policies should take into account not only the present situation but the dynamic nature of the problem. In these countries unemployment of school leavers is cumulative: the rate at which young people are leaving schools and seeking work continuously outpaces the capacity of the economies to provide employment outside farming. This type of unemployment, moreover, is not self-correcting, nor will any simple expedient solve it. For the individual—the young African hoping to place himself in the modern world—a long period of unemployment may undermine his self-confidence and turn his optimism to disillusionment. For the nation, unemployment of any kind represents a high waste of human resources. As increasingly large numbers of potential workers do not contribute to the productive system, they become a heavier burden on those who are working.

When urban areas become seriously overcrowded, with consequent unhealthy conditions, governments are often pressed to provide expensive amenities. And although these are certainly part of long-term development, heavy expenditure on them at a critical period may be diverted from the more fundamental aims of building a productive "infrastructure," encouraging new industries, and improving agriculture. And if policies are

Reprinted, with permission of the author and publisher, from the JOURNAL OF MODERN AFRICAN STUDIES, Vol. 1, No. 3 (1963), pp. 351–371.

not achieved to balance rural and urban development, then providing amenities in large cities becomes self-defeating: more and more people are attracted from the countryside.

Politicians are keenly sensitive to the threat of jobless literate youth to stability, particularly at a time when many African countries are going through a period of intense political re-alignment. Thousands of idle young men, dissatisfied with their lot and prospects, aware of the widening gap in incomes between the highly paid and the less fortunate, might well rally around a self-appointed leader to press for a radical change in the established order. And in an age of rapid communications, political agitation can erupt quickly among young discontented literates.

Then, there is the further danger that if long-term solutions in harmony with the general pattern for economic advancement are not designed now, some countries may be pushed during an emergency to adopt stopgap, or even coercive, measures that could turn out to be very costly. Temporary set-ups organised under pressure have a way of turning into permanent institutions—which may not be the ones desired by the architects of national progress.

BACKGROUND FACTS

The background to this problem of unemployed school leavers combines two facts: the widespread popular demand for education together with the rapidly rising populations in all these countries. These account for the multiple expansion of facilities for basic education in both rural and urban areas. But facilities for secondary and vocational education have by no means developed in the same proportion. At present, out of every 1,000 primary school children, no country has more than 10 per cent going on for further formal education. This means, quite simply, at least 900 young people looking for jobs or for training leading to jobs. And even with steady expansion of secondary, technical, and university education, still a large number of primary school leavers will be seeking work. At the important Addis Ababa conference in May 1961 on the development of education in Africa, a plan was presented for universal primary education in all participating countries by 1980, with 23 out of every 100 advancing to second-level education, and two out of every 100 reaching the higher education level. These are admirable objectives, yet the plan for attaining mass education might well be accompanied by a twin plan for achieving large-scale employment of its products.

The sharp rise in the rate of population growth is largely explained by the wider dissemination of health education and services. Most African countries today have an annual population increase of from two to three per cent. Recent estimates show: Uganda, two and a half per cent; Kenya and Tanganyika, around two per cent; while Ghana and Nigeria both exceed two per cent. The 1960 population of the 34 countries represented at

Addis Ababa was estimated at 172 million, with the figure of 281 million projected for 1980.

In contrast, European nations during similar stages of economic change seldom exceeded one-per-cent yearly increases in population, and then only for short periods. As late as 1900 Great Britain had a yearly increase of slightly more than one per cent, while Germany, Austria, Italy, and the Scandinavian countries were all less than one per cent. Another perspective: capital accumulation in the economies of nineteenth-century Europe not only happened over many decades, with low population increases, but also well before public funds were spent in any great amount on health services or widespread primary education. African countries are attempting to speed up capital formation, with high population increases, and at the same time allocating heavy public expenditures to provide primary education for high proportions of school-age children. This comparison gives a hint of the immense task ahead.

Populations of the new African nations are thus becoming younger—with 35 to 40 per cent now under the age of 15. Of course, there is nothing necessarily ill-advised about having such increases in population and sending such a large number of children to schools. At least in human terms, both can be a source of much joy. The question is whether individual countries have the capacity to achieve the higher rate of economic progress necessary to match the expectations people have of improvements in their living standards. Can economic development more than keep abreast of the rising population of, say, two per cent every year? And, related to this, can the administrative ability be developed—together with the techniques and the financial resources—to provide the opportunities for training and constructive work so eagerly sought by the younger generation? The problem is not so much one of setting up targets but of finding the means to reach them.

Progress in basic education in Africa has three distinct stages. In the first stage only a relatively small proportion of school-age children attend school: perhaps no more than 10 to 30 per cent. The second stage comes when some 50 to 80 per cent or more receive this elementary schooling. The third stage is reached when nearly the entire population has passed through primary education and is literate; there is then acceptance by the whole community that all people, including farmers, need preparation for their economic tasks through exposure to the disciplines of formal school work.

In the first stage, those who pass through primary schools, even without attending secondary or vocational schools, are usually able to find work at a regular income outside farming. They find jobs as clerks in central and local governments and trading firms, as messengers, as assistants to produce buyers, and so on. In the second stage, the number of school leavers has been multiplied by three or four while the number of jobs has increased only slightly. Mass unemployment of school leavers then prevails and may last a long time. The advance towards universal primary education thus reveals itself as an opportunity—but also a dilemma.

A few tropical African countries are still in the first stage. Most, however, have reached the second, and from all points of view—social, economic, and political—this is the most difficult stage. Few will reach the third stage before the year 2000. In the meantime, no government can remain passive to the dangers implicit in this transition from stage two to stage three.

Although the pace of educational change differs among and within countries, the elements of the school leavers' employment problem are much the same everywhere. Formal education—because its disciplines, ideas, and goals are alien to the traditional culture of African peoples—everywhere disrupts the cohesion of tribal societies. For example, only a few parents—most of whom are farmers—want their school children to become farmers. Compared with the possibilities that education can lead to, farming—however necessary—is downgraded. The village school is more often thought of as a symbol of the means of freeing the younger generation from the drudgery of farming. These parents pay the modest school fees—often a considerable amount of the income that comes from local sales of surplus produce—with the hopes that their children later on will gain jobs that provide financial rewards and prestige.

The school leaver himself has become aware of the workings of the exchange economy. He has seen bicycles, transistor radios, and gramophones, the fashionable clothes of those with steady incomes. But the material goods are not the greatest attraction. (In many cases, those school leavers who have found paid work show remarkable restraint and save a high proportion of their low incomes, often sending money back home for the education of younger brothers or sisters.) The main thing is that the school leaver cannot see any progressive future for himself in the village. And though he may have heard that jobs are difficult to find in the city, he is young and ambitious and fired with possibilities. With the blessings of his parents, he starts out on the long adventure.

Consider a school leaver who comes in search of work to the sprawling city of Ibadan, in Western Nigeria. He stays with his relatives, sometimes doing some domestic chores in return for his food and shelter. He becomes an "applicant," first making contact with the wage-paid members from his home area, who form a kind of network for spotting potential openings. He fills up applications to the departments of government, to the few new industries. Most mornings he joins the crowds at the youth employment exchange. Then he roams the streets, sauntering past the mechanic workshops and the small craft industries—the carpenters, tailors, sandal-makers. If his parents can afford the fees, he can compete to become an apprentice, perhaps to a motor mechanic. As an apprentice, his training might be negligible or it might be an excellent beginning to a career as a skilled craftsman. After he has worked faithfully for three to five years, he may then be given enough tools by his master and help by his parents and relatives to become a type of journeyman with the prospect later of becoming a master and starting business of his own. But there are examples of former school-leaver apprentices, too, who are not able to make the transition between training and gainful work—and who are now unemployed.

Or this school leaver may pay a few shillings a month to learn typing in one of the many establishments found in the city. Even if he learns to copy-type, he is still one of many, with similar rudimentary skills, meeting the ever-hardening employment market. If he is strongly built, he may be able to get occasional work as a daily-paid labourer. But this is often not enough to buy food, much less the new shirt he would like to have. After a year or so, the relatives with whom he is staying may treat him in a less friendly way. He may then even move on to another city to stay with other relatives. Recent sample surveys taken in Ibadan and in the nine other principal centres in the Federation of Nigeria show that many school leavers have been unemployed for two or three years, or even longer.

The decision to return to the home village comes hard. Those school leavers from areas where land is plentiful and where cash crops are grown can go back, however reluctantly, to the security of the farm. Others have strong negative feelings: "I cannot go back. To confess failure would be a disgrace to myself and my family." Still others come from areas where land is scarce and drained of fertility; there are no farms for them to return to.

Because of the unevenness of the spread of education within and between countries, there are consequent disparities in the patterns of migration. Centres of attraction are the principal administrative and industrial cities. By and large, school leavers follow those relatives and other village people who have gone before them. In this way, "lines of migration" become established. Where—as in East Africa—there is considerable migration between countries, school leavers cross national boundaries to stay with their wage- and salary-earning relatives. They go to Nairobi, Salisbury, and the copper belt towns. For example, some 50 per cent of all wage-paid workers in manufacturing industries in Salisbury came from outside Southern Rhodesia.

The extent of the unemployment of school leavers can be measured by the number of applications that are made to employers in the few large establishments, by the increasing time individual school leavers spend without work—and ultimately also by the statistics of delinquency and vagrancy. Particularly when relatives are no longer able to help and the school leaver is forced to live on his wits, then sometimes he crosses the line into delinquency. This marks the slow weakening of tribal disciplines and the rise of the individual on his own.

Who are these unemployed school leavers? They are mostly those who have completed, or nearly completed, their primary schooling. Because in many countries the average age of primary school leaving is falling (from 16 to 14 in some areas), most of these young people have very little qualification for many of the jobs they apply for. They are both young and untrained, whatever may be their potentiality for improvement. In some areas standards have declined as a result of the rapid expansion, and also the shortening, of primary school courses.

In some countries those who have been forced to withdraw from secondary schools in the early years are finding difficulty in getting jobs, as are, for example, those who complete the course in the 600 secondary modern schools in Western Nigeria. Even those who complete secondary grammar school take much longer to find positions which a few years ago they would have spurned.

Unemployment among school leavers is not the only form of unemployment in these countries. In most African cities today there are increasing numbers of formerly wage-paid adult workers without jobs. Another indication of the pressure for employment, their condition is particularly poignant because after years in the cities they have adopted an urban pattern of living and, in many cases, have accumulated family responsibilities. Having lost intimate contact with the land, their return to rural areas where their costs of living would be lower is not easy to accomplish. And in some areas—though usually of less importance—there are unschooled youths too who hope to find work in the cities. The setting to these forms of "open unemployment" is provided by the widespread "latent unemployment" represented by the multitude of those on farms and in other small enterprises whose labour contribution is never fully used, or is relatively ineffective—either at particular times of the year or all the time. They are the under-employed.

Thus the employment problem of school leavers—caused by the impact of education on a background of traditional society and an underfunctioning economy—aggravates the existing latent and open unemployment. Because of their rising numbers and the related social pressures, however, the unemployment of school leavers calls for the closest attention.

TOWARDS PRACTICAL SOLUTIONS

Since the problem of large-scale unemployment of primary school leavers is a new one, answers cannot be found by a scrutiny of the development patterns of other countries. Practical solutions can be arrived at only by closely examining structures of the individual African economies, by analysing points of growth in relation to potential employment absorption, and then by considering priorities of government expenditure and effort.

The reason for the relative shortage of wage-paid jobs, and of apprentice places, lies within the nature and rate of expansion of the economies concerned. The pace of change is limited by the available capital, managerial experience, agricultural and industrial skills—and all these are in critically short supply to meet the requirement of accelerated development. From the employment viewpoint, these African economies have certain significant characteristics in common: large agricultural sectors, accounting for over half of each country's total produce and engaging 75 per cent or more of the working population; small industrial sectors, with, in most cases, only two to five per cent of the working population actually engaged in manufacturing or mining.

Creation of modern industries, so often thought of as a panacea for solving the employment problem, is a slow process. And since the trend in industry is for greater mechanisation with proportionately fewer—more highly skilled—workers, the capital investment needed to employ one worker often amounts to between £500 and £5,000. In the crucial decade that lies ahead, the flow of internal savings, together with foreign loans and investments, will create jobs in modern industry for only a small fraction of those demanding work. Even by 1980 it is unlikely that many countries will have more than seven or eight per cent of gainfully-employed people working in factories—the probable exceptions will be those countries which already have a head-start, such as Ivory Coast, Kenya, and Southern Rhodesia. After some decades there will no doubt be instances of self-generating economic systems, but in the meantime the few large-scale industries with secondary effects arising from their establishment cannot come near to solving the problems of mass unemployment.

Setting up new factories depends not only on the available capital and skills but also on the ability of the local market to buy the products. And the local market is where the bulk of the population is: in agriculture. One spur to development, then, is to invest money wisely in agriculture, thus raising incomes, and achieving the conditions for encouraging new industries. Most of these countries have what might be described as "export economies," with one or two commodities relied upon to provide well over half their total earnings from world trade. Improvements to agriculture can boost the quality and quantity of the existing main crops and bring a healthier diversification, thus increasing the export proceeds and lessening the risks of crop failures or fluctuating world prices. With the rise in national income, more funds—both public and private—come forth for investment in industries, perhaps in association with foreign capital and technology. At the same time, the incomes of farmers rise, and the individual family can now buy plastic buckets, aluminum cooking utensils, locally-made shoes—the products of the new industries. But this economic cycle takes time.

In the meantime, during the next few years, where can the jobs be found for young, literate Africans? Because of the huge areas covered by most of these countries, a comparatively large number of people are required for government administration, for public utilities, and for communications. But, while African university graduates and trained technicians are urgently needed for positions at the higher echelons, there is neither the expansion nor the turnover at the lower levels to allow employment for any great numbers. Public services in many countries, in fact, have too many employees and a push for efficiency often brings painful reductions in the need for lesser-skilled labour. Banks and the bigger commercial enterprises are not likely to need young recruits in any great quantity. Large plantations require many labourers at the beginning, during the planting period, but after that not many for maintenance. The large mines have, for the most part, stabilised their labour forces and are able each year to take only a few replacements; and these are usually selected from the miners' sons who have grown up on the mine compound. The modern building and construction industries hold greater prospects for wage-paid employment, but they are dependent on private and public funds as well as a continuing climate of political stability and business optimism.

Since there are no bright possibilities for providing employment on a sufficiently large scale in these more modern establishments, are there opportunities in the more traditional activities? Here, the economies of these countries of tropical Africa show marked differences—in the variety and vitality of the "transitions" between family subsistence farms and modern industrial units. And it is here that government employment policies have been weakest.

These "transitions" include the small business of traders, self-employed artisans, and craftsmen, and the smaller firms of builders, transporters, and processors of agricultural products. This whole array of indigenous enterprises represents the only really competitive element in these economies as they vie with each other for customers and strive to provide the most attractive price and quality of goods or service. What is the capacity of these "transitions" to absorb more African young people into profitable work? They take far more workers in proportion to each unit of capital than do the large modern factories; they also often provide low-cost training within the traditional apprenticeship patterns. And they are of fundamental importance to the progress of any country both in conveying a flow of incentive goods to farmers and in creating the atmosphere for entrepreneurial talent to develop.

But there are wide differences between countries in the strength of these small enterprises. In Eastern and Western Nigeria, for example, colourful markets thrive with the vigorous exchange of goods, and in every town and city small entrepreneurs energetically advertise their goods and services on a myriad of signboards. These traders and craftsmen and artisans struggle against obstacles and use brave initiatives in the attempt to move ahead. And there are cases of those who have made the breakthrough from small beginnings to large-scale operations—in transport, building, and road contracting, and in modern furniture making. The mammy traders—with their shrewd intelligence and aggressive business sense—add an extra vitality to the West African scene. Not only do they train and employ girls in their activities, but they often accumulate large sums of capital for further investment.

In Northern Rhodesia, on the other hand, where school leavers set out from their villages and trek as their adult relatives before them to the "line of rail," these small enterprises do not flourish with such strength or variety. Because of the low order of exchange in local markets and the lack of transport facilities, the local economy in farming is less advanced. In many parts of the country the task is to *create* an agricultural economy—to encourage the production of surpluses for local and export markets.

The scene changes again in East Africa. Here the Asian members of the community have for several generations carried out the activities of produce buying, selling imported articles, and manufacture in small industries such as tailoring. Against this accumulated experience, it is difficult for Africans to start in competition, or to win their way forward once having started. And most parts of East Africa show restrictions on trading in urban areas, especially as to location, that are unknown in West Africa.

It is true, of course, that the impetus for these small enterprises to emerge and develop derives from the general strength of the economy of which they become a part. They are especially sensitive to movements in export trade and to the often related rise or fall in government spending on general development. But governments might now begin to think of industrial policy on a gradation stretching all the way from the modern large enterprises to these backstreet small industries. The aim of policy should be to help improve the techniques and management of these small concerns, to blur the edges of this so-called "technological dualism." After all, careful examination will reveal that in some instances this is occurring naturally. For example, a mechanic working in a small workshop in the back streets finds employment with a modern motor works; after some years of service and of saving, he returns to set up his own improved workshop. The old takes from the new and narrows the differences that exist.

Depending on local variations, governments can—at low cost—design policies to improve the functioning of these smaller enterprises which will in turn provide training and employment for some of the school leavers coming forth. There are the familiar arguments that in the long run raising productivity in these small industries will lower employment needs. But certainly, in the meantime, employment opportunities will rise. As the cost of production falls and the design and quality of products improve, the smaller industries are better able to compete against the cheaper range of imported goods. This should mean a saving on foreign exchange, making more capital imports possible.

A Small Business Extension Service might be formed to give advice to selected small industries—on designing more attractive products, improving techniques of workmanship, marketing more successfully, and organising the business more efficiently. Another scheme might be to recruit some of these masters and apprentices on a highly selective basis for short-term courses on the pattern set by the French-speaking West African countries. Efforts might also be made to interest some of the larger trading establishments, as well as the biggest consumers—the various departments of central and local governments—in purchasing those products and services that meet specified standards. And finally, governments should not impede the emergence and growth of these small enterprises by too hastily adopting imported notions about the need for strict apprentice laws.

One aspect of development, then, is to find out what already exists and learn to work with it. Improving what is already functioning is often a much less costly operation, both in money and in human effort, than starting something completely new.

Even if there is a healthy growth of the "transitions"—the smaller units of commerce and industry within the traditional structure—the chances of training and work for the rising numbers of school leavers will still be limited.

IMPROVING AGRICULTURE

The greatest number of employment opportunities must therefore be found within agriculture. But it is no use telling school leavers to go back to farming without any plans for them; they will need some practical help at the beginning, some on-the-job training, even if only by regular visits to ensure continuous improvement, which in turn gives them greater rewards and makes farming worth while from their viewpoint. In farming, after all, there is an essential difference between one year's experience 20 times and 20 years' experience.

There are many who believe that the most fundamental approach to creating modern farmers is through curriculum reform in the thousands of primary schools. By making the schools more farm-centred, it is said, the employment problem will solve itself. The arguments are that schools should be made more "environmental," should foster the idea of the dignity of labour, and should encourage greater realism and resourcefulness among pupils in their home surroundings. The school farm plot should serve as a training ground for improved farming while the school workshop should develop skills in such general crafts as carpentry and bicycle repair, and in the local crafts, which might be pottery-making and weaving. Academic subjects should be related to the local scene: mathematics to include simple account-keeping, using local farm and market examples; language lessons to be developed from African life and literature; geography and history to begin with reference to the local and national scene; science studies to start by analysing the world around them. Certainly the trend for African education is in this direction. But curriculum reform *alone* will not solve the employment problem.

The fact is that school leavers' views of their vocation in life are determined largely by what happens outside the school, in the society and economy. As long as they see in farming a poor and stunted life, they will seek for what seem to them the better opportunities of the cities. What is wanted, first of all, is a really effective general policy towards agriculture which would demonstrate that improved farming can bring as much money and as rewarding a life as other occupations.

Yet, at the outset, countries are faced with what seem to be intractable problems in achieving low-cost changes within traditional farming patterns. Africans farm mainly for subsistence food, with some surpluses going to local and export markets. These export crops are valuable providers of foreign exchange: cocoa, cotton, groundnuts, for example. But most farming puts family needs first; specialisation among farms is very small. Human power and the use of "the blade system" are everywhere; animal power is seldom used, and mechanical power rare. And the pattern of shifting cultivation is universal. While suited to a low density of population, such a system is subject to strains when population is rising at present rates. Then the cycle of fallow and cultivation gets shorter and shorter, which means eventual deterioration of soil by over-cropping. Fragmentation of holdings is also widespread. Much African farming thus demands very hard work; and, when measured against the handicaps, it is often efficient. But productivity per person and per acre is low everywhere.

In the present context, what *specific* policies can be worked out that have meaning both for improving this system of farming while at the same time providing a future for young school leavers? Experiments already under way in tropical Africa show some possibilities: first, establishing large farm settlements on unused tracts of land which might draw young farmers from a radius of, say, 40 miles; second, encouraging smaller farm settlements on unused land close to their present villages; third, helping individuals to introduce improved methods while engaged on family holdings.

Northern Rhodesia and Western Nigeria, for example, took a courageous and imaginative approach to the problem in establishing large farm settlements. Congo (Brazzaville) also plans to creat new village settlements. The Northern Rhodesian scheme at Mungwi (which accepts illiterate farmers as well as school leavers) and the Western Nigerian settlements were financed on a long-term loan basis. They have new model villages with such modern facilities as tap water. The 13 farm settlements spaced throughout W.estern Nigeria began in 1959 with large sections of donated land—from 4,000 to 6,000 acres for each settlement, allowing some 200 school leavers (after two years' instruction in farm institutes) to be settled on individual holdings of from 20 to 30 acres. All-out efforts have been made to use modern technology (a tractor pool, for example) and tested scientific approaches in deciding on the combination of arable and tree crops, techniques of planting, possibilities of raising livestock, and co-operative marketing. These settlements are expensive: from £2,000 to £3,000 per settler, repayable over a period of 15 years beginning from the time the tree crops come into production. On the grounds of finance, of the concentration of scarce administrative talent, and of the many human problems that emerge—when youths are striking out for themselves away from their familiar environment—the direct employment possibilities of schemes of this size are necessarily limited. Their demonstration effect, however, can be considerable; by showing what modern farming in the tropics can be, they make more modest follow-up schemes easier to execute.

Although these large farm settlements are too expensive to be widely imitated, some of their features can be retained in a greatly modified version. Experiments have begun in which villages provide land for their own school leavers and the government gives initial support with subsistence payments to the settlers, subsidised seedlings, and advances for buying tools. Settlers then pay their own way as they go along. Agricultural extension advises on blocking out the land into individual units of economic size which allow for expansion over a series of years and which combine suitable crops for the area in a judicious selection between income now and income later. Co-operative buying of requisites and selling of products is introduced. Since in the early stages the young farmers live with their own families in the village, the costs are kept to a minimum. Yet these young farmers make a distinct break with traditional farming. And when the farm unit reaches its full size and the cash crops come into full bearing, they will have an income equal to, if not above, the lower wage-earners in the cities. They will also have the greater security of growing their own food, ultimately living in their own houses, and not worrying about losing their jobs.

For those school leavers who start on their family land, agricultural extension can make regular visits to encourage them, individually or in groups, in overcoming the obstacles they meet in trying to put into practice the improved methods learned in schools. Small amounts of credit may be given, and advice on techniques of production and marketing. Such an approach to specialised training and settlement in existing villages has been tried out, for example, in Dahomey and Ivory Coast. These examples show that much can be accomplished under existing land tenure arrangements—without waiting for big change-overs in these patterns.

As sufficient farm extension staff becomes available—we could call them *les animateurs,* to use a descriptive expression from French-speaking West Africa—a start can be made in using visual aids and perhaps introducing local and national merit awards for high performances. Such awards can have immense incentive value during intense periods of innovation in farming. Finally, young farmers' clubs can be expanded everywhere to extend instruction, encouragement, and group feeling through the period after the youth leaves school and before he is ready to start farming on his own. And, of course, after beginning on his own as well.

Any realistic programmes for helping to create young modern farmers based on arrangements of low cost and community self-help will be steps in the right direction. The aim is two-fold: to initiate expanding economic farm units and to furnish a local exhibition of what improved farming could look like. Where new nutritional crops, higher-yielding strains of existing crops, better poultry, and more skilful methods of management are introduced by these young settlers, they represent an effective demonstration to local villagers. Adult farmers will take greater notice of the accomplishments of their own sons than the work of government demonstration farms. They will then be more willing to meet farm extension officers and try out some of their suggested improvements.

GOVERNMENT PLANS AND PROJECTS

Most economic plans in tropical Africa (and in other continents, for that matter) treat the objective of creating more employment as peripheral to the main theme of economic advance. To some extent this is justified—at least it is understandable—because development normally does create some employment now, with the prospect of more later. Government policies derived from the economic plan are those which have to do with the general conditioning of the economy (for example, by tariffs, regulation of money supply, trade agreements) and those related to spending on capital projects. Since most African governments account for over half of the total capital formation in their countries, government spending is a major stimulus to the working of the economy. The more immediate results can be measured: the lift in output, income, and number of wage jobs. But the less immediate results arising from the response of private enterprise to government participation in the economy are much more difficult to assess. These responses may be illustrated by countless examples from African countries. A new feeder road brings multiple results: transporters and traders move into the villages; more consumer supplies flow in; higher surpluses move out; a co-operative for marketing farm produce is started; farm extension work becomes more effective. And as incomes rise, more money is spent locally: the tailor has more orders; the carpenter has more business; more apprentices are required; more jobs are available. Or take another example. Government initiates a highly selective programme for technical and other aid to small industries. After a time several firms meet success; others emulate; output and employment rises. By taking sufficient examples, gradually a record can be built that would be valuable in helping to determine future public spendings or to adjust present ones for maximum results in both productivity and employment. In achieving economic growth, the objectives of higher output and higher employment can co-exist much more harmoniously than is commonly supposed.

When weighing the priorities of public spending, however, African countries have a difficult choice to make. The more money that is spent on education (and other social expenditure including health measures), the less there is left to spend on promoting economic development, which could provide more employment for school leavers. This conflict lies at the centre of all planning throughout tropical Africa.

In these countries at present the most compelling reason for education is to provide the high-level skilled people to take over responsibilities in the expanding public services, in firms, in the professions, and in politics.

All concerned with education in Africa today agree that many more young Africans must go through the universities and higher technical institutes; and in order to provide a broad enough base for selection, many children will need primary schooling. But the large percentage of those who cannot go beyond the primary stage must not be considered merely "discards" in the process of educating a few to the highest level. The paradox, now and for some years ahead, is the shortage of university graduates and the over-supply of primary school leavers. And governments must discover the means for doing something about both problems simultaneously.

In an attempt to solve this quandary, a few countries have already made the difficult decision to reduce the rate of expansion of primary school opportunities for the time being, thus allowing more resources to go into the establishment of secondary and technical schools and universities. Even so, as mentioned before, all countries subscribing to the May 1961 conference at Addis Ababa endorsed the ideal of universal primary education by the year 1980. Carrying this out will require vast expenditures. Already some countries have between 20 and 30 per cent of their national budgets devoted to education. Having accepted the goal of a widely-based educational pyramid, governments must now find the means to pay for it, without compromising the chances of raising employment opportunities for the primary school leavers.

Thus the question is: How can rising education costs, both capital and recurrent, be met in the years ahead? It is clear that because of unequal endowments in natural resources among African countries the probable course and pace of economic progress will vary; and the ability to press on with expanding education will be a greater or lesser burden. Capital and recurrent costs per pupil also vary by country. But there are certain common elements in the problem. In every country there is a need to achieve the extra revenue required without at the same time destroying incentives to work and earn. To accomplish this, more responsibility for paying education costs must be devolved to the local areas—both for capital and recurrent costs. People are much more willing to contribute towards something they value highly which is close at hand. On the capital side, many thousands of schools could be built by voluntary contributions in money and labour (with government standards observed and survey services provided by local governments). For recurrent expenses, special education rates or fees could be introduced, or present systems strengthened. Where some farm areas are devoid of money circulation—depressed areas—governments can obtain a higher contribution through labour donations in building, compensated for by grants-in-aid for recurrent costs.

When this has been done, not only will central governments be in a better position financially to afford positive programmes to increase employment opportunities for the ever-increasing numbers of primary school leavers, but the case of African countries for international aid for higher education will be all the more valid.

Difficulty sometimes arises at policy level because unemployed school leavers are thought of as *surplus labour*. "Make-work" schemes may then be hastily designed, often with little attention to their economic value to the community or their training value to the individual. Part of the confusion on this basic principle comes from the fact that individual school leavers may often be surplus to their home farms as at present organised. To the nation as a whole, however, unemployed school leavers cannot be surplus. The problem requires a different perspective: the task is not how to absorb surplus labour but rather *how to make the best use of scarce resources*. The desired solutions, therefore, are those which make the fullest use of limited resources—financial and other—for the economy as a whole; in this way productivity reaches towards its maximum and many more school leavers are employed to greatest advantage.

Another fallacy sometimes occurs: it is thought that short-term solutions can alleviate present pressures and the problem will later solve itself. But solutions worked out on this premise usually will be quite costly and will serve only to aggravate the problem in a few years' time. These projects tend to band young people together as if they were homogenous units possessing equal abilities and gaining equal rewards. From the point of view of the nation and of the individual, policies towards raising employment for school leavers must be regarded as *long-term*. There are no short-term solutions. The youths want an outlet for their ambitions, opportunities for self-improvement, recognition of the diversity of their talents. Clearly, policies that do not purposefully relate special short-term experience to the expected employment scene later run counter to these individual goals. Even those projects that admittedly are experimental (and the right to experiment should be guarded jealously in any African country) are better conceived with reference to their likely employment outcome.

Again, there are the despairing cries, "School leavers only want white-collar jobs." Naturally enough, youths want the highest-paying jobs they can get, and as long as the returns of a clerk or a messenger are considerably higher and steadier than those of a subsistence farmer, they will seek these jobs first. But this is an indication of their economic alertness, certainly not a sign of character defect or laziness. In fact, close enquiries show that African school leavers are most realistic and quickly revise their expectations when they find that these jobs are not available. But it is no use expecting them to go "back to the land" unless there are positive policy measures to improve agriculture.

In the same way, control of the influx of school leavers into cities, perhaps with forced repatriation, is ultimately futile. Such controls not only create dissension but also are usually inefficient in their operation; moreover, they merely pass the problem back to the rural areas. They are no substitute for real incentives: in particular, a detailed agricultural policy encouraging self-improvement on the job.

If such a policy does exist, then the need is to pass on the information to school leavers. In more general terms, vocational education and counselling about employment and training opportunities can be conducted in schools and in the labour exchanges, both in rural and urban areas. This flow of information, in fact, is an integral part of any country's bid for awakening and harnessing its people in national drives towards economic improvement.

In recent years the gathering concern for idle urban and rural youth has given rise to a variety of schemes in almost all countries of tropical Africa.[1] Kenya, for example, began in 1957 and now has over 160 Youth Centres throughout the countryside and main cities, training some 14,000 young people up to the age of 19. The name is appropriate: the Youth Centre provides a place for unoccupied youths to come together to improve themselves. In a school-like atmosphere they do some general academic work, learn improved farming, and work at a variety of trades. They also take part in sports and in recreation, such as playing in a band. For girls, there is special emphasis on the home sciences. The ideal of community service is upheld; individual pupils are encouraged to give care to old people and the sick in their villages. In Nairobi, the Youth Centre has pioneered in providing a home for orphans and in helping to rehabilitate vagrant and delinquent youngsters. The unique feature of Kenya's movement is the remarkable response from local communities: they donate the land, construct the buildings, and—through local authorities—pay staff salaries. Further funds have been contributed by commercial firms in Kenya and, recently, by overseas foundations. The central government contributes a minimum of direct aid.

A quite different plan has developed in Mali. In 1960 the Civic Service began with 1,500 young men in some 37 camps, mostly situated in rural areas. Here the minimum age is 20, and the service period of two years begins with three months' training conducted by military officers. The main object is to perform work of national importance—such as building roads, dams, and bridges—as specified in Mali's five-year development plan. At the same time, the youths are trained in modern agricultural methods and in trades, so that they can settle back in their villages with increased skills. This Civic Service has been worked out at a modest cost. Youths are housed in simple buildings and huts, and they sleep on mats. They receive free clothing, small monthly allowances, and a bonus at the end of their service in the form of tools. This plan was designed in the hope that the value of the public works accomplished by these youths will match the costs of their training period.

These are only two of the many projects designed to meet the pressures of the 1960's. What lessons can be drawn from the variety of experience in all these African countries? By and large, the projects are too recent for any clear prototype to have emerged that could have wide validity as a guide for the future. Some are markedly experimental in design; there is a groping for correct procedures. This is a field, however, in which even the exchange of facts and events could be most valuable. And the schemes that failed are as instructive as those for which some success is claimed. But in testing the validity of any scheme there is always one ultimate question: What is the best use of the nation's scarce resources, particularly of capital and organisation?

Although the range of these projects in tropical Africa is very wide they fall roughly into two categories: (*a*) largely works schemes, usually of a temporary nature, in which vocational training is sometimes provided, and (*b*) largely specialised training schemes, which may include practical work. Some schemes emphasise social objectives such as the discipline and dignity of work; they stress the idea of national service for its own sake, at the same time as building new skills. The great diversity in characteristics is revealed in the manner of recruitment (age of entry, whether selective, whether voluntary or with some degree of coercion); in the manner of operation (the proportions of training and work involved, money or other allowances, the means to enforce discipline, the length of time school leavers are associated with the scheme); and in the provision, if any, made for helping these school leavers later in their attempts to find suitable work.

Among the largely works schemes are: national construction, human investment, workers' brigades, compulsory national service, civic service, labour volunteers. Most of these are found in French-speaking West African countries; a notable exception is Ghana's Workers' Brigade. Some of these include unschooled youth and adults. Some involve military-type discipline. A general recognition is growing, however, that when dealing with youth the less coercive the methods the more effective the responses; in particular, almost all tropical African countries have agreed to the important conventions 29 (1930) and 105 (1957) of the International Labour Organisation on compulsory labour. Dedicated to the idea of national service, these schemes usually involve youth in physical work in creating national assets; such as building roads, dams, and irrigation systems. And usually whatever training exists is gained while working on these projects.

On economic grounds, these schemes may lend themselves to criticism because of their high public cost and because they often divert scarce capital and administrative talent from more urgent development tasks. And often such labour-intensive works can be accomplished more cheaply by the use of machinery and perhaps with more experienced labour. Another difficulty frequently occurs in introducing specialisation and differential rewards for work done; without these, youths have less spur to self-improvement. Then, also, there are problems in finding continuous work that has meaning within the general development of the area and for which recurrent costs can be borne once the capital works have been completed. If a scheme keeps school leavers for a very long period, or has no definite time limit, the best answer may well be simply to recruit them into central and local government service for public works—as apprentices of various kinds—and thus give them the benefit of training on the job, participation in specialised work, with rewards changing as they gain ability and experience. But against these economic appraisals should be weighed the less measurable social gains of improved personal discipline and attitudes towards society.

Specialised training schemes, on the other hand, include youth centres, youth clubs, civic centres, trade centres, and trade schools. They are usually on non-military lines, and are voluntary, with selective recruitment. Some give attention to furthering general education; some are "correctional"; all provide training in skills—usually farming or trades, or both. These schemes vary in the extent of local self-help, the contribution of voluntary workers (by missionaries and others), and the amount of finance and organisation provided by the local or central government. A few of these institutions aim to be self-supporting by charging fees to trainees or making products for sale.

Experience all over Africa suggests one big problem related to both kinds of youth schemes: What happens to the school leavers once their courses of training and work have finished? Have the conditions of these camps and special schools made them better or less able to meet the competitive job market? Are those with farm training more or less willing to undertake farming in rural areas? How many later rejoin the ranks of the unemployed? Almost universally there is lacking an effective follow-through system which could both guide these youths and evaluate their experience.

YOUTH EMPLOYMENT PLAN

In order to provide a focal point for the multiple policies having to do with the employment of school leavers, a Youth Employment Plan might be worked out and kept continuously under revision. With manpower and education assessments, it would form an integral part of the nation's general economic planning. The Youth Employment Plan would bring together all the aspects of the problem into a meaningful pattern so that, instead of fragmentary solutions based on limited perspectives, the solutions will be viewed as reinforcing each other within the whole process of development. Thus, the difficult balance between rural and urban advancement will be more correctly appraised. Curriculum reform will be seen in its relation to agricultural extension; vocational guidance and a flow of information can take place in relation to government schemes for helping young farmers and aiding small businesses; the respective roles of central and local governments can be worked out to mesh with the contributions of local self-help and voluntary organisations. The Youth Employment Plan would sponsor continuous research to determine the relative costs of various training and work schemes, to review pilot projects in terms of costs and results, and to exchange information with other countries.

Unemployment among school leavers is perhaps the most serious long-run socio-political problem facing African countries. Governments, obviously, have a decisive role in determining the many-dimensional policies to meet these employment demands. Meaningful solutions can be achieved, consistent both with national goals and with the aspirations of individuals.

FOOTNOTE

1. An excellent—though somewhat incomplete—survey is given in "Youth Employment and Vocational Training Schemes in the Developing Countries," in *International Labour Review* (Geneva), LXXXVI, no. 3, September 1962.

*The Israeli School as a Selective Institution**

CHAIM ADLER

A. INTRODUCTION

IN PRE-MODERN SOCIETIES, education played (and still plays) only a slight role in social selection or in elite formation. The elites of the different institutional spheres are mainly selected by ascriptive criteria—descent and class origin. In modern societies, however, universalistic patterns and achievement orientations predominate in role allocation. As a result, education's power as an agent of social selection, and its impact on elite formation, have grown considerably.

A different development ought, however, to be mentioned in this respect. Educational systems are expected to play a decisive role in mobility, mainly for students of lower class origin; in other words, it is expected that schooling provide equal chances of mobility for all. For this reason, once new social groups emerge in society's foreground and confront its "center," the children of these groups are exposed to the existing school systems. These school systems are, as a rule, associated with the middle class (historically and functionally), and their content and ethos seem to be congruent with the conditions and requirements of middle class behaviour patterns, modes of belief and role structure. It has become a commonplace that the democratically motivated exposure of a nation's entire child population to a somewhat non-differentiated school system is related to a disproportionate scholastic failure of students of lower class origin. Contrary to official ideology and popular expectation, education does not significantly alter the social composition of society's elites. Two major modes by which the schools can remedy this situation are open and are frequently applied simultaneously. First, the standards of scholastic requirements may be lowered in order to achieve higher rates of success for students of disadvantaged backgrounds. This measure may, however, diminish the school systems' role in development or modernization. Alternatively, one may allow for considerable differentiation in the structure of education offered (mainly at the post-primary level); such a move will usually lead to a con-

* This article is a revised version of a paper submitted to the Fifth World Congress of Sociology, Washington, D.C., U.S.A., August 1962.

centration of students of disadvantaged backgrounds in one specific type of education—as a rule the non-prestigious type. This second alternative is therefore hardly in line with the ideal of democratization and again does not basically change the composition of the elite. As indicated earlier, school systems often attempt both to channel the highest possible proportion of lower class students into all types of post-primary education (including that which is most prestigious) and to maintain as high a scholastic level as possible. It is hoped, as a result, that democratization and development may take place concurrently. It is expected, in other words, that society will maintain its rate of expansion and development on the one hand, and—on the other—absorb new social elements into elite positions as a result of the education they have undergone.

In the following pages we shall analyse this dilemma as reflected in a specific society—that of Israel.

B. EDUCATION IN ISRAEL

The Jewish population of the "National Home" in Palestine was about 700,000 in 1948,[1] the year of Israel's establishment as a state, and the overwhelming majority of the adults in the community were immigrants. The Zionist colonization movement differed from other such movements not only in the motives of many of the settlers, but also in its aspiration to create an egalitarian society in which the free play of economic factors should be controlled and the individual socially insured. A strong pioneering spirit prevailed in the small community. The majority of the initial settlers were young, from an extremely homogeneous European environment and—as a result of the altruistic motive for immigration—rather select.

Throughout the period of the British mandate—from 1919 until the establishment of the State of Israel—there existed a voluntary, autonomous educational system in the Jewish community. Since this school system was sponsored by the three main political blocs, it was of a rather diffuse, preparatory nature with a highly ideological tinge. On the other hand, however, the community aspired from the moment of its inception to as high an educational standard as possible both in content and in the span of education regarded as necessary.

In a homogeneous and select community, with the high cultural and educational background of a great many of its adult members, a uniform and prolonged school system with a diffuse cultural inclination could probably answer the society's needs most successfully.

The establishment of the independent State of Israel (in May 1948) brought about changes in two main directions.

First, there was a rapid development towards a more differentiated social framework. Not only did each institutional sphere develop indigenous criteria of functioning, but the establishment of state machinery encouraged an increasing institutionalization of activities which had previously been performed voluntarily and on the basis of ideological motivation. The emergence of more universalistic and specific value orientations was the result.

The second change was of a demographic nature, inasmuch as the population more than tripled in the course of the first fifteen years of the State's existence. More important, probably, than the numerical significance of this immigration, was its ethnic composition. Whereas about 20 per cent of the resident Jewish population of pre-State Palestine were of Asian or African origin, 55 per cent of the 1,130,000 immigrants between 1948 and 1963 were of Asian or African origin, as compared with 45 per cent of European or American origin.[2] The motivation of most of the immigrants now was the search for a haven rather than the previous aspiration towards ideological self-fulfillment. The vast influx of Middle Eastern Jews from highly traditional cultural backgrounds brought about an unprecedented heterogeneity in the society. Large sections of these immigrants came to Israel lacking education, occupational training or experience, capital, political awareness and other features necessary for successful integration into a Western industrial and democratic society. As a result many moved into the lowest strata of society. The new trends in the institutional development and the drastic change in demographic composition were the cause of much social tension.[3] The impact of these developments on the educational system was considerable.

Though the Jewish population of Palestine managed to provide universal schooling on an elementary level for its children, it was felt that one of the first laws of the newly established state should provide for the free, universal and compulsory education of primary school age-groups. In September 1949 the Israel Knesset (Parliament) passed the Compulsory Education Law, which applied to children from five to thirteen years of age (i.e., a span of 9 years of compulsory education). Responsibility for the provision of free primary education rested with the State, maintenance to be shared with local authorities. This first education law officially recognized the three political "trends" in schooling already referred to. Only in 1953 was the State Education Bill enacted, thus abolishing the multi-trend system.[4]

These two basic laws governing education in Israel laid the foundations of a highly centralized and uniform educational system, under the control of the Ministry of Education (which has the second largest budget among the Ministries—9 per cent of the State budget).[5] The structure, pedagogic procedure, educational aims and curriculum of the educational establishments are largely similar and draw heavily on the educational ideology and experience of the pre-state era.[6]

Post-primary education covers four years and is neither compulsory nor free. Yet over 80 per cent of all primary school graduates proceed to one of the various types of post-primary school; and of the entire 14-17 age-group, about 60 per cent are undergoing some kind of education.[7] A number of post-primary schools are municipally run, but generally speaking 60 per cent of the rather high tuition fees are covered by parents, 20 per cent by local authorities and 20 per cent by the State (through a scheme of graded tuition fees). There exist two major types of post-primary school: academic or pre-university (comprising about 50 per cent of the students in post-primary education) and vocational or agricultural schools (covering about another 35 per cent). In summing up, we may, therefore, say that in the pre-state period formal education played only a partial role in elite formation. Being of a rather diffuse and ascriptive ideological nature, it lacked, to a certain extent, a selective emphasis based on the individual's scholastic ability. The educational system, however, had an indirect impact on elite recruitment due to its political affiliation, and to its commitment to both general cultural values and the revival of Jewish culture; identification with such political and cultural aspects was among the main criteria of elite recruitment.

With the social developments resulting from the foundation of the State a major change took place. A basic transformation of the criteria of elite recruitment occurred with an ever-growing emphasis on specific knowledge, individual achievement and universalistic role orientations. As a result, the role of ascriptive and diffuse patterns in elite selection diminished. The educational system has not yet, however, been fully adjusted to these changes, and a full awareness of its selective functions and a readiness to implement them has not yet developed.

The problem, however, is even more complicated by an additional phenomenon. The school system of the State of Israel was expected to offer "equal educational opportunities to all," in the light of the demographic growth and the change in the "ethnic" composition of the population. It therefore tended to refrain from introducing measures which would emphasize its selective significance. It is this specific dilemma which we shall now proceed to investigate.

We shall first analyze the extent and rate of adaptation of the Israel school system to the new social conditions and its function in placement in elite positions. We shall then turn to the attempts of the Israel school system to function as an agent of democratization to advance students of disadvantaged backgrounds, and to the impact of these policies on elite formation.

C. THE SELECTIVE FUNCTIONS OF THE ISRAEL SCHOOL SYSTEM

In the following remarks we shall try to show that the Israel school system has so far adapted to the vast social developments of the last twenty years only reluctantly, even though it has demonstrated a considerable degree of flexibility and readiness for change. It seems that—as in other comparable cases—the school system has been heavily preoccupied with the implementation of the Law of Compulsory Education, the Law of State Education and the adaptation of their frameworks to a five-fold expansion of the student body over a period of 17 years.[8] The major field of this development was elementary education. It is therefore not surprising that the system has not developed the mechanisms of selection required to answer the manpower needs of a rapidly developing society and ensure the most efficient preparation and selection of candidates for the elites. Moreover, as will be noted shortly, the educational heritage of the pre-state era could, to a certain extent, be regarded as a handicap as far as these needs are concerned since it was a non-differentiated educational system, with distinct emphasis upon the high quality of the educational product and a diffuse cultural orientation. Finally it seems that the major efforts of Israel's educational system so far have been made in facing the challenges of democratization in general and the challenge of social integration in particular. (See Section D, page 216.) It seems to be evident that educational efforts aimed at democratization and integration may well contradict the attempts to adapt an educational system to the needs of development and elite formation.

1. *Elementary Education.* Primary schools are, with very few exceptions, eight-year schools. Without going into the pedagogical implications of such a structure it must be mentioned that as a result the entire span of free, compulsory education is taken up by kindergarten and primary school. A large part of the population is, however, still economically incapable and/or culturally unprepared to undertake the burden of the rather expensive post-primary education. Such a structure is therefore bound to have a negative effect on transfers to post-primary schooling, particularly in those strata of the population where potential mobility is crucial. This problem is accentuated if we consider the economic waste of child-labour and the loss of potential talent among the children who do not go beyond the eight-year primary school.[9]

2. *Selection for Post-Primary Education.* At the end of primary school studies (i.e., at the age of 14) a nation-wide examination is held for all children. The final mark is computed on the basis both of the average of students' last mark in grade-cards, and the mark obtained in the examination (at a rate of 50:50 approximately). Success in the examination entitles the student to participate in the scheme of graded tuition fees referred to above.[10] A few selective problems of sociological significance are thus created.

First, students who fail in the examination have considerable difficulty in being accepted by an academic secondary school (even if money is no obstacle) and turn mainly to either vocational or agricultural secondary schools. As a result, the existent ambivalence towards technical occupations is accentuated by the pattern of directing students of lower intellectual abilities into technical occupations.[11] A certain proportion of the students, therefore, who in general show a very high level of aspiration, probably turn to vocation education with a rather negative motivation.[12] It may be assumed that some of the difficulties which Israel encounters in the development of a technically trained elite have their roots in this phenomenon.

Another consideration must be the nature of the examination, which is of an academic character, mainly of a multiple-choice type, based on material taught in grades 6 and 7 of primary school. The chances of success for students from primary schools of a lower standard are obviously smaller than those of students who attended better schools; the former, however, are usually the very students who are in greatest need of scholarship aid, according to their position in the stratification system and in view of the official egalitarian philosophy. Thus, whereas the drop-out in secondary schools raises serious doubts as to the validity of this selection,[13] the character of the examination raises doubts as to its success in transferring lower-class—even if talented—graduates of mediocre primary schools into secondary education.

To sum up, it is to be doubted whether the mechanism of selection which governs the transition from primary to post-primary education is congruent with Israel's manpower development and elite recruitment needs. Such doubts relate a) to the overcrowding of academic secondary schools, indicating that students of superior ability are only seldom directed into technical education, and b) to the uniform and academic character of the qualifying examination, which may, in numerous lower-class cases, turn into a barrier even for talented students, and which may be one of the causes for its rather limited validity as a predictive test.

3. *Post-Primary Education.* As we have seen in the preceding pages, elementary education is the main arena of "democratization" where it is believed that equal educational chances for all are provided. The analysis of post-primary education, in comparison, shows a considerable degree of ambivalence regarding the redefinition of its goals and functions. We have already seen (in section b) that as far as transition to post-primary education is concerned, a serious and honest effort is being made by the authorities to offer financial assistance where needed in order to encourage the democratizing function of post-primary education as well. We have, however, also seen that little has so far been done to adapt post-primary education in general and the highly prestigious academic secondary school in particular, to the new social conditions, thus enabling it to make a genuine contribution to the efforts at democratization. The institutionalized emphasis on "quality," or "high standards" still persists, lending it an "elitist" flavour and orientation.

As indicated earlier, about 60 per cent of the 14-17 age group do attend schools, in spite of the fact that this education is neither compulsory nor free. However, only about one-half of these students (or 30 per cent of the 14-17 age group), study in the academic secondary schools. Moreover, of every two students who go into an academic secondary school only one successfully graduates. In other words, only 15 per cent of the 18-year-olds are successful graduates of academic secondary schools. The selective function of drop-out in post-primary education calls for a few remarks.

As indicated, drop-out rates in academic secondary schools have in the last few years been about 50 per cent.[14] (E.g., 48 per cent of students who started ninth grade in 1957 dropped out and did not graduate from secondary school in 1961; similarly 53 per cent of those who started ninth grade in 1960 and should have finished secondary school in 1964 dropped out.) Among students who started secondary vocational education in 1957, and those who started secondary agricultural education in that year, 68.5 per cent and 61 per cent respectively did not complete 4 years of post-primary education.[15]

We cannot discuss here all the pedagogic and sociological aspects of school drop-out. There is little doubt that the selective function of school is, *inter alia,* the "sifting out" of all those students who are incapable of making satisfactory progress. The question, however, is both one of magnitude and of the existence of meaningful absorptive mechanisms for those students who do drop out. It may well be possible to trace some of the causes of a rather high drop-out rate to some of the features peculiar to the Israel school system, and to two in particular: a) the tradition of a high valuation of education, with the resultant pressure on post-primary schools (mainly those of an academic nature); and b) the fact that post-primary education is crammed into a short span of four years, and is more or less uniform in structure, philosophy and curriculum. As a consequence, the school system lacks structural and pedagogical flexibility and the capacity to adapt to the atypical student. It would seem that in view of the social and demographic changes we have mentioned, such flexibility and adaptive power are especially essential.[16] It happens, therefore, that a rather severe problem of drop-out is caused without any planned direction to another school of those students who discontinue their studies. The problem of an ever-growing group of adolescents whose formal education is incomplete and who are, therefore, unequipped with the skills necessary to face a modern society, has to be considered. Of even greater importance in this context is the possibility of loss of talent, with its obvious impact upon the composition of the elite.

In the same field, the "peak" of secondary education merits a few remarks. A matriculation examination is held by the Ministry of Education at the end of academic secondary education. The Matriculation Certificate is a prerequisite for all higher education and entitles the successful examinee to enter major branches of it. Matriculation may be taken externally by those students who have not attended a regular secondary school.

As a result, the pressure on academic secondary education is heightened by the fact that this is the main channel to a certificate which is a pre-condition for all higher learning and for many desirable positions. It has been turned, in consequence, into a highly selective bottleneck, with neither equally prestigious alternatives nor official mechanisms for re-directing the rejected applicants, the drop-outs and the unsuccessful examinees.

In summing up these points, we want mainly to pinpoint the probable source of the dilemma in the following situation. On the one hand there is the tendency towards democratization and educational development—the scene of which is elementary education, and the main spokesmen for which are the directors and leaders of the central educational administration. One possible effect of the prolongation of a uniform elementary education might be the lowering of standards and the insufficient motivation of the highly gifted. On the other hand we have shown the rather elitist structure and orientation of secondary education; the main spokesmen here are the secondary school principals and a certain section of the universities' faculties. Thus, although the entire student body is brought to the verge of post-primary education at the age of 14, only about one-third of this age group enters academic secondary education, 50 per cent of these drop out and an additional, smaller group fails the matriculation examination.

Our doubts as far as elite formation is concerned, relate therefore to a) the numbers of graduates "supplied" by the educational system, especially in view of the needs of an expanding society; b) the problematic job satisfaction of students who have absorbed the egalitarian philosophy of the elite, have subsequently dropped out of, or have not reached academic secondary education, but have nevertheless arrived at positions in the technical elite; c) the elitist attitudes and orientations of the minority who have "arrived."

We shall now turn to another aspect of elite formation in Israel, connected with the demographic changes it has undergone.

D. THE ISRAELI SCHOOL SYSTEM AS A FACTOR IN THE INTEGRATION OF NEW IMMIGRANTS

In the previous section we discussed mainly problems concerned with the structure of the Israeli educational system, and analyzed their impact upon selection processes in general and on elite development in particular. Since Israel is a country of immigration our discussion would be deficient if it did not view problems of elite formation in the light of the resultant demographic changes.

Education has always been regarded as an important instrument of immigrant absorption. We shall not analyze here the Israeli definition of "absorption," but assume that whatever the ideological implications may be, mobility—particularly into the elites—is an integral part of this concept. Such mobility, no doubt, depends, among other things, upon proper and adequate education. If we discover that in the selective processes, new immigrants' children, or certain groups among them, are significantly under-represented in school—this would indicate that the problem under discussion is becoming aggravated. It is, moreover, logical to assume that serious tensions threaten any society in which ecological concentration, educational failure, cultural lag, and economic and vocational inferiority, all coincide with ethnic origin. It is only natural that in such a situation education is viewed as a major potential vehicle of change.

A large number of investigations have shown that new immigrants' children, mainly those of Oriental Jewish[17] origin, have a high rate of failure in the Israel school system.[18] We shall not repeat the arguments advanced as possible explanations of this educational backwardness;[19] we shall limit ourselves to observing that as a result of this scholastic failure among Israel's "disadvantaged groups" (mainly children of Middle-Eastern and North African Jewish origin, whether born in Israel or not), these groups are still significantly under-represented in post-primary and higher education. Thus, whereas 14-17-year-olds of such Oriental Jewish origin now constitute between 50-55 per cent of their age groups, they comprised only 25.9 per cent, 28.5 per cent and 32.0 per cent of the post-primary school population in the years 1963/4, 1964/5, and 1965/6 respectively; in academic secondary education alone, which as we saw is not only prestigious but a prerequisite for mobility, the percentage of these students in the years mentioned was only 17.8, 20.0 and 23.4 respectively.[20] (There are unfortunately no detailed statistics available of the proportion of these students in the last—and decisive—twelfth grade of post-primary education. It may safely be assumed, however, that it drops to about one-half on the above figures so that in 1965/6, for example, the proportion of these students in the last grade of post-primary education was probably about 16-18 per cent of the total student body, and in academic secondary education about 12-13 per cent.) Even though a consistent growth in the proportion of Oriental Jewish students in post-primary schools is discernible, growth is slow and their significant under-representation is still a fact. It follows logically that the same situation prevails in institutions of higher education.

In analyzing the serious efforts of the education authorities to compensate for this state of affairs, the uniformity of the Israeli school system comes into focus once again. The contention was—and to a large extent still is—that for the school to fulfill its "absorption" mission, one rather demanding type of curriculum should guide all schools, so that all students go through the same kind of elementary school and qualifying examination. One of the basic ideologies governing education has been "educational equality," or "equal education for all." Equal opportunity for educational achievement and success, however, implies the adaptation of structure and curricula to different aptitudes and to individual needs and goals, in order ultimately to give each student an equal chance of mobility. However, when the problem first arose this was not admitted as a guiding principle because of the dominant egalitarian ideology which imposed a uniform system of education. The latter calls for the immigrants' adaptation to a rigid structure and therefore limits their potential chances of mobility.

The large gap in scholastic achievement between students of Middle-Eastern or North African origin and those of European or American origin which was discovered in the early fifties seriously alarmed the veteran elite, which committed itself to the rapid elimination of this phenomenon.[21] An analysis of the measures applied to alleviate the situation shows three main phases.

1. The first phase was marked by two related features: the basic assumption was that "closing the gap" meant the adaptation of the new types of students to the existing system. Secondly, in order to achieve this as rapidly as possible mainly administrative measures were applied. Even though these measures barely touched the causes of the scholastic difficulties, they fairly rapidly abolished some of the *symptoms* of the problem, without, however, changing or adapting the educational system itself.

One of the best examples of the measures used is the following: To increase the percentage of students of Oriental origin in post-primary education, a lower norm of an ascriptive nature was introduced for this group in the qualifying examination taken in the final year of elementary school. In other words, these students were to be entitled to the advantages of the graded tuition fees scheme even if their score in the exam seemed to cast doubts on their chance of succeeding in future studies. This is therefore a mechanism which transfers non-qualified students to post-primary education by administrative manipulation, without having educationally relieved the causes of their handicap. The school system into which these students were escalated made almost no attempt to adapt itself to their needs, so that quite obviously they were likely to drop out.

2. The second phase started towards the end of the 'fifties[22] and its main feature was the readiness of the educational authorities, for the first time, to apply differential educational measures in an attempt to diminish the gap in scholastic achievements. As in the previous phase, however, this permissiveness was intended to help students of Oriental origin to adapt to the *established* educational frameworks.

The best example of these measures is special boarding schools set up for the most talented and promising students of Middle-Eastern and North African origin. The idea was, that with special care and enrichment programs, as well as training in group life and self-government, these students could successfully adapt to the existing and—as we have shown, quite elitist—secondary educational system. From the scholastic point of view this was a successful measure for the students involved: there was hardly a drop-out in the first groups to try the experiment. However, since only a small proportion of students from these groups can be classified at the end of elementary school as highly talented and thus qualify for such a project, it hardly seems possible that this method could produce a change.[23]

3. We are today in the third phase and there is as yet very little information available on which to base an evaluation. This stage is characterized by two related phenomena: firstly, the readiness of the educational authorities to introduce differential educational frameworks, methods and content for the entire population of disadvantaged students, and not for the highly talented minority only; and secondly, the awareness of the educational planners that this will not result in the students being "adapted" to the existing, institutionalized educational system. In other words, it implies a growing flexibility as to structure, method and content and an acceptance of the fact that the "educational product" cannot and will not be of a uniform character.

The major innovation in this phase might well turn out to be the introduction of a system of "setting": during the last three years of elementary education the class (mainly in the heterogeneous schools) is subdivided into three scholastically more homogeneous groups for three subjects only;[24] students may be placed into different groups for each of these subjects. At each level teaching is conducted by different methods, at a different pace, and even according to different curricula.[25]

In conclusion, one can say that the Israeli school system has displayed a remarkable capacity for absorbing an unprecedented demographic expansion, and considerable flexibility and readiness to experiment in order to make school a decisive factor in democratization in general and in the development of students from disadvantaged backgrounds in particular. It would seem, however, that in order to fully adapt the educational system to the new social conditions in general and to elite recruitment in particular, radical changes will have to be introduced. On the one hand there will have to be a readiness to introduce differential methods, content and even institutions, as early in the educational history of the child as possible (to include his mother, preferably before the first birth); and on the other hand, a readiness to limit the elitist character of secondary and higher education, not necessarily by lowering standards, but by opening up different possibilities of educational mobility without any one of them having a marked superiority over the others. In view of the degree of flexibility and adaptability in the system up to now, there would seem to be a good chance of future successful adaptations along the lines we have indicated.

FOOTNOTES

1. *Statistical Abstract of Israel,* No. 17, 1966, p. 20. Published by the Central Bureau of Statistics, the Government Press, Jerusalem.
2. *Statistical Abstracts of Israel, Ibid.,* p. 96.
3. For a full sociological analysis, see S. N. Eisenstadt, "Israel," in A. M.

Rose (ed.), *The Institutions of Advanced Societies,* University of Minnesota Press, Minn., 1958.

Also Eisenstadt, S. N., "Patterns of Leadership and Social Homogeneity in Israel," *International Social Science Bulletin,* V. 8, No. 1, 1956.

Frankenstein, C. (ed.), *Between Past and Future—Essays and Studies on Aspects of Immigrant Absorption in Israel,* Henrietta Szold Foundation, Jerusalem, 1953.

Matras, J., *Israel: Absorption of Immigrants, Social Mobility and Social Changes,* The Free Press, Chicago, Ill., 1962.

Shuval, J. T., "Emerging Patterns of Ethnic Strain in Israel," *Social Forces,* V. 40, May 1962.

Shuval, J. T., *Immigrants on the Threshold,* Asherton Press, New York, N.Y., 1963.

4. Bentwich, J., *Education in Israel,* Routledge and Kegan Paul, London, 1965.

5. *Statistical Abstracts of Israel, Ibid.,* p. 550.

6. Avidor, M., "The General Education System," in M. Smilansky *et al.* (eds.), *Child and Youth Welfare in Israel,* The Henrietta Szold Institute, Jerusalem, 1960 (pp. 55–56).

7. *Statistical Abstracts of Israel, Ibid.,* No. 12, 1960–61.

8. While the number of students in all educational frameworks was about 140,000 in 1948–49, it was about 730,000 in 1965–66. It should also be mentioned that the Law of Compulsory Education (covering 9 years of schooling) had been almost fully implemented and enforced by the early fifties. (See *Statistical Abstracts of Israel, Ibid.,* p. 587.)

9. The main reason for retaining this structure seems to be of a political nature: the extremely strong elementary school teachers' organization has refused to have its power curtailed through the process of turning the last two years of elementary education into junior secondary education. It is, however, almost definite that within the next few years free, compulsory education will be raised to the age of 15 with elementary education ending at the age of 12 so that all students will have the opportunity of at least partial post-primary education, compulsory and free.

10. The limit of success depends on the amount of money the Ministry of Education may make available for the scheme and the number of students in the eighth grade of that particular year. It is worth mentioning that in the eight years this scheme has existed the number of students aided has grown more than tenfold.

11. Of the students aided through the graded-tuition fees scheme, 70 per cent were in academic secondary schools in 1964–65. This is additional evidence of the fact that the better students are being directed into academic secondary schools.

12. Ortar, G., "Primary School Graduates in 1956: Their Scholastic Aspirations and Achievements," *Megamot,* V. 8, No. 1, 1957 (Hebrew, with English summary).

13. For example: of all primary school graduates who passed this qualifying examination successfully in 1957, only 40 per cent had reached the stage of matriculation—for which the examination ought to have been a predictor—in 1961. These percentages are not higher than those from the period before the existence of the selective examination. [Muhsam, H. V., *et al., The Supply of Professional Manpower from Israel's Educational System,* Jerusalem, 1959 (Hebrew, with English summary).]

14. These figures do not take into account students failing the matriculation examinations.

15. Calculated from *Statistical Abstracts of Israel,* No. 13, 1962, p. 456; and *Statistical Abstracts of Israel,* No. 16, 1965, p. 581. Vocational and agricultural schools have lately introduced two- and three-year courses, in addition to the full four-year course. The above statistics also include, therefore, students who did not go beyond the second or third year, being students of such shortened programs.

16. For a detailed analysis of this problem, see the author's (unpublished) Ph.D.

dissertation, *Secondary School as a Selective Factor, from a Social and Educational Point of View,* Jerusalem, 1965 (Hebrew, with English summary).

Also the author's paper, "Some Social Mechanisms Affecting High School Drop-outs," submitted to the 6th World Congress of Sociology, in Evian, 1966.

17. Mainly Iraqui, Persian, North African and Jemenite.

18. Adar, L. "A Study of the Scholastic Difficulties of Immigrant Children in the Fourth Grade of the Elementary School," *Megamot,* V. 7, No. 2, 1956 (Hebrew and English summary).

Also Simon, Arie, "On the Scholastic Achievements of Immigrant Children in the Lower Elementary Grades," *Megamot,* V. 8, No. 4, Oct. 1957 (Hebrew, English summary).

Smilansky, M., "The Social Implications of the Educational Structure in Israel, *Megamot,* V. 8, No. 3, July 1957 (Hebrew with English summary).

Although there is little statistical evidence, it may be assumed that similar problems exist for children of established residents of Oriental origin.

19. We shall only indicate some of the Israeli work done in this field. For a general analysis of the Israeli literature in the field, see:

Adar, L., and C. Adler, *Education for Values in Schools for Immigrant Children in Israel,* published by the School of Education of the Hebrew University, Jerusalem, 1965 (in Hebrew; 153 pp.).

Dror, R., "Educational Research in Israel," in *Scripta Hierosolymitana,* V. 13, 1963, Jerusalem.

Frankenstein, C., "On the Concept of Primitivity," *Megamot,* V. 2, No. 4, 1961 (in Hebrew only).

20. *Statistical Abstracts of Israel, Ibid.,* p. 600 and *Information in Educational Statistics,* No. 14, July 1966, p. 44; occasional bulletin published by the Central Bureau of Statistics and the Ministry of Education, Jerusalem.

21. It is of interest to note that the newly coined Hebrew term for "disadvantaged" (especially tailored for the Israel case) literally means "those who are in need of development."

22. We are not implying that with the onset of each such phase, the methods used in the previous one were removed, but only that additional methods were introduced into the educational scene.

23. For a similar project, see Smilansky, M., *et al.,* "Regional Enrichment Centres for Disadvantaged Children in the Upper Grades of Elementary School," in *Pupil, Teacher and School,* edited by M. Chen, published by the Henrietta Szold Institute for Child and Youth Welfare, Jerusalem, 1966.

24. Hebrew, English and Mathematics—the subjects which seem to be most difficult.

25. In view of the meagre information available about this new move we shall refrain from evaluation. It does, however, seem that the method is being applied too late. Toward the end of universal compulsory education the chances of a real change in the scholastic fate of the lowest level are slim. Much earlier intervention of this kind—pre-school programs, and planned and intensive education of parents—seems to be called for.

For a full analysis of the sociological implications of the problem, see Chaim Adler, "Education and the Ingathering of Exiles," paper presented at Hebrew University's Conference on "The Ingathering of Exiles," October 25–26, Hebrew University, Jerusalem, Israel (Hebrew).

*Comprehensive Education**

ANTHONY CROSLAND

I WANT TO TALK about comprehensive reorganisation—a subject on which, apart from the Circular itself, there has been no Ministerial statement for a year. It is a subject which arouses intense discussion, and now absorbs much time and effort on the part of Local Education Authorities. I think it only right, therefore, to try and put the basic issue in perpsective, and to report to you on the progress so far made.

In doing so, I must warn you that I shall talk also about social and even political values. A few people still think that social and political aspirations can and should somehow be kept out of education. But of course they cannot and should not. Education and society interact on each other at every point. The structure of education must have a profound effect on the social structure—on the degree of equality, of equity, of opportunity, of social mobility; similarly, the content and character of education must profoundly influence the values and standards of adult society. Conversely, the social class structure will affect the demand for education and the pool of ability available; likewise, the values and character of the society must affect what is taught in the schools and generally, indeed, the national attitude to education. And I hesitate to mention the further mundane but crucial fact that only elected politicians (and not, dare I say, even the wisest Royal Commission) can and should decide how much shall be spent on education as compared with other claims on our resources—health, housing, pensions, roads, defence, or personal consumption.

It is for these reasons (obvious enough in all conscience) that in every society decisions about education—about priorities in spending or the organisation of the school system—must have a social dimension and reflect value judgments about justice, class, equality, ethics, or economic growth. It is for this reason that every educational philosophy, from Plato through Arnold to Dewey, has articulated the social and moral values of its time and of its author. And it is for this reason that every educational system in recorded history—whether of Athens or Sparta, of New Guinea or the Pueblo Indians, of Russia or America today—has mirrored the needs and aspirations of the community which created it. And as these needs and aspirations change, so the system must be changed if dangerous tensions are to be avoided.

It is against this background that we must see the movement towards comprehensive education. For I believe this represents a strong and irresistible pressure in British society to extend the rights of citizenship. Over the past 300 years these rights have been extended first to personal liberty, then to political democracy, and later to social welfare. Now they must be further extended to educational equality. For until recently our schools have been essentially middle-class institutions, and our educational system essentially geared to educating the middle-class, plus a few from below who aspired to be middle-class or looked like desirable recruits to the middle-class. The remainder were given cheaper teachers and inferior buildings and were segregated in separate schools. But today the pressure of democracy, under either political party, insists on full civil rights and full incorporation in the educational as in other fields.

However, let me now try to make the more specific case for comprehensive education and against the tripartite or bipartite system of schools which we have had since 1944. In summary, I believe this system to be educationally and socially unjust, inefficient, wasteful and divisive. I doubt if any indictment could be more wide-ranging than that.

First, and to me most important, I assert that separatism is socially unjust. Now to demonstrate this, I must ask you to consider what it is that we are measuring when, at 11-plus (and however careful our selection procedures), we get out our labels and ticket our children—or most of them—for life: when, in Sir Frederick Clarke's phrase, we divide them up between the unselected goats and the carefully selected sheep.

Fifty years ago everyone, and even 20 years ago most people, would have answered that we were testing something—whether we called it measured intelligence, ability or aptitude—which was biologically inherited and fixed in a child for life. That was the philosophy which underlay the Hadow and Norwood Reports and the 1944 Act—that we were faced with children who differed from each other genetically and permanently, and who therefore needed to be educated in separate schools. By a further divine dispensation, fortunate indeed for the educational administrator, the differences fell into a precise numerical pattern—25 per cent academic and 75 per cent non-academic—which most conveniently fitted the existing pattern of schools.

Today we see matters quite differently. The researches of sociology and psychology have taught us, what only a few pioneers like Burt proclaimed in the past, that measured intelligence, unlike specific gravity, is not a fixed and innate quantity. It is not something given in limited measure in the genetic make-up of the new-born child. What is given is a bundle of assorted potentials, and what happens to them is a matter of nurture, of stimulus and response. The intelligence quotient is a function partly, of course, of inheritance, but also of environment and background.

SOCIAL CLASS

Moreover, the environmental factors which exert the strongest influence on measured intelligence and hence on educational performance—the factors of home and neighbourhood, of size of family and parental aspirations—are all strongly linked to social class.

The first clear demonstration of this link between measured performance and social class came within 10 years of the passage of the 1944 Act. The "Early Leaving" report of the Central Advisory Council in 1954 concluded, on the basis of careful statistical research, that by the time of the 11-plus examination, the children of certain social groups had begun scholastically to outstrip those at the other end of the social scale. It further concluded that the improvement between 11 and 16, which raised many pupils from the bottom selection group to the highest academic categories, was also most common among those from professional and managerial occupations. "The boy," said the Central Advisory Council, "whose father is of professional or managerial standing is more likely to find his home circumstances favourable to the demands of grammar school work than one whose father is an unskilled or semi-skilled worker." Thus it appeared that quite apart from any hereditary differences, the working-class boy suffered under a clear social handicap; and that what we were testing by examinations was perhaps as much home background as innate intelligence.

I have mentioned this official inquiry, carried out for the Central Advisory Council 12 years ago, because it demonstrates that the challenge to the existing structure came quite early on from the heart of the system. Two years later the Floud and Halsey work on "Social Class and Educational Opportunity" was published; a year later the British Psychological Society inquiry, edited by Philip Vernon, on secondary school selection; in 1963 the immense analyses in the Robbins appendix by Professor Moser and the Ministry of Education statisticians, measuring the pool of unused ability; and in 1964 Dr. Douglas's work on "The Home and the School." All this has reinforced the view that I.Q. and educational performance are heavily influenced by environment as well as by heredity, and that many working-class children suffer a pronounced environmental handicap as compared with middle-class children of the same ability.

What then are we doing when, at the age of 11, we divide our children into 25 per cent grammar and 75 per cent secondary modern? It is not, I suppose, in dispute that the grammar school offers more in terms of life-chances. The grammar school child—and I am talking now of children of the same level of attainment and the same potential when they start at secondary school—has a statistically much greater chance than the secondary modern child of going on to higher education, and of commanding therefore a wide choice of occupations. He is four or five times as likely to be prepared by subject specialists for the examinations which lead to higher education. He will generally be taught in smaller classes: the pupil-teacher ratio in January, 1964, was 17·5, compared with 20·3 in the secondary modern schools. The latest salary analysis shows that over 70 per cent of grammar school staff are paid salaries above the basic scale, compared with 45 per cent in secondary modern schools. John Vaizey suggested in 1958 that the average grammar school child received 170 per cent more a year in terms of resources than the average secondary modern school child; and there is no reason to think that the differential has been narrowed since then.

This is in no way to minimise the remarkable efforts of the secondary modern schools in recent years. It is to their enormous credit that without the stimulus of the top 20 per cent of ability they have nevertheless helped able youngsters to get good G.C.E. results and to go on to higher education. But this has been in spite of the odds being loaded against them. Given, then, that the grammar school offers more ample chances and opportunities in after-life, and given that I.Q. at 11 reflects home background as well as innate intelligence, what the 11-plus is doing is this: on the one hand, it penalises the working-class boy not necessarily for innate stupidity but partly for his social background, for his less educated parents, his larger family, his crowded home, his slum neighbourhood, his generally less favourable environment.

At the same time we diminish his opportunities for improving his ability by continued education. Already in the 18th century no less an authority than Dr. Johnson said: "I do not deny, Sir, but there is some original difference in minds; but it is nothing in comparison of what is formed by education." Now in the 20th century research has confirmed that measured ability is a function not only of heredity and environment, but also of the educational process itself. Whatever may be the endowment at birth, and however social environment may smile or frown upon it, good schooling will make more of it than poor schooling, and longer schooling will take it further than schooling cut short. This influence of educational stimulation on intelligence grows more profound with age, and may well be decisive in the years from 15 to 20. Yet we deny the opportunity for this stimulus to large sections of our population because of their social background at the age of 11.

Thus, we punish the working-class boy for his social origins not once but in a series of successive stages. For under the present system, with streaming in primary schools followed by selection at 11-plus, the working-class child of similar abilities to the middle-class child at the age of eight does progressively worse at the primary school, has less chance of obtaining a grammar school place, and falls still further behind from 11 onwards.

EQUALITY OF OPPORTUNITY

Now of course we cannot wholly correct an unfavourable background by a change in school organisation. The argument goes far wider than educational policy. To make equal opportunity in education a reality we shall have not only to eliminate bad housing and inadequate incomes, but steadily to make good the educational deficiencies of parents who cannot give their children the encouragement they need. True equality of opportunity cannot be accomplished in one generation, or by education alone; it needs a wider social revolution.

But as soon as we concede that measured intelligence is not a quantity fixed for life, and that it depends moreover partly on the child's environment, we must surely think it indefensible to segregate children into different schools at the age of 11. It is, of course, in the nature of things that as we grow to manhood we go different ways. Life itself is a selective process. But we must allow that process to work fairly; we must allow time for the beneficial influence of education to compensate for the deficiencies of upbringing and early circumstance. Segregation as early as 11-plus is indefensible. We must keep the choices open, and defer as long as possible the irrevocable selection. Amid all the shifting contours of educational planning I am certain of this: that the system must allow the individual to pick up, to make good, to try again. You do not feed a child less because it grows slowly or has some initial handicap to overcome.

To me, then, the central and irresistible argument against the 11-plus lies in the denial of social justice and equal opportunity which it implies. And as though this denial were not enough, we superimpose on it, as you all well know, a further geographical inequity. I refer to the notorious fact that, in what passes for a national system of education, there are 13 authorities providing selected places for less than 15 per cent of pupils, and 29 authorities providing for over 25 per cent—and one of them almost 40 per cent. These facts alone would impel us to change, not for the sake of administrative tidiness but for the sake of the youngsters whose life-chances are so arbitrarily determined according to where they happen to be born.

However, perhaps arguments based on social justice will seem too remote to hard-headed educational administrators—though I have never noticed, happily, that such people in England are lacking in principle or idealism; far from it. But lest we still have left a nucleus of conscienceless bureaucrats, I turn now to my second argument against separatism. This is based on the inefficiency implicit in it. I refer especially to the extreme fallibility, the hit-and-miss nature, of the process of selection. Wherever you draw the line there will be people on either side of it with very little between them, quite apart from the fact that from one test to another a child's I.Q. performance can and does vary considerably.

In the early 50's, as you know, intensive research was carried out which showed that while the procedures applied by local authorities—using standardised tests and teachers' assessments—were in one sense highly efficient, there were still about 10-12 per cent of "wrong" allocations made each year. That is to say, for every 100 children, some five or six were allocated to secondary modern schools who, had they been sent to grammar schools, might have been more successful than another five or six who were in fact sent to grammar school. And if we allow for the fact that children actually allocated to grammar schools would be expected to show up better than those who were not, the results suggest that the number of really "wrong" allocations may have been much larger. I may add that subsequent transfers enabled only one or two children per 100 to move into grammar schools from secondary modern. This shows the acute danger of miscalculation at the age of 11; it also shows how hard it is to correct the miscalculation if you segregate children into different schools.

SOCIAL WASTE

But there is also—and this is my third argument—a wider social waste involved. If ever there was a country which needed to make the most of its resources, it is Britain in the second half of the 20th century; and the chief resource of a crowded island is its people. Moreover the proportion of relatively inexpert and unskilled jobs to be done declines from year to year. To behave in these circumstances as though there were a fixed 25 per cent of top ability at 11 not only flies in the face of the evidence which I have quoted; it amounts to feckless prodigality.

The extent to which we are wasting good educational talent for what are in part social causes was fully and horrifyingly documented in the Crowther and Robbins Reports. Not all the waste, of course, is linked with the 11-plus; some is due to early leaving or poor performance in grammar school. Yet it is also clear that, despite all that has been done in the secondary modern schools by able and devoted teachers to minimise the damage, there has been a frightful waste of latent talent through the sheer fact of segregation, through the discouragement put upon a large group of the population by the label of failure. The proof lies in the subsequent upgrading in comprehensive schools of the 11-plus failures, and indeed in the award of some of our highest academic honours to those who at 11 had fallen on the wrong side of the line.

There are, I believe, two ways in which a fully comprehensive system will minimise this waste. One relates to the element of self-fulfilling prophecy in the educational system. We know from researches how vital are the expectations of parents and teachers to the performance of the children. Children expected to do well, on the whole, do well; children marked with the brand of failure on the whole will fail.

Failure in the 11-plus—the only exam, as has recently been pointed out, in which three-quarters of those concerned know they must fail—is conspicuously such a brand. If anyone doubts this they have only to see the effect of failing the 11-plus on the morale of both parents and children.

But if, by eliminating early selection, we could also lessen the early sense of failure, we might not only avoid a lot of unnecessary human misery; we might also find a sharp increase in the performance of many of the 75 per cent who now so often fulfil the gloomy prophecy made about them at the cruelly early age of 11.

In addition, the truly comprehensive school is given an enormous impetus and inspiration by having within it the full range of ability. The secondary modern schools have, to their credit, introduced G.C.E. courses for the benefit of those who could profit by them; but without the example of the top range of ability as pace-setters, it is all too easy for children not to make the effort, to accept society's verdict and let it go at that.

For we all know how much students learn informally rather than formally, from each other rather than from their elders. We know that standards in a school are partly set by what sociologists call "the student culture," by the young taste-makers and opinion-moulders. If these are hostile to brains, hostile to school and the teacher, then intellectual standards will be low. But to the extent that an academic stream exists, setting at least one model and acting as intellectual pacemaker, to that extent the standard will improve. It must, surely, be the experience of many of you here, as it is the finding of studies on both sides of the Atlantic, that the achievement of those who would otherwise be in a secondary modern school, and notably those in the middle ranges of ability where the greatest waste is now, is markedly higher in a comprehensive school—due to the extra stimulus, the fizz (in Mr. Mason's graphic phrase), the upgrading imparted by the academic stream.

THE BRIGHT BOY?

But what of the bright boy? Will he not suffer? And, more generally, is not an elitist system, a Platonic meritocracy, essential to efficiency and survival in a competitive and scientific world? As to the latter point, I have little anxiety. We have long combined almost the most elitist educational system, with almost the slowest rate of economic growth, of any advanced industrial nation. Both America and Sweden with their comprehensive systems have outstripped us in efficiency. I should suppose that what we most need from this point of view is a huge widening of educational opportunity. There is no evidence at all that we need to preserve selection at 11-plus.

And why should the bright boy or girl suffer by attending a comprehensive rather than a selective grammar school? Exact comparison is difficult in Britain, because most comprehensive schools operate in areas where the grammar schools still cream off a large proportion of the brighter pupils. But there is some evidence from a large-scale international research project, not yet published, that in mathematics at least the bright pre-university pupils in countries with a comprehensive system do just as well as similar pupils in countries with a highly selective system such as our own; moreover, to support the point which I have just made, the mathematics performance of pupils of lower ability is much higher in the comprehensive countries than in selective countries. This would suggest both that "more" does not necessarily mean "worse" for brighter pupils, and that the total "yield" may be greater in a comprehensive system.

In Britain, indeed, the comprehensive schools may be so concerned to do as well academically as the grammar schools that the danger may be the opposite one—too much concentration on the bright pupils. But this danger will no doubt be counteracted as the need to compete narrowly with the grammar schools disappears.

A particular fear is also expressed, which one must again respect, that the grammar or direct grant schools provide the only opportunity for bright working-class boys to rise out of their class and obtain an academic education. I think the point I have just made largely answers this. And there is this further point. One must not disregard the wastage of working-class children which already occurs from the grammar schools, where they are much less likely than boys from better homes—even when they have gained admission—to stay on and do well. This may be bound up with one of the weaknesses which the grammar schools have developed under the selective system—namely, a comparative neglect (sometimes an almost callous neglect) of their lower streams who are thought not to be up to the G.C.E.

SOCIAL DIVISIONS

I pass now from social waste to my fourth argument—a more controversial one, though I personally feel it deeply: that separate schools exacerbate social division. It cannot be denied that the 11-plus divides overwhelmingly according to social class: indeed, because of streaming in the primary school, social class division in schools begins to operate at the age of eight. What we euphemistically describe as educational selection is for the most part social selection; and our educational division is largely a class division.

This is so partly for the perhaps natural reason that schools and teachers react to social as well as to educational factors. As Dr. Douglas reminds us, *children who come from well-kept homes and who are themselves clean, well clothed and shod, stand a greater chance of being put in the upper streams than their measured ability would seem to justify*. But of course the more fundamental cause is the one which I have already stressed: that measured intelligence at 11 is partly a function of environment, and that environment is closely linked with social class. What we are testing at 11, therefore, is to a large extent social class background.

Now by selecting for a superior school children who are already well-favoured by environment, we are not merely confirming, we are hardening and sharpening, an existing social division. This can surely not be thought desirable. I will not argue the point in terms of equality. But I will argue it in terms of a sense of community, of social cohesion, of a nation composed of people who understand each other because they can communicate. If the only time we can, as a society, achieve this common language is when we go to war, then we are at a much less advanced stage than many societies which the anthropologists describe as primitive. We have only to consider our industrial relations, and the lack of communication and mutual understanding reflected in them, to see the depth of social division in Britain today. Of course, education alone cannot solve this problem. But so long as we choose to educate our children in separate camps, reinforcing and seeming to validate existing differences in accent, language and values, for so long will our schools exacerbate rather than diminish our class divisions.

STREAMING

Of course the elimination of separatism at 11-plus is only a necessary, and not a sufficient, condition of reducing the divisive effect of our school system. We should not much improve matters if selection gave way merely to rigid streaming within a strictly neighbourhood pattern of schools. This would re-create many of the old evils within a comprehensive system.

When I speak of streaming, I naturally do not mean to imply that it can or should be avoided totally and at every age. I refer to unnecessarily early and rigid streaming. Here of course there must be an improvement as a result of comprehensive reorganisation, and in the place that matters most—the primary schools. We all know what strains and rigidities the 11-plus has imposed on the primary schools—the over-emphasis on tracking and streaming and cramming. But the case for early streaming will disappear as the 11-plus disappears. There will, indeed, be much wider scope in the primary schools for innovation and experiment and the release of creative ability—from teachers and pupils alike. The newer and better methods of teaching, in mathematics, in English and in French, are more likely to be tried and more likely to bring good results; and subjects like music are less likely to get crowded out of the curriculum.

And as far as the comprehensives themselves are concerned, I am most interested, as I go round the country to find how strong is the reaction against some of the early practices of rigid and premature streaming. There seems to be a general loosening-up and a greater willingness to experiment.

The problem of the one-class neighbourhood school is more intractable. It is not, of course, a problem created by going comprehensive: four out of five secondary modern schools are neighbourhood schools, and most grammar and direct grant schools are predominantly middle-class—they do not become classless merely by having a small working-class stratum, any more than the House of Commons became truly representative of British society 60 years ago merely because Keir Hardie was elected to it. The problem is the result of gross social inequality combined with bad town-planning. In the long term the mere fact of wider educational opportunity will gradually improve matters. In the short term it is for the local authorities to give close attention to the boundaries of catchment areas; and in Circular 10/65 I have urged them to make such schools as socially and intellectually comprehensive as is practicable, perhaps by linking together two districts of a different character. This is very much the kind of problem on which further light will, I hope, be thrown by the special programme of research that we have launched.

Even with rigid streaming and neighbourhood schools, it would be hard to maintain that a comprehensive system could produce as sharp a social cleavage as the present division into separate schools. But with the elimination of streaming in primary schools, the movement against premature streaming in the comprehensive schools, and the growing realisation by Local Education Authorities of the need to make their new comprehensives socially heterogeneous, I think I may reasonably claim that the new system will reduce the sense of social division and increase the sense of social cohesion in contemporary British society.

11-PLUS ABOLITION

It was, I think, these various considerations—of equity, efficiency, avoidance of waste and social cohesion—which produced over the last decade an increasing revulsion against the 11-plus, and a gathering movement towards comprehensives. And it was they which caused this Government to set the seal of national approval on this movement by the issue of Circular 10/65.

There were, of course, those who urged us not to act—in particular, the melancholy waiters: "wait for Plowden," "wait for research," wait for something or other. Of course they were too late. Whatever the Government did or did not do, reorganisation schemes were being prepared at local level; it was surely not proposed that the Government should veto them all when they arrived in Curzon Street.

"Waiting for Plowden" was in any case an impractical suggestion. The Council is not due to report until this summer. Any proposal for an altered age of transfer would arouse, I imagine, strong controversy throughout the educational world. The Government would have to allow an ample period for argument, debate and consultation with all the interests concerned. At the end of this period, any decision to change the national age of transfer would require the lengthy process of a new Education Act. We are surely talking here in years, not months. I could not allow hundreds of thousands of children to suffer the injustice and fallibility of the 11-plus for this long period.

Again, it is said that we should have awaited the results of research. This is not a suggestion which I will accept from my political opponents. For no previous educational change—including the 1944 Act—ever waited on the results of research; nor, if it comes to that, did previous Ministers, when they approved many comprehensive schools and schemes.

But I would not criticise them for this, because the "waiting for research" argument betrays a misunderstanding of the nature both of educational research and of our political system. Educational research, in any case a very new tool, can give us new facts, illuminate the range of choice, tell us how better to achieve a given objective. But it cannot tell us what the objective ought to be. For this must depend, as I tried to make clear earlier, on judgments which have a value-component and a social dimension—judgments about equity and equal opportunity and social division and economic efficiency and all the other criteria which I have mentioned in this speech. These judgments cannot be made in the National Foundation for Educational Research. They can be made only in Parliament and the local Council chamber.

The purpose of research is quite different. It is, by fact-finding surveys and evaluative studies, to help local authorities, and their administrators and teachers, to carry out this major reform more effectively. I delight in the fact that for the first time in our educational history such studies will be built into a major reform from the outset. We owe it to those who will be running the education service, and teaching in its schools, a generation hence, that we make proper provision now for informed policy-making in the years to come. But it can be no substitute for taking those decisions in our own generation which must be taken, in common fairness, to give those children now in the schools the best opportunity we can to advance themselves and their society. Those decisions are a part of the political process; there is nowhere to take them for settlement except into the political arena. . . .

FOOTNOTE

* Speech by Anthony Crosland, Secretary of State for Education and Science, at the North of England Education Conference, January 7th, 1966.

Part Four

Sub-Cultural Variations and Education

A society is an aggregate of persons who possess in common certain characteristics. Yet these characteristics are never uniformly shared. Within societies, people may be divided by race, ethnicity, urban-rural setting, region, social class, or differences in technology. People thus divided tend to behave rather differently, even though collectively they may associate with a common culture.

Modernization usually aims at molding the patterned behavior of sub-populations into a national culture. It seeks also to erase the inequities among sub-groups *vis-à-vis* social and economic opportunities. In modernization the school is an acknowledged agent of national goals and is expected to perform an integrative role. Yet the school can also be divisive, exacerbating existing cleavages and thwarting the efforts of other modernizing agents. This section deals with the school's function as an agent in social change and acculturation.

Sub-populations are often discriminated against; yet discrimination is not always intentional. Schools can be principal offenders, unmindful that they are curtailing opportunities for social and economic advancement of sub-groups whose position they avowedly wish to better. In the United States, for example, although distinctions adverse to Negroes have been frequently invidious, they sometimes have been made unwittingly. Negroes have been deprived, collectively and individually, of equal educational opportunities by even well-meaning people and institutions. Providing them with more schools has not always led to more of them being educated. Without appropriate models of middle-class behavior, Negro children have often lacked the incentive to take advantage of the facilities offered them.

In Ghana we find another instance of unintentional discrimination against sub-groups. For that country Philip J. Foster notes that inequalities in the distribution of schooling have encouraged ethnic conflicts. Those ethnic groups exposed early to formal education have had a competitive advantage in a newly aligned social structure; further extension of schooling to them has been considered discriminatory to other groups. Yet to equalize effectively the provision of schools among major ethnic groups would require placing rigid checks on school development in areas already favored with schooling, a move that would be disastrous politically. The schools in Ghana have not been able to pursue fruitfully national social and economic aims and simultaneously circumvent political exigencies. Schools in Ghana, as in the United States, have worked to defeat some of their own objectives.

The essays in this section suggest that disparities in schooling may be unavoidable in countries experiencing a differential internal rate of economic and social change. As Manning Nash observes for Mexico and Guatemala, village life is often far removed from the national culture. The schools, being extensions of the national culture, are culturally distant from the local communities which tend not to be receptive to their efforts to induce new ways. The smaller the schism between village culture and national culture, or, alternatively, the more social change that has already taken place, the more effective the school is in infusing new ideas. This is not to say that schools must be tied closely with local institutions in order to be innovative. Indeed, as in the case of Burma, when village schools are closely bound to village life and are not so much extensions of national culture, they tend to be unoriented to change.

The school as an agent of modernization promotes change. Yet precisely how is innovation accomplished through schooling? Evidently the adoption of new values attendant with social change rewards social and economic achievement, and individuals find in the school a means of achieving. Schools can be innovative in affording individuals the training necessary to obtain newly satisfying rewards. Achieving the objectives promoted by modernizing agents encourages further change. Obviously, however, formal education cannot be a mediator of social change unless schools are provided. Yet even if schools were to be extended equally to all sub-groups of a nation, the effectiveness of schooling as an instrument of change would probably vary. Social change is inhibited when communities oppose schools. Sub-populations resistant to formal education because of their culture become deprived of the rewards change brings elsewhere in the nation.

Warren Hagstrom suggests that the point at which schooling is likely to become innovative is when the roles of teacher and student are incompatible with the roles of parent and child, when technological change dictates that complex and objective skills be taught outside an emotionally charged setting such as the family. The acceptance of schools in preliterate societies reflects social change insofar as parents allow their traditional task of teaching youth to be largely pre-empted. This suggests that sub-groups marginal to the national culture may resist formal education, because their technology is not sufficiently complex to require objective instruction. When technologically complex skills become valued, communities become in need of teachers not only because they are endowed with desired skills but also because they can instruct at an emotional distance. The conclusions reached by Nash and by Hagstrom lead us to believe that for the school to be effective in fostering change it must neither be very remote from nor very intimate with the community.

Insofar as technological change increases receptivity to schooling, towns offer more visible rewards for education. Phyllis Goldblatt notices that for Mexico, receptivity to education in urban areas depends on individuals' perceptions of the school's potential to increase personal income. In rural areas, on the other hand, foregone income, or the income that would be gained were the individual to be working rather than attending school, is salient. Whereas in urban areas receptivity is largely a matter of achieving a positive reward, in rural areas it is more a matter of not finding satisfying alternatives to schooling.

Clearly, variations in race, ethnicity, region, urban-rural setting, and technology influence schooling. Yet other variations can be significant. Sterling Fishman infers that at certain times in particular countries less universal cultural distinctions are occasionally salient. For example, Germany at the turn of the century experienced a movement toward dilettantism which, although not intended to be class oriented, increased the cultural alienation of the proletarian masses. The movement took root and a rather respected and numerous group, schooled in artistic grace, emerged before the outbreak of war in 1914. Though ephemeral, the movement had an impact on education and thought at an important period in Germany's history.

The essays in this section suggest that difficulties in promoting schooling often can be attributed to sub-cultural variations. When these variations are substantial, schools are likely to be differentially effective in fostering their objectives. As long as leaders sincerely desire that schools implement national goals, they can little afford to ignore the subtle effects of population differences on education.

Ethnicity and the Schools in Ghana

PHILIP J. FOSTER

ONE OF THE MOST SERIOUS PROBLEMS confronting many of the newly emergent nations of Africa is that of reconciling pronounced regional and ethnic loyalties with broader national requirements. In the past, colonial expansion had often created political units from agglomerations of peoples possessing distinctive language and culture while, conversely, homogeneous groupings were frequently divided by the arbitrary drawing of colonial boundaries. During the colonial period such artificial units remained viable but, with the achievement of independence, ethnic minorities have often asserted their political rights in such a manner as to threaten the continued existence of some new nations. Pressures from these groups have ranged from demands for the devolution of central government powers and the establishment of loose forms of federation to outright secession and the creation of primarily ethnic states.

Most of these movements have been subsumed under the heading of "tribalism." This is a misleading term. To be sure, certain groups with secessionist tendencies stress their cultural "differentness" from other peoples with whom they have been fortuitously associated. However, quite frequently so-called ethnic conflicts mask lines of fission which arise for other reasons. Issues may arise between primarily urban ethnic groups and rural minorities or between peoples who produce lucrative cash crops and others who have not been so fortunate. In the Congo a massive cleavage has occurred between those who have gained from regional industrial development and the remaining peoples. It is possible in many such cases to show that long-standing economic differences constitute the basis for "tribal" movements. In virtually every new African nation highly uneven internal patterns of change have occurred and it is unfortunate that a host of disparate causes for conflict are couched in ethnic terms and diverse issues concealed under the label of "tribalism."

Ghana has had its share of these problems; although one of the smallest nations of West Africa, it presents a picture of considerable ethnic diversity. Covering most of the southern portion are the Akan peoples

Reprinted with permission from the COMPARATIVE EDUCATION REVIEW, Vol. 6, No. 2 (October, 1962), pp. 127–135.

who constitute some 44 per cent of the total population.[1] The Akan are themselves subdivided into numerous clusters, many of which originally constituted distinct political units; most important among these are the coastal Fanti and the Ashanti who occupy the central area of Ghana. East of the Fanti and centering on Accra and the coastal littoral as far east as the lower Volta are the Ga-Adangme (about 9 per cent). Across the lower Volta and extending some eighty miles inland are the Ewe people (numbering just under 13 per cent) who form the third major ethnic grouping. The final distinctive set of peoples, residing to the north of Ashanti and occupying about half the total area, are the northern peoples, primarily Gur speakers, who form over 30 per cent of the peoples of Ghana.

These four major groupings are distinctive in language and culture, but they are supplemented by other minorities such as the Guan and peoples of the Volta remnant. Not only this, each major group is subdivided into a bewildering number of smaller units, many of which formerly constituted autonomous and quasi-autonomous polities. It is not surprising in this situation that the present government of Ghana has had to meet determined opposition from certain segments of the population, notably from the Ashanti and the Ewe. However, regionalist pressure has been by no means absent among the Ga, Fanti, and the northern peoples. The defeat of regionalist political leaders at the polls does not prevent the conflict between ethnic groups manifesting itself in other forms. In the struggle for power the educational system has played a significant if only partially understood role. We attempt here to delineate some relationships between the schools and contemporary ethnic conflict in Ghana.

Most observers would agree that, in the long run, the extension of formal education among the masses tends to lessen many intercultural differences and helps to replace particularistic and local values by attitudes more consonant with the needs of the whole nation. This view may be correct but some caution is needed, since by no means do all regionalist movements draw their leadership or support from the least educated segments of a population. Indeed, in Uganda, Baganda separatism stems partly from the fact that they are the most highly educated segment of the population. We shall argue here that in the short run (and the short run can be a very long time) regional inequalities in the distribution of schooling can exacerbate ethnic conflicts. Further, it will be indicated that regional inequalities in provision of schools are virtually inevitable in areas where there has been a differential internal rate of economic and social change. This has been the case in virtually every African territory; we use Ghana to illustrate one of the latent or, perhaps more appropriately, one of the unanticipated consequences of Western formal education when it is transferred to societies possessing distinctive forms of social and political structure.

Historically, the peoples of Ghana have been exposed to European contact in a highly differential manner. Increasingly close contact was made with the coastal peoples from the late fifteenth century onward, largely through the medium of trade. A Portugese school existed in Elmina in the early sixteenth century and Danish, Dutch, and British educational institutions maintained a precarious existence in the coastal forts during the seventeenth and eighteenth centuries. By the end of the nineteenth century, after the British annexation of the whole coastal zone in 1874 and its designation as "the Colony," enrollments in Government and assisted schools stood at something over 11,000—with an unknown but probably equal number of pupils in unassisted institutions.[2] The major recipients of Western education were unquestionably the Fanti, the Ga, and the Akwapim, all of which groups were on or adjacent to the coast.

It should not be supposed, however, that the demand for Western education was initially high. The earliest representation in these coastal schools was from groups who were peripheral to traditional social structures. These were "Castle Mulattoes" and the children of African traders.[3] Indeed, although at a later stage Western education became important in succeeding to chiefly office, there is evidence that in some areas possession of schooling disqualified individuals, otherwise eligible, from assuming high status roles in traditional society. It can be argued that Western education could not have established itself without considerable difficulty in the coastal zone but for the operation of three major catalytic factors: the growth of urban centers depending on trade and exchange; the development of cash-cropping (particularly cocoa) which developed in the Akwapim area in the last decade of the nineteenth century; and finally, of course, the superimposition of effective British rule from 1874 onwards. These three factors to a varying degree were dysfunctional to the persistence of traditional social structures while, at the same time, they created new occupational and status roles, access to which was facilitated by the possession of formal education. Within this emergent context the schools could become "meaningful" institutions and there was an increasingly rapid acceleration in the level of public demand for education.

The Colony or southern portion of Ghana therefore represented the area of maximal change and the development of education was necessarily intertwined with the factors indicated above. By the middle of this century, shortly before the effective achievement of internal self-government, it was clear that the popular demand for education had far outstripped the supply, reflecting a widespread consciousness, particularly in the towns, of the occupational and status advantages accruing from education.

The position in Ashanti, however, was very different. Throughout the greater part of the nineteenth century the military power of the Ashanti Confederacy kept British interests pinned to the coastal zone and even threatened the continued existence of the Fanti states. The Ashanti resolutely opposed mission activities and the construction of schools within the Confederacy, and it was not until Ashanti was annexed in 1900 that the process of change, which had long been operative in the coastal region, began to manifest itself. The pattern of educational demand in Ashanti tended thereafter to parallel, but lag behind, that in the coastal zone. Paradoxically, therefore, the prolonged military success of the Ashanti operated to their disadvantage in the long run, since the imposition of British rule placed them in an adverse position vis-à-vis the coastal peoples in the acquisition of new occupational and status roles for which education was increasingly essential. The Ashanti were not perceptive of the instrumental importance of education until quite late in the colonial period and educational demand tended to lag some way behind that in the Colony.

If the Colony represented the area of maximal development and Ashanti an intermediate zone, then the "Northern Territories" was a region of minimal change. Up till 1900 contact there with the British was almost nonexistent, and even after its annexation in that year it cannot be said that the rate of change was marked. The development of a systematic pattern of indirect rule and the relative absence of economic change elsewhere generated by cash-cropping implied that traditional social structures remained virtually intact until the very end of British hegemony. The demand for schools remained remarkably low and many of the institutions that were created in the north remained partially empty. For these traditional societies the schools remained "meaningless" institutions that could not be functionally incorporated into their culture.

By 1948 the geographical pattern of inequality was very clear. The proportion of the population with six years of education or more stood at 5.8 per cent in the Colony, 3.9 per cent in Ashanti, but only 0.21 per cent in the Northern Territories. The continuing close association between education and urbanization processes stood out very clearly; average education levels in the larger towns were between two and three times that for the population as a whole.[4]

This kind of picture is common enough in most parts of Africa and is inevitable so long as local rates of social and economic change differ so markedly. The Ghanaian situation, however, was complicated by the coincidence of major zones of differential change with major ethnic divisions. Thus in speaking of the Colony we are also implying that it was particular ethnic groups, notably the Fanti, Ga, and Akwapim, who provided the bulk of enrollments in the few highly selective and highly prestigeful secondary schools. The Ashanti lagged behind, particularly at the secondary level, while education among northern ethnic groups was limited at all levels.

It should be clear, therefore, that these marked inequalities in educational provision might have provided a focus for the manifestation of ethnic rivalries in the competition for the very limited number of new occupational and status roles generated by British penetration and overrule. That this did not arise during the colonial period was due to the fact that there was a variable perception of the instrumental value of education among the different ethnic groups. This was greatly reinforced by the pattern of British administration itself. In general, the Colony, Ashanti, and the Northern Territories tended to be governed as distinct units with a minimal degree of "national" as opposed to local patterns of administration. In Ashanti and the Northern Territories, particularly, more systematic policies of indirect rule favored the persistence, in modified form, of traditional authority structures and political units. This policy tended to insulate the three major segments of the Gold Coast from each other and to place a premium on immediate ethnic ties and localized forms of authority. In this kind of situation overt conflict between ethnic groups for access to limited occupational opportunities was minimized and "particularistic" safeguards ensured that the "backward" areas could maintain their own local forms of administration and policies of recruitment to office based on ethnic criteria with formal education as a secondary rather than primary criterion. Though ethnic conflict was inhibited, at the same time, regional differences tended to be perpetuated.

Since the achievement of effective internal self-government in 1951, British colonial policies in this respect have been largely reversed by the government in its policy of nation building. It has tended to consistently de-emphasize the role of ethnic units as a basis for local administration and has rather stressed the importance of a far more unitary and centralized pattern of administration. To this end the former native authorities, based partially on traditional groupings, have been swept away and replaced by a secular system of district councils functioning largely on the British pattern. Although chiefs still play a considerable informal role, at the legal level their traditional authority has been minimized and they have been stripped of all but vestigial ceremonial roles. The notion of regional assemblies and the devolution of central government powers has been generally discountenanced. Above all the government has been consistent in its policy of downgrading ethnic factors in recruitment. Formally, at least, it has emphasized a policy of occupational recruitment by "merit," irrespective of regional or ethnic origin. Clearly, the primary criterion of merit is the possession of formal educational qualifications so far as government is concerned.

This policy of de-insulation has clearly placed an immense premium on schooling as a means of individual or *group* mobility, and clearly it confers marked advantages on the more educated sections of the population who come from southern ethnic divisions. During the colonial period, low levels of education among particular ethnic groups did not necessarily militate to their disadvantage, but there is now a belated recognition by some of these groups, particularly in the north, that ethnic demands for educational parity in the schools must be asserted if they are to achieve their share of the "commanding heights" in the new polity. Consequently, the present government has had to face the criticism that it has discriminated against certain ethnic minorities in the provision of education. That such criticisms are largely unjustified in view of the historical evolution of Ghana is beside the point. Inequalities do exist and provide powerful weapons in the hands of separatist or regionalist political leaders.

Paradoxically, immense government activity in education has exacerbated the situation. Between 1951 and 1960 the administration launched a massive expansion of the six-year system of primary schools and the four-year program of middle schools (Table 1). Although rates of expansion were greatest in the north, the greatest absolute increase in schooling occurred in the southern area; there was a greater volume of unmet demand for education in the south. However, in consequence, although actual levels of educational provision have arisen in all areas, the relative differences as between major ethnic groupings have also tended to increase. This result could have been forestalled only by placing rigid checks on school development in the south—a course of action that would have been politically disastrous.

However, public criticism on this score has been less than might have been expected. Since 1951 debate in the Legislative Assembly has shown an increasing preoccupation with secondary rather than with primary or middle school education, and local representatives have been far more active in criticizing the government for not providing this highly selective type of schooling. The reasons for this emphasis are not hard to discover. Traditionally, the schools in Ghana have been utilized by individuals to obtain access to prestigeful and well-paid occupations within the "modern" sector of the economy. There has correspondingly been a movement away from traditional subsistence activities among the products of the schools.

TABLE I. ENROLLMENTS IN THE GHANAIAN PRIMARY AND MIDDLE SCHOOL SYSTEM 1952/3 TO 1959 (IN THOUSANDS)[a]

	Area[b]				
Year	*The Colony*	*Ashanti*	*Trans-Volta Togoland*	*Northern Territories*	*Total*
1952/53	234	116	72	8	430
1959	335	170	101	32	638

NOTE: Since 1953, changes have been made in the designation of the various sections of Ghana but to avoid confusion earlier terminology has been adhered to here.

[a] Computed from Gold Coast, *Education Statistics 1952/1953* and Ghana, *Education Statistics 1959* (The Office of the Government Statistician, Accra).

[b] The figures here relate to a twelve-month period; the differences in dating arise from changes in the official school year. 1959 represents the last year for which comprehensive statistical returns are available.

There is little hope that such perceptions of the instrumental role of education can be readily modified. The dilemma arises that the wage-employment sector of the economy has grown at a consistently slow rate throughout the colonial and postcolonial period. At present, occupational opportunities in both the private and public sector are only expanding at a rate of between fifteen and twenty thousand per annum.[5] Meanwhile, the vast expansion of lower levels of education has raised the annual output of the middle schools alone to approximately 40,000 per annum. Excluding individuals leaving school with a six-year primary education, it is probable that not over a third of middle school leavers can find paid employment of any variety in this emergent sector of the economy. This phenomenon is not, as some observers have assumed, due to literates wishing to obtain "white-collar" employment or refusing to "work with their hands." [6] It is a more serious phenomenon of generalized unemployment due to dysfunctionalities existing between the gross rate of school expansion and the over-all rate of growth of the exchange sector of the economy.

Thus, as the volume of primary-middle school education has risen, its social and occupational "value" has drastically declined while, correspondingly, increasingly massive pressures have been generated for access into the public secondary schools. These 59 schools contained approximately 15,000 pupils in 1961, but increasingly a secondary school education is the only guarantee for obtaining adequate employment. At present, only about 6 per cent of middle school scholars can obtain entry into them and, in consequence, there has been a rapidly spreading awareness of their strategic position with respect to the whole process of occupational mobility. Indeed their importance is heightened by the fact that government controls approximately 60 per cent of employment opportunities while a high proportion of the private employment sector is dominated by larger commercial companies. These types of employer tend to stress universalistic patterns of occupational recruitment based on education. It is not surprising, therefore, given the combination of limited opportunities and a stress on educational criteria for obtaining a job, that the educational qualifications for entering many occupations are as high, if not higher, in Ghana than they are in many economically developed nations—notwithstanding the low general level of education among the population as a whole.

Just as individuals have perceived the strategic importance of secondary schools so also have ethnic groups. Criticism has been forthcoming from the Northerners, the Ashanti, and the Ewe that the government has been tardy in its plans for secondary schools in their areas, and charges of ethnic discrimination have been easy to raise. To be sure, since the bulk of these institutions (particularly those of high caliber) are in the southern section of the country, it is easy enough for the secondary schools to become pawns in a political game when secondary school programs are being considered. We must now examine, on the basis of empirical evidence, how far ethnic claims for parity in secondary education are being met and to what extent unintentional "discrimination" may exist.

First, one point must be made clear. Regional disparities in secondary school provision are large: over two-thirds of these institutions lie in the extreme southern zone. However, none of these schools recruits on a local basis in the sense that it can draw its pupils only from its immediate locale. The schools are "national" institutions in that they are free to enroll pupils from all parts of Ghana. All middle school pupils who wish to be considered for entry to a public secondary school enter for a national common entrance examination, once a year. At present, some 25,000 pupils annually compete for approximately 2,500 available places in the junior forms of public secondary schools. Thus only about 10 per cent of examinees actually obtain places.

The actual allocation of successful candidates among individual schools is the result of two major factors. The first is over-all standing in the ranked examination lists. The second is the choice of secondary schools as expressed by the students themselves when they apply for entry to the examination. It is perfectly permissible for a student to nominate a school at great distance from his home rather than one in closer proximity and, consequently, there is a tendency for more established secondary schools with long traditions of academic success to receive a high proportion of choices from pupils all over Ghana. Naturally, then, prestigeful institutions are able to freely choose from among the academically promising candidates while less established secondary schools are obliged to accept poorer scholars from lower levels on the examination rankings. The system thus tends to perpetuate a hierarchy of secondary schools differing markedly in levels of academic achievement. To a considerable degree, therefore, the occupational future of students is determined as much by the particular secondary school they attend as it is by the fact that they have completed a secondary education *per se*. Indeed it is perfectly possible to point to a cluster of high-prestige secondary schools whose students are able to obtain university entrance in proportionally greater numbers and a number of low-status schools for whose students a secondary education is becoming increasingly terminal.[7]

However, given marked geographical inequalities in the distribution of secondary schools and given also that the system tends to perpetuate academic inequalities, it is still possible to argue that the system is likely to minimize patterns of differential ethnic recruitment. A "national" system is less likely to be open to charges of ethnic discrimination than is one where the schools are unevenly distributed and recruit only from local districts or regions. Conversely, it can still be argued that the present system of academic selection tends to favor the examination success of students from occupationally and educationally superior familial backgrounds which would *pari passu* be reflected in ethnic inequalities favoring such minorities as the Ga, Fanti, and Akwapim.

We are, fortunately, in a position to test partially some of these hypotheses as a result of our comprehensive survey of social and ethnic selection into secondary schools. Thirteen of the 59 schools in the public secondary system were excluded from the study on the grounds that they were very new and not yet established institutions, while of the remaining 46 schools,

23 were selected on a stratified basis.[8] Within these schools a sample of 963 senior pupils was taken—775 boys and 188 girls, roughly in the proportions in which the sexes are distributed in the public secondary school system as a whole. The sampling procedure provided a widespread geographical distribution of schools and also gave a very representative picture of both "elite" and "low-status" institutions.

The general picture of ethnic recruitment as revealed by the survey is given in Table 2. Column *i* indicates the proportional representation of

TABLE II. ETHNIC ORIGINS OF STUDENTS COMPARED WITH THE DISTRIBUTION OF ETHNIC GROUPS IN THE TOTAL POPULATION

Ethnic Groups by Area	*(i) General Population Proportion %*	*(ii) Male Sampled Students %*	*(iii) Selectivity Index*	*(iv) Female Sampled Students %*	*(v) Selectivity Index*
Southern	*47.0*	*64.2*	*1.4*	*77.4*	*1.6*
Akwapim	2.2	5.0	2.3	10.5	4.8
Fanti	11.3	17.5	1.5	24.9	2.2
Other Akan	10.0	9.9	0.9	6.7	0.7
Ewe	12.5	16.7	1.3	11.6	0.9
Ga-Adangme	8.9	10.9	1.2	21.1	2.1
Guan	1.0	2.1	2.1	0.5	0.5
Nigerian	1.1	2.1	1.9	2.1	1.9
Central	*20.7*	*28.2*	*1.4*	*20.0*	*0.9*
Akim	3.2	3.2	1.0	5.7	1.7
Ashanti	14.1	21.9	1.6	13.2	0.9
Brong	3.4	3.1	0.9	1.1	0.3
Northern	*30.7*	*6.3*	*0.2*	*2.1*	*0.06*
Other	*1.6*	*1.3*	*0.8*	*0.5*	*0.3*
Total	*100.0*	*100.0 (775)*	*—*	*100.0 (188)*	*—*

subpopulations in terms of three major clusters and distinct ethnic divisions. Results are shown for male and female students separately since the sexes present markedly different patterns of recruitment (columns *ii* and *iv*). In order to facilitate more direct comparisons, "selectivity indices" have been computed by taking the ratios between proportions in the student bodies and in the total population.

If male students are considered first it should be clear that there is no difference in over-all selectivity as between the southern and central groupings taken as a whole. To be sure, individual ethnic variations exist and, as might be expected, the Fanti and Akwapim show somewhat higher selectivity indices than other groups. However, so also do the Ashanti, and it would seem that the present system of selection has tended to minimize major differences between ethnic groups in these zones. The same generalization does not apply to the North; here the representation is far below the mean for other areas. Northern access to secondary schools is extraordinarily limited and in this case the data do provide material supportive of regionalist dissatisfactions.

Columns *iv* and *v*, however, reveal that a very different situation prevails in patterns of female recruitment. In this case, gradients are everywhere much steeper and inequalities more marked. Distinct differences appear among the three major zones, while no less than 56.5 per cent of the students consists of Fanti, Ga, and Akwapim who together only account for 22.4 per cent of the total population. Conversely, the selectivity index for northern girls drops to a minute 0.06. This kind of picture is to be expected since female enrollments have always lagged behind male representation in Ghanaian schools and it is to be anticipated that female students will initially be drawn from the more highly urbanized and educated groups among the southern ethnic population.

This contention would tend to be confirmed by the major divergences in male and female recruitment in terms of urban/rural origin and parental level of occupation and education. A fifth of the fathers of male students but nearly half of the fathers of girls had more than ten years of schooling. A third of the boys and over half of the girls come from homes located in towns with at least 20,000 inhabitants. The fathers of one-third of the boys and two-thirds of the girls were employed in clerical or professional occupations. Girls tend to be drawn from much narrower segments of the population. Though space precludes fuller analysis of the data, there is little doubt that apparent ethnic inequalities are almost entirely explainable in terms of these other variations in student background. This type of evidence accords well with our general hypothesis that ethnic inequalities stem largely from differential internal rates of social and economic change and are not attributable to the operations of ethnic factors *per se*.

Another point of considerable significance is to consider to what extent certain ethnic groups appear to obtain preferential access into certain types of elite secondary school as measured by the latter's over-all academic success, the quality of their teaching staff, etc. Interestingly enough, when the schools were divided into elite as against low-status schools it was not possible to perceive any preferential relationship emerging. In general, ethnic groups were very evenly distributed among the two types of school. It has sometimes been suggested that the better schools do tend to draw heavily on certain ethnic groups but this was not supported by the evidence. Indeed, there was a clearly marked tendency for the better schools to include a far greater number of representatives from different tribes than did the poorer institutions which tended to draw more heavily on their immediate ethnic hinterland. These latter institutions were essentially "ethnic" schools in spite of the nature of the common entrance examination. Thus, for example, in the elite institutions the mean number of ethnic groups represented stood at 13 and in no case did a particular group provide a clear majority of scholars. Conversely, in the low-status schools the mean number of groups stood at only 6, and in every case the "local" tribe formed the majority of the sample. There is, therefore, a marked tendency for poorer institutions to increasingly become "ethnic" schools and to provide a totally different type of cultural atmosphere from that prevailing in elite schools.

In summary, therefore, the study indicates that so far as boys are concerned patterns of ethnic recruitment are rather more even than has been supposed (except for the north). Patterns of female recruitment are much more uneven, largely due to the operation of nonethnic factors. It is doubtful, indeed, in the short run that the pattern of female recruitment will change rapidly given present social and economic divergences in Ghana. A rather more disturbing phenomenon is the degree to which certain institutions are becoming more "ethnicized." Such a situation is not so serious where secondary education is in ample supply but where provision is limited the persistence of particularistic and ethnic tendencies in recruitment is to be deprecated.

It may be possible to indicate very rational causes for such inequality but such explanations do not satisfy ethnic minorities who perceive the issue as one of discrimination. Although the Ghanaian case has been studied in some detail here, it is probable that the situation is likely to repeat itself in wide range of the new nations of Africa given conditions of uneven change. Though education is by no means the only factor involved, it too presents an issue about which lines of cleavage can occur.

Perhaps the greatest tragedy is that the immediate requirements for maximal economic growth sometimes suggest that inequalities in educational provision are not disastrous and are themselves a necessary, if temporary, corollary of development. However, such judgments do not determine the nature of educational expansion and run counter to the political aspirations of the masses. For them parity of access and the universal diffusion of formal education is the point at issue. Indeed, political demands so frequently run counter to actual development requirements.

REFERENCES

1. Ethnic distributions have necessarily been computed from the 1948 Gold Coast census; these estimates are likely to be revised on publication of the Census of 1960.

2. F. Wright, "The System of Education in the Gold Coast Colony," *Special*

Reports on Educational Subjects (London, H.M.S.O., 1905), Vol. xiii, Part II, p. 3.

3. Without doubt the most valuable material on early patterns of recruitment is to be found in F. L. Bartels, "The Provision and Administration of Education in the Gold Coast, 1765–1865" (unpublished Master's thesis, Institute of Education, University of London, 1954).

4. Gold Coast, *Census of Population 1948.*

5. Some indication of trends in employment can be derived from *Ghana Quarterley Digest of Statistics* and *Economic Surveys,* 1955–1958.

6. Previous research by the present writer utilizing a substantial sample of middle school pupils indicated that there was an overwhelming preference for manual trades.

7. Thus in a sample of 366 sixth-form students studied in 1961 by the present writer, over 70 per cent were drawn from a small group of high-status institutions. The sixth form essentially constitutes the pre-university group.

8. It should be noted that there are a number of private secondary schools in Ghana but these were excluded from the sample since, generally speaking, their social role is quite insignificant compared with that of the public secondary schools. Many of them are little more than middle schools.

The Role of Village Schools in the Process of Cultural and Economic Modernization

MANNING NASH

WHEN A NATION embarks on a deliberate course of modernization there is a clear and broad mandate for the educational system. Education serves as one of the principal means of social transformation. In a newly developing nation education is viewed by the elite and their planning agents as having two chief tasks: (1) to instil the skills required for the movement of the economy from a raw-producing, agricultural-export one toward an industrial, processing and diversified agricultural economy; and (2) to produce a modern nation of dedicated citizens from a population of peasants who have small experience and understanding of civic, consensual or mobilization politics. These tasks stem in part from the elite vision of the future and in part from their appraisal of the contemporary social structure.

The universities and secondary schools in nations like Mexico, Guatemala and Burma—the nations I shall use in this paper as empirical referents for the propositions advanced—are fairly amenable to planning, to elite control and to government pressure to get on with the tasks of modernization. Of course, I do not mean that the government can or does have its way easily with the universities and secondary schools. Indeed, the recent history of universities in Southeast Asia—especially Burma—and events in Guatemala during the 1950's, indicates that universities have a built-in dynamic of independence, of resistance, and of political criticism. However, the universities, their faculties and student bodies are visible, centralized, and, even if opposed to the government or the elite, are at least speaking and acting in the same idiom and in the same universe of expectations as those who seek to find the path and means toward modernity. Universities are, in fact, one of the spearheads of modernity in any developing nation, and however ineffectual they may be at one or another moment, they are ineluctable sources or reservoirs of the culture of modernity and of the skills for economic transformation.

The village schools, on which I concentrate, are in a different relation

Reprinted, with permission of the author and publisher, from SOCIAL AND ECONOMIC STUDIES, Vol. 14, No. 1 (March, 1965), pp. 131–145.

to the government and the elite, and play a more problematic role in the process of modernization. The village schools are numerous, decentralized, less open for inspection, less amenable to manipulation, and most importantly, they are set into local communities. Higher education, in most cases, forms its own community and relates to the world community of like institutions. But the village school is embedded in an organized local community and it has neither the resources nor the ability to set itself against, or apart, from the social system of which it is but an aspect. Not only is the village school part of a locally organized society, but the community itself is but an aspect of a complex nation, a larger social and cultural system.

In order to assess the possibilities and the probabilities of various local systems of education in the process of social change aimed at speeding modernization, the first tasks are the exploration of the relation of the school to the local community, and the stipulation of the place of the local community in the complex society that is the nation. Earlier, I have had recourse to the concept of a "multiple society with plural cultures," as one attempt to conceptualize the nature of social integration in Mexico and Guatemala,[1] and I have subsequently extended and modified this notion in trying to account for the peculiar articulation of Burma.[2] And I have found the concept to be heuristic in making a comparison between Latin America and Southeast Asia,[3] so I propose to use it now to see in what manner it helps to elucidate the role of village, local education in the process of modernization. The multiple society may be defined as:

> . . . a segmented social order welding a territory and its population together by a single set of political and economic bonds. There is a class, or segment, which commands resources of national scope, carries in it the idea of nation, maintains relations with other nations, and is in some sort of touch with scientific, economic and political developments of the international community. It is this group, spread out through the national territory, in whom political control is vested and among whom political power is contested. The other segments of the multiple society are organized for regional or local purposes. They do not command political or economic power of national scope. They are, in contrast to the national elite, of small scale in social organization. Plural cultures are sometimes found in the multiple society. Not only is the political, economic, and ideological scope of the segments different, but their cultures may be also (e.g., in Burma the Kachins, Karens, and Shans are cases [and in Mexico and Guatemala the various Indian cultures are like this]).
>
> The multiple society is different from our own in that the social and cultural variations are not class variations on a basically common culture in a single social structure, but rather the society exhibits poor articulation between segments, disparities in the principles of social structure from segment to segment, and allows only the national, elite elements to be organized for purposeful political action.[4]

In treating Mexico and Guatemala, the data comes from the far end of the multiple society continuum. The Guatemalan community is a mixed Indian and Ladino *municipio* in the Western Highlands, and details of its society and culture may be found in *Machine Age Maya*.[5] The Mexican Indian community of Amatenango del Valle is an extreme instance, even for Mexico. These Indian societies are in a tense bi-cultural situation and there is much antipathy and hostility between the Indians and the environing, super-ordinate Mexican nationals (here also called, as in Guatemala, *Ladinos*. The term Ladino is primarily cultural, not biological, and it means any person who speaks Spanish as the chief language, who dresses like a member of the national society, and who is culturally indentified with a society beyond the local community. Indian-Ladino are polar opposites, and for the purposes of this paper the Ladino-ized Indian, who does exist, will be ignored). In Amatenango, there is but a single resident Ladino family, that of the school teacher.

Amatenango is a municipio with a town centre of 1,469 persons and a rural periphery of 2,529. It is an all-Indian community, and more than 90 per cent of its population are born in the municipio and spend their lives there. It is, like other Mayan Indian communities in Meso-America, a distinct local society, united by blood and custom, living on its own territory and conscious of itself as an ethnic entity. The community makes its living by agriculture on a small plot system combining the subsistence crops of maize, beans and squash with a cash wheat crop. It also is the pottery producing centre for a region between Tuxtla and Comitan. The community has many of the defensive features of the Indian peasantry of Meso-America, but it is none the less tied into the national society in at least three distinct and significant ways. First, the economic ties stemming from its relationship in the regional market economy give rise to the fact of the circulation of Mexican currency, the consumption of items produced in the national economy, the price levels being set by the forces of supply and demand on the larger stage of the region, and tenure of land being defined by the national legal code. Second, like other communities, Amatenango has been the object of special government attention. The *Instituto Nacional Indigenista* (INI) has for more than a decade carried out in this region a programme of education, road building, sanitation, medical care, and agricultural and industrial innovation. Amatenango, for example, has a clinic sponsored by INI, a store and credit society, and a piped water system installed by the agency. Thirdly, Amatenango is affected by the politics of Mexico, for the programme of "incorporation" of Indians into the national society is implemented or ignored according to shifts in politics at the national level. Also, the *ejido* (government grant of communal land) is in the political arena, and some Amatenangeros have *ejido* land in the hot country about a day's distance from the municipio. And finally, just how the Indian will fare with the police, the courts, and in the myriad legal and contractual relations Indians make with Ladinos is a function of the political climate of the nation as that is refracted in the backwoods of Chiapas.

Left on its own, that is, making a mental abstraction and eliminating from the scene all Ladinos, a community like Amatenango would not have any school at all. For the community itself continuity in culture and development of the skills needed for the maintenance of the society come through the informal means of ordinary socialization and enculturation. What is needed to be an Amatenangero is learned in the local social system, while what is needed to deal with outsiders may be learned in the local school. This puts the school and schooling in perspective: it is an extrinsic agency, part of the larger society, transmitter of a different cultural tradition, and by nature an agent of change and a source of new and wider mental horizons. That the school has not radically transformed the community, or in fact made much of a dent in its illiteracy is a function of two facts: the major concerns of the people of Amatenango, and the character of the incumbent school teacher.

The people of Amatenango are, because of their place in the multiple society and due to the long history of acrimonious ethnic relations in Chiapas, not concerned with becoming Ladinos, and the process of acculturation over nearly 400 years has not eroded the ethnic distinctiveness of the society, whatever cultural items and traits they have borrowed and accepted from Ladino society. The Amatenangeros have major interests in making a living, a mundane business of getting along with neighbours, and keeping the proper relations between the society and the supernatural. For these ends, the school counts little. Nothing in the curriculum implements the ends of Amatenango Indians.

The school itself is set in the central square of the town centre in an adobe building. The Ladino teacher and his family (his wife and daughters serve as assistant teachers) make their residence in the school compound. About 280 students (130 girls and 150 boys) are usually enrolled in the three grades that the school offers. (There is another school of about 50 students in the rural *barrio* of Madronal.) The major tasks of the school are the teaching of Spanish and the elementary skills of reading and writing. The normal language of the household and the streets of Amatenango is Tzeltal, and if anybody learns Spanish it is as a second language. Men in Amatenango have a much higher fluency in Spanish than do women. By rough percentages, for the town centre, better than 85 per cent of the men are to some extent bilingual, while just the reverse is true for women, of whom more than 85 per cent are mono-lingual in Tzeltal. Among children from six to twelve years of age (in 1959, when all of these data were collected in the field) the percentages of bi-linguality of both boys and girls was about 75 per cent. What is clear from this figure is that the three or four years of school does instil some basic Spanish language skills in both boys and girls, but that men, because they travel, meet Ladinos, sometimes work for them and have other contacts with them, while women do not; hence men increase their Spanish over their lifetimes, while the Spanish of the women tends to erode and decay from lack of occasion for use.

The literacy rates, even in the most loosely defined notion of functional literacy, are about 15 per cent for the males, and under 5 per cent for the females, indicating the difficulty of transfer of the skills from school to everyday life, where they are not called for at all. The only reading matter I ever observed in Amatenango were comic books in simple basic Spanish, an occasional newspaper, and government decrees. Outside of the Indian officials in office, it is safe to estimate that the population of the town centre, collectively, spends less than one hour a day in contact with the printed word.

The innovative potential of village education—for the school does follow the national curriculum and does try to instil some history, some geography, some patriotism, and some arithmetic as well as the national language and literature—is thus clearly circumscribed by the total operation of Amatenango as a society with its given value system and its place in a multiple social structure. It is further hampered by the character of the school teacher himself. The teacher and his family are socially isolated from the Indians. At night he locks up his school and his house, and given the numerous guns he has, the place has something of the aspect of a fortress. The analogy is deliberate. The teacher is an alien in the midst of a people he does not understand and does not completely trust. On their side the Amatenangeros neither respect nor trust the school teacher. He leaves on any occasion, his life is tied to the nearby city, not the village, and even if he should wish, he could not get into the intimate daily life of the community. He is overbearing, authoritarian, and not particularly gentle in his relations with the Indians. Furthermore he is a state of Chiapas employee, and hence not responsible to the local community, and they in no way influence the conduct or the content of teaching. The school scratches the surface of Amatenango life, because that life is oriented to its own concerns, and because the teacher is a social irritant in an alien community, not the representative, however humble, of a respected *literati.*

What revolutionary or innovative potential schooling may in fact have when it is divorced from the constraints of local society is exemplified by a social experiment carried out in Indian communities about 20 years ago. There was a programme of boarding schools (*internados*) instituted by the Mexican government to train some Indians in each community in Spanish speech and literature. Young boys and girls were taken from their families and put into boarding schools and kept from four to six years. Of the ten taken from Amatenango into the programme, all are now resident in Amatenango, all of them are still bi-lingual, and all of them are literate. Furthermore they have worked out to be something of an elite, in the sense that they relate the community to a Ladino world that they understand much better than their fellow villagers, and they have held the top offices in the village civil and religious hierarchy. They have, at least some of the men, moved over to a Ladino style dress, and have a comparatively expanded view of the world. Also some of them have taken on jobs (like store keeper) that no other Indian could handle, and furthermore they are the people who have married outside of the habitual rule of village endogamy. They have married Indian women from other communities who were ladinoized enough to give up traditional Indian costume.

The boarding school experience does indicate that elementary schooling can result in important social change, even for people at the end of multiple society, but that it must be withdrawn from the community constraints, when the community is organized as is Amatenango.

By way of contrast of Amatenango, but still in the same social species or type, is the Guatemalan Indian community of Cantel. Cantel is a more sophisticated community of Maya Indians in a double sense than is Amatenango. It apparently had a richer Mayan heritage (in the area where Quiché was and is spoken), and it has been in longer, more intimate contact with Guatemalan Ladino society than has Amatenango. If I can hazard a forecast, when the road net around Amatenango now in construction gets to the level that Cantel has enjoyed for 20 years, Amatenango will begin to approximate many of the structural and cultural features of Cantel. The municipio of Cantel is also more populous. Its town centre (in 1954, when the field census was taken) had a population of 1,910 and its outlying areas had 6,585 souls. In the town centre (*pueblo*), on which I shall focus, the Indians accounted for 96.2 of the population, and the remaining 3.8 were Ladinos. In the pueblo, 17.7 of the population were engaged in specialist occupations (not all of them full time) and more than a quarter of the work force was in the textile factory just across the river from the town centre. In short, the town centre was a bustling, cosmopolitan, and specialized place compared to the agricultural village of Amatenango. But still Cantel was a distinct social and cultural entity, both in objective fact and in their self perception as Cantelenos whose customs were different, not only from Ladinos but, say, from their Zunil, Almolonga, Totonicipan, or Quezaltenango neighbours.

There were in Cantel two schools. One was the national school, the other run by the factory for children of factory workers. The school attendance in Cantel was slightly better than that of Amatenango (my remarks and data are restricted to the town centre and the canton of Pasac), but the difficulty of meeting the compulsory attendance of children from age seven to age fourteen was about the same. Where school and work conflict in societies at this level of income, work always wins. Poverty coupled with familial agricultural production has the effect of drawing children out of school as soon as they are useful in the fields. Cantel's schools offered up to sixth grade education. But the enrolment figures are revealing: in the first three grades are 300 pupils; in the fifth and sixth grades combined there are only 20 pupils. Still, the fact that 20 students a year get up to the sixth grade level gives Cantel a greater edge on the modernity and national integration scales than Amatenango.

By the same loose definition of literacy, about 60 per cent of the Cantelense are illiterate, and this is about the national average, while Amatenango was above the reported Mexican average. Bi-lingualism in the town centre is much greater for women than it is in Amatenango, and most men can handle elementary Spanish.

The schools are, as they are in Mexico, agencies of the national government, transmitters of the national culture, and divorced from the community in regards of support or of control. The school teacher is a Ladino, somewhat marginal to the community but not so nearly an alien as in Amatenango.

That the schools have not been more of a radical agent of social change than in fact they have been in Cantel is accounted for by two major facts. First, the poverty of the community and the nation keeps many children from more than three years of education, where they barely learn the elementary skills; and secondly the national government is, and has been, hesitant about how to incorporate Indians into the political society of Guatemala. Thus the schools are not seen, nor used as catalysts in social change, but are confined to transmission of elementary skills, some patriotism, and some minor facts about history and geography. But these schools could, if an ideology activated them, if more resources were poured in, if more teachers were assigned, if more books . . .—but why catalogue the needs of any underdeveloped country?—act more forcefully as agents of change. This requires not only the necessary expenditures, but a clear and definite programme among the national segment as to the role of the Indian in Guatemalan society. This programme is but vaguely enunciated and defined, and this very hesitancy, plus the lack of scale in investment, keeps the schools in a marginal role in fostering modernity.

One strong index of the impact of both schools and factory on the children of Cantel is found in the occupational aspirations of school children. Interviewing (in 1953-54 when all of the data were collected) 136 boys and girls between the ages of 10 and 15 in both the Pueblo and Pasac schools, for job preferences, revealed the predominance of a preference for artisan or specialist occupations. These occupational aspirations are at variance with the chief uses of manpower in the community and far exceed the foreseeable demand for the kinds of jobs and services selected by school children. What these aspirations seem to indicate is a continuance of the basic community values of self-employment and economic independence or self-sufficiency. Formerly these values were expressed in terms of land holding, but the pressure of a growing population on a fixed land base has moved the loci of the values to artisan or specialist occupations. This younger generation of school-educated are willing to try occupations which may cut them off from some of the roots of community life and possibly alienate them from the local society. It appears that schooling, even under the restricted conditions of Cantel, does have the potential for social change and mental expansion.

Part of the receptivity to change in the economic sphere among the school-educated of Cantel is intimately linked to the political events of the preceding decade, and points up again the fact that, in multiple societies structured like Guatemala, political events on the national scene are likely to be decisive in social and economic change in local communities. The school can and does act as agency of the national society, and in the interaction between the school and the community lies an important source for receptivity or resistance to change.

In Cantel, the generational differences of the effect of both educational and political change are fairly clearly marked. The older generation lost much influence, power and respect to the younger more literate and less traditional members of society,[6] and this is echoed even in the consequences of schooling. Of the adults attending a night school for literacy, only one thought of an occupation outside of the traditional roster of Cantel (and, of course, those willing to come to night school on their own for the rewards of literacy represent the most progressive of the older generation). In short, those who are "well built-in" members of the society and of middle age cannot afford the risks of mobility, of loss of social obligation and support and the adventures of new careers. This generational difference underlines yet another important generalization: in local communities the village school begins to instil different values from those of the local community, but adulthood, the claims of mundane life, the competition of the known with the unknown, and the absence of supporting institutions beyond the schools make these values, in most instances, atrophy and eventually disappear.

Through a contrast with another newly developing nation, Burma, the highlights of the place of village education in modernization may be, I believe, better approximated. The value of contrasting such culturally and historically disparate societies is akin to the role of litmus paper in bringing out the special ingredients of the differing social mixtures. And, of course, one reason for attempting the contrast is that I have field work experience in Burma, so that comparability comes as much from the general categories of social prehension as it does from the simple fact that the same mind and methods have gathered and interpreted the data of observation.

A review of the recent history of Burmese education is available in Tinker[6] (1962), and the current state of the University is well summarized in Fischer.[7] The description of the village schools I give is restricted to Upper Burma (above the 40 inch *ishopyet*) and stems from the period 1960-61.

Burma, as a new nation, fits within the general category of a multiple society,[8] but its multiplicity is different from that of the Meso-American societies sketched earlier. Elsewhere, the multiplicity of Burma a decade after independence was characterized as:

> A thin modern elite was the national segment of the new nation. There were administrators from the old civil service, the politicians schooled in agitational politics, the army officer corps, and a sprinkling of intellectuals, professional and businessmen. This group has been

> called the political class. It ruled over a peasantry, the "hill peoples," and the other non-national indigenous peoples. In lieu of the former colonial civil servants, nationals now filled all the ranks, and a single political party, driven by internal strife and jealousies, emerged as the legitimate political custodian of sovereignty . . . The key to membership in the national segment is the command over some of the skills needed to run large and complex organizations of persons and resources . . .[9]

Within this multiple, poorly articulated society, the peasants of Burma were to be turned into modern farmers, or industrial workers, and responsible dedicated citizens, enlisted in and implementing the elite's drive to the Burmese version of a welfare, socialist society. (All of this refers to a time before the second take-over of General Ne Win. His military coup does not much, so far, affect the structure of Burmese society. It has merely changed or eliminated some of the personnel in the elite segment, but it, too, seems to be groping for the keys to giving social vitality and meaning to slogans and programmes of contemporary Burma.)

Burma is a relatively poor nation, and given the war time devastation, it has not the capacity to give all of its citizens a primary education. School attendance cannot be made compulsory. In 1960-61, in Burma, of 30,000 village tracts, only about 10,000 of them have primary schools, and some of them have neither primary schools nor monastic schools (*kyaung* is Burmese for school and *pongyi kyaung* is school run by monks in which literacy, some religious knowledge and some Pali are taught). There are not enough facilities to take all the children who are eligible for education, physical plant is likewise insufficient, and finally there is a shortage of qualified teachers.

I do not want to concentrate on the constraints in resources and personnel, but rather to characterize village schooling in Upper Burma to show the place of the school in the community, the relations of the community to the larger society, and possibilities of the educational system as a means of implementing a transformation in the basic structure of Burmese values and social organization. The data come from two villages, one a mixed, dry crop community south and west of Mandalay in the Sagaing region, the other a wet rice farming community in the Mandalay district about seven miles south of Mandalay. Between these two communities they approximate the range of social and cultural variety among the peasantry of Upper Burma. Unlike Meso-America, the village and communities of Upper Burma are not distinct cultural entities, rather they are variations on a common regional culture, located expressions of cultural organization of a tradition deep and widespread in the region. Further, villages do not have the restrictive, bounded social corporateness of Meso-American Indians. These villagers are inhabitants of a country known to them, the rural extension of Burmese society and culture. They are much more akin in their status to the Ladino in Guatemala than to the Indian, although even this analogy is somewhat misleading.

In the mixed crop village there are two schools, one a government school, the other a *pongyi kyaung,* although both schools are housed in *pongyi kyaungs.* The physical plant of the schools is a modest wooden structure raised high on stilts. The government school contains both *koyin* (novices in the Burmese Buddhist order of monks the *sangha*) and *kyaungtha* (secular students). In the village primary school there are 70 students (15 girls and 55 boys), while in the *kyaung,* taught only by monks, are 15 students. The whole school population is then 106 students. With a population of 553, this is virtually everybody in the community who is eligible for school, even though attendance is not compulsory. This attendance reflects the greater wealth of a Burmese peasant village compared to a community like Amatenango, and it also indicates the high value placed on literacy and the role of the religious heritage of Buddhism which for centuries has schooled the peasantry in the rudiments of reading and writing, and also it marks the great differences between being a multiple society with plural cultures when one of the cultures (as in Amatenango) is subordinate, and being the rural component of a continuous social organization (as in the Burmese peasantry).

Education for the village boy or girl virtually stops at the fourth standard and in the last two years only 4 students (2 boys and 2 girls) have gone beyond the fourth standard.

The two schools are virtually identical in method and content of teaching, although the *pongyi kyaung* teaches some Pali, and the Buddhist cosmology while the state primary school includes some history, arithmetic and general science. *Pongyis* occasionally strike recalcitrant students; state teachers have given up that practice. In a Burmese village the teacher's role is one of great respect and the social distance between teacher and pupil is correspondingly great. In traditional Buddhist belief the objects of great honour are: the Buddha, the Sangha, the Dhamma (the teaching of the Buddha) the parents and the teacher. At many public ceremonials children give honour to these five worthy objects. Teachers are considered the repositories of knowledge. The job of the teacher is to lead the student forth into the exploration of a fixed body of knowledge. The role definition of the superordinate, learned teacher *vis a vis* subordinated pupil, with the task structure of communicating fixed knowledge, makes teaching a rather rote business. Students have the goal of acquiring knowledge letter-perfect, not to challenge, innovate or question either the teacher or the information he transmits. The teacher and his teaching are traditional authorities and the psychological stance of the pupil is that of "traditionality," a reverence for authority and for the pastness of things. Hence the method of teaching is oriented to train the memory, to stuff the mind, and to fix a respect for what is already known. Students are rewarded for feats of memory, for long letter perfect recitations, and for knowing answers to standard questions.

The method of teaching is much more suited to social continuity and stability than it is to social change and innovation. The village educational system is one of the agencies for cultural transmission; it is a means for the maintenance of the traditional culture. Other educational agencies in the village exhibit the features that the school does: learning goes from respected elder to reverential junior, stress on learning by rote, and reward for traditional knowledge. The village school is not detached from other educative agencies of the community, and hence does not have its own standards, ethics or momentum. It is only an extension of a local society teaching its young to be members.

In the abstract, education is one of the most highly valued things in Burmese life; in fact, support for schools and teachers at the local level is meagre. Villagers do not support by contribution, by labour, or through organization in the local schools. That is the government's job and they have no social sense about government projects. The operative values of villagers are plain enough, both in their speech and in their activities when they are faced with real choices. They want to make a living, get along with relatives and neighbours, earn respect and honour, and lay up a store of *kutho* (merit), so that in the next life they may have a favourable rebirth. If education does not implement or bear on these concerns, it does not engage the interest of the villagers. As a consumption good, education is not in village purview. Education should conduce to economic gain, and that is why village boys go beyond the fourth standard, to be clerks, teachers, or civil servants, to take on a middle-class style of life in an urbanized setting. Or education should lead to the enhancement of one's chances for favourable rebirths, and that is why monastic education is pursued. Finally education means a display of refined handling of common knowledge, for that is how an educated man gets respect. An education oriented to manipulating nature, changing the world, intellectual curiosity and exploration is not worth the villagers' time and resources. From this value stance it follows that girls get less education than boys, that attendance is spotty, and that every household or religious task has priority over education.

The teachers in this village are not native to it; they come from a nearby village. This may, in part, explain their inability to get local support for the school, but it does not account for their equally bad luck with national authorities. The village teacher is the lowest rung in the educational bureaucracy. Before making any demands his request must be processed through a bewildering hierarchy of officials. As the student before the teacher, so the teacher before superordinate officials: a feeling of powerlessness. His only means of coping is compliance in the official context. The teacher is aware that the basic educational decisions are political events. For him the educational system is at once too much and too little politicized; too much so because the political parties decide on the principles of education, and too little so because the teachers are an ineffective political organization.

A poor village in the Mandalay district, which makes its living by wet rice farming, amplifies and extends some of the contentions made above. This village has a primary school, and it exhibits the same teacher-pupil relationship and the same traditionality. It has that same element of *anade* —a complex value and attitude implicating reluctance or shame if a junior should question a senior or contradict his teacher. The school is also an embedded institution lacking autonomy or a dynamic of its own. The villagers do not control it, barely support it, and they expect the school to give their children only the minimal skills of functional literacy.

In the four standards of this school there are 110 children on the rolls: the first has 82, while the fourth has but 10. In the first are 36 boys and 46 girls, in the fourth, 8 boys and 2 girls. The sex and numerical skewing manifests the economic facts of life in this community. It is poor. Many of the people do not have enough land to meet even the modest demands of the Burmese peasant. Rice growing is a labour-intensive activity for several months of the year. Education competes with child labour in the fields, and at age 10 or 11 (the fourth standard) children are useful field hands. Girls can help their mothers, as well as work in the fields, so they drop out more drastically than do boys. In the lower standards attendance is episodic, and for the four months I have data, daily school attendance never exceeded 80 of the 110 on the rolls. Regular attendance is a problem unsolved.

The school is scheduled to have three teachers, but there is only one. There is a teacher shortage at the village level, and its causes are not obscure. The teacher who remained in this village is native to it; her family and friends live in it. Her job as teacher is a second income, for her husband also teaches in a nearby community. She does not have a modern, nor heavy investment in her teaching skills. She has only a seventh standard education, plus a year training course taken in the late 1930's. For her, village teaching is a reasonable, useful and not unexciting life. For the young graduate from a teacher training school life in a poor village is repellent. Being assigned to a strange village is almost a sentence to exile, boredom and frustration for a young graduate. The salaries and life-style of beginning teachers do not compensate for these evils. It takes devotion and idealism for a rural school teacher to persevere with an assignment in a village.

This rice village indicates the pressure of poverty upon the Burmese village school. Poverty does not shape the Burmese village school, it is not the root of its difficulties; it merely exacerbates them. The point is here laboured because there is a prevalent belief that money and means would solve all the ills of local education. What increased investment would do, in the absence of social and cultural change, is merely to shift schools like the one in the rice village toward the full achievement of the Burmese pattern as exemplified in the mixed crop and in the 36 villages I surveyed.

The comparisons in this paper may be summed up in two columns:

BURMA	MEXICO-GUATEMALA
Education tied to rest of institutions	School as extension of national society
Main task, enculturation	Oriented to change of values
Knowledge is not a novelty, does not touch major concern	Local support not relevant
Unoriented to change	Authoritarian teacher-pupil relations
Authoritarian teacher-pupil relations	Knowledge not fixed
Completion of primary school depends on economic opportunity	Motives for completion economic
Local support minimal	Image of educated man partly traditional
Teachers barely trained	Teachers undertrained
Resource poor	Major value: creation of citizens
Image of educated person traditional	Minor value: literacy

What this profile shows (providing, in fact, it does fit more than the data from which it is derived and justifies the bold use of national society labels) is that the educational system in Burma is a different species from that of Mexico and Guatemala, which latter both belong together. The similarities in the profiles stem from the relative poverty of the nations and the tremendous costs of implementing a primary education programme at such a late stage in national history. The differences in the educational systems are reflections of the larger social and cultural differences, and spell out at a micro-level the meaning of a recently sovereign nation in Southeast Asia, with a Buddhist cultural tradition, oriented to reaching a form of democratic socialism, as against two Latin American societies with a Spanish-colonial heritage, being strongly involved in both Westernization and modernization. These differences affect the method of teaching, the content of reaching, and the place of the village school in local communities and in national plans. The contrast also underlines the different potentials for a given local system of education to absorb and use creatively more investment. The mechanical formula of pouring resources into schooling is hence recast into a broader framework of viewing a set of social and cultural consequences and possible economic payoffs.

Three very general propositions about village schools in the process of social change may be hazarded on the basis of the foregoing:

1. It is change in the economic, religious and interpersonal relations on the local and regional levels which are antecedent to change in the educational system.
2. Local schools tend to be conservative agents, transmitting by means that reinfórce local tendencies toward stability.
3. Education becomes a force for social change only when the process of social change is well underway.

The practical and procedural consequences of these propositions are fairly self-evident. What is needed is to verify them with a wider sample than that given here. However, it is clear that the diagnostic tools of social science, its abilities to distinguish between types of poverty and types of social system are valuable ingredients in translating any plan into practice, and even in foreseeing, however opaquely, some of the consequences of a given course of action.

FOOTNOTES

1. Manning Nash, "The Multiple Society in Economic Development. Mexico and Guatemala." *American Anthropologist,* Vol. 59, pp. 825–33, 1957.
2. Manning Nash, "Southeast Asian Society Dual or Multiple." *Journal of Asian Studies,* Vol. 23, pp. 417–423, 1964.
3. Manning Nash, "Social Prerequisites to Economic Growth in Latin America and Southeast Asia." *Economic Development and Cultural Change,* Vol. XII, pp. 225–42, 1964.
4. Manning Nash, "The Multiple Society in Economic Development." *op. cit.*
5. Manning Nash, *Machine Age Maya.* Glencoe, Ill., The Free Press, 1958.
6. Hugh Tinker, *The Union of Burma,* Chatham House, 1962.
7. Joseph Fischer, *Universities in Southeast Asia.* International Education Monograph No. 6. Columbus, Ohio, Ohio State Press, 1964.
8. Manning Nash, "Southeast Asian Society Dual or Multiple." *op. cit.*
9. Manning Nash, "Social Prerequisites to Economic Growth in Latin America and Southeast Asia." *op. cit.*

*Deliberate Instruction Within Family Units**

WARREN O. HAGSTROM

EDUCATIONAL PLANNERS and administrators have neglected the family as an educational resource. This may be a justifiable neglect, but it has not been justified. Behavioral scientists, if they have studied the relations between the family and education, have been primarily concerned with *motivation* and with *opportunities*. They have not considered the family as an arena in which persons may teach and be taught. I shall be concerned here with deliberate instruction in complex skills in family settings. By "deliberate instruction" I mean situations where one person seeks to give another competence in certain skills and knowledge, where both teacher and taught recognize this as a primary purpose of the interaction, and where this instruction is neither incidental to practical activities nor part of play and games. By "complex skills" I mean motor and conceptual skills persons seldom acquire on their own—skills such as reading, performing music, driving an automobile, sailing a boat, or performing a magical rite. Both the "deliberateness" of instruction and the "complexity" of skills are variable. An examination of instruction in families suggests new ways of relating such topics as education in primitive societies, tutoring, apprenticeship, and the social psychology of interpersonal relations.

What I shall argue is that deliberate instruction in complex skills very rarely takes place in families. A possible explanation is that persons find the roles of teacher and student incompatible with the roles of parent and child. This role conflict may take different forms in traditional and modern societies, but the effect is similar. Nevertheless, learning obviously occurs in families. *Moral* instruction is probably universal. Technical learning may occur often as an incidental aspect of practical work in traditional societies, and it may occur often as an incidental aspect of play in both traditional and modern societies.

Instruction in the family can be studied in developed societies; some technical skills, such as driving, are commonly taught, and in some exceptional families, such as those of child prodigies, great competence in some skills is achieved after parental instruction. However, the skills taught or the families in which they are taught may be quite unusual, and such studies cannot give us an idea of what it would be like if families were schools. I have chosen instead to examine two social contexts in which familial instruction might be more typical, primitive societies without schools and the aristocratic strata of societies without boarding schools. Each of these will be discussed in the following pages. I shall then briefly discuss a social psychological theory of the role conflict between teaching and familial roles. Finally I shall summarize some of the major changes occurring in all societies with industrialization and relate them to the preceding.

ETHNOGRAPHIC DATA

Many societies make no arrangements for "education" outside the nuclear family of parents and children. Complex skills in hunting, agriculture, construction, religion, and other subjects are transmitted to children largely from parents. Thus, such societies should be excellent "natural experiments" for the study of systematic instruction in family settings. However, a search of ethnographic studies reveals that little attention has been devoted to the subject by anthropologists. In their detailed and extensive studies of infant and child care, one can find meticulous descriptions of weaning and toilet training, punishment, patterns of deference, children's work and play, but few references to instruction in complex skills. The reason for this is clear: *In societies without schools, instruction in complex skills (and in general skills) is seldom differentiated from other social activities.* If children learn, they learn as an incidental aspect of their play, or productive work, or even more casually.[1] Such "education" is evidently quite effective.[2] However, the fact remains that we do not know why education in families takes only these forms. An answer may be obtained if the question is turned around. Under what conditions is education in the family found wanting? Why do societies establish schools?

Anthropologists have attempted to answer these questions by invoking the development of social stratification, the decline of the extended family, or the growth of political complexity. The first was emphasized by Margaret Mead, who argued that the development of social classes caused societies to introduce schools (or, more generally, extra-familial instruction) (Mead, 1943). Stratification creates the possibility of a difference in social rank between parent and child. Then, according to Mead, individuals recognize this and recognize that educational experiences or the lack of such experiences may lead to a shift of class position. Some extra-familial agency is required to give these educational experiences, since real or potential discontinuities mean that parents are not considered able to teach their own children. While in the modern world this agency is usually the secular school, in highly stratified pre-industrial societies it may be a religious organization, a "bush school," or some form of apprenticeship.

A second hypothesis about the origins of schools can be obtained by generalizing the argument made by the historian Bernard Bailyn with regard to American schools (Bailyn, 1960, pp. 15-25). He argued that the function of education was discharged by the extended family in seventeenth-century England; such a family, including several adults well integrated in the larger community, had the resources and the power to perform essential educational functions. For various reasons this family could not be maintained in the American environment. Instead there developed the "isolated nuclear family" of parents and young children. This family lacked the resources to educate its own children, and in the American environment schools were developed to fill the gap. More generally, one can advance the hypothesis that extra-familial educational institutions will tend to be present in societies in which the extended family is weak and the nuclear family is relatively isolated.

This hypothesis was tested and found wanting by John D. Herzog (Herzog, 1962). Herzog studied ethnographic reports of 119 societies and used them to classify the societies by type of instructional system, type of family, political integration, and other variables. He recognized three classes of "deliberate instruction": by kin, by non-kin without change of residence of the student, and by non-kin with a required change of residence.

Before considering the bearing of Herzog's findings on the hypotheses of Mead and Bailyn, some of his results must be examined. Herzog found deliberate instruction by kin present in 59 per cent of the 79 societies for which information was available. This contradicts the assertion above about the absence of deliberate instruction by kin in known societies. To resolve this contradiction would require at least a re-examination of the ethnographic reports used by Herzog in classifying all 79 societies. Even this would probably not be enough, since the ethnographic reports are often very sketchy. Herzog himself reported that the classification of societies according to the presence or absence of instruction by kin was "intuitively unsatisfactory." For example, he classified the Balinese as a society in which children were instructed by kin; the basis for this was a report devoting less than two pages to the education of children, and the description of education by kin is vague enough to permit the interpretation that such "education" is not deliberate but is instead an incidental aspect of play and work.[3] While many of the ethnographic reports are equally sketchy, some provide stronger evidence for the presence of deliberate instruction by kin. Holmberg's description of the way a Siriono boy learns to hunt strongly suggests that he is taught by his father (Holmberg, 1950, pp. 77-80). Wallace and Hoebel (1952, pp. 126f.) assert that the Comanche boy was deliberately taught tribal lore and hunting by his grandfather. Leighton and Kluckhohn (1947, pp. 50-59) write that the Navaho child is taught agricultural and household skills primarily by his parent of the same sex. Clearly, in some societies some complex skills are deliberately taught by kin. But while the ethnographic accounts may establish the fact of instruction, they do not describe it; they do not adequately describe the content of the instruction (perhaps the skills are not especially complex and are easily learned), the pedagogical techniques (perhaps instruction often occurs in a play setting or is an incidental aspect of work), or the interpersonal strains instruction may produce. In any case, the scanty attention devoted to instruction in most ethnographic reports strongly suggests that deliberate instruction, even when it exists, is not a salient or important activity in the societies described.

Herzog's other types of deliberate instruction involve teaching by non-kin. His data show the reverse of the hypothesis extracted from the work of Bailyn: instruction by non-kin is *less* likely in societies in which the nuclear family is relatively isolated and *more* likely in societies with strong extended families. Even so, the correlation between type of family and type of instruction is smaller than the correlation between "political integration" and type of instruction; the former correlation is greatly reduced when political integration is held constant. Political integration goes along with social stratification (cf. Chaney, 1966, p. 1465), and these results thus tend to confirm Mead's hypothesis about schools.[4] Herzog, however, seeks a psychological explanation of the correlations. Basically he argues that the family household structure—the role of extended kin, residence rules, the economic roles of mothers, and the presence or absence of polygyny—plays a large role in determining psychological relations between parents and children. Extra-familial deliberate instruction may function to weaken the dependency of children on their parents (or, more particularly, their mothers). This can be stated most clearly for extra-familial instruction with a required change of residence. In many societies children live with their mothers apart from their fathers; this is especially common in polygynous societies. Given this type of "mother-child" household, instruction by non-kin with a change of residence is very likely. More or less severe initiation ceremonies are likely to be found in the same societies. This type of instruction has the same function as the initiation ceremony; it reduces the boy's dependence upon and identification with his mother, which is likely to be especially strong and problematical in this type of family system.

Herzog has attempted to extend a theory of initiation ceremonies to the educational context. The theory of initiation ceremonies is itself suspect and is the subject of numerous polemical articles.[5] Furthermore, Herzog's study exemplifies many of the serious defects of the cross-cultural approach (cf. Zelditch, 1964). The most serious of these is the placement of grossly different phenomena into the same class. Thus, the West African bush school (Watkins, 1963) as well as the English Eton are both extra-familial instruction with change of residence, and the American public school and the Kikuyu initiation school are both extra-familial instruction without change of residence. Moreover, different persons reading the same ethnographic accounts classify a society differently; the scheme is relatively unreliable (Herzog, 1962, p. 309). The sampling procedure treats as "independent cases" societies which may very well have influenced one another; thus, Herzog's sample includes both the Serbs and the Bulgarians, both the Tlingit and the Yurok (Indians of the Northwest

American coast). An example of the type of problem this produces is Herzog's classification of the Mixtecans (a Mexican Indian people) as a society in which extra-familial instruction is present. The ethnographic account (in B. Whiting, 1963) clearly indicates that the Mixtecans have been compelled to send their children to school by Mexican government authorities. A final defect this study shares with other cross-cultural studies is its attribution of "stability" to societies undergoing rapid change; colonization and industrialization have been transforming educational practices for two centuries or longer in many of the societies in Herzog's sample, but the possibility of change is neglected in his classification procedures.

Despite these serious defects, Herzog's study is valuable as a pioneering effort in an important substantive area. More important, his theory includes a significant insight: an important latent function of schools may be to make children less dependent on their parents. As Herzog points out, the importance of this function, and the way in which it is performed, will depend upon the nature of the family; this should hold true both between societies and within a particular society (Herzog, 1962, pp. 333-336).

The anthropological data referred to in the preceding pages can be summarized in the following three propositions:

1. In societies without schools, instruction within families is seldom "deliberate" but occurs in the course of ordinary work and in play and games.
2. Societies are likely to establish schools or other forms of extra-familial instruction when they reach a stage of complexity such that children will often play different adult roles than their parents; this stage is typically associated with the development of social classes and political centralization.
3. Education in the family is likely to be associated with the prolonged emotional dependence of children on their parents (either both parents or, in some cases, the mother); schools and other forms of extra-familial education, like initiation ceremonies, may have the function of attenuating this dependency.

These hypotheses emerge from a relatively gross and superficial comparison of societies with and societies without schools. Some anthropologists have given us more detailed reports of schools in more or less primitive and traditional societies. These reports lead to a qualification and extension of the hypotheses just stated.

First, the obvious idea that schools exist in societies because parents are themselves not proficient in essential skills and cannot teach them is supported by the critical role of reading and writing in the schools of pre-industrial societies. These are the major skills learned (if they are learned), and most children do not continue their education beyond this elementary stage. They are the clearest examples of "impractical" skills for children. A child's ability to read is unlikely to help his family perform the adaptive tasks of an agrarian or extractive society. Thus, the child is taught to read in order to benefit him at some indefinite future time; his family will benefit indirectly, if at all. Literacy cannot be acquired merely by participating in work and play. These aspects of literacy training are in accord with Margaret Mead's hypothesis about the social function of schools: the child must learn to read in order to play a potentially *different* role from that of his parents. It is also true that the literacy of a society is associated with its political centralization and its stratification.[6] If Herzog is correct, and the development of schools is more strongly correlated with the political centralization of societies than with other variables, the specific instructional tasks will be in the area of literacy. Herzog's own sample of societies can be used to test this type of hypothesis. While the ethnographic data do not give the extent of literacy in societies, a crude indicator of the importance of literacy is the presence or absence of a "book religion"—Christianity, Islam, Buddhism, or Hinduism. Preindustrial societies without book religions are likely to place less value on literacy or even to be without a written language. When the societies in Herzog's sample are classified by the presence or absence of a book religion, it is found that this variable has a much higher correlation with the presence of extra-familial instruction than political integration or other variables.[7] The data suggest the importance of a written language in causing societies to have schools: literacy skills are not readily acquired in family settings.

A second insight into the relations between schools and families that is provided by detailed ethnographic reports concerns the assistance given by the family to the school. Most reports suggest that parents are either unable or unwilling to assist children with school work. In colonial situations parents may oppose the goals of the schools; even when they do not, parents are unlikely to assist their children in homework or to encourage them to do homework. (See the reports in B. Whiting, 1963, and Fischer, 1963.) Parents are not necessarily indifferent to the school success or failure of their children. Usually, however, success and failure are not clearly marked. Societies with strong extended families evidently do not encourage competitiveness in children, and their schools usually do not do so either. Herzog's impression is that schools in such societies have a "very different flavor" than our own. " 'Rote learning' is emphasized; the status differential between teacher and pupil is relatively larger; a variety of levels of achievement is not recognized, as a rule, all students striving to meet the same tradition-decreed goals" (Herzog, 1962, p. 326). A common pedagogical technique is for the entire class to recite in unison with or for the teacher.

When failure is clearly marked, parents tend to react either fatalistically or with hostility toward the child. On the one hand, some parents do not believe that a child's school success is greatly influenced by his own endeavors. On the other, some may believe that success results from obedience; failure is attributed to disobedience and may lead to parental rejection.[8] If these reactions are a serious problem when schooling is largely segregated from family life, they would undoubtedly be a much more serious problem if parents themselves attempted to instruct children in complex skills such as reading.

The importance of reading and writing in the schools of traditional societies at first seems to provide support for the hypothesis that extra-familial instruction exists to train children in skills in which the parents are not adept. A closer examination, however, leads to a qualification of this point of view. The importance of reading lies not only in the fact that parents are not skilled in it, but in the fact that reading cannot readily be learned as an incidental aspect of work or play. When reading is taught in schools, parents are not likely to become highly involved; school learning and family life are segregated, so segregated, in fact, as to produce serious problems for the school. If the parent does become involved because of a child's failure, he is likely to react by attributing disobedience to the child instead of by giving him emotional support and helping him with his work.

HISTORICAL DATA: MORAL INSTRUCTION IN THE ARISTOCRATIC HOUSEHOLD

Societies without schools have been considered as one natural experiment for the study of deliberate instruction in family settings. A similar experiment is provided by the aristocratic family of the West from ancient Greece to the present day. These families usually have existed in societies with schools, but the resources of the families have been such that instruction could be carried on in the household by the parent and by the tutor, who has often been as emotionally close to the child as the parent himself. Although aristocratic families have not been "typical," examination of them may provide insights into the nature of the family as an educational institution.

The aristocratic family has had a number of distinctive features relevant to the education of its children. First, marriages are often arranged for the good of the larger family group; these arranged marriages have often been associated with emotional distance between husbands and wives and an almost institutionalized mistress role. Second, these families have been able to delegate to servants many of the tasks usually performed by parents. Third, sons often have been almost assured of rights to succeed their fathers, and this has been associated with rebelliousness; England's Henry V, the Prince Hal of Shakespeare, was not an unusual case.

Taken together, these characteristics have led to highly formal relations between parents and children. They are probably associated with the distinction between "moral instruction" (*Erziehung, formation*) and "technical education" (*Unterricht, instruction*)—a distinction still of great importance in European educational thought. (See Metraux, 1963, and Broudy, 1963.) The aristocratic child must be brought up to be loyal to the "house" whose interests he can so easily harm and to the upper status group of which he is a member. Until boarding schools were developed, he was usually brought up by specialists employed by his father for these purposes. Teaching roles in aristocratic education were divided between "personal tutors" and "technical instructors." The child had first a tutor or "friend," usually of reputable status, who, however, did not engage in the deliberate instruction of complex skills. Those who did teach complex skills usually have had low status. Let us consider some of the historical variations in these two roles.

"Personal tutors" have often been emotionally close to their charges; they may have been closer to children emotionally and more important for personality development than the parents.[9] However, tutors in such positions probably were not engaged directly in teaching skills such as reading, mathematics, and foreign languages. Rather, such tutors saw to the employment of specialized instructors for such skills and supervised the instruction given. The personal tutor was primarily interested in the moral development of children. (Cf. Ariés, 1962, pp. 194, 269, 270.) In less wealthy families, unable to afford more than a single tutor, the personal tutor was probably compelled to be the technical instructor as well. Probably such tutors were not emotionally close to their students; outside of novels like Fielding's *Tom Jones*, I have not discovered reports of their positions in families.

The references in the preceding paragraph concern Western Europe in the sixteenth and seventeenth centuries, but similar roles have been present throughout Western history. Marrou suggests that the relation between tutor and taught in Greece about the time of Plato was not so much quasi-paternal as erotic; nevertheless, the relation was one of emotional intimacy and was oriented more toward moral instuction than "instruction in techniques" (Marrou, 1964, pp. 56f.).[10]

Those actually engaged in teaching complex skills to the young in Greece and Rome were held in low esteem. (The Greek sophists seem to be an exception, although they seldom taught the young, and the "philosophy" they often taught may not have been a "complex skill" in the same sense as most of the other skills discussed here.) In ancient Greece such teachers were likely to be downwardly mobile and ill paid. (Marrou, 1964, pp. 204f.) In the Middle Ages and Renaissance the technical instructor—a secular master for such skills as reading, writing, dancing, and fencing—still had the low status of a tradesman (Ariés, 1962, pp. 296ff.). These teachers either instructed young children, a task associated with low prestige in almost every society, or they taught older children and youths, more or less at the demand of the students. The *flow of demand* in instruction is a useful concept in this and other contexts. Information, requests, complaints, or orders may either issue from the teacher to the student or the other way around. With young children the flow of demand is likely to be from the teacher to the student; problems of discipline may be serious. In aristocratic instruction, a personal tutor may assure obedience by the student to the technical instructor and protect the student from harsh physical punishment. With older students, the flow of demand in instruction may be reversed. This seems to happen infrequently, although it may have been common in aristocratic instruction. Since the source of demands usually has higher status than the recipient (Homans, 1950), this would further contribute to the low status of the teacher. However, it would probably also serve to reduce interpersonal strains in instruction.

The technical instruction of aristocratic children was in all likelihood not carried on in familial or even quasi-familial relationships. Furthermore, the existence of the personal tutor role suggests that even moral instruction was not given entirely in familial contexts but that much of it was given in quasi-familial ones. The tutor was a member of the aristocratic household and was a quasi-parental figure, but he was not a parent.

The same pattern is manifested in the "apprenticeship" of aristocrats. Philippe Ariés has pointed out that in the Middle Ages even aristocratic children were sent away to serve families in other homes—"serve" in the literal sense of waiting on tables and performing other similar activities. Ariés suggests that the pattern was probably common throughout the West during the Middle Ages and that its goal and function was what some contemporaries said it was: "In order that their children might learn better manners" (Ariés, 1962, p. 365). Instruction in elaborate rituals of etiquette as well as technical skills is likely to generate interpersonal strains in families, and sending children to other families for such instruction is one way of avoiding these strains. In addition, the practice of apprenticeship may have served the function of reducing the dependency of children on their parents; this may be a more serious problem for sons who succeed to the role of their fathers.[11]

The extension of education in schools, especially residential schools, almost eliminated this form of apprenticeship by the late eighteenth century, although it continued in the working classes well into the nineteenth century. The interpersonal aspects of working class apprenticeship deserve more intensive study. It is often argued that the master-apprentice relation was almost identical with the parent-child relation (cf. Bailyn, 1960, p. 17), but the point of view advanced here suggests that such descriptions must be mistaken. The master was a *quasi*-parental figure and could probably give certain types of instruction with less interpersonal strain than an actual parent.

In summary, an inspection of the education of aristocrats does not show that parents or quasi-parental figures usually gave instruction in technical skills. Aristocratic families were no more likely to be "schools" than the families in preliterate societies. Furthermore, even moral instruction in aristocratic families involved a complex division of labor, with personal tutors, lower status technical instructors, and apprenticeships in other families. Tutors and apprenticeships may have had the function of reducing the dependency of sons on their parents—to the effect that the son could later enact a family role which was at one with a political role in society. In this respect, these practices may have been similar in function to initiation ceremonies in primitive societies and schools in many societies.

ROLE CONFLICTS IN INSTRUCTION

In all societies relations between parents and children are expected to be permanent and based on respect and affection. Continuation of the relationship is not contingent upon satisfactory performance in the respective roles; one does not fire a child or a parent for incompetence. Nor does one explicitly *evaluate* his child's performance of a certain activity in the same way, according to the same criteria, as one evaluates unrelated persons. Of course, the relationship is not permanent; children do become independent of their parents, sons do not marry mothers. But achieving independence is not a process without complications.

Relations between teachers and students are inherently temporary;[12] at best they are based upon approval and esteem. Teachers typically deal with an age-graded set of students, and they evaluate them according to purely universalistic standards, standards quite independent of the particular relationship between the judge and one judged. Even if instructional and examining roles are differentiated, instructional technique requires evaluation of performance according to universalistic criteria; even the most humane teachers motivate students by withholding approval when the student fails to perform as one in his age-ability category can generally be expected to perform.

Hence the roles of parent and teacher are incompatible. The parent who tries to become a teacher must tend to make the continued nature of his relationship with his child contingent upon the child's performance as judged according to criteria the parent might use with just anyone else. One might expect such a procedure to arouse anxiety in the child, an anxiety expressed in terms of overdependency or perhaps rejection of the parent. The parent himself will be ambivalent in such situations—on the one hand his instruction is devoted to making the child capable of acting independently of him, while on the other hand he expects the child to remain in a dependent position. One might expect parents to be easily irritated, regardless of the outcome of the instruction. Failure of the student will have latent gratifications for both teacher and taught: it will reinstate the bond of dependency between them.

Technical instruction is quite different in these respects from moral instruction. Parents frustrate and evaluate children in the course of normal socialization, especially in the area of "moral instruction." But moral instruction in the family does not involve the postponement of gratification: typically it involves the expression of his feelings by the parent. Moral instruction is typically diffuse and relevant to the particular relation between parent and child. Its positive "outputs" are the expression of love by the parent and the establishment of authority or nurturant relations from the parent to the child. (Moral instruction also has a more generalized aspect, relating to the child's position in some larger collectivity—the larger family, the community, or the status group. But elements of authority and dependency are still involved.) The positive output of technical instruction is different: it is the ability of the child to perform a task *independently*. While the parent may reward the child with expressions of affection, this is an indirect consequence of the activity; the direct consequence is to reduce the authority-dependency relationship.

These considerations suggest that when complex skills are learned in family settings it is because the strains associated with the parent-teacher, child-student role conflict are controlled or avoided. Strains can be controlled when the instruction is of short duration, when the payoff can be expected quickly and is large compared to the frustrations experienced during the instruction. Strains can be avoided when learning occurs in the contexts of practical activities or games. While parents frustrate and evaluate children according to universalistic criteria in the course of practical activities, in such activities the performance of the child is relevant as means, not ends. The consequence of the child's failure is typically to have the task performed by someone else; it does not signify failure of the entire activity, as it does in instruction. Just as the goal of the activity is not to change the child's capabilities, failure to perform has less effect on the child's self-concept and status. Conversely, a child's successful performance in such activities does not make him independent of the group but instead makes him a more valuable member of it.

Games are different from instruction in that they are a kind of pretended practical activity. Once players sit at a table to play anagrams or Monopoly, they are governed in part by values like those of practical activity: they defer immediate gratification to win, they utilize universalistic criteria in selecting moves, they relate to other players in terms of actual or potential performances only, and their obligations to other players are strictly limited by the rules of the game. Families often play games, and the games of children are very important learning experiences for them. But any consequences of games, outside of "fun," are incidental. (On this and the following see Goffman, 1961, and the sources cited there.) Games are by definition "non-productive." They are not expected to have consequences outside themselves, and external reality is not expected to influence play. Family members can be "impersonal" and "competitive" in games simply because games are denied serious reality. This is probably the reason for the importance of games in familial education. However, games are often inefficient ways of learning, and games that are superior for learning purposes may be difficult to play in families because parents cannot become genuinely involved in them.

When the parent attempts to deliberately instruct his child, he must basically change his role. Sometimes such changes in roles can be tolerated, as they are in the game or in practical activity. The role conflicts involved in the parent-teacher, child-student situation are more severe because the situation is treated as having important consequences, because it jeopardizes the child's security, and because it may threaten the parent's authority.

The theoretical considerations discussed above might be tested in a variety of ways. While systematic data collection remains to be performed, I have elsewhere reported some explanatory studies (Hagstrom, 1965). One can study situations in our society where parents frequently teach children, such as auto driving or music; or exceptional cases, such as children who learn to read before attending Grade One or those well-known child prodigies who have been instructed by their parents.

1. I interviewed some professional music teachers and found only a few who had taught their own children successfully. Those who attempted instruction and failed reported that they had difficulty in controlling their own irritation and that their children became anxious (much more anxious than other students) when corrected. Those who succeeded reported that instruction proceeded much more easily after the child had become sufficiently skilled in performance to direct specific questions to the teacher; interpersonal strain was greater in the early stages of instruction, when the teacher more closely monitored the behavior of the student.

2. Auto driving is usually taught successfully by parents to children, in the sense that the skill is acquired. Sons learn fairly readily from their parents, with only a minority of my informants reporting serious interpersonal strains; when parents attempt to teach daughters the attempt more often fails and serious strains are likely, but most attempts are successful and without serious strain; high strain is typical and failure is common when husbands attempt to teach wives. These differences can perhaps be accounted for in terms of relative authority and dependency. Husbands and wives are formally equal and it is difficult for one to assume the authority of teacher over the other. Daughters, and perhaps wives to some extent, are expected to be dependent, and instruction tending to make them independent causes more serious strains than when sons are taught.

3. Studies have shown that between 1 and 4 per cent of American children learn to read before Grade One; but the same studies show that this learning is seldom the result of deliberate instruction by parents. Usually the child initiates interaction in the instruction (Durkin, 1961, 1963).

4. Biographies and autobiographies of child prodigies who were instructed by their parents—persons ilke John Stuart Mill, Norbert Weiner, and Ruth Slenczynska—report that instruction was very stressful. The parent teacher (who was the father in every case I have discovered) tended to be authoritarian and punitive, and only the child's satisfaction at gaining the exclusive attention of his parent permitted the instruction to proceed. Typically the child found it difficult to achieve independence from his father; gaining independence was associated with personality crises in early adulthood. (These strains and problems are probably not universal; Wolfgang Amadeus Mozart, for example, was taught successfully by his father without any apparent serious interpersonal strains or serious problems of dependency.)

These types of data cannot substitute for systematic studies of the consequences of parental attempts at instruction, but they do suggest that the nature and consequences of the role conflicts occurring when parents attempt to become teachers deserve systematic study.

SOCIAL CHANGE AND PARENTAL ROLES

What has been asserted so far is perhaps just as true of parent-child relations in primitive as in urban-industrial societies. Parent-child relations are everywhere particularistic and diffuse, and technological change does not produce basic changes in these respects. Obviously, technological development implies that skills of greater complexity must be acquired by children. Possibly most skills in pre-literate societies are no more complex than driving in our own: instruction may produce interpersonal strains, but the strains can be controlled since the instruction can be completed quickly and the payoff to student and teacher is clear and quick. Technological development also tends to divorce the family and the economic productive unit, and this means that children are less likely to learn complex skills as an incidental aspect of cooperating in productive work. But technological change is also associated with changes in the family that may relate in other, less obvious, ways to education.

William Goode (1963) and others have amassed much evidence to show that industrialization is associated with a decline in the importance of extended kinship organizations and joint households. The power of elders is reduced, and there are fewer economic controls over mate choice. Interpersonally, this means the growth in the likelihood and importance of conjugal love, greater emotional interdependence of spouses, a decline in the division of labor between spouses in child rearing, and a decline in parental power over older children. The link between parents and adult children becomes primarily sentimental and not instrumental.

If this is true, the theory of role conflict sketched above may be true especially of families in urban-industrial societies. Parental roles are always differentiated to some extent, but perhaps some types of differentiation may make it possible for a parent to play the role of teacher.[13] The argument presented above was in terms of incompatibility of the teacher role with the primarily "expressive" and "nurturant" role of the parent. If, however, the mother plays a primarily "expressive" role and the father a primarily "instrumental" role, why may not the father be an effective teacher? The father's instrumental role might be characterized by a tendency to be unemotional and to emphasize evaluation based on the performance of specific tasks, even in relation to his children, just as the teacher's role. It might be hypothesized, then, that the instrumentally oriented father could teach his children complex skills without generating interpersonal strains. A similar hypothesis, which can be tested readily, is that instruction in American families will be most successful when parental roles are highly differentiated. Preliminary observations provide no support for these hypotheses. E.g., the fathers of child prodigies tended to dominate their children in both the instrumental and the affective areas of life, with the mothers remaining very much in the background; there was in fact little effective role differentiation. There are also some cogent theoretical arguments against these hypotheses.

The differentiation of parental roles in a society is inversely correlated with potential disjunctions in the roles of parents and children. High differentiation occurs when sons succeed to the positions of their fathers, less differentiation when they do not. (This proposition is suggested by the theory of Bott, 1957; see also Slater, 1961.) Thus, when there is high parental role differentiation, the father is likely to be a continuing authority over his sons and a member of the same kinship and political units as they are. Even such "instrumentally" oriented fathers are likely to stand in a particularistic relationship to their sons; the fathers will be primarily oriented to their sons' ascribed statuses and will not expect mutual obligations to be restricted to a few specific areas of life. Problems of authority and loyalty will be more salient than problems of competence in the performance of important tasks. In such societies relations between fathers and sons tend to be highly structured; social distance is high, and patterns of deference are elaborated and formalized. (See Stephens, 1963, chs. 7-8.) Fathers in such societies will be unlikely to give sons the independence required of students. Good descriptions are provided by Oscar Lewis (1962) in his descriptions of Mexican families.[14] It has been shown that paternal autocratic dominance is associated with the dependency of sons in industrialized societies (Elder, 1965).

In summary, deliberate instruction in societies with high parental role differentiation is likely to produce strains because of the importance of filial obedience and loyalty. Deliberate instruction in societies with low role differentiation is likely to produce strains because of the importance to children of parental nurturance and security.

Thus, in both traditional and industrialized societies the transmission of complex skills will require something like schools, even if parents themselves possess the skills to be transmitted. The skills to be transmitted in traditional societies are fewer and less complex than in industrial societies, and the schooling will be less extensive and intensive. As a society attempts to move rapidly toward industrialization it may attempt to extend schooling, but attempts to transmit only complex skills will probably be unsuccessful. Some of the limitations of schools in such societies have been noted above; they tend to be authoritarian and to reinforce a traditional lack of innovativeness and traditionally low aspirations. Under some conditions, however, schooling may promote basic changes in personality as well as the acquisition of complex skills. On the one hand, if the family structure is changing in such a way that fathers exhibit either what Everett Hagen calls retreatism (lack of aspiration to achieve traditional goals) or a non-traditional capricious and arbitrary authoritarianism,[15] children may accept the competing authority of the school and the different identity it offers. On the other hand, the school may sometimes assist in undermining paternal authority. Following the implications of Hagen's theory, one might suggest that schools in developing societies will be most effective among those strata suffering most from the "withdrawal of status respect"—a withdrawal of customary recognition of merit brought about by a change in the power structure, derogation of institutionalized activity without a change in the power structure, contradiction among status symbols, or nonacceptance of expected status on migration to a new society (Hagen, 1962, pp. 185-193).[16] The schools would be most effective in such strata precisely because traditional paternal authority will be weakest in them.

NOTES

* Portions of the research reported here were supported by the U.S. Office of Education and the University of Wisconsin Alumni Research Foundation, whose assistance is gratefully acknowledged. An earlier version of this paper was read at the Meeting of the Midwest Section of the Comparative Education Society in Madison, Wisconsin, in April, 1966. Participants at the Meeting offered many valuable suggestions, for which I wish to express my appreciation.

1. For typical examples, see Firth (1957, pp. 134f.); Stephens (1963, ch. 8); B. Whiting (1963); and Herzog (1962, pp. 301–307).

2. Some doubts may be expressed about the effectiveness of primitive education. Writing about the Alorese of Indonesia, Cora DuBois noted a "general underdevelopment of mastery techniques. It is patent that in practically all specialties there is a singular slovenliness of achievement. . . . Their mythology is confused and unstructuralized. Their knowledge of genealogies is . . . deficient. . . . Little is done by way of elaboration, and no effort is made to master the resources of the environment. . . . Consistent training and the assurance of reward (or penalty) are essential to learning. These two factors are largely absent." DuBois gave a psychological explanation of this lack of achievement motivation. (DuBois, 1961, pp. 134f.)

3. See Covarrubias (1942, p. 133).

4. However, Erwin Epstein reanalyzed some of Herzog's data and obtained only a small correlation ($Q = .15$) between degrees of social stratification and presence of instruction by non-kin. (Epstein, 1965)

5. On this controversy, see J. Whiting *et al.* (1958); Young (1962); and Cohen (1964).

6. For an exaggerated argument to this effect, see Lévi-Strauss (1964, pp. 291f.).

7. For details, see Hagstrom (1965, pp. 12–14).

8. An Israeli study documents these reactions for parents of first-graders. See Smilansky and Adar (1961, pp. 5, 9ff.).

9. For a good description, see a biography of the seventeenth-century English Dukes of Bedford: Thomson (1959, p. 72, passim.).

10. Note should be made here of Marrou's contrast of Greece and Rome in this respect, since his description of Rome makes it seem an exception to the generalization that parents are seldom engaged in the deliberate instruction of their children. Marrou asserts that the Roman boy's "real teacher" was his father (Marrou, 1964, p. 314). However, none of the sources he cites show that it was *customary* for fathers to deliberately instruct their sons in complex skills. Rather, Pliny, Aulus Gellius, Quintilian, and Plutarch seem to have been discussing exceptional cases, or an idealized past when fathers really were such teachers, or instruction by tutors in the home as opposed to instruction in schools. While further examination of Roman

literature might be more revealing, the primary sources available to me do not seem to support the view that Roman fathers typically gave instruction in complex skills to their sons.

11. There are, however, other explanations for this practice of apprenticeship. Up through the sixteenth century even well-born men could be political and economic dependents of the greater aristocrats. Apprenticeship at a young age may have been one way of firmly establishing a patron-client relationship.

12. Cf. Matthew B Miles' treatment of "temporary systems," where he suggests reasons why systems temporary in time and isolated from other relations are effective in producing change, including the changes in persons usually sought by schools. (Miles, 1964.)

13. The argument here is somewhat contrary to that presented by Talcott Parsons and his colleagues (Parsons and Bales, 1955, ch. VI), who assert that in every society the father plays a primarily instrumental role, acting as an authority figure, while the mother plays a primarily expressive role, acting as a nurturant figure. They argue that this differentiation is functionally necessary, both to maintain the instrumental adequacy and integration of the family as a group and to adequately socialize the children. Philip Slater has argued against this functional theory very effectively (Slater, 1961). He shows that the modern American family is relatively "dedifferentiated," and he presents a great deal of evidence to show that children in American families are less adequately socialized when parental role differentiation is high than when it is low. He does suggest, however, that high role differentiation may be more functional in some primitive societies.

14. Cf. also Hagen (1962, ch. 7–8). In a traditional society such as Burma, "The parents can hardly be said to train the children. Rather, they rule them, perhaps laxly, perhaps amusedly. However, against one manifestation of rage, rage toward one's parents, there is severe training. Great importance is attached to teaching the child deference toward his elders. . . . Boys become unable to function independently in the presence of elders or superiors, relying on the elders or superiors for judgment." (p. 165)

15. See Hagen (1962, ch. 11) on these types of paternal behavior, which he suggests are typical in societies on the verge of change.

16. The transformation of the English aristocracy in the seventeenth century may illustrate Hagen's thesis. With the rise of the Tudor monarchy in the sixteenth century, the aristocracy lost their traditional roles of military and political leadership. Concomitantly, the status respect awarded them in society was jeopardized. The aristocracy weathered the storms of the seventeenth century and emerged as the wealthy elite of a capitalist economy and bureaucratic state. In the transition, aristocratic families changed: conjugal love became the norm, parental authority over children declined—and the English boarding school became an established part of the life of aristocrats. See the excellent treatment by Lawrence Stone (1965).

REFERENCES

Ariés, Philippe. *Centuries of Childhood.* New York: Knopf, 1962.

Bailyn, Bernard. *Education in the Forming of American Society.* New York: Vintage Books, 1960.

Bott, Elizabeth. *Family and Social Network.* London: Tavistock, 1957.

Broudy, Harry S. "Historic exemplars of teaching method." In N. L. Gage (Ed.), *Handbook of Research on Teaching.* Chicago: Rand McNally, 1963, pp. 44–93.

Chaney, Richard P. "Typology and patterning: Spiro's sample reexamined." *American Anthropologist,* 1966, *68,* 1456–1470.

Cohen, Y. A. "The Establishment of Identity in a Social Nexus." *American Anthropologist,* 1964, *66,* 529–553.

Covarrubias, Miguel. *The Island of Bali.* New York: Knopf, 1942.

DuBois, Cora. *The People of Alor, Vol. I.* New York: Harper Torchbooks, 1961.

Durkin, Dolores. "Children Who Learned to Read at Home." *Elementary School Journal,* 1961, *62,* 15–18.

Durkin, Dolores. "Children Who Learn to Read Before Grade One: A Second Study." *Elementary School Journal,* 1963, *64,* 143–148.

Elder, Glen H., Jr. "Family Structure and Educational Attainment: A Cross-national Analysis." *American Sociological Review,* 1965, *30,* 81–96.

Epstein, Erwin. "Cross Cultural Sampling and a Conceptualization of 'Professional Instruction.'" *Journal of Experimental Education,* Summer 1965, 33, 395–402.

Firth, Raymond, *We, The Tikopia.* Boston: Beacon Press, 1957.

Fischer, John L. "The Japanese Schools for the Natives of Truk, Caroline Islands." In Spindler (1963), pp. 512–529.

Goffman, Erving. *Encounters.* Indianapolis: Bobbs-Merrill, 1961.

Goode, William J. *World Revolution and Family Patterns.* New York: The Free Press of Glencoe, 1963.

Hagen, Everett E. *On the Theory of Social Change.* Homewood, Ill.: Dorsey Press, 1962.

Hagstrom, Warren O. *A Study of Deliberate Instruction Within Family Units.* Mimeographed Report to U.S. Office of Education on Cooperative Research Project No. S-184.

Herzog, John D. "Deliberate Instruction and Household Structure: A Cross-cultural Study." *Harvard Educational Review,* 1962, *32,* 303–342.

Holmberg, Allan. *Nomads of the Long Bow: The Siriono of Eastern Bolivia.* Washington: U.S. Government Printing Office, 1950.

Homans, George C. *The Human Group.* New York: Harcourt, Brace, and World, 1950.

Leighton, Dorothea, and Clyde Kluckhohn. *Children of the People.* Cambridge: Harvard University Press, 1947.

Lévi-Strauss, Claude. *Tristes Tropiques.* New York: Atheneum, 1964.

Lewis, Oscar. *Five Families.* New York: Science Editions, 1962.

Marrou, H. I. *A History of Education in Antiquity.* New York: Mentor, 1964.

Mead, Margaret. "Our Educational Emphases in Primitive Perspective." *American Journal of Sociology,* 1943, *48,* 633–639.

Metraux, Rhoda. "Implicit and Explicit Values in Education and Teaching as Related to Growth and Development." In Spindler (1963), pp. 121–131.

Miles, Matthew B. "On Temporary Systems." In Matthew B. Miles (Ed.), *Innovation in Education.* New York: Columbia University Teachers College Bureau of Publications, 1964, pp. 437–492.

Parsons, Talcott, and Robert F. Bales. *Family, Socialization and Interaction Process.* Glencoe, Ill.: The Free Press, 1955.

Slater, Philip E. "Parental Role Differentiation." *American Journal of Sociology,* 1961, *67,* 296–308.

Smilansky, Moshe, and Leah Adar (Eds.). *Evaluating Educational Achievements: Summaries of Some Studies Carried out by the Henrietta Szold Institute of Schooling in Israel.* Paris: UNESCO Educational Studies and Documents, 1961.

Spindler, George D. (Ed.). *Education and Culture.* New York: Holt, Rinehart and Winston, 1963.

Stephens, William. *The Family in Cross-Cultural Perspective.* New York: Holt, Rinehart and Winston, 1963.

Stone, Lawrence. *The Crisis of the Aristocracy, 1558–1641.* New York: Oxford University Press, 1965.

Thomson, Gladys Scott. *Life in a Noble Household.* Ann Arbor, Mich.: University of Michigan Press, 1959.

Wallace, Ernest, and E. Adamson Hoebel. *The Comanches.* Norman: University of Oklahoma Press, 1952.

Watkins, Mark H. "The West African 'Bush' School." In Spindler (1963), pp. 426–443.

Whiting, Beatrice (Ed.). *Six Cultures*. New York: Wiley, 1963.

Whiting, John W. M., R. Kluckhohn, and A. Anthony. "The Function of Male Initiation Ceremonies at Puberty." In Maccoby, E. E., Newcomb, T., and E. L. Hartley, (Eds.), *Readings in Social Psychology*. New York: Holt, 1958, pp. 359–370.

Young, Frank W. "The Function of Male Initiation Ceremonies: A Cross-cultural Test of an Alternative Hypothesis." *American Journal of Sociology*, 1962, 67, 379–390.

Zelditch, Morris, Jr. "Cross-cultural Analyses of Family Structure." In Harold T. Christensen (Ed.), *Handbook of Marriage and the Family*. Chicago: Rand McNally, 1964, pp. 462–500.

*The Geography of Youth Employment and School Enrollment Rates in Mexico**

PHYLLIS GOLDBLATT

IF THE PEOPLE of a country are caught up with the rising expectations for development, they must be ready to adopt changes. The ways in which new ideas spread across a country and the readiness with which people utilize them will determine how successful a nation will be in the total process of modernization.

Primary schooling is often viewed as an agent of change. It is presumed to promote new skills, to allow people to consider alternatives to old ways, to offer incentives to greater efforts, and to encourage national unity through a common language and familiarity with other parts of the population. But primary schooling in developing countries may also be viewed as the dependent variable, the new trait or innovation that diffuses through the society in various patterns. This paper is concerned with an analysis of factors that explain spatial patterns in the diffusion and distribution of primary school enrollment rates in Mexico. The principal methods used are factor and multiple regression analyses.

The theoretical framework takes as its starting point the diffusion theories of certain human geographers, derived in part from the "gravity models" of central-place theories but as modified by work at Lund, Sweden.[1]

Scholars working with central-place theory have developed a technique for measuring the influence of one population aggregate upon another as a function of size and distance. It has been assumed that the larger a population of place B the more influence it will have on a population in place A. The greater the distance from A to B the less is B's effect on A. To obtain the "population potential" of A we would divide the population of each other place, B_1, B_2, B_3 by its distance from A, distance $_{1}$, $_{2}$, $_{3}$, etc. and sum the results. Fattahipour[2] tested out this concept of population potential in a study of the diffusion of education in Iran but found it inadequate: both the central and intermediate cities remained self-contained with little spillover of educational stimulation to the hinterlands.

The Lund geographer Hägerstrand has applied a rather different model, embracing "information fields" and "resistances" to the study of diffusion in space. He found a remarkable stability in the geographic pattern for the diffusion of many innovations (including schooling) over a two-hundred-year period. He identified established centers from which innovations spread, and these centers appeared to form a status order. Ideas from the innovation centers were more likely to be accepted. What he calls information fields are communication channels; the most effective flow of information followed the "tellings"[3] between people. As indexes of these interpersonal linkages he used telephone usage and migration routes. Mass media appeared to promote new ideas only when supported by person-to-person communication.

But people do not always accept new ideas when they first hear of them. Reactions depend upon the economic and cultural setting and how a particular innovation fits into that setting—hence the concept of "resistance," the degree of ease with which particular new ideas are accepted for any given intensity of "tellings." Some new ideas may be adopted almost immediately, some only after repeated tellings, some not even then.

Education fits into this model in several ways: First, using Hägerstrand's general model as a guide, this paper discusses the enrollment of 6-14 year olds in the states of Mexico as the innovation being diffused. Spatial variation in enrollment will be treated first as a function of information fields, approximated by patterns of communication from urban to rural areas and across regions of the country. These variations will then be examined from the resistance side of the model, examining traits of populations in one area versus another that affect parental decisions to enroll their children in school. In many instances, direct measures of information fields and decision factors cannot be obtained and indirect indexes must be used.

The spatial distribution of educational attainments of adults can fit into the Hägerstrand model in other ways. Thus, rather than the enrollment rates of children (treated as the innovation or dependent variables) the education levels of adults may be viewed as a proxy variable for "intensity of tellings." That is, it is assumed that educated adults have more contacts with new ideas, and a locality with a large proportion of educated adults would have a more rapid rate of interchange of information relevant to decisions about schooling.

The level of adult education can be considered from the resistance side also, making people more eager or more opposed to keeping their children in school for both economic and non-economic reasons: the more educated the adults the greater the presumption that aspirations for children's education will be high, simply viewing education as a value in itself, any economic returns aside.[4]

Mexico provides a good case for this kind of analysis, apart from the unusual amount of information available. In the early 1900's Mexico was characterized by a population 80 to 90% rural. Rural Mexico was backward and underdeveloped, inhabited largely by poor, illiterate peasants, under the domination of *hacendados* or owners of manorial estates. About 85% of the population was illiterate, and only one quarter of the school age children were in school. During the past third of a century or more there has been rapid development on all fronts. The leaders of the 1910 Revolution attempted to break down the restrictions of class and region surrounding education and to use the schools as instruments of change.

THE GEOGRAPHIC PATTERNS OF PRIMARY SCHOOL ENROLLMENT RATES

Though access to schools has broadened over the past generation or more, wide variation in their use and effectiveness persists. Some states remain almost wholly traditional while others have most of the earmarks of modernity, and the Federal District is one of the most modernized urban areas in the world. It is in the North generally and in particular parts of the central plateau (mainly in the capital district) that progress has been most marked. The three states facing south on the Pacific are most retarded: Guerrero, Oaxaca, and Chiapas. The northern states are better off than most of the central plateau, the latter displaying extremely diverse levels of development within a densely populated region.[5]

The three illustrative maps showing proportionate enrollments of 6-14 year old children in urban (Map 1) and rural (Map 2) areas highlight the diversities of development among the parts of Mexico. The overall enrollment rate (Map 3) provides a good general image of regional development, both cultural and economic. In the South there is also a clustering of states, but this time at low levels of school enrollment. The extreme diversity between North and South and the complex variations in the central group of states suggest that the gradient patterns implied in conventional population-potential models would not provide an adequate explanation for the observed pattern.

A first survey of some of the factors that can be presumed to underly the geographic pattern portrayed in the maps is provided by the correlation matrix (Table I). The literacy of urban males 40-49 years old has a positive association with enrollment of 6-14 year olds in urban areas (.385). The proportion of urban males literate in the 40-49 year old age group has a negative relationship to the employment of 8-11 year olds (—.512). With rural males the pattern is the same, a low (but positive) association between the literacy of older males and enrollment of youth in school (.105). At the same time there is a negative relationship between literacy of older men and the employment of children (—.777). Adult literacy clearly enhances enrollment of children in school and is associated with low enrollments (—.315) in urban areas and even more strongly in rural areas (—.571).

In the zero-order correlation matrix (Table I) traditionalism, as indicated by going barefoot,[6] has little connection with either urban or rural enrollment rates (.004 and .112 respectively).

Yet there are negative correlations between going barefoot and adult literacy, which is correlated with enrollments. (The proportion of males barefoot is related to the literacy of older urban males —.656 and to the

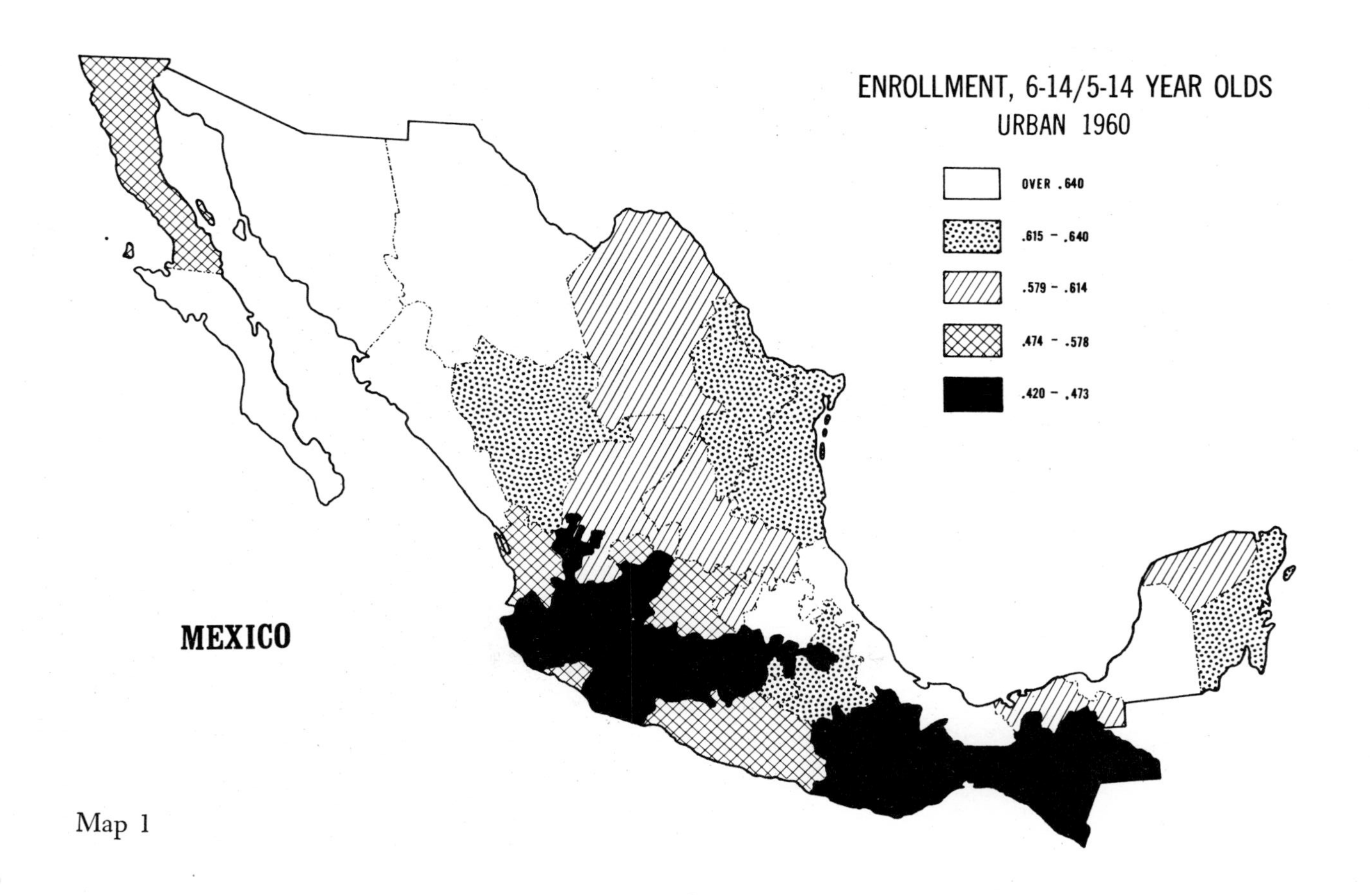
ENROLLMENT, 6-14/5-14 YEAR OLDS
URBAN 1960
OVER .640
.615 - .640
.579 - .614
.474 - .578
.420 - .473
MEXICO

Map 1

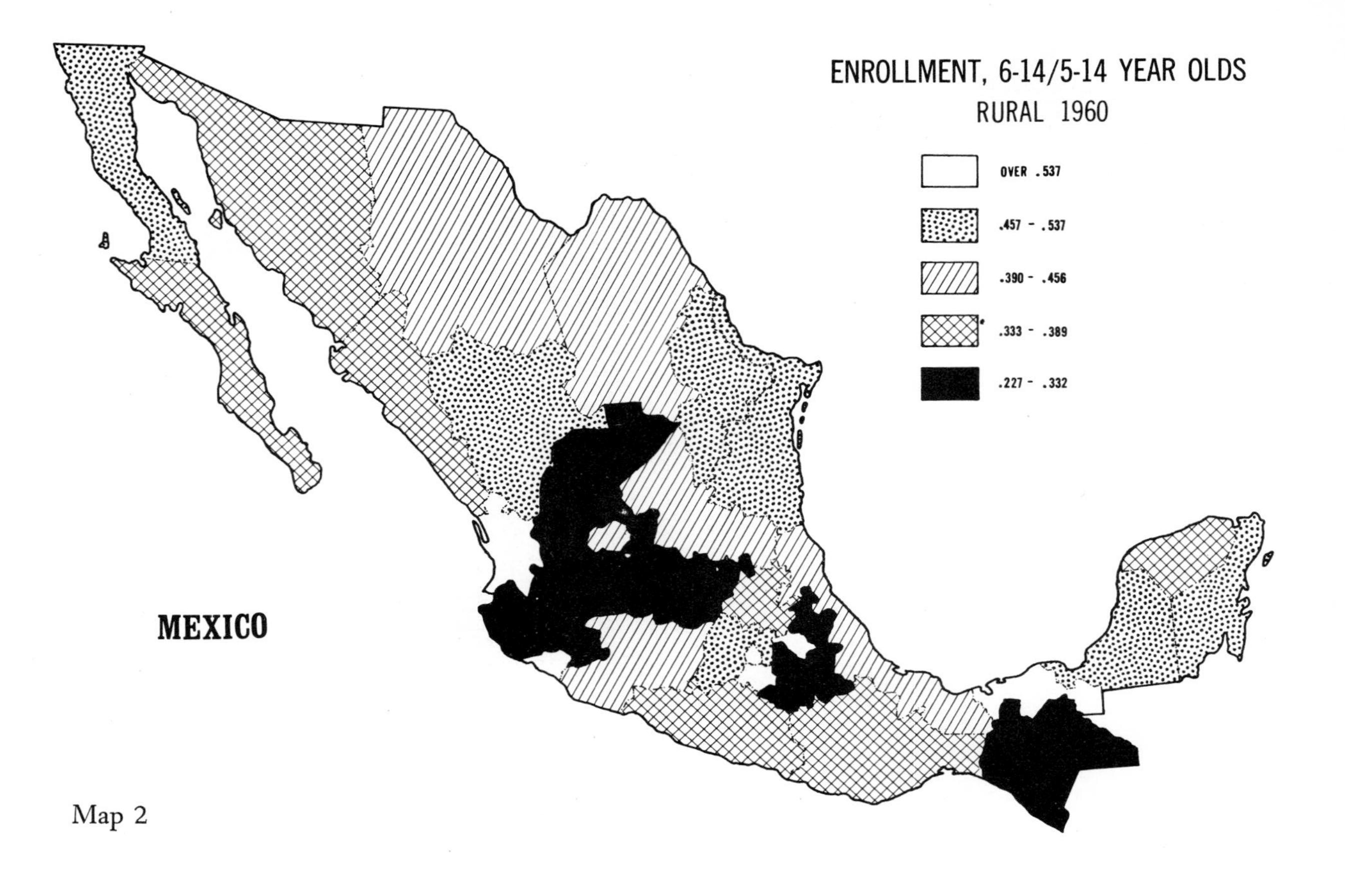
ENROLLMENT, 6-14/5-14 YEAR OLDS
RURAL 1960
OVER .537
.457 - .537
.390 - .456
.333 - .389
.227 - .332
MEXICO

Map 2

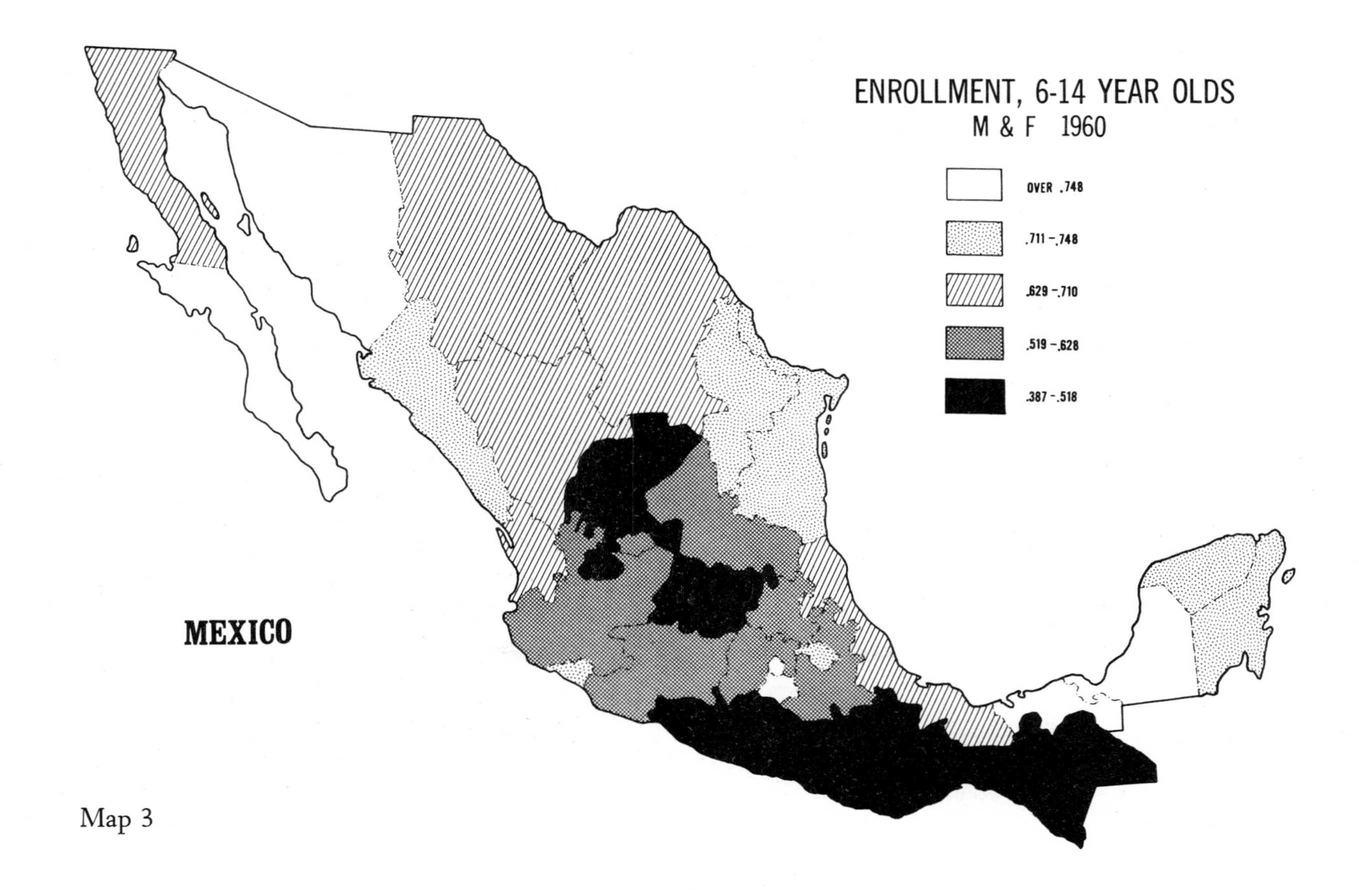
ENROLLMENT, 6-14 YEAR OLDS
M & F 1960
OVER .748
.711 - .748
.629 - .710
.519 - .628
.387 - .518
MEXICO

Map 3

TABLE I. ILLUSTRATIVE CORRELATIONS BETWEEN EDUCATIONAL AND OTHER VARIABLES—MEXICO (UNITS = 32 STATES)

	1	2	3	4	5	6	7
1. Enrollment, 6–14's—urban	—						
2. Enrollment, 6–14's—rural	−.085	—					
3. 8–11 year old males employed	−.315	−.571	—				
4. Urban males age 40–49 % literate	.385	−.055	−.512	—			
5. Rural males age 40–49 % literate	.105	.490	−.777	.463	—		
6. % males employed, agriculture	−.129	−.338	.679	−.580	−.663	—	
7. % males barefoot	.004	.112	.480	−.656	−.492	.606	—
8. Not immigration	−.016	.417	−.542	.501	.458	−.568	−.504

literacy of older rural males —.492.) This prepares one for the reordering of some of these relationships that will emerge when some multiple regressions and partial correlations are explored below.

VARIATIONS IN ENROLLMENTS AS AN ASPECT OF RURAL-URBAN COMMUNICATION FIELDS

Two diagrams were drawn to represent the "information" and the "resistance" sets of factors respectively. The actual variables available for analysis are put in the rounded boxes and the concepts or hypothetical variables in the square boxes. The goal is to explain enrollment of children in school, and the network of relationships displayed reflects the causal hypotheses derived from the Hägerstrand model and other sources. Although we may start with overall enrollment rates by states, there are distinctive characteristics of the rural as against the urban patterning of influences and behavior that are especially interesting.

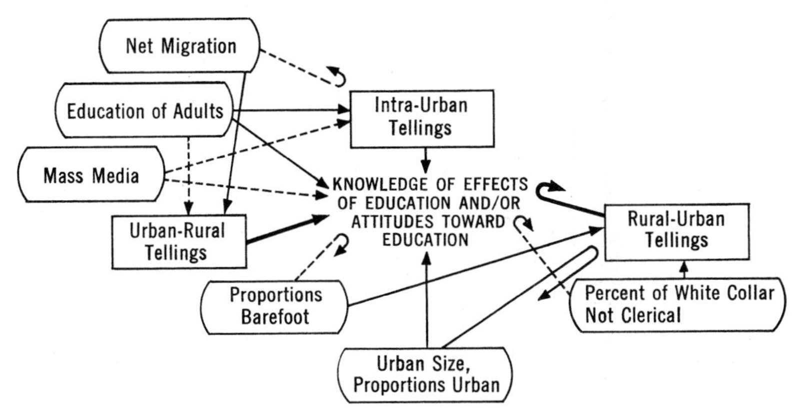

FIGURE 1. INFORMATION AND COMMUNICATION.

We begin with Figure 1 on information and communication fields. Information can flow within either urban or rural areas and between them —through intra-urban and intra-rural tellings. The intra-rural tellings were not put in the diagram, however. The straight arrows indicate positive influence on diffusion of knowledge about the effects of education and tellings that convey attitudes favorable toward education. The arrows that turn back on themselves indicate negative effects. When an element in the chart has a traditionalist influence, arrows from it to Knowledge of Effects of Education and/or Attitudes Toward Education turn back or reverse themselves. Here we have factors that impede or delay the spread of information and the orientations to education upon which the decisions to enroll and continue in school are based. Hereafter we will refer to such arrows as "reversing arrows."

One would expect innovations to diffuse mostly within and among urban places with weaker influence to the surrounding hinterlands. Also, areas with high rates of immigration presumably have greater opportunities and higher levels of economic modernization; a priori we would expect higher enrollment rates. These assumptions were generally upheld in zero-order correlations. However, more refined analysis points to distinctive urban types. Controlling for other key variables, the simple relationships may not hold. Thus in Table II, regression in urban enrollment rates of children 6-14 were depressed by large immigration rates in cities of any given level with respect to manufacturing incomes and percentage of men in white-collar jobs. Given these controls, the less the immigration rate in the state the higher the enrollment (partial correlation —.506). Figure 1 shows a reversing arrow from net migration to intra-urban tellings. Evidently, newly arrived migrants bring their traditional rural culture, tend to live in self-contained neighborhoods, and only belatedly accept the emphasis on schooling. Where there are many of them they pull down enrollment rates.

In pursuing the time dimension further, contrasting 1960 with 1940 enrollments as dependent variables, enrollments at the later date were not as well explained as were the 1940 enrollments. There were heavy migrations over that twenty year period, but while residences may change families may retain contact with their former localities. Thus with movements of people subareas become less homogeneous and the spatial web of "tellings" lose some of their previous distinctiveness and clarity.

When we consider rural-urban tellings we are thinking of towns that are strongly influenced by their surrounding rural areas. There is both persistence of indigenous traits and low levels of income. Thus a high proportion of males going barefoot suggests the presence of towns functioning as trading places for rural people. Examination of the occupation mixes within the white-collar category reveals distinctive urban types.

One might expect a high proportion of white collar workers to be related to areas of high literacy of adults and high enrollment rates of children; i.e., areas that are progressing. Instead (Table II, regression 1) high enrollments appeared with high manufacturing incomes (.486) but a low proportion of males in white collar occupations (—.318). The anticipated facilitating effect of white-collar employment was not revealed. A reexamination of the underlying data showed clearly that the regressions were confounded where many traders outweighed the other non-manual categories in the white collar occupational group; proportions of clerical workers give quite different results.

A high proportion of the state population residing in urban places presumably diffuses knowledge about education, and the proportions living in cities has been growing rapidly. That proportion is higher in the northern states, which also display a closer connection between urban and rural

TABLE II. PARTIAL CORRELATION COEFFICIENTS (SELECTED FROM BEST REGRESSIONS) BETWEEN ENROLLMENT RATES FOR 6–14 YEAR OLDS AND OTHER FACTORS (*SIGNIFICANT AT .05; **SIGNIFICANT AT .01)

	Urban	*Rural*
(1) % of males in manufacturing with incomes over 500	.486**	
% of males in white collar occupations	−.318*	
$R^2 = .248$		
(2) % of males in manufacturing with incomes over 500	.651**	
% of males in white collar occupations	−.311*	
Immigration rate of state	−.506**	
$R^2 = .441$		
(3) % of males barefoot	−.586**	
Literacy %, urban females age 40–49	.688**	
$R^2 = .473$		
(4) % of males barefoot		−.465**
Literacy %, rural males age 40–49		.629**
$R^2 = .404$		
(5) % of 8–11 year olds employed (outside family) (with employment of children included, the literacy rate of 40–49 year old rural males dropped out)		−.571**
(6) Literacy %, rural females age 40–49		−.270
% of 8–11 year olds employed		−.581**
$R^2 = .372$		
(7) % of 8–11 year olds employed		−.561**
% of dwellings with radio		−.223
$R^2 = .360$		
(8) % of males in agriculture with incomes over 500		−.305*
% 8–11 year olds employed		−.608**
$R^2 = .389$		
(9) % of males barefoot		−.536**
% of 8–11 year olds employed		−.717**
$R^2 = .520$		

Note: Regressions were programmed to drop out variables the partial correlation of which had an F value less than 1. In selecting variables for regressions, no two variables with loadings of over .8 on the same factor were used.

development. However, development in rural areas may reflect special irrigation projects, for example, rather than the spread of modernizing influences from the urban center. In other parts of Mexico, and especially in the South, urban places as yet seem to exert comparatively weak modernizing effects upon the surrounding rural people.[7]

DETERMINANTS OF "RESISTANCE" TO DIFFUSION OF EDUCATION AND VARIATIONS IN ENROLLMENT RATES

Some clues to the factors that influence people when they decide whether or not to send their children to school have emerged from these data. The data for the most part referred to spatial aspects of communications and the direction and intensity of tellings; i.e., the information field. Within any

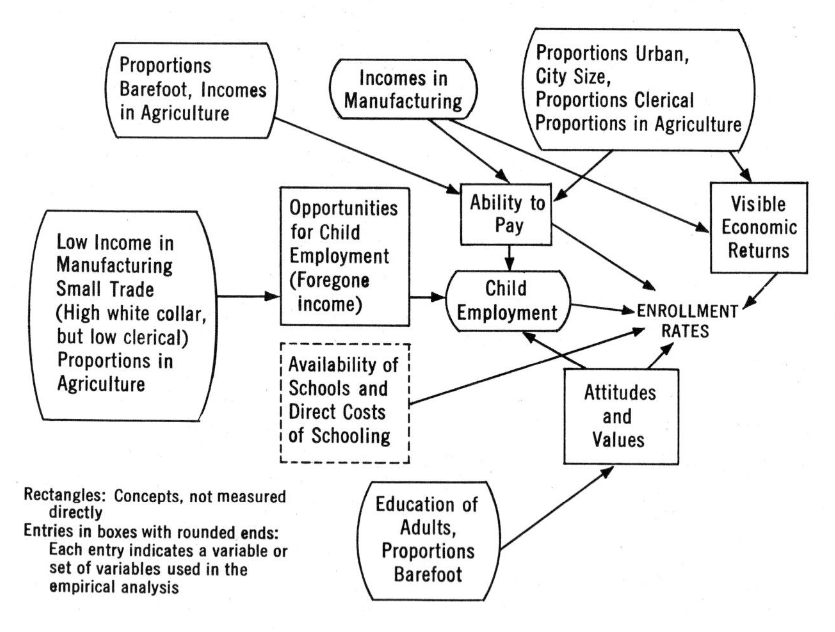

FIGURE 2. RESISTANCE (PLUS AND MINUS).

such field, how readily an innovation is adopted depends upon the factors that determine resistances; these latter are explored as a decision model in Figure 2. Again the rectangles are concepts and the rounded boxes are independent variables that proved to be important. Two of the rectangles refer to costs and availability of schooling. One is ability to afford schooling, one is the visibility of economic returns to schooling, and one is value attitudes or cultural traits and non-economic preferences.

The direct costs of schooling (in the rectangle with dashed lines) were not represented by any variable. At the level of elementary school such costs are small and differ little from one area to another. For availability of schools we had one variable: proportions of elementary schools that did not contain the full range of six grades. However, that variable is ambiguous in that it may be as often an index of pace of expansion as of availability. Furthermore, local availability is itself a function of local pressures for schooling. More important on the cost side are opportunities for child employment and the costs in foregone income that such opportunities entail. Though children legally are not to be employed, child employment is widespread enough for the census to tabulate the 8-11 year olds separately among the economically active population.

Levels of income in agriculture and in manufacturing were used as indicators of ability to pay for schooling. In this context the proportions of males going barefoot can be interpreted as a level of living index though it is also a cultural index.

I will first discuss the urban patterns. In the urban setting a high level of income for employees in manufacturing was a powerful stimulant to enrollment of children. In the multiple regression analysis for urban enrollments this index of ability to pay for education was more important among urban populations than the levels of employment of children (which was dropped by the F test). The influence of parental education came in with a strong positive value in regressions that included proportions of males barefoot. The latter was a strong depressant on enrollment rates when controlling for parental education (see regression 3). Whether children in towns go to school is a function predominantly of parental economic ability, the visibility of education pay-off in future earning power, in the immediate environment, and a positive attitude toward education on the part of adults (as inferred from adult literacy and urban style of dress).

In the factor analysis a strong modernization factor emerged; it had high loadings for urban population, high manufacturing income, clerical employment, few males in farming—and high enrollments of children. Juxtaposing regressions 1 and 2 leads to identifying a type of city with high manufacturing incomes, a small newly arrived or transient population, and a large proportion of other than tradesmen among the white-collar men.

In parallel fashion, an effort was made to isolate elements of the rural social structure that could explain variability in rural enrollments. The proportion of males in agriculture, the level of farm mechanization, and the proportion of agricultural laborers showed little influence upon enrollments (these variables were eliminated by the F tests at 1.00).

Level of incomes from agriculture had virtually no effect upon enrollment except when we controlled for the proportion of males in agriculture and employment of children. Doing this, income worked in reverse; thus low farm incomes actually raised enrollment rates at any given child-employment level (Table II), regression 8. Although we could speculate concerning the complex of factors that lie back of this result, the data do not permit any firm explanatory inference.[8]

Child employment is placed centrally in the diagram on resistance because of its logically key place in the schooling decision matrix. Yet this variable washed out in the urban regression even as it dominated the rural ones. Does this mean that foregone opportunities for child employment are unimportant in cities? That clearly is not the case. Martin Carnoy[9] found that employed children earned substantially more in the cities he studied than in his rural localities. Among urban populations foregone earnings are a relatively large cost in the last years of elementary school. Nevertheless, he found that despite high urban foregone incomes, urban rates of return to investment in the 4th to 6th years of primary school run to 30 or even 40%. This finding is consistent with our regressions. Despite high opportunity costs, relatively fewer children are employed in Mexico's cities than in rural areas, and rates of child employment fail to explain differences in urban enrollment rates precisely because other factors dominate: visibility of returns to schooling, high parental incomes, parental education and participation in modern culture *versus* many unassimilated immigrants living (barefoot) in the poorer residential areas of cities.

In rural areas, where returns to schooling are less visible, ability to pay is generally lower, and there is less variation in these traits. Here the extent of opportunity for child employment comes to play a pervasive part in determining school enrollments. While the opportunities themselves cannot be measured directly from the available data, the uses people make of those opportunities and the correlates of such use can be studied. The data indicate that such use and the extent of such opportunities in rural areas are greatest where there are moderate proportions of males in agriculture, low incomes in manufacturing, and many small traders (indicated by high white-collar but low clerical proportions). Among rural populations, once factors inducing child employment are allowed for, male literacy disappears and female literacy becomes an insignificant factor (regressions 5 and 6). When child employment is not taken into account, the degree of cultural traditionalism and adult literacy are important (regression 4). Indeed, cultural traditionalism retains an influence even after the factors producing high employment of children are allowed for (regression 9).

In summary, the Mexican data support Hägerstrand's emphasis on face-to-face "tellings" as the crux of the functioning of an information field. Evidence on this includes low correlations of urban with rural enrollment rates and low adult literacy correlates in the central area. Even more strongly, this thesis is supported by the negative immigration effect. In contrast to Sweden, however, Mexico is a bicultural land and has recently been experiencing a shaking loose of old geo-cultural patterns as sub-cultures move into new locations. Thus we find that 1960 trait clusters are geographically looser than those for 1937. Mexico displays strong culture change.

The "urban" settings range from the so-called "urban" that is essentially the gathering place and community crossroads of traditional rural society (which still lag in enrollments) to modern cities where incomes are high and returns to education are clearly visible.

Variations in school diffusion among rural populations suggest that opportunities for child employment play a key role, with ability to pay and visible returns generally too low to neutralize deterrent effects of foregone income opportunities.

Throughout, in both rural and urban life, the importance of cultural variabilities is clearly evidenced. The adoption of urban ways and the literacy of the older generation act as supportive factors in receptivity to the education of youth. Urban enrollments had the best R^2 with the culture variables, adult female literacy and proportion of males barefoot; and the barefoot variable came through in almost every rural regression in which it was included.

The implementation of centrally designed plans for education may meet countless hidden constraints among groups of illiterate people bound to a traditional culture. In designing programs, central planners must be aware of the subtleties in the diffusion of education and its relationship to the socio-economic structure, both in deciding goals and in determining the most effective areas on which to focus their efforts.

FOOTNOTES

* The author is indebted to Mary Jean Bowman for her helpful comments on the manuscript. The author however is solely responsible for any deficiencies in the text.

1. Torsten Hägerstrand, "Quantitative Techniques for Analysis of the Spread of Information and Technology," *Education and Economic Development,* ed. C. Arnold Anderson and Mary Jean Bowman (Chicago: Aldine Publishing Company, 1965), pp. 244–280.

2. Ahmad Fattahipour-Fard, "Educational Diffusion and the Modernization of an Ancient Civilization: Iran" (Unpublished Ph.D. dissertation, Department of Education, University of Chicago, 1963).

3. "Tellings" refers to the exchange of information between people who meet and talk informally.

4. Of course there are also correlations between education attainments of adults and other variables, like occupations, that affect demands for educated people and enter into the content of the tellings. However the pertinent variables in this connection are those providing more direct indications of demands for educated people.

5. In most of my analyses the Federal District has been omitted, for it would distort most of the distributions and often lead to overstated correlations. It would have been preferable to use *municipios* (counties) as units rather than states, but the labor entailed in handling thousands of *municipios* would have been prohibitive—and fewer items of information are available for *municipios* than for states.

6. The proportion of males going barefoot as opposed to those wearing *huaraches* or shoes is used as a proxy variable for adherence to the traditional culture.

7. The mass media—as exemplified by movie attendance and possession of radios—did not stimulate enrollments; this is consistent with Hägerstrand's emphasis upon person-to-person communication.

8. In equations (6), (7), and (8), the negative partial correlation coefficients for females literate, dwellings with radios, and males in agriculture with incomes over 500 pesos seem surprising. While no one is significant (with the partial exception of agricultural income over 500 pesos), the fact that all three have negative associations is something of a puzzle. Other correlations suggest that each of the independent variables is a reasonably firm one, but rural enrollment rates have a wide range of error. What equations (6), (7), and (8) do demonstrate, is that once account has been taken of 8–11 year olds employed, the other variables add little to the explanation of rural enrollment.

9. Martin Carnoy, "The Return to Education in Mexico: A Case Study" (unpublished manuscript, The Brookings Institution, March, 1966).

Crisis in German Culture: The Art Education Movement

STERLING FISHMAN

PERHAPS NO single historical abstraction has been the subject of so much criticism as that misbegotten child known as "modern technology." Despite the wealth which modern technology has created, critics have risen on all sides to attack it. Each fights his own war with the monster and tries to make his own peace. For instance, to Charlie Chaplin in his film, *Modern Times,* modern technology meant an assembly line and a creative fury that tortured and dehumanized its human creator. To Karl Marx, it did not mean the oppression of the worker by the machine, but by the evil capitalist. To Henry Ford, it meant a dangerous urban rootlessness that had to be combatted as well. To Karel Capek, the Czech playwrite, it meant an eventual tyranny of mechanical robots.

To none of these men, however, was the *ugliness* of modern technological society its principal evil as it was to the English critics, John Ruskin and William Morris, and to the German museum director, Alfred Lichtwark. To these men, the Frankenstein of modern times was the tastelessness of the new masses and the aesthetic horror of the goods they produced and the cities in which they lived. It is to the last of these figures, Alfred Lichtwark, and his outrage at modern ugliness that this study is devoted.

I

Alfred Lichtwark (1852-1914) grew up in a Germany that was still rural and parochial. His father was a miller and small land holder and provided young Alfred with a comfortable home, two sisters, and a brother. His mother, a descendant of Johann Sebastian Bach, brought the family cultural distinction.[1]

As a young man, Lichtwark seemed destined to become a teacher. He had already embarked on this career in 1878 when he encountered Justus Brinckmann, the founder and Director of the Hamburg Museum of Arts and Crafts (*Museum für Kunst und Gewerbe*). Lichtwark saw him as a genius who fully recognized the importance of artistic taste in the daily affairs of life. Brinckmann frequently lectured on the development of form and the use of artistic materials in common household utensils. His aim was to maintain and restore taste in the manufacture and use of everyday items. He committed himself to the preservation of craftsmanship at a time when factories were just beginning to flood Germany with their hordes of goods.[2]

With the approval and support of Brinckmann, Lichtwark decided to pursue a career in museum work. Leaving Hamburg, he studied and worked in Leipzig and Berlin where he changed and expanded the ideas of his mentor to suit his own personality. In Berlin, he witnessed the growing pains of the capital with its new political power and flourishing industrial wealth. The increasing interest in art collecting among the *nouveaux riches* delighted him, but their lack of taste appalled him. Art critics whom Lichtwark considered "loud half-blind little grumblers, with enormous pretensions,"[3] imposed their opinions on this vulnerable public. Lichtwark listened painfully to the comments made by middle class Germans as they observed the works on display in Berlin museums. Supposedly well-educated citizens seemed to lack any aesthetic appreciation for form, light, or color. He became convinced that German schools had completely failed to develop artistic taste. To him, Germany with all of its new industrial wealth and technological power stood on the brink of an era of ostentatious ugliness and cultural decline.

What most concerned Lichtwark was the failure of the German middle classes to develop artistic sensitivity. He began to regard his countrymen as "learned barbarians," who were well educated in that they knew a great deal of information, but who were totally deficient in matters of taste. And it was the general level of popular taste which determined the true measure of a people. What the new Germany required was a cultural crusade in the name of taste so that all Germans would care enough to keep themselves well groomed and surrounded with tasteful tools and furnishing.

In addition, he saw the development of artistic sensitivity as a way to restore social unity to Germany. Art provided a means to bind the various social classes to one another. The growing alienation of the German factory worker would cease, if he could feel joined in a common cultural community with the middle and upper classes. Lichtwark was not greatly moved by the poverty of the poor, only by their tastelessness. He saw the failure of German technological society in terms of its inability to produce good taste and refinement rather than its inability to alleviate its social and economic ills. He opposed social legislation, whether initiated by Bismarck, whom he admired, or by the Social Democrats, whom he detested. Although he occasionally lectured to groups of workers in Berlin about art, he eventually concerned himself chiefly with the cultural role of the gifted and the wealthy. He believed that the greatest achievement of a people was the production of genius and beauty, not literate masses. Thus, he seems to have considered it more important to beautify the Berlin slums than to eliminate them, to fill the windows of the poor with flower pots rather than their cooking pots with chickens or their pay envelopes with money.

II

In 1885, Lichtwark was asked to return to his native city and become Director of the Hamburg Art Museum (*Kunsthalle*). He enthusiastically accepted the post and determined to use his new position to launch a cultural crusade that would sweep across all of Germany.

In several speeches, which he delivered to groups of prominent Hamburgers at the outset of his new career, he clearly defined how he hoped to accomplish this.

First, Lichtwark proposed to popularize "dilettantism." Germans, he charged, were unsure of themselves in matters of taste. An enormous increase in artistic amateurism would correct this, especially in the plastic arts. This would not only make dilettantism more respectable and good taste more widespread, but it would also create a more sophisticated public for professional artists.[4] Furthermore, he argued, the general improvement in taste caused by increased dilettantism would improve the quality of German manufactured goods as well. "The future of our art and our industry," he asserted, "depends on whether we know how to educate a critical and demanding buying public." [5]

Second, Lichtwark demanded a reorientation of German education. German education, he charged, had become a crude form of head stuffing by means of memorization. This was not education, but instruction, he asserted, making a clear distinction between the German words, *Unterricht* and *Bilden.* Thus, the average German never developed any taste or aesthetic sensitivity, but merely acquired information. "This lack of aesthetic education which is so strikingly evident in the negligence of our outer-selves makes us appear as half-barbarians to more highly civilized nations." [6]

Lichtwark proposed to correct this deficiency by rearing German children in an artistic environment. In order to produce a new generation of tasteful and cultured Germans, walls, furniture, toys, picture-books, schools, parents, and teachers must all be artistically purified. Increased dilettantism would do much to achieve this end. The proper use of the Museum would do more.

Third, then, Lichtwark envisioned an active educational role for the Hamburg Art Museum. The Museum had to be more than a storage vault and display case for the art of times past. If its halls and walls were available to contemporary local talent as well, a new interest in art would follow. In addition, parents and teachers could be re-educated by means of special courses. Students could be brought to the Museum for lectures and discussions. In the end, a richer artistic life would result. Furthermore, if local art were properly displayed and appreciated, students would gain an awareness of the beauties of Hamburg and other Hanseatic towns and seek to preserve them.

III

Between 1886 and 1901, Lichtwark turned the Hamburg Art Museum into a novel kind of art-educational institution. He spoke regularly to children and adults and became renowned as a virtuoso lecturer and educator.[7] In addition, he opened the rooms of the Museum to a variety of unusual local exhibitions, each designed to stimulate popular interest.

Of these, the most important was undoubtedly the First Exhibition of Dilettante Art in 1893. On this occasion self-professed amateurs proudly exhibited their artistic works in the halls of the Museum. As might be expected, Lichtwark's dilettante movement appealed to those who enjoyed the leisure to dabble—especially wealthy women. He did not regard this as an undesirable situation, however, but rather as a welcome one. "All of those assumptions which are accepted by the women of today," he astutely noted, "will be absorbed by the next generation with their mother's milk." [8]

Other exhibitions gained equal success. In 1893 the First International Exhibition of Amateur Photography opened in the Museum. This encouraged local interest in the new medium and resulted in a group of amateur camera buffs who not only broke the hold of professionals in the field, but initiated an exciting naturalistic trend in their unposed photographs as well. By 1898 they hung their own remarkable exhibition in the Museum. Other amateur groups devoted to gardening, book-binding, pottery, and needlework followed a similar pattern of development.

These activities principally involved adults. With respect to children, Lichtwark's influence was less direct, but equally as pervasive. Inspired by the Museum Director, reformers gained confidence and boldly assaulted the hide-bound schools and homes of Hamburg in a myriad of ways. Some campaigned for better teaching methods in literature and drawing, others for more tastefully decorated nurseries and schoolrooms. Although the attackers were loosely organized and poorly coordinated, they quickly succeeded in altering the status quo. A brief examination of three of these efforts to transform the schools and homes can best illustrate how these kinds of reform were achieved: first, in the unusual matter of school decor; second, in the selection and teaching of German literature; and finally, in drawing instruction.

IV

It should be noted that German schools had looked like dreary factory sweat shops long before the industrial revolution. The only principle which had been followed prior to Lichtwark's arrival in Hamburg was not a decorative principle at all, but a hygienic one. For some unknown reason the Hamburg school administration considered drab gray more germ resistant than other colors; hence, the universal application of this color to all school walls.

Lichtwark achieved remarkable success in his campaign to beautify the schools, since there were few vested interests to oppose him. After he prevailed upon many of his wealthy friends to donate paintings, the cost of redecorating promised to be small. The Hamburg school administration quickly agreed that the schools could be both hygienic and colorful and adopted the following resolution: "The interior decor of the schools should not distract the child by its obtrusiveness, but should make the school rooms more homelike while also awakening an aesthetic consciousness in the child." [9]

In addition, Lichtwark won an energetic champion to his cause in Meir Spanier of Münster, whose lengthy pamphlet, "Artistic Picture Decorations for Schools" (*Künstlerischer Bilderschmuck für Schulen*) appeared in 1897 [10] and quickly went through several editions.

Spanier, like Lichtwark, believed that an artistic environment exercised a more profound effect on the growing child than did any art appreciation course. According to him, "A work of art provides a secret education that is usually more lasting than conscious pedagogical efforts. . . . The artistic instincts of young people must be ennobled so that they are repelled by bad art whenever it appears." [11] In a third edition of his pamphlet Spanier also attacked the hygienic purists, who apparently still had their spokesmen as late as 1899. One of the most outspoken of these advocated order and cleanliness as the only suitable principles of classroom decor and pictures of Christ and the Kaiser as the only suitable decorations.[12] Spanier retorted by suggesting that the Kaiser prohibit the sale of tasteless pictures of himself to such people.

Spanier was influenced not only by Lichtwark, but by similar men and movements in England and America as well. He warmly admired John Ruskin's efforts to bring art to the poor people of London and sought to do the same for Germany by encouraging publishers to print inexpensive reproductions of masterpieces. Like Lichtwark he saw art as the all-purpose social cement which would re-integrate the poor into German culture. He also praised the American struggle against cultural barbarism, which he saw centered on the figure of Ross Turner and a meeting of artists and teachers held in Boston in 1892.[13] Only Russia, he sadly reported, remained untouched by the new interest in art and classroom decor.

Spanier foresaw remarkable results if his picture programs succeeded. Parents and children would join hands and rush to the nearest book store to purchase the inexpensive reproductions which publishers, at his urging, would have made available. A masterpiece would then hang on every wall of every home and school in Germany reflecting the good taste and culture of German citizens, and combatting the growing industrial ugliness.

If Spanier vented his spleen on drab walls, Heinrich Wolgast, a Hamburg teacher, turned his on bad literature. The crusade for better books, which he initiated, vividly illustrates how Lichtwark's influence permeated the literary arts as well as the plastic.

Wolgast attacked the unrestricted use of literature for religious and nationalistic ends with little or no regard for its literary merit. In essence, he agreed with the moralists of ancient Greece and Rome who rejected the notion that poor literature could teach good behavior. Sound moral values could not be presented in shabby literary dress; one could not freely separate the ethical from the aesthetic. Similarly, Wolgast attacked memorization as being no substitute for understanding. Memorization and repetition led eventually to a sense of literary saturation and revulsion.

In his pamphlet "On Picture Books and Illustrations," Wolgast asserted that the first six years of a child's life were crucial to his cultural development. He reiterated Lichtwark's concern for the nursery and urged that the pages of the child's first book be filled with true art. Undoubtedly, Wolgast had met Lichtwark prior to publishing this pamphlet and was already influenced by the Director. Although their relationship never ripened into close friendship, Wolgast acknowledged that Lichtwark's presence and inspiration was crucial.[14]

For the most part, however, the "Children's Literature Movement" (*Jugendschriftenbewegung*), which Wolgast founded, prospered without Lichtwark's participation. Wolgast provided this movement with inspiration and a manifesto when he published his most successful work, *The Horror of Our Children's Literature*, (*Das Elend unserer Jugendliteratur*), in November of 1896.[15] In this book he pleaded with parents and teachers to put better literature in the hands of German children. He centered his thrust on poetry, demanding that "Adolescent literature in poetic form must be a work of art." [16] This meant that it should be written by poets, not by moral zealots or patriots. He also called for livelier teaching, more and better school libraries, and good inexpensive editions so that book owning and collecting could become popular among all classes. Wolgast especially attacked that genre of children's literature which appealed to the "baser instincts" and singled out the extremely popular travel and adventure books of Karl May at literary anathema. May's books, he charged, peddled a vicious brand of pious sadism wherein righteous heroes sadistically mauled and tortured their villainous enemies.[17]

A third movement for reform which Lichtwark inspired and encouraged focussed on drawing instruction. Its avowed purpose was to transform drawing instruction from copying into creative self-activity. The method of instruction which had dominated Hamburg schools until the mid-90's bore the name of its author, Stuhlmann. Stuhlmann claimed that his system was based on Friedrich Fröbel's idea of learning basic forms—squares and circles—by drawing cubes and balls. The spirit of Fröbel was lost in the transmission to Stuhlmann, however. Students instructed in his quaint method usually lost their eyesight as well as their interest in drawing.

They carefully drew curved and straight lines with the help of dotted paper. The lines were abstract and meaningless. Teachers required no special drawing instruction in order to inflict this stigmatic system on their helpless wards, only an instruction sheet, dotted paper, and discipline, all of which were plentifully available in Hamburg schools. Inspired and assisted by Lichtwark, two Hamburg teachers, Karl Götze and Johannes Ehlers, led the assault on the Stuhlmann method.

Ehlers had begun to teach drawing in 1887. Quickly recognizing the evils of the existing method, he introduced reforms into his own classes which he then refined throughout the 90's. Ehlers' reforms centered in the third and fourth years of the elementary school. He provided his students with a familiar object to observe—an egg, a radish, or a lemon, for example. He then removed these objects and asked the students to draw them from memory. This demanded precise observation and *Anschauung*, perception, on the part of the students. In order to avoid rigidity Ehlers employed various muscle exercises and soft drawing materials like chalk or charcoal in his instruction. Students then sketched an imaginary outline of the object in the air before committing their drawing to paper or slate. In the development of this system, Ehlers was influenced by the work of an American, J. Liberty Tadd, whose book on drawing instruction was translated into German and published in Hamburg in 1900.[18]

Ehlers' colleague, Karl Götze, on the other hand, was less concerned with the methodology of drawing instruction. For him drawing served as a form of free self-expression which permitted the child to develop his personality fully. In his most important work, *The Child as Artist* (*Das Kind als Kunstler*),[19] Götze asserted that the technical achievement in learning to draw was not as important as the creative activity involved. The teacher, therefore, should never judge or criticize drawing as a technical achievement. Thus, he strongly advocated artistic permissiveness.

In order to popularize his ideas, Götze helped to found the Teacher's Union for Art Education (*Lehrervereinigung für kunstlerische Bildung*) in 1896 and the art education journal, *Der Sämann* (*The Sower*). In 1898 the Teacher's Union sponsored the first exhibition of children's art in the Art Museum, an exhibition which took its title and rallying cry from Götze's book, *The Child as Artist*. *Der Sämann*, on the other hand, quickly became one of Germany's leading educational reform journals. Although its life was short, its impact was great, and Lichtwark was one of its leading contributors.

Where Lichtwark hesitated was when he feared that his efforts might be expanded prematurely or transformed into a purely pedagogical movement devoted to making art a child-centered activity. He lacked Götze's Rousseauean faith in the developing natural genius of the liberated child. The evangelical enthusiasm of Götze could not be restrained, however. He acted to expand the Hamburg successes into a nation-wide movement. Faced with the prospect of control slipping from his hands, Lichtwark reluctantly joined Götze in founding the Art Education Movement at the turn of the century and sponsoring a series of national meetings of prominent artists and educators to discuss the cultural problems of the Fatherland. The first meeting was scheduled for the fall of 1901.

V

Lichtwark had sown his seeds of reform among the wealthy and the well established. On Sunday, September 29, 1901, he reaped his rewards. Chatting amiably with one another as they arrived, two hundred and fifty German notables in the fields of art and education assembled in the Royal Sculpture Museum in Dresden for the opening of the first Art Education Meeting. Their broadly defined purpose was the rejuvenation of German cultural life. Specifically, they came to save the plastic arts—drawing, painting, and sculpture.

Who were these champions of cultural reform? They were middle-class men with official positions, titles, fixed incomes, and future pensions, educational administrators representing thirty-four German states and towns, teachers representing twenty teacher's associations as well as artists, professors, and other cultural luminaries. All had achieved status and recognition in Imperial Germany. The high priests had assembled to reform themselves. They performed the necessary rites, danced the necessary ritual dances, and pontificated pompously about art and education. As might be expected nothing very spectacular resulted—not even a good rain shower.

Lichtwark valiantly sought to save the day. He delivered the opening speech entitled, "The German of the Future" (*Der Deutsche der Zukunft*). In so doing he hoped to create a dialogue about an ideal German cultural type, a German version of the English gentleman, and thereby prevent the meeting from becoming merely a discussion of pedagogical problems. His effort failed. Not only was he unable to save the Meeting from becoming a genial social gathering for established educators and artists, but his German of the future essentially turned out to be a Prussian officer with artistic inclinations, hardly an inspiring ideal.

Two further meetings in 1903 and 1905 revealed the full extent of the disaster. The 1903 Meeting convened in Weimar and the 1905 Meeting in Hamburg, with the Weimar Meeting devoted to literature and the Hamburg Meeting to music, dance, and gymnastics. Karl Götze delivered the final platitudinous post mortem to the third meeting on October 15, 1905. In glowing terms he recounted a decade of success and predicted a glorious future. A powerful revolution has transformed our external lives, he asserted, and "now seizes our inner life with a formative life principle." One searches in vain, however, for any proposal to convene another meeting.

The Art Education Movement proved more lasting and successful than the meetings. Although it never developed a tightly knit organization, it continued to center its activities in Hamburg. It provided a title under which a myriad of loosely connected reform groups worked. Lichtwark remained its dominant personality. Under its auspices, museums assumed a more active role in community life, publishers provided inexpensive editions of German literature and reproductions of paintings, school boards repainted walls and hung more and better pictures in schools, teachers employed new and livelier techniques to teach the arts, psychologists researched the relationship between the personality of the child and artistic expression (Georg Kerschensteiner collected over 6,000,000 children's drawings by 1906 which he puzzled over for years afterwards), and dilettantes became more respectable and numerous. Due to the Movement's loose organization, it easily spilled its members into other reform movements as well. The Movement failed, however, to alleviate the drabness of technological society principally because it never made contact with Germany's proletarian masses. Nor did it succeed in healing the breaches in German society as Lichtwark hoped it would by reintegrating the industrial worker into local cultural life. Rather, the cultural alienation of the workers increased.

Lichtwark had believed that if he saved the growing German middle class, he would save society. The new scions of taste would emerge from this group and cast their spell over the workers and other alienated peoples. Class differences merely represented a loss of community awareness. Once the middle class had been reintegrated into its historic context, it would influence other disaffected groups as well. As a matter of course, an improvement in the general level of artistic taste would follow. A new sense of community and a new sense of beauty would grow hand in hand with each other. This great faith in the restorative powers of art appears in the long run to have been ill-founded. Art has at times strengthened community ties, but it has hardly healed the great social schisms of our age.

Finally, it should be noted that Lichtwark's crusade was not directed solely against technological ugliness and social disunity, but against middle-class Philistinism and educational pedantry as well. Lichtwark accepted a set of absolute standards with respect to art, taste, artifacts, and dress. His anger was directed against all those who fell short of these standards or who refused to recognize their existence. He saw the new kind of Museum, the artistically reformed school, and the highly motivated dilettante as the means by which these standards could be imposed on the rest of German society, the only way by which Germany could be saved from the crassness and ugliness of a new age.

No one ever declared that the Art Education Movement had completed its task or that there were no more learned barbarians in Germany. With the outbreak of the War in 1914 and the death of Lichtwark in that same year, it merely disappeared, as it had appeared, in a haphazard and disorganized fashion.

FOOTNOTES

1. There are two biographies of Lichtwark: Julius Gebhard, *Alfred Lichtwark und die Kunsterziehungsbewegung in Hamburg* (Hamburg, 1947); and Anna von Zeromski, *Alfred Lichtwark, Ein Führer zur deutschen Zukunft* (Jena, 1924). Gebhard's book is more thorough and critical while von Zeromski's is more laudatory and readable.
2. Alfred Lichtwark, "Justus Brinckmann—Der Typus," in *Das Bild des Deutschen* (Langensalza, 1931), pp. 65–66.
3. Gebhard, *op. cit.,* pp. 35–40.
4. Quoted in Gebhard, *op. cit.,* pp. 44–45. See also Alfred Lichtwark, "Das Aufleben des Dilettantismus," in *Das Bild des Deutschen* (Weinheim, 1962).
5. Quoted in Gebhard, *op. cit.,* p. 20.
6. Alfred Lichtwark, "Die Kunst in der Schule," in Alfred Lichtwark, *Eine Auswahl seiner Schriften* (Berlin, 1917), Vol. I, p. 32.
7. The famous artist, Max Liebermann, admiringly called him a born educator. See Zeromski, *op. cit.,* p. 115.
8. Quoted in Marcks, *op. cit.,* pp. 42–47.
9. Quoted in *Ibid.,* p. 93.
10. The 3rd enlarged edition (Leipzig, 1902), is quoted hereafter.
11. Quoted in Gebhard, *op. cit.,* p. 89.
12. Spanier, *Bilderschmuck,* p. 6.
13. *Ibid.,* p. 49.
14. Quoted in *Gebhard,* p. 104.
15. The 6th edition (Leipzig, 1922) is quoted here.
16. *Ibid.,* pp. III–VIII.
17. See the defense of May in Ludwig Gurlitt, *Gerechtigkeit für Karl May* (Radebeul bei Dresden, 1919).
18. J. Liberty Tadd, *Neue Wege zur Künstlerishen Erziehung der Jugend Zeichnen—Handfertigkeit—Naturstudium—Kunst* (Hamburg, Leipzig 1900).
19. (Hamburg, 1898).

Part Five

Religion and Education

Religion and religiously oriented organizations have often been closely associated with education and schools. In Christian communities until quite recently, education was largely a function of churches. Similarly, in the Islamic lands of the Near East, Asia, and Africa, religious bodies controlled schools which often adjoined mosques; religious functionaries acted as teachers; and religion predominated in the curriculum. Similar close relationships between religion and education have been found in areas characterized by other religious faiths—Buddhism, Hinduism, and Judaism, for example.

The educational functions of religious bodies were also intertwined with their missionary and proselytizing activities. Missionaries in Africa, the Near East, Asia, and Latin America provided various types of education along with their sermons on the Gospel or the Koran.

Where churches or equivalent religious organizations assume other than purely religious functions they may be described as "non-specialized" social units. This was true, for example, of churches in medieval Europe and in the Byzantine and Ottoman Empires, and of the missionary churches in Africa and elsewhere. With social and political modernization, which, among other things, has meant the emergence of nation-states, the functions of the church have been circumscribed. The task of nation-building inevitably entailed a more active part by the government or the state in educational affairs. In several cases, this development gave rise to conflicts between what is often referred to as "state" and "church." This has been particularly evident in Western nations—Britain, the United States, France, the Scandinavian countries, the Netherlands, and others. With the consolidation of modern polities it was inevitable that conflicts over education would arise. On the one hand, the cohesiveness and solidarity of a modern nation-state presuppose a trained, competent "electorate" and explicit and positive attempts by the state to recruit and train the young to the tasks and responsibilities of citizenship. Invariably in all these nations it has been assumed that the basic desideratum for induction into citizenship and the national culture was universal, compulsory schooling which only the state could make possible. The viability of religious organizations, on the other hand, presupposes new generations who are trained in the specific beliefs and practices of those organizations. While each church calls for "particularistic" forms of education, specific to the content of its doctrines, and controlled by it, the state calls for more "universalistic" forms. To illustrate the church-state conflicts over education in the West, two political democracies have been chosen: England and the United States.

Both countries have been characterized by religious pluralism and, in the last hundred years or so, by religious toleration and the principle of parental freedom in education. Both countries have had stable political institutions and a party system of government. In both countries there has been a noticeable absence of the anti-clericalism that has rocked France. In both cases conflicts over the church-state-school issue have been resolved through the functioning of "routine politics," i.e., through accepted channels of public and legislative debate. And generally the issue has revolved around two major problems: (a) religious instruction in the state or public schools; and (b) public support of denominational schools. While the processes at work may have been the same, the arrangements regarding the two thorny problems have varied.

Herbert Kliebard analyzes the issue in the United States by focusing on the major court cases and by placing the issue in its historical context. He points out that in the interpretation of the Constitutional principles, the Supreme Court has recently viewed the role of the state as one of religious "neutrality" rather than as a strict "wall of separation." As the role of the government extends to all facets of social life, there seems to be more elasticity in extending benefits to denominational schools. On the other hand, the Court has upheld the principle of absence of religious instruction and observances in the public school.

In examining the "religious question" in English education, Andreas Kazamias concentrates on the major legislative enactments, e.g., the Acts of 1870, 1902, and 1944. He discusses the issue as an integral part of British politics and shows the interplay of social, political, and religious forces over education as the country moved from laissez-faire political liberalism to the Welfare State. He also suggests that the differences in the arrangements concerning religion and education between England and the United States must be sought in the differing political and educational roles that religious organizations have traditionally played, and the variations in the concepts of education. From the experience of these two countries, one could hypothesize that changes in the functions of school are accompanied by concomitant changes in the relationships between religion and education.

European metropoles transplanted their educational ideas and institutions into their colonies. David Scanlon points out that the patterns of church-state-school relationships in the African colonies reflected those of England, Belgium, and to a lesser extent, France. Shifts in policy at home were accompanied by changes in the colonies. Because of the predominant role in education played by religious bodies (missions) and the practical obstacles faced by the African nations after independence, education continues to be largely provided by religious organizations. Scanlon implies that a process similar to that described above seems to be at work, namely, that as state authority consolidates, and as education is perceived to contribute to nation-building, the educational functions of religious bodies are likely to be circumscribed.

Daniel Creselius' essay on the Moslem university Al-Azhar provides another variation of the interplay between religion—this time Islam—education, and the state. More explicitly than in the other selections of this section, Creselius analyzes this interplay in terms of traditionalism and modernization or cultural change. Religion and religiously oriented organizations by and large have been conservative factors in the push toward social and political modernization. This has been especially true of Islam, a religion much more rigid, encompassing, and "other-worldly" than Christianity or Buddhism, for example. Al-Azhar for centuries trained Islamic religious leaders (*ulama*) who generally performed other than purely religious functions. It was also the custodian of Islamic traditions and doctrines. The emergence of liberalism, secularism, and nationalism in the twentieth century unavoidably created cleavages and bifurcations in the Egyptian society. Al-Azhar, representing tradition, became a reactionary force seeking to ward off change. Following the Revolution of 1952, the modernist leaders of the new state proceeded to change the structure and functions of the university in order to bring it more within the mainstream of the new revolutionary ideology. Creselius' study should provide the springboard for other similar inquiries into the dynamics of modernization involving religious institutions.

Religion, the State, and Public Schooling: The American Context

HERBERT M. KLIEBARD

Supreme Court decisions of the 1960's have dramatically brought to the fore the question of the relationship between religion and the schools in the United States and made it the subject of heated public debate. Sometimes obscured by immediate questions of Bible-reading and prayer in public schools is the fact that these questions are really part of the larger issue of church-state relationships in this country, an issue with a long and complex history. In some countries, like England, where a tradition of a state church has been maintained, the analysis of legislative enactments on church-state questions provides a convenient vehicle for understanding the development of the issue. By contrast, the central issue which dominates the question of church-state relationships in the United States, is the meaning and/or the wisdom of the prohibitions set forth in the First Amendment to the Constitution, particularly the so-called Establishment Clause.

The First Amendment says, in part, "Congress shall make no law respecting an establishment of religion, or prohibiting the free exercise thereof." It is with these words that the framers of the Bill of Rights sought to insure religious liberty against infringement by the federal government. It is clear from the wording that governmental coercion with respect to religious beliefs or religious practice is forbidden, but what is forbidden by the prohibition of establishment laws is the subject of much debate. This is partly because establishment apparently meant many things in the period before the First Amendment was drafted.

In the early years of the Commonwealth of Massachusetts, establishment took a form that in some respects was similar to establishment practices in England, although, of course, the Congregational Church was established, not the Church of England. As in England, however, financial support for the church, including pay for clergymen, came from public taxes, and those who were not members of the established church were denied certain civil liberties. This establishment pattern was modified in the charter of 1691, however, so that other Protestant citizens could vote, and it even became posssible in later years for the state to support clergymen who were not Congregationalists.

Some colonies such as Pennsylvania and Rhode Island developed traditions of religious liberty, and, although nominal religious establishments existed in the Middle Colonies, they frequently took the form of governmental support for a variety of recognized religions. At times, this pluralistic form of establishment adopted the practice of permitting each individual community to choose the particular minister who would receive public support. Such a practice was widespread, for example, in New York.

Virginia and other southern colonies initially established the Anglican Church but did not maintain any important ties with the church hierarchy in England, and, like the other American colonies, slipped into a pattern of broad religious toleration and support for a variety of churches. By the end of the eighteenth century, Virginia chose to disestablish entirely. A clear-cut choice was available to the Virginia legislators between James Henry's "Bill Establishing a Provision for Teachers of the Christian Religion" and Thomas Jefferson's "Bill for Establishing Religious Freedom." The former, if passed, would have supported virtually all of the recognized religions in Virginia at the time, perpetuating a pluralistic form of religious establishment. The latter prohibited any governmental support of religion even of a nonpreferential kind. With the help of Madison's "Memorial and Remonstrance Against Religious Assessments," James' bill died, and Jefferson's bill was passed in 1786. This was just three years before the debate over the Bill of Rights began.

Although we have no verbatim record of the debate in the First Congress, it is clear from available data that the wording of the First Amendment was the subject of great concern to the framers of the Bill of Rights. Some wordings which would have unquestionably permitted governmental support of religion on a nonpreferential basis were rejected, as were wordings which would clearly have prohibited such a relationship. An additional factor involved, emphasized by Professor Katz in his interpretation of the debate,[1] was that the Bill of Rights was designed as a limitation on the power of the federal government, not that of the states. The framers of the First Amendment, then, had to be careful not to interfere with existing state establishments of religion, of which there were five at the time. When the House and the Senate passed different versions of the Amendment, a committee was appointed to resolve the differences. Madison, who led the delegation from the House, was apparently successful in achieving a consensus favorable to the House of Representative's more separationist version. It should be emphasized, however, that the Amendment was in no way intended to interfere with the right of individual states to maintain establishments of religion.

No mention was made of education or schooling in the Constitution proper, or in the Bill of Rights, or in any of the subsequent Amendments to the Constitution. This means, of course, that education is a power reserved for the states, and, furthermore, that the prohibitions contained in the First Amendment to the United States Constitution have no relevance to the manner in which the states conduct schools. Even this question, however, was largely academic throughout the first part of the nineteenth century because there were no state systems of schools as we know them today.

Much of the credit for developing a free and universal system of schools belongs, of course, to Horace Mann, who is largely responsible for accomplishing this task directly in Massachusetts and, by example, in the rest of the country. Mann served as secretary to the State Board of Education in Massachusetts from 1837 to 1848, and worked tirelessly to develop a system of common schools that would serve the Commonwealth's various social classes and diverse religious population. As such, he realized that the public school, if it was indeed to serve all, could not engage in direct sectarian teaching, as was practiced in private schools sponsored by religious groups. To leave religious teaching out entirely, however, given Mann's strong Christian commitment, would have been completely out of the question. Mann compromised by eliminating the teaching of particular religious dogma, but retaining the Bible, read without note or comment, as the basic core of religious teaching in the public schools of Massachusetts. This compromise laid Mann open to criticism that he was anti-religious and anti-Christian, and he was continually defending himself against such charges in his annual reports to the Board.[2]

Mann's compromise, however, turned out to be a rather practical one. Most citizens seemed satisfied with this form of religious instruction, with the only significant opposition coming from the growing Catholic minority. Here and there, particularly in the latter half of the nineteenth century, we find Catholics challenging the practice of Bible-reading in the public schools and some of these challenges reaching the state courts. One of the most important of these state cases is the famous Edgerton Case.[3] Here, five Catholic residents of the city of Edgerton, Wisconsin objected to the fact that two public school teachers had taken it upon themselves to begin each school day with a recitation from the Bible. Their objection was based on several religious grounds. First of all, they pointed out that the King James version was being used, a translation that was not approved by their Church. Furthermore, they argued that the Bible, according to their religion "ought not to be read indiscriminately" and that only duly authorized interpreters of the Bible are entrusted with this responsibility according to Catholic practice. The Wisconsin State Constitution is more clear-cut than is the United States Constitution on the intermingling of church and state, and the Wisconsin Supreme Court, basing their decision on the State Constitution, ruled unanimously in favor of the petitioners. Bible-reading in the public schools of the State of Wisconsin was therefore ruled unconstitutional in 1890.

One of the most important events insofar as making the schools the setting for much of the church-state controversy occurred in 1868 with the passage of the Fourteenth Amendment. This post-Civil War measure, designed to guarantee certain civil liberties to the newly freed slaves, stated, in part, "No state shall make or enforce any law which shall abridge the privileges and immunities of citizens of the United States."

Many years later, the Supreme Court was to interpret the Fourteenth Amendment as making the prohibitions of the First Amendment applicable to the states. The states, then, became subject to the same limitations that had been imposed on Congress by the adoption of the First Amendment. It is the combination of the Fourteenth Amendment and the First Amendment, then, which has served to make the schools the major arena for the church-state controversy in America.

The first major Supreme Court cases involving the relationship between church and state, however, were based not on the First Amendment (made applicable to the States by the Fourteenth), but on the "due process clause" of the Fourteenth Amendment. This portion of the Amendment was designed to protect citizens of the United States by prohibiting the state from depriving "any person of life, liberty, or property without due process of the law. . . ."

In 1923, the Supreme Court was called upon to decide whether the State of Nebraska had violated the terms of this Amendment by passing a law which restricted the teaching of "languages other than English" to pupils who had completed the eighth grade.[4] The law, a product of World War I, was aimed at curbing private foreign language schools. These schools, it was felt, were thwarting the public schools' efforts to Americanize immigrants. The statute was violated by a teacher at the Zion Evangelical Lutheran School, and he was subsequently fined in accordance with the law. Essentially what the Supreme Court was called upon to decide was whether the Nebraska legislature had exceeded its power to control school affairs by preventing Robert T. Meyer from teaching German to pre-adolescents. The Court ruled that the state's power must give way in this instance to the appellant's individual rights since it could not be shown that the teaching of modern foreign languages had a pernicious effect on the individual or society.[5]

Another case which was to have a profound effect on the limitation of the states' power with respect to education is the famous Oregon case which was decided in 1925.[6] A referendum had been passed in the Oregon election of 1922 which would have required all children between the ages of eight and sixteen to attend public schools only. Like the Nebraska law, it was directed at private sectarian education in general, although the active support of the measure by the Ku Klux Klan would seem to indicate a distinct anti-Catholic bias. To private schools, one run by the Society of Sisters of the Holy Names of Jesus and Mary and the other, a non-sectarian military academy, sought to prevent Governor Pierce, a strong supporter of the law, from carrying out its terms. The Constitutional grounds were the same as in *Meyer,* the Fourteenth Amendment's due process clause, and again the Supreme Court ruled that the state had exceeded its power by, in effect, disenfranchising private schools and creating a kind of state monopoly in education without "due process of the law." Stated differently, the decision required that the State of Oregon, and by inference all other states, recognize private schools, secular and religious, as qualified to provide the education that is required by the compulsory education laws of the state. Both *Meyer* and *Pierce* illustrate a limitation on state power which not only involves the right of religious schools to exist but to constitute a recognized alternative to the education that the state provides.

A further limitation on the states' power to control educational affairs, this time within the context of the public school itself, is to be found in the Supreme Court's rulings on the question of the compulsory flag-salute. A kind of confrontation between state power and individual religious freedom developed when members of the Jehovah's Witnesses faith refused on religious grounds to salute the flag in certain public schools where this was required. In the first of these cases, the Supreme Court upheld the right of the state, through its duly constituted educational authorities, to prescribe those practices it deemed necessary to attain legitimate educational objectives.[7] The tone of the decision indicated a deliberate attempt to keep the Supreme Court from becoming a kind of national school board. Three years later, however, when the refusal by Jehovah's Witnesses to salute the flag in public schools was considered again, the Supreme Court dramatically reversed itself on this question.[8] This time the Court held that state power must give way when it conflicts with Constitutional guarantees of religious freedom. Taken together, the *Meyer, Pierce, Gobitis,* and *Barnette* cases clearly indicate that, in mid-twentieth century, the Supreme Court was to become the forum and the schools the setting for the debate over the definition of church-state relationships in this country.

The relationship between church and state in America affected school affairs in two ways: The first was related to the legal role and status of religious schools in this country. Their right to exist as an alternative to public education had already been established in *Pierce,* but the further question of whether they were legally entitled to support out of public funds, and if so what kind and in what manner distributed, was yet to be resolved. The second revolved around the issue of the kinds of limitations that the First Amendment imposes on the conduct of *public* school affairs when made applicable to the states by the Fourteenth Amendment. At stake was Horace Mann's attempt to include a common core of religion as part of the program of the public schools. Given America's political and judicial traditions, questions of this scope could hardly be decided once and for all time by passing a law or issuing a ruling. Instead, interpretations of these issues would be progressively developed as the Supreme Court was faced with specific litigation arising from actual events.

The first time the Supreme Court considered the question of state aid to religious schools was in 1930 when several citizens of Louisiana objected to a state law which made publicly owned textbooks available to students attending religious schools. Their challenge was not based on the prohibitions set forth in the First Amendment, but on the Fourteenth Amendment itself. They argued that, under the Louisiana law, their taxes were being used to support private education. Public taxes, therefore, were being used for a private purpose, not a public one. The Supreme Court disagreed with the petitioners and unanimously held that *children* were being benefited by the law, not religious schools.[9] This is the first official recognition of what has come to be called the "child benefit theory."

The "child benefit theory" was revived and reinterpreted seventeen years later when the Court was again faced with a challenge to the use of public funds for religious education.[10] This time the immediate question was not textbooks, but the reimbursement to parents by the state for the cost of sending children to and from parochial schools. A New Jersey law permitted such a practice, and the Board of Education in Ewing Township had implemented it. This time, the petitioners based their case not only on the Fourteenth Amendment, but, for the first time, on the First Amendment made applicable to the states by the Fourteenth. The question in the *Everson* case, then, was not just whether public funds were being used for a private purpose, but whether the prohibition against a governmental establishment of religion could be interpreted as making the practice unconstitutional. This time the Supreme Court was sharply divided over the issue. In a five-to-four decision, they upheld the New Jersey statute again invoking the idea that children were being benefited (this time by being protected from traffic hazards) not the religious schools. In the course of this decision, however, Mr. Justice Black, speaking for the majority, offered a far-reaching interpretation of what the establishment clause of the First Amendment meant. Paradoxically, it was a strong separationist interpretation, declaring that, "No tax in any amount, large or small, can be levied to support any religious activities or institutions, whatever they may be called, or whatever form they may adopt to teach or practice religion." Here for the first time in a court opinion, Mr. Justice Black used Jefferson's old metaphor "a wall of separation between Church and State" to describe the relationship. Dissenters in this case were quick to point up the seeming inconsistency between the interpretation given and the actual findings in the case.

In 1948, just a year later, however, the "wall of separation" interpretation was used to strike down a religious program in the public schools of Champaign, Illinois.[11] The program involved the use of school grounds for conducting classes in religion sponsored by a nonsectarian group called the Champaign Council of Religious Education. The classes were conducted on a voluntary basis, but Mrs. Vashti McCollum, an atheist, nevertheless felt that the cooperation of school authorities and the use of school property constituted a violation of her rights under the establishment clause of the First Amendment. A majority of eight Supreme Court Justices upheld Mrs. McCollum's petition citing the "wall of separation" phrase as basic to their interpretation.

When a similar case arose four years later, however, the Supreme Court retreated slightly from the strong separationist position they had taken in *McCollum*.[12] The main difference between the New York released-time program being considered and the religious program in Illinois was that religious classes were held off school grounds in New York. The New York program, nevertheless, represented close cooperation between school authorities and religious groups and the adaptation of public school functions in order to insure the success of a religious program. As in *McCollum,* the petitioners in *Zorach* argued that the coercive power of the state was being used to further sectarian education, a violation of the First Amendment. The Court disagreed, finding instead that some forms of cooperation between church and state were normal and natural. To find otherwise, they thought, could be interpreted as hostility to religion. Such a decision represented, however, an apparent contradiction. Either the "wall of separation" metaphor represented an accurate way to describe church-state relationships in this country as suggested in *Everson* and *McCollum,* or the absolute separation implied by that term constituted a form of hostility which was contrary to the American religious tradition. Taking *Cochran, Everson, McCollum,* and *Zorach* together, it is clear that the Court had found on both sides of that issue.

In the 1960's, the Supreme Court reexamined their interpretation of the church-state question in the light of two celebrated cases. The first of these, *Engel* v. *Vitale,*[13] involved a "non-sectarian" prayer composed by the New York Board of Regents and recommended for daily recitation in the public schools of that state. The prayer said simply, "Almighty God, we acknowledge our dependence upon Thee, and we beg Thy blessings upon us, our parents, our teachers, and our country." Several parents of children attending the New Hyde Park public schools objected on the grounds that, although the prayer was supposed to be voluntary, the state through the schools had directly involved itself in religious affairs. Such interference by the state in religious matters, they claimed, violated the establishment clause as interpreted in *McCollum.* In a six-to-one decision, the Supreme Court held simply that the government is not in the business of writing prayers or recommending their use. The decision offered no important extension of the "wall of separation" doctrine nor did it modify it in any significant way. Nevertheless, it stimulated a major controversy across the country, and many public officials felt impelled to issue statements sharply critical of the Court's decision. Charges of "atheistic Supreme Court" and "Godless schools" were frequently made. Actually, however, the practice of reciting government composed prayers in public was an isolated one, and in that sense, at least, the implications of the *Engel* decision were not very far reaching.

In 1963, a year later, however, the Court was faced with a case which, in effect, challenged a long-standing practice in American public schools, recitation from the Bible without note or comment.[14] It will be remembered that Bible recitation was the heart of Horace Mann's solution to the question of religious and moral teaching in the public schools and was still a widespread practice in many states. In some states, it was even compulsory. The challenge to this practice came from two sources: The Maryland case arose when Mrs. Madalyn Murray, active in atheist causes, kept her son out of Woodbourne Junior High School in Baltimore because school officials refused to excuse him from the compulsory Bible recitation. In Pennsylvania, Ellory Schempp, a practicing Unitarian, refused to participate in a similar program in Abington Senior High School. Both cases reached the Supreme Court at about the same time and were argued on successive days.

The Supreme Court, in one decision covering both cases, held that the practice of Bible-reading as a school exercise, whether compulsory or not, represented a violation of the establishment clause of the First Amendment. Not only was this decision much more significant than *Engel* in terms of the particular practice involved, but Mr. Justice Clark, speaking for the Court in *Abington* ventured a kind of reinterpretation of the establishment clause. Rather than using "wall of separation" as his theme, he built his interpretation on the term *neutrality*. He argued, in effect, that neutrality more accurately describes the relationship between church and state in America than does "wall of separation." By way of interpretation, the majority decision in *Abington* created a new test of constitutionality under the First Amendment.

> The test may be stated as follows: What are the purpose and primary effect of the enactment? If either is the advancement or inhibition of religion then the enactment exceeds the scope of legislative power as circumscribed by the Constitution. That is to say that to withstand the strictures of the Establishment Clause there must be a secular legislative purpose and a primary effect that neither advances nor inhibits religion.[15]

Clearly, under such an interpretation, some kinds of relationship between church and state are possible. It is in that sense a more accurate and realistic interpretation than "wall of separation" given the increasing tendency in modern times for government to touch almost all facets of our lives. The neutrality principle, however, clearly forbids governmental preference in religious matters even to the extent of preferring those who believe over those who do not believe. In that sense, it is not certain how the Court would decide if it were to reconsider the *Zorach* case, for example, in the light of the neutrality principle. At any rate, Bible-reading as well as other school-sponsored religious exercises, could not "withstand the strictures" of this interpretation of the establishment clause.

It is difficult to determine from our present vantage point whether the neutrality principle will be quickly replaced by a new interpretation or whether it will be consistently applied and perhaps extended in subsequent cases involving church-state relationships. The present American posture on matters of church and state has emerged in small increments with much backing and filling. It was not brought about by sweeping executive pronouncements or by major legislation. Although the ultimate source of our interpretation has been the First Amendment to the Constitution, that interpretation has been progressively built and modified only when substantive legal questions about concrete rather than abstract issues have reached the courts. Any effort to take it out of that context of decision-making would be a most radical undertaking.

FOOTNOTES

1. Wilbur Katz, *Religion and American Constitutions* (Evanston: Northwestern University Press, 1964), pp. 8–10.
2. See, for example, Horace Mann, *Eighth Annual Report* (1950), p. 75 and *Twelfth Annual Report* (Washington, D.C.: Hugh Birch–Horace Mann Fund of the National Education Association, 1952), p. 116.
3. *State ex. rel. Weiss et al* v. *District Board of School District No. Eight of the City of Edgerton* 76 Wis. 177 (1890).
4. Another section of the law required that English be the language of instruction in all the schools of the state, but this section of the law was not challenged.
5. *Meyer* v. *Nebraska,* 262 U.S. 390 (1923).
6. *Pierce* v. *Society of Sisters, Pierce* v. *Hill Military Academy,* 268 U.S. 510 (1925).
7. *Minersville School District* v. *Gobitis,* 310 U.S. 586 (1940).
8. *West Virginia State Board of Education* v. *Barnette,* 319 U.S. 624 (1943).
9. *Cochran* v. *Louisiana,* 281 U.S. 370 (1930).
10. *Everson* v. *Board of Education,* 330 U.S. 1 (1947).
11. *Illinois ex. rel. McCollum* v. *Board of Education,* 333 U.S. 203 (1948).
12. *Zorach* v. *Clauson,* 343 U.S. 306 (1952).
13. *Engel* v. *Vitale,* 370 U.S. 421 (1962).
14. *School District of Abington Township* v. *Schempp,* 374 U.S. 203 (1963).
15. *Ibid.*

Religion and Educational Policy in England

ANDREAS M. KAZAMIAS

> It was when William Temple "kissed Cowper-Temple" that my settlement was found.
>
> R. A. Butler

BUTLER'S METAPHOR dramatized the last major confrontation of powerful interest groups over an issue which erupted in 1870 but whose roots lay deep in the English past. The issue may be simply described as the role of religion in education, and the interest groups as lay and ecclesiastical organizations or churches. On the Education Act of 1944 (the settlement), Dr. William Temple, Archbishop of Canterbury, represented the interests of the Church of England (the Anglican communion), whose involvement in education stretched as far back as the middle ages. Cowper-Temple symbolized the compromise dating back to the Education Act of 1870, which protected the interests of dissenting denominations and other religious or lay groups; and R. A. Butler, the President of the Board of Education in 1944, spoke for the State. This essay concentrates on three major episodes or phases in the history of what is known as the "religious question" in English education, and on the current situation. The episodes are the three Education Acts of 1870, 1902, and 1944 respectively; and the purpose is to analyze and illuminate each phase through historical comparison. This entails an analysis of each episode both in its contemporary politico-religious and social context, and in its relation to the others.

THE FORSTER AND BALFOUR ACTS

Sensitive to demands for expanded popular education arising out of industrialization, and responding to continued agitation from the Nonconformists and other social groups, Gladstone's Liberal government enacted the famous Education Act of 1870. The Forster Act, named after W. E. Forster, the Vice-President of the Committee of Council on Education, laid the foundations of a national system of education. This entailed a reorganization of the arrangements by which education was provided, aided, or supported. In essence it signalled the entrance of the State in a social activity which had heretofore been based on parental responsibility and voluntary associations, mainly the churches. Specifically, the Forster Act provided the framework for the emergence of a "dual system" of schools: those supported by voluntary bodies and those supported (out of local rates) by locally elected *ad hoc* bodies called "School Boards." Board schools were to be established where voluntary efforts were found not to be "sufficient, efficient, and suitable." Two features in the Act reconciled the contending positions on religious instruction. One was the "Conscience Clause" and the other the "Cowper-Temple Clause." According to the first, all schools (denominational included) receiving government grants would see to it that religious instruction were given at special times to allow for the easy withdrawal of those children who objected on religious or other grounds. The Cowper-Temple Clause, pertaining to Board schools, read as follows: "No religious catechism or . . . formulary which is distinctive of any particular denomination shall be taught in the school."

The political and sectarian conflicts that surrounded the Bill have been discussed in several studies.[1] Anglicans battled with Nonconformists, secularists with orthodox, Liberals with Conservatives, radicals with reactionaries, and progressives with traditionalists. Religion in the schools became an arena of curious political coalitions between Catholic and Protestant, socialist and conservative, and between Unitarian and High Churchman. Unlike the American experience, there was no Supreme Court to render a decision on the legality of the issue, based on constitutional principles. Religion in education was a national political issue to be fought in the political forum, the Parliament. Tradition weighed heavily and both voluntarism and parental responsibility were "safeguarded." At the same time, however, changes in the power structure and in political ideology challenged the strict voluntarist educational arrangements. The position of the victorious Liberals was strengthened by the support of the Nonconformists. Both groups espoused the new doctrine that educational deficiencies could not be corrected unless the State assumed a more positive role in providing education. Forster argued that the education of the people was a matter of the utmost significance for national, political, and economic reasons. Education, in short, was by 1870 perceived to be more than just a church function aimed at the moral rescue of the unfortunate. According to Forster:

> Upon the speedy provision of elementary education depends our industrial prosperity. It is of no use trying to give technical teaching to our artizans without elementary education; uneducated labourers . . . are for the most part, unskilled labourers. . . . Upon this speedy provision depends also . . . the good, the safe working of our constitutional system. . . . [N]ow that we have given them (the people) political power we must not wait longer to give them education.[2]

The arrangements of 1870 created an educational competition between School Boards and the churches. Supported by the growing power of the Nonconformists, and always relying on public money, Board schools grew at an unprecedented rate. By the turn of the twentieth century, they claimed about half of the total number of children in elementary schools. In contrast, after an initial spurt, voluntary schools had by 1880 reached their peak expansion. Voluntary schools run by Nonconformist denominations started decreasing in both numbers and enrollments, while Church schools labored under what was referred to as "intolerable strain." Rather than capitulate, however, the Anglicans were determined to fight for their schools; and politically, they still had the backing of the Conservatives and the Establishment. In 1895 Lord Salisbury, a Churchman and an avowed enemy of the School Boards became Prime Minister of the New Unionist Government, and the Duke of Devonshire, another Churchman, became President of the Privy Council and *ex-officio* chairman of the Education Committee. Four months later a deputation of the Anglican clergy headed by the Archbishop of Canterbury demanded from the new leaders support for their schools. The hopes of the Anglicans were raised when influential members of the new government such as A. J. Balfour spoke out openly in support of voluntary schools and against what they called the extravagance of the School Boards. After an unsuccessful attempt in 1896 to "rescue" the voluntary schools and introduce changes in the governance of education, as well as in religious instruction, the Unionist government under Balfour successfully enacted the Education Act of 1902.

In condensed form, the Balfour Bill included the following provisions:

1. The Councils of every County, Country Borough, Borough and Urban District were to be the Local Education Authorities (LEA's), each of which would appoint an education committee to supervise the schools.
2. Schools were to be differentiated into two categories: "provided schools," supported entirely from funds controlled by the LEA's (from local rates and government grants), and "non-provided schools," whose continuing expenses would be met by the LEA, but whose expenses for capital improvement would be met by the sponsoring voluntary agency.
3. Provided schools would be managed by boards of no more than four LEA-appointed members and two members appointed by "minor local authorities," and were to provide only non-sectarian instruction (the Cowper-Temple Clause).
4. Non-provided schools would be managed by boards of no more than four foundation and two LEA-appointed members, and could provide denominational instruction subject to the Conscience Clause.

As in previous similar episodes (the 1870 Act and the abortive 1896 Bill), the Balfour measure aroused bitter controversies, sectarian strife, and political rancor. Liberals were pitted against Conservatives, Anglicans against Nonconformists, and Board School supporters against voluntarists. But by 1902 the political power structure had changed. The Liberals had in the meantime split over other issues, and they were in the minority. In contrast, the Conservative party in power and their Anglican allies presented an impregnable solid front. Further, the government enlisted the support of other groups—the Fabian socialists, the National Union of

Teachers, and even some dissident Liberals—who seemed to have been moved more by their concern for a national system of education than by the issue of sectarianism. Placing educational responsibility on local government units was a more effective way to promote national education than if it were left to *ad hoc* bodies like the School Boards. The Bill was also supported by the Roman Catholic Church, which had by then grown in numerical strength and political power.

Under the 1902 Act the dual system was strengthened; henceforth it became a permanent feature of the English educational system. So did Cowper-Templeism and the Conscience Clause. The non-denominational schools were to be under different authorities, thus strengthening the foundations of a national system of education encompassing secondary education as well. The Act provided relief for the voluntary schools, but did not go beyond that. Clearly the more universalistic elements inherent in the idea of a national system were strengthened. To what extent the individualistic character of the education provided by the religious organizations could successfully compete with that of the State system remained an open question. The Act was not a victory for the nonsectarians, nor for those who espoused more radical secularist doctrines. Yet in the competition between State and voluntary education those who favored the latter were clearly at a disadvantage. At a time when there were even whisperings of a Welfare State the omens for the ultimate victory of State education could already be discerned.

THE BUTLER ACT AND TODAY

By 1944, English social, political, and religious life had undergone major transformations. Liberalism as a political force had all but disappeared, and Labour emerged as the undisputed second major political party. Labour was anxious not to reopen the religious "hornet's nest," and instead pushed for more opportunities in education. The power of religion over the people had waned and the churches suffered in membership and resources. There were signs of a spirit of cooperation among the Protestant churches; and both Anglicans and Nonconformists were less militant on the religious question in education than before. The general public became more interested in the social advantages of education for their children and were less likely to be aroused by the religious aspect. The two wars rallied the people together, blurred social distinctions, and created an atmosphere of consensus rather than discord. Moreover, these overwhelming events dramatized the significance of a truly national system of education. In introducing the Bill of 1944, Butler stated that the aim was not to eliminate the dual system, but "to bring the church schools along with us in as close a degree of partnership as possible, and to eliminate as much of the friction involved in the operation of the dual system as we can." Nevertheless, he was also explicit that only a "nationalized" system of education could meet the social and economic needs of the postwar period. Voluntary school managers had shown that they were unable to discharge their "statutory liabilities." The objective, therefore, was to set up "a new framework for promoting the national growth and development not only of children, but of national policy itself towards education in the years to come." Accordingly, it was incumbent upon the State to assume "the duty of promoting the education of the people." The Local Education Authorities were to be placed under the Minister's (note the change from a Board to a Ministry) "control" and "direction," and their duty was to establish a "national policy for providing a varied and comprehensive educational service in every area." [3] The new policy offered the official benediction to collectivism in education in contrast to nineteenth century laissez-faire liberalism.

The Butler Act provided the following:

1. Schools established by the LEA's were to be known as county schools; schools otherwise established as voluntary schools.
2. There were to be three categories of voluntary schools: (a) controlled schools, (b) aided schools, and (c) special agreement schools.
3. Controlled schools were to be supported entirely by the LEA, which would also be responsible for the appointment and dismissal of teachers, but subject to consultation by the managers about the appointment of the Head teacher and "reserved" teachers.
4. An aided school was to be one responsible for half the cost of structural improvement and external repairs, and in which managers would appoint the teachers.
5. Special agreement schools were schools which had made proposals for support under a previous Act (Act of 1936). In such cases, the LEA would pay not less than 50 percent and not more than 75 percent of the capital costs, and appoint and dismiss teachers "subject to the managers to be satisfied as to the fitness and competence of the reserved teachers."

As to the religious instruction in the various types of schools, the Act included the following provisions:

1. In all state-aided schools (county and voluntary) the school day must begin with a "collective act of worship" and religious instruction must be given subject to the Conscience Clause.
2. Religious instruction and worship in the county schools must not be "distinctive of any particular denomination," but must be conducted in accordance with a non-sectarian "agreed syllabus" to be drawn up by representatives from the various important religions in each area, from the teachers' associations, and from the LEA.
3. In all controlled schools denominational instruction might be given by reserved teachers twice a week; otherwise religious instruction was to be in accordance with an agreed syllabus.
4. In aided or special agreement schools denominational religious instruction might be given in accordance with the trust deed.

It is interesting to observe that the 1944 Act made no provisions concerning the content of education except in matters of religious observance and instruction. The 1944 Concordat is in force today, except that by the Education Act of 1959 grants payable to aided and special agreement schools can be increased to 75 percent.

Of all the religious organizations the Roman Catholic Church was the most reluctant to accept the Bill. The Catholics rejected the Bill on doctrinal and ideological grounds as well as on grounds of distributive justice and individual freedom. They were against the "agreed syllabus," and against what they called "the excessive influence of State officials in the determination of the type of school to which a child must be sent." Moreover, they strongly felt that the proposed financial conditions were intolerably unjust to a religious minority which by right and belief wished to maintain its own schools. "Whatever the issue," the Catholics said, "we shall do our best to keep pace with any national advance in the educational system, but we shall never surrender our schools." When the Bill was passed the Roman Catholic Church opted under protest to place its schools under the category of "aided." [4]

The Concordat of 1944 and the 1959 Act should not be interpreted as the final solution to the problem. Churches have not relinquished their traditional role of influencing educational policy. Through educational policy committees, they have sought to improve the agreed syllabus for inter-denominational religious instruction, and to combat secularism and materialism in education. Counting all types of schools (aided, controlled, and special agreement), the churches still provide education for about 22 percent of the school-age population. The Roman Catholics have pushed vigorously for denominational schools and greater support. While Anglican schools, and more so Free Church schools, have shown a marked decline, Roman Catholic schools have registered dramatic increases. Since 1911 enrollments in the former have decreased by about 30 percent, while those in the latter have increased by about 250 percent.[5]

The position of the Catholic Church since 1944 and the rapid increase in its schools indicate an important shift in the politico-religious controversy over education. On both the Forster and the Balfour Acts the Catholics allied themselves with the Established Church and with the Conservatives. Their political power during that period was rather weak. In interest and ideology the Catholics stood at opposite ends from the Nonconformists. But by 1944 their political strength had increased and along with it their militancy over religion and the schools. This, coupled with a decline in the Anglican and Free Churches, revived the spectre of renewed conflicts. Concern and potential discord today would be less among Protestant denominations (Anglicans and Free Churchmen) and more between Protestant and Catholic groups.[6] Among the Protestant churches the previous sectarian strife has dissipated and there are more points of agreement than disagreement.

But the most noticeable shift since 1870 has been the ascendancy of the State in education. In short, education has become a State rather than a church function. And as education has become a "social service" and a matter of public policy, different arrangements have been made with respect to religious instruction in the schools and the administrative relationships between religious and state organizations.

COMMENTS AND OBSERVATIONS

It is too tempting to view the religious question in English education simply as a conflict between Church and State or between secularism and sectarianism. But it is relevant to point out that thorough-going secularism in England has not met with wide support. Nor does one observe the intense anti-clericalism of other countries such as France or Turkey. All along the general assumption has been that some sort of religious instruction should be part of a child's education in schools. The question has not been religion or no religion, but *what kind* of religion and by whom. When education was in the hands of religious bodies, the answer was relatively simple. The schools taught the doctrines and precepts distinctive to the denomination that administered and supported them. Objections were raised by one religious group (mostly the Dissenters) against another (the Church of England). Dissenters objected to the privileges enjoyed by the Church of England and to the fact that in certain localities only Church schools existed. This forced Nonconformist parents to send their children to schools run by another denomination, thus exposing them to Anglican proselytism. Hence they called for support to build their own schools, in order to teach their own religion, and for the removal of other "disabilities." But when in 1870 state authorities extended their educational responsibilities, the question of what kind of religion should be taught in the "new" schools and what the arrangements were to be on matters of administration and control became the object of fierce animosity.

Sectarian strife had been characteristic of British society since the Reformation. With the suppression of Catholicism, the major conflicts had been between the Established Church and those groups which dissented from it, i.e., the Dissenters or Nonconformists. But the cleavages between "Church" and "Chapel" did not revolve solely around matters of religious dogma; they were also enmeshed in social and political differences as well. The Nonconformists drew their greatest support from the middle and upper urban commercial classes and from the laboring groups. In the nineteenth century, they became more and more associated with the Liberals in both interest and ideology. The Established Church, on the other hand, was associated with privilege, political conservatism (Toryism), and the landed aristocracy. Hence, sectarian disputes over religion in the schools were compounded by considerations of social and political power. In supporting a nondenominational type of religious instruction in the "new" schools after 1870, and the Cowper-Temple and Conscience clauses of the Education Act of that year, the Nonconformist-Liberal groups were also safeguarding their political interests against an Anglican-Tory alignment.

Students of the American variation of the church-state-school problem are apt to view the English parallel in American terms. Certainly, unlike France, Italy, Spain, Greece, and Latin American countries, England and America are alike in that they are both religiously plural societies. But compared to America, England has not had the clear separation of church and state, often sanctioned on the authority of a constitution. Moreover, despite the existence of several churches, England has also had the tradition of a "national" church, the Church of England. Prior to the nineteenth century, the Church controlled most of education, Catholicism was severely restricted, and Nonconformism suffered from certain disabilities, for instance, denial of posts in the civil service and admission to certain schools. Since then, such handicaps have been removed, the privileged position of the Church has been considerably restricted, and all churches have enjoyed religious toleration and freedom.

Yet the English situation remains rather "untidy" and paradoxical. The Church of England is "by law established." The Queen or King bears the title "Defender of the Faith" and is a member of the Church of England. In theory, the Queen (the State) has considerable powers over the Church, particularly in episcopal appointments. But in practice, the powers of the State are in the hands of a lay body, the House of Commons, exercised through a lay figure, the Prime Minister. And the Prime Minister, as well as the majority of the House of Commons, may not be Anglicans. Hence a Church that is "by law established" may be, and often is, under the authority of a lay, non-Church Prime Minister. But one must be careful about the nature and scope of this authority. In theory, the State lays down (through Acts of Parliament) what the Church professes (its articles of faith) and how it shall conduct its public worship. But, as D. W. Brogan notes, "only the most old-fashioned and unrealistic lawyer now believes that this picture has any relation to the facts." [7] The State does not support the Church, nor are clergymen civil servants.

On the other hand, the State still retains the important function of appointing Church leaders (bishops), and twenty-six bishops (including the Archbishops of Canterbury and York, and the Bishops of London, Durham, and Winchester) sit in the House of Lords. Further, although in both membership and sphere of influence it does not occupy the previous position of power, compared to other religious groups the Church of England continues to be "national" in character and predominant in prestige. Brogan put it as follows:

> The Church of England is still for most Englishmen the national and proper way of rendering to God the things that are God's even if that belief involves another: that Caesar is to determine what things are God's and what his.

And again:

> The Church of England is the *normal* form of religion; even the Dissenter who dissents from its claims, like the earliest Nonconformist who refused to conform to its practices, admits, by his protest, its predominant place. An Anglican bishop, even in a city like Liverpool, where his Roman rival has more adherents, is by national custom the chief representative spokesman of the Christian viewpoint.[8]

Under such circumstances, it is understandable that Butler's solution in 1944 depended to a large extent on the support of all religious denominations, especially the Anglican communion. Yet by then it was clear that, despite the force that religion still exerted in the fortunes of English educational policy, the churches, including the Church of England, were fighting a rearguard action. No longer were church organizations major arbiters in the moral and ethical teachings of schools, let alone in the values of society. Morality and the values of society became a matter of a more universal national concern, in which the State had the most vital interest. Schooling was no longer the responsibility of pious gentlemen eager to rescue the people from their moral weaknesses by instilling particular brands of religion. It was a public concern, a matter of public policy, whose aim was to promote national growth, consensus, and development. A national system of education could not be provided by the churches. They were beset by financial strains; they were challenged by secularism and a diminution in membership, and their aims were particularistic. They realized that if they were to preserve what they had they must cooperate with the State.

The English case also furnishes an example of how change and continuity involving powerful institutions operate within a political democracy. Despite major cleavages along religious, political, and social lines with concomitant variations in interest and ideology, there was what might be called a routine functioning of the political process. There was no evidence of disintegration or disruption of the political system, of complete withdrawal on the part of particular contending groups, or of complete separation. Conflicts were contained and resolved through acceptable norms of political behavior. And once an agreement was reached all parties sought ways to operate within the revised structure.

FOOTNOTES

1. See, for example, Marjorie Cruickshank, *Church and State in English Education: 1870 to the Present Day* (London: Macmillan & Co. Ltd., 1964), pp. 14–38, and C. E. Bidwell and A. M. Kazamias, "Religion, Politics, and Popular Education: An Historical Comparison of England and America," *Comparative Education Review,* Vol. 6, No. 2 (October, 1962), pp. 97–111.
2. Hansard, 3rd series, 199, 1870, p. 465. Also see Brian Simon, *Studies in the History of Education, 1780–1870* (London: Lawrence and Wishart, 1960), pp. 354ff.
3. *Hansard,* Fifth Series, Vol. 396, 1943–1944, pp. 221–226.

4. For the position of the Roman Catholic Church, see *The Times (London)*, January 6, 1944, p. 2. For the Anglican position, see *The Times (London)*, February 17, 1944, p. 2. For the position of the Free Churches, see *The Times (London)*, January 14, 1944, p. 7, and *The Times (London)*, February 3, 1944, p. 2.

5. In 1911 there were about 1,750,000 in Anglican and about 300,000 in Roman Catholic schools. In 1960 enrollments in the former dropped to about 1,275,000. In 1964 the Catholic schools enrolled about 777,000 children. See A. Stafford Clayton, *Historical and Social Determinants of Public Education Policy in the United States and Europe,* Cooperative Research Project, No. F-017, Office of Education, U.S. Department of Health, Education, and Welfare, 1965, p. 92.

6. *Ibid.*, p. 91.

7. D. W. Brogan, *The English People: Impressions and Observations* (New York: Alfred A. Knopf, 1943), pp. 59–60.

8. *Ibid.*, pp. 59, 66–67.

Church, State and Education in Sub-Sahara Africa: An Overview

DAVID SCANLON

IN DECEMBER 1962 the *All Africa Churches Conference on Christian Education in a Changing Africa* met at the University of Rhodesia and Nyasaland. For the student of African education this was an historic meeting. The date marked the 107th anniversary of David Livingstone's famous speech at the Senate House of Cambridge University, a speech that sparked the missionary invasion of East Africa and contributed greatly to the expansion of missionary effort in West Africa. However, for the contemporary historian the Conference marks the beginning of a new period in African educational history. The very title of the sponsoring agency, the *All Africa Churches Conference,* suggests a shift in the locus of power from churches in England, France and the United States to those of Africa. The Conference, representing practically all the Protestant churches and countries of Sub-Sahara Africa, was organized and run by the distinguished African educators D. Z. K. Matthews and Dr. Donald M'Timkulu; the majority of the delegates were Africans. In the literature, the working papers and resolutions passed by the Conference, one seldom found the terms "missionary" or "mission school" but rather "teacher" and "church-related schools." While the Africanization of the churches has been going on for many years, the Salisbury Conference represented the clearest expression of African control over the vast church-related educational system that stands even today as the foundation of education in Africa. Many African delegates at the Conference could recall the founding of the apex schools in Africa that were to produce many of the African nationalist leaders. It was possible to look at David Livingstone's speech 107 years ago and compare the enthusiasm with which young Englishmen responded by organizing the Universities Mission to Central Africa with the current enthusiasm of American youth in the *Peace Corps, Teachers for East Africa, African American Institute* and similar projects. Between the time of Livingstone and Salisbury the face of Africa had changed. First, the great areas indicated in the maps of 1865 as simply forests or, in some cases, Abyssinia, became, by the turn of the century, Nigeria, Gold

---

Reprinted with permission of the author, from the INTERNATIONAL REVIEW OF EDUCATION, Vol. 9, No. 4 (1963–1964) pp. 438–446.

Coast, Senegal and Congo. By 1962 Africa was, for the most part, independent and the standardized colors used to indicate Colonial holdings, pink for the British, green for the French had disappeared. While colors may change, the institutions introduced by the metropolitan powers remained, for the most part, intact. With few exceptions, it was easy to Africanize the administrative and legal structure of the countries. Legislative assemblies, courts, and establishments concerned with finance, transportation, agriculture had always been considered as part of the ordinary machinery of Colonial government. The rules, regulations and procedures for the operation of these branches of government were clear. However, when one examined the educational structure, the situation was not as clear and in many cases blurred. For the one section of government that had traditionally been run by voluntary agencies was the educational system.

In depending upon voluntary agencies, which meant, for the most part, religious organizations, Britain, Belgium and, to a lesser degree, France were reflecting what had been the traditional pattern of church-state relationship in education in Metropolitan countries. In France and Belgium the Catholic church was subsidized by the state for educational purposes, and this same pattern was repeated overseas. While Church and State were officially separated in France in 1903, the governments never cut off completely the subsidies paid to religious groups maintaining schools in Africa. In England the "dual" system which supported both government schools and schools maintained by religious groups was transported to Africa and became the pattern for church-state relations in education. Until World War I, there were few schools run by the government in Sub-Sahara Africa. Statistics would vary from country to country, but it would be difficult to find a country where missionaries were not operating 98% of the schools. From the viewpoint of governments the arrangement was a satisfactory one. Ordinarily, social services were paid for out of local revenue, and as there was little local revenue, governments were willing to have religious organizations operate and maintain schools.

It was only after World War I that Colonial Bureaus of Education were established. Missionary societies had indicated at the famous Edinburgh Conference of 1910 the impossibility of missions bearing the full responsibility for education, and it had been mission groups that had urged the investigation of education in Africa conducted by the Phelps-Stokes Fund in the early 1920's.

In the Colonial offices of France, Belgium and England, special committees and commissions were appointed to investigate education in the colonies, and all three countries issued policy statements that indicated the responsibility of the government in the field of education. In the three statements there is a clear indication that governments would support the established schools which meant mission schools. In country after country in Africa, the first departments or bureaus of education were established in the 1920's. The departments of education asserted the primacy of the government in educational matters but the management, the operation of the schools, remained in the hands of the missionaries.

From the viewpoint of the governments, schools managed by religious groups were much less expensive to operate than government secular schools. In England Lord Meston's report *Aspects of Indian Education* was quoted to illustrate the low cost of mission schools compared to government schools. In addition, there was the existing pattern in Britain and Belgium of a church-state relationship that supported schools by religious groups.

In most cases the missions welcomed the new financial assistance although it meant closer supervision by the government. The mission schools that had started with a few children at the turn of the century were faced with increased demands by African parents for education for their children. There was a clear understanding by the missions of the interaction of religion and education. Most mission groups would perhaps have agreed with the Apostolic Visitor who advised a meeting of Bishops and Missionaries in Dar-es-Salaam in 1928, "Collaborate with all your power; and where it is impossible for you to carry on both the immediate task of evangelization and your educational work, neglect your churches in order to perfect your schools." [1] To qualify for grants from the government, missions had to comply with minimum standards. To prepare students for the examinations that would lead to higher education, the missions followed the curriculum of the metropolitan power.

From the 1920's until independence the Colonial departments of education took a more active role, but time was short and funds were scarce. The plans drawn up by the Colonial powers in the 1920's were ruined by the world-wide depression of the early 1930's.[2] Plans were again postponed by World War II, and it was only in the World War II period that governments began the rapid expansion of education in Africa. While government schools (non-mission) were developed, the basic policy of support to mission schools continued. Thus, upon achieving independence, African countries found they had inherited the "dual" system of the European power. In most African countries the church-related schools are in the majority. In the minds of many Africans there is no real difference between grant-aided, financially subsidized church-managed schools and secular schools. In the education reports published by Ministries of Education, it is often difficult to differentiate between strictly government schools and schools sponsored by voluntary organizations. However, despite the unanimity that does exist in many countries, there is the possibility of conflict if the aims and objectives of the government appear to be in conflict with the aims of the church responsible for the management of the school.

To the observer it appears obvious that the schools throughout Africa will be used to a much greater degree than they have in the past in the process of nation building. Citizenship training will become an important aspect of education, and it is in this area that there is the possibility of the greatest conflict between the church and the state.

Under the present conditions in Africa, there are four possible variations in the relation of church and state.

The first is the system in which the state recognizes the church's right to participate in providing the national system of education and gives financial support in varying degrees.

In Uganda, for example, the central government pays the salaries of all teachers in church-run secondary schools, junior secondary schools, teacher training colleges and technical schools. In addition, the government pays the school a capitation grant per student, and as the majority of schools are boarding schools, a boarding grant is made. The costs of new buildings and expansion of existing buildings, if approved by the ministry, is financed by the central government.

On the primary school level, it has been customary for the local church to provide a school building (or build one) in cooperation with the local education authority. After the school has been in operation for a year or two and has proved to be necessary, the government contributes toward the cost of operating the school. Statistics for school enrollment in Uganda indicate the strength of voluntary agencies on the primary school level. Of the 6086 primary schools with a predominantly African involvement, Protestant, Catholic or Muslim agencies run 5700. The concept of voluntary agencies operating schools can result in a proliferation of schools within a small geographical area. In the city of Kampala, for example, there were government primary schools for Africans, Protestant primary schools for Africans, Catholic primary schools for Africans and Muslim primary schools for Africans. In the large Asian community in Kampala there were different primary school systems. The Hindus divided into two groups, each managing its own primary school system. There were two major Muslim groups in the Asian community, the Suni and the Ismailia Khoja, followers of the Aga Khan—each with its own primary school system. The Sikhs divided into two groups, and there were two Sikh primary school systems. The Goan community, because of its religious and cultural background, had had its own primary school system. In addition, the government maintained a primary school that had a predominantly Asian enrollment.[3]

Religious groups depend upon government grants for maintenance of schools, and there are few groups that could maintain schools without government support. In most of Africa, this has meant that the churches accept the regulations and requirements established by the ministries in order to receive grants in aid. But to date, the regulations and requirements have been concerned primarily with the physical plant of the school and the professional staff. The content of the curriculum has been determined by the examination system that has been, for the most part, non-political. The one example (under this category) of a direct clash between the government and the church has been in South Africa. With the passage of the Bantu Education Act in 1953, Protestant and Catholic groups responsible for managing schools were faced with a dilemma. Could they accept a curriculum that was, in the minds of most observers, designed to keep the African in an inferior position? All schools managed by churches depended heavily on the grants in aid. After reviewing the possibilities, some Protestant communities decided (1) they could not operate the schools without government support and (2) they could not accept the curriculum the government would insist upon in order to receive funds. Therefore, the only alternative was to close the schools. The Catholic church joined the Protestant community in opposing the curriculum. However, it has been trying to maintain schools without government aid. As it does not receive financial aid, it is relatively free to select its own curriculum.

A second possible variation is in one sense a corollary of the first. Under this arrangement, the state would recognize the church's right to participate in education but only at its own expense. This approach, which has been labelled, "The American Plan," would result in the closing of the vast majority of church-related schools. No church or consortium of churches could possibly maintain the schools without the grants in aid they are now receiving. However, the churches in Africa and the overseas churches are also making a financial contribution. Unfortunately, there are no reliable figures on the amount of money expended annually by African and overseas religious groups.

A third approach would be one in which the state refuses the church any role in education at all. To date, only one country has taken this position and that is Guinea. In January 1959, three months after Guinea gained its independence, President Sékou Toure announced that within two years his government would nationalize the entire educational system. During the two-year interval the state, he explained, would continue to subsidize church schools. There is little doubt that the movement on the part of President Toure was one calculated to bring greater control by the state over the curriculum of the school. Toure, more than any other leader, has made full use of the school in citizenship training and nation building. It is difficult to judge whether the nationalization process carried on by Toure could be as easily repeated in other African countries. First, there was the fact that Guinea had fewer schools maintained by missions than practically any other country in Africa. Only 1500 students in 1958, the eve of independence, qualified for the Elementary School Certificate. Therefore, there were no strongly entrenched interests to contend with. Secondly, the dramatic move by President Toure led to offers of assistance from hundreds of French teachers in France and in other West African French-speaking countries. Commenting on the role of politics in education in Guinea, Professor L. Gray Cowan wrote, "The party (the Democratic Party of Guinea) sees education not as an end in itself but as a tool for the forging of a new national purpose and for the attainment of those ends which the party and the mass have agreed upon. Education of the mass, therefore, is just as important as is the formation of the new elite with the technical training that is necessary for industrialization and modernization of the economy. The educational revolution in Guinea must be seen as part of that country's larger transformation of society, but in an even wider context it may well illustrate the direction to be taken in education by many other African states." [4]

A fourth possible variation is the plan whereby the state recognizes for education purposes only one religion or denomination and withholds recognition from others. It appears unlikely that this approach will be used in the foreseeable future. Christian denominations are in a minority in African countries, and there is certainly no indication that political leaders, the decision-makers, are anxious to support denominational Christianity. The same could be said of those countries that have an overwhelming Muslim majority both in terms of population and political leadership. There is no indication that any school system will be operated exclusively by the Muslim community.

Historically the country that is now independent and that came closest to this approach was the Belgian Congo. In May 1906 the Independent State of the Congo and the Holy See concluded a concordat that recognized the exclusive right of the Catholic missions in operating schools. Catholic mission schools, subsidized by the government were considered the official schools of the Congo. In 1924 this arrangement was reaffirmed by the Belgian government with Catholic missionary societies and became the *modus operandi* until 1948. At this time the government agreed for the first time to support Protestant mission schools. It was not until 1954 that the first public secular school was opened in the Congo.

In reviewing the possibilities of future church-state relations, it would appear that practically there are only two possibilities. The first is to continue the traditional pattern of church-related schools. The second is to nationalize the school. From the viewpoint of many churches in Africa, the nationalization of primary education would relieve the churches of administrative and financial costs. And there were some at the Salisbury Conference, a minority, that suggested the abdication of church activity in education in areas that were clearly governmental responsibility and in which the churches are simply providing a service function. (However, the majority favored a continuation of the present policy.)

The future of church-state relations would appear to depend on whether or not church-related schools are considered a genuine part of the national education system. In this the churches throughout colonial Africa have the disadvantage of being viewed as part of the colonial apparatus and as such may be suspect in countries with a bitter history. A "dual" system could operate in most African countries if the church-related schools are genuinely viewed as part of the *modernization* apparatus of the country and not simply an extension of *westernization*. In the process of nation building in Africa, it will be most unusual if the schools are not viewed as an integral part in building a philosophy of government. But the entire process of "citizenship" training in education is foreign to most church-related schools that are operated with a background of European missionary sponsorship. The basic problems, therefore, are of a political nature. Conflicts in the future will occur when the political philosophy of the government appears to be in contradiction to the philosophy of the church-related schools.

The fact was realized by those leaders responsible for the Salisbury Conference. Dr. Donald M'Timkulu, Director of the Planning Committee expressed this view when he said, "I am one of those who believe very firmly that the provision of educational facilities is pre-eminently the responsibility of the State. The State has a duty to educate its citizens. This is its right and it is one of the distinguishing marks of good government. We as Christians, should be deeply concerned with good government, and so our greatest service to the nation would be to see to it that the State provides the best possible education for its citizens, thus providing a base on which good government can be established.

If the Church as a whole, through all its members, seeks to fulfill its true mission of service to the nation, it must above all avoid the danger of parallelism—the provision of services which the State is willing and able to provide. The priorities have now changed and the best contribution in the service of the nation, at present, lies elsewhere. We must seek carefully to find where priorities lie and discover anew the need that is greatest in the total service of the nation.

It is important to stress, as a basis of policy, this involvement of the Church with the world. This is part of the process of change that we must come not only to recognize but to accept. As a result of the historical associations connected with the bringing of the Gospel to our continent, African Christians have tended to regard themselves as a community apart from their society—a people pure and apart from the rest of the society from which they have been drawn. The temptation for the Church has been to isolate its membership in a religious enclave intent on preserving its own purity of faith and its own chosen standards of life. This attitude was not only a mistaken one in that it failed to understand the true nature of the Church—for whilst the Church is not "of this world," it is yet "in the world." It also tended to make us inward looking, thus divorcing the Church from the nation, and yet it is this fruitful tension which characterizes the Christian way of life, and from which stems the power of the Church.

Withdrawal from the world has been the weakness of the Church in Africa, and this weakness we must now eradicate if the Church is to have any future in the changed conditions of the Africa of today. The rise of new nation-states, the tremendous force of nationalism seeking to weld together nations from what was heretofore a heterogeneous assembly of tribes, makes demands on all to give their varying contributions to this tremendous task of nation-building. Our willingness to make this contribution to the total life of the nation, or our failure to do so, could mean the success or failure of all the well-laid schemes we have heard about." [5]

FOOTNOTES

1. Quoted in Roland Oliver, *The Missionary Factor in East Africa* (London: Longmans, 1952), p. 275.
2. See Advisory Committee on Native Education in the British Tropical African Dependencies, *Education Policy in British Tropical Africa* (London: His Majesty's Stationery Office, 1925); Gouvernement Général de l'Afrique Equitorial Française, *Instructions Relatives à l'Application de la Circulaire du Mai 1925 de M. le Gouverneur Général R. Antonetti Réorganisant l'Enseignement en Afrique Equitoriale Française* (Brazzaville: Imprimerie du Gouvernement Général, 1936); *Projet de l'Enseignement Libre au Congo Belge avec le Concours des Sociétés de Missions Nationales* (Bruxelles, 1925).
3. Since 1957 the Government has made an effort to integrate schools, and today the majority of schools are integrated.
4. L. Gray Cowan, *Guinea, African One Party States* (ed. by Gwendolyn Carter, Cornell University, 1962) p. 213.
5. *Policy and Planning in Christian Education in Africa,* by Dr. Donald M'Timkulu. All Africa Churches Conference, Conference on Christian Education in a Changing Africa. Mimeographed statement.

Al-Azhar in the Revolution

DANIEL CRECELIUS

I

ON THE EVE of the Young Officers' *coup d'état* in July, 1952, al-Azhar was suffering from the consequences of more than half a century of spasmodic reform and severe political crises arising from the general conflict between Egyptian modernists and traditionalists, a conflict which naturally revolved around al-Azhar and its system of education.[1] For both groups this ideological confrontation had been crystallized in specific issues concerning the control of al-Azhar and the diminishing availability of satisfactory jobs for al-Azhar's graduates.[2] This struggle, then, between the two competing ideological orientations, influenced the issues and described the lines of battle for the more intense political struggle between parliament and king for control of al-Azhar and its system of religious education.

Egyptian politics after the First World War can be characterized as a triangular struggle for authority among the British, the king and the parliament. As the instrument for the centralization of authority, parliament generally had the support of modernists who wished to counteract the influence of the British, to limit the power of the king in the British manner, and to unite the independent system of religious education with the newer system of government controlled education.

The fluid state of political relationships in this unstable system forced a constant realignment of political alliances. In attempting to bolster his own insecure position the king thrashed about for temporary allies, one time invoking British aid against a rebellious parliament, one time packing parliament with politicians faithful to himself, another time standing with parliament against the British. But throughout the period of these realignments one ally remained constant. The active antagonism of the group of *'ulamā'* to both the British and parliament turned al-Azhar into a royalist bastion. It often provided his only support in simultaneous struggles against the British and parliament. But this alliance between the throne and al-Azhar had the unfortunate result of setting the modernizing nationalists against both institutions. Since 1919, al-Azhar's participation

Reprinted, with permission of the author and publisher, from the MIDDLE EAST JOURNAL, Vol. 20, No. 1 (Winter, 1966).

in the nationalist movement quantitatively and qualitatively lessened as it came under attack from the Egyptian nationalists themselves.[3] Parliament and the political parties now became the instruments to control the throne and al-Azhar and to introduce reforms into Egyptian society.

The cleavage in Egyptian society influenced by the process of "modernization" grew ever wider as the modernists and traditionalists found no common ground for agreement or cooperation. The majority of conservative 'ulamā' rejected any thought of a reinterpretation of unalterable Islamic tradition or doctrine and successfully disciplined or ostracized from their body reformers of all attitudes,[4] such as Muḥammad 'Abduh, 'Alī 'Abd al-Rāziq, Ṭāhā Ḥusayn, Rashīd Riḍā, Sa'd Zaghlūl, Muṣṭafā al-Marāghī, and Khālid Muḥammad Khālid.[5] The 'ulamā' continued to ward off serious reform by insisting that any attack on al-Azhar or its traditions was an attack on Islām itself, but their successful defense of al-Azhar's independent position under the patrimony of the king, coupled with their rejection of any but token structural reform, further alienated the religious community from the modernizing Egyptian élite, aggravated this wound in Egyptian society and forced the modernizers to work their way *around* al-Azhar and religious questions.[6]

By their refusal to countenance reform the shaykhs denied themselves the opportunity to help shape the course of the reform movement which nevertheless evolved. A continuous battle was fought over the issue of reform along a myriad of fronts, but the major confrontations were centered on the question of education. Two opposing systems of education, each based on a specific set of values and judgments, had developed, but the process of modernization was tipping the balance ever more positively toward the government controlled system.

Since 1900, the modernists have revitalized and expanded the embryonic government school system as a way of introducing modern ideas without actually touching the traditional religious system. A government directed school for *qāḍis* was developed in 1907 in an attempt to expose *qāḍis* to a broader curriculum. The Egyptian university which opened in 1908 has had an enormous rôle in training generations of Egyptians dedicated to reform. As these and other modern institutions took root in Egypt they began to limit the functions of traditional Islamic institutions. The ruling élite, drawn almost exclusively from the ranks of those who had a significant exposure to Western education,[7] used these new institutions, and especially parliament, as the instruments for the development of their programs. Parliament continually expanded the jurisdiction of the civil court system at the expense of the *sharī'ah* system as Western-inspired law encroached upon the domain of the sharī'ah.

In a direct attempt to subject the entire Azhar system to its will, parliament appropriated the Azhar budget to itself and claimed responsibility for key appointments at al-Azhar in the famous law Number 15 of 1927.[8] When it found itself thwarted by the combined opposition of the king and the shaykhs of al-Azhar, parliament retaliated against all shaykhs by discriminating against Azhar graduates when they sought government positions and held up appropriations for the Azhar budget, thereby forcing the king to subsidize al-Azhar from his private treasury. The king and the shaykhs were now thrown into a tight embrace.

As the Azharis withdrew from public affairs under the attacks of the nationalists the cleavage between the two general orientations grew ever wider. The 'ulamā' jealously guarded that which they had and obstinately opposed any suggestion that might compromise their authority, but their own strength was weakening in direct proportion to the growing strength of the modernist movement.

The march of reform within al-Azhar itself was tedious and hard fought, supported as it was by such a small group of reform-minded 'ulamā.' The battle was, however, over structural organization rather than substantive issues. Despite appearances of far reaching change between 1908-1936, such as the addition of modern courses to the curriculum, reorganization along the lines of a modern university and the regulation of diplomas and faculty ranks, al-Azhar in 1952 was little changed in substance and sadly out of touch with Egyptian realities.[9] As an indication of the slow pace of actual reform beneath al-Azhar's public espousal of reform, one can mention that English, which first appeared in the curriculum as early as 1901 and which King Fārūq *ordered* to be taught, along with French, Hebrew, Persian, Chinese, and Turkish, was not taught at al-Azhar until 1958 when Maḥmūd Shaltūt, then Vice-Rector, announced that English instruction would begin immediately.[10]

It can be seen, then, that the Young Officers inherited a nation deeply split over modernist and traditionalist orientations, an unreformed Azhar, and a religious class which was desperately trying to defend its own crumbling position while refusing to participate in the modernization of Egyptian life and thought.

II

Religion was one of the most explosive issues the Revolution had immediately to face. The threat to the Revolution was not from al-Azhar, however, but from the highly organized, powerful and aggressive *Ikhwān al-Muslimūn,* the Muslim Brethren. Faced with the Ikhwān desire for power, the Free Officers made obvious overtures for al-Azhar's support and allowed the idea of religious reform to lay dormant until their own position was secure.

Using General Nagīb as their symbol and spokesman, the clique of Young Officers gave public assurances to the 'ulamā' of al-Azhar that they stood for and would uphold sound Islamic principles. Besides paying frequent official visits to al-Azhar's shaykhs, the Free Officers made it a conspicuous collective habit to pass the important Friday prayer at al-Azhar itself or one of the other great mosques of Cairo where the shaykhs and public could bear witness to their piety. Although the Free Officers early showed themselves willing to cooperate with the Ikhwān to gain their support, their aversion to the extremist principles of the Brethren,[11] coupled with their unwillingness to share power, drove them to strengthen their ties with al-Azhar, to which the Ikhwān organization was generally opposed.[12]

The mutually antagonistic aspirations of the Free Officers, now reconstituted as the Revolutionary Command Council (RCC), and the Ikhwān led ultimately to the assassination attempt against 'Abd al-Nāsir as he addressed a mass Alexandria audience on October 26, 1954. Although the subsequent destruction of the Ikhwān organization and the adherence of al-Azhar to the principles of the Revolution had the effect of relieving the RCC of immediate political pressure from religious groups, the continuing question of Egypt's basic religious orientation was potentially dangerous enough to cause the RCC serious concern. The destruction of the Ikhwān, however, was the key which unlocked the door to general religious reform and offered the opportunity of bringing religion under the control of the Revolution. But, though the RCC was devoted to bringing al-Azhar and the religious hierarchy under the firm control of the government, it did not force the issue of reform until two years later when it finally felt secure in posing the problem of the sharī'ah court system.

The second stage of reform was reached when the autonomous communal systems were officially absorbed into the national system of secularly oriented courts. In an atmosphere of revulsion against the shaykhly class, especially created by the government press when the police arrested two *qāḍis* who were giving favorable judgments in return for favors from their women litigants, the government summarily announced in September, 1955, the abolition of all religious courts as of January 1, 1956. Despite the fact that it was an attempt to create a unified legal system for the modern Egyptian state and was aimed primarily at the autonomous sharī'ah system, the Western press generally missed the important consequences this action had for the Muslim community in Egypt because it overplayed the significance of the law for Egypt's Coptic community.[13]

The shaykhs made no defense of the sharī'ah system on theoretical grounds, for justice has traditionally been within the jurisdiction of the political authority. Publicly the shaykhs made no defense whatsoever. All Egyptian dailies of September 26, 1955, carried congratulatory statements from various highly respected shaykhs who supported the government's program. On September 28, the major Egyptian daily, *al-Ahrām,* accompanied a picture of Shaykh al-Azhar 'Abd al-Raḥmān Tāj shown congratulating President 'Abd al-Nāṣir, with this leading shaykh's thanks to the President for having taken the "liberating step" of abolishing the courts. Shaykhs beyond the reach of the RCC, however, raised a public outcry over the government's move and protests came in from all parts of the Islamic world, notably from Syria where the Ikhwān still had a strong organization.

Behind the headlines, the Egyptian shaykhs complained that Azhar graduates, already heavily discriminated against in their search for government jobs, would find it impossible to compete with government trained lawyers for positions in the combined system because they were unfamiliar with the Western bases of modern Egyptian law. The job future of Azharis, they said, was becoming desperate. The government made only a small concession to the 'ulamā' in guaranteeing that no *qāḍi* presently employed in the sharī'ah system would lose his job; he would be retrained to sit in the combined system. To further allay shaykhly fears, the RCC emphasized that sharī'ah law had not been abolished; the sharī'ah system had simply been "absorbed" into the national system where sharī'ah "principles" would still be applied. Nevertheless, the government made it clear that there would be far fewer jobs for Azharis who continued to concentrate solely on traditional studies.

With the crisis of diminishing job futures for Azharis as a backdrop, the military leaders decided to complete the absorption of the religious hierarchy into the revolutionary system by bringing to an end the semi-independent position of al-Azhar itself. The RCC had begun this campaign to subvert al-Azhar's autonomy in the early days of the Revolution by seeking out cooperative shaykhs to act as the channels for government policy at al-Azhar, but its own precarious position cautioned a careful approach to this bastion of tradition.

Although we have little data on the personal and institutional conflicts between the men of the Revolution and the 'ulamā' of al-Azhar because of the public support the 'ulamā' were forced to give to the Revolution, we get some indication of the intensity of the struggle waged in the halls of al-Azhar by the spate of resignations submitted by highly placed 'ulamā' as protests against government "meddling" in religious affairs, the temporarily successful passive resistance of the shaykhs to reform or control (the government representatives found it impossible to work with the shaykhs) which delayed reform for several years, and the rapid succession of military leaders appointed to control al-Azhar.

The attempt by some of the highest ranking revolutionary leaders to subvert al-Azhar's independence continued for years and sharpened already violent personality conflicts at al-Azhar. Though the march of reform was seriously delayed by the resistance of the 'ulamā', its final outcome was never in doubt. Only the terms of the capitulation had to be agreed upon. After the example given to the men of religion by the severe destruction of the Ikhwān al-Muslimūn, the government was always able to count on the official public support of al-Azhar for its revolutionary programs, but the succession of military men appointed as Director of al-Azhar Affairs was nonetheless unable to overcome the traditional suspicions of the 'ulamā' toward reform or government interference in the internal affairs of al-Azhar.

Kamāl al-Dīn Rif'āt (2/11/59-10/23/59), Aḥmad 'Abdallāh Ṭa'īmah (10/24/59-10/17/61), Ḥusayn al-Shāfi'ī (10/18/61-10/23/62), three leaders from the military establishment, and Dr. Muḥammad al-Bahai (10/29/62/-3/25/64) were all unable to create a satisfactory working relationship with the conservative shaykhs of al-Azhar.[14] Lacking any foundation for opposition to the Revolution, the 'ulamā' temporarily thwarted government programs for al-Azhar by simply failing to cooperate with their appointed directors. These personality conflicts led in extreme cases to further resignations of highly placed shaykhs who preferred this path to the ignominy of presiding over al-Azhar's end as an independent institution. This strategy could not change the course of events, however; it could only delay it. The government took advantage of these resignations to appoint Western educated Ph.D.'s of a more liberal outlook to these important vacant positions. Although the obstacles to reform were slowly being removed, the government had to continue to move cautiously, for it knew full well that any violent attack against al-Azhar would be construed as an attack against religion itself.

The government sought cooperation among a few progressive shaykhs at al-Azhar who desired reform even at the expense of government interference, for the tortuous course of reform at al-Azhar had shown that significant changes could only be imposed upon al-Azhar by government action.[15] Notable among these shaykhs was Dr. Muḥammad al-Bahai, German educated, who was later promoted to the position of Minister of Awqāf and Director of al-Azhar Affairs. He is now professor of philosophy at Cairo University. Dr. al-Bahai prepared the ground for reform at al-Azhar by gathering about him a group of administrators similarly devoted to reform and by presiding over the passage of certain fundamental legislation that laid the groundwork for the total reorganization that was to engulf al-Azhar. The half century of delayed religious reform dammed up behind al-Azhar finally burst upon the institution in the summer of 1961, sweeping away the dead past but leaving the foundations for the erection of a new al-Azhar. The total reorganization of this great Muslim institution to which the government had for so many years been pointing was announced in June, 1961.

III

The atmosphere of great urgency which surrounded the National Assembly meeting on June 22, 1961 was evoked by the fact that the Assembly had to complete its last order of business, the reorganization of al-Azhar, in this, the last meeting of the parliamentary session. Preliminary documents outlining a reform had supposedly been worked out, for a government committee and a committee representing al-Azhar presented their respective versions of a reform bill for consideration. It is obvious, however, from the similarity of these two bills in their original form that the version supposedly representing the views of al-Azhar had actually been prepared by the government and handed to the Azhar committee at the last moment.[16]

This judgement is substantiated by the unpublished minutes of this momentous meeting which clearly reveal that the Azharis did not know what was in their version.[17] They asked for adjournment in order to study its contents.

The government representatives treated the shaykhs harshly, hidden as they were from public scrutiny behind the closed doors of parliament. They did not debate the issue of reform with the shaykhs; they accused them and demanded that the reform be passed. As President of the Assembly, Anwār al-Sadāt controlled discussion of the government proposals; rather, he guided the "explanation" of the reform. The shaykhs were also handicapped by a lack of knowledge concerning parliamentary procedure and were constantly being silenced by al-Ṣadāt on points of order. An excellent example of the military's attitude toward the shaykhs occurred when one venerable shaykh digressed from his lengthy speech into a *ḥadīth* concerning the Prophet, which he used to support his point. No sooner was the *ḥadīth* out of his mouth when al-Ṣadāt, impatient with the shaykh's verbosity, insisted that this was a *ḥadīth* about Umar and not the Prophet. The shaykh's composure left him. He stammered, then retreated, saying that, anyway, it was one of those unsure *ḥadīths* which only Allah knows. Then the shaykh sat down, totally embarrassed.

Despite the efforts of al-Ṣadāt, the shaykhs showed themselves unhappy and opposed to the law, for they knew it meant the end of al-Azhar's quasi-independent existence. In an effort, then to impose the law upon al-Azhar, the government enlisted the support of some of its most important leaders. In addition to the aforementioned al-Ṣadāt, Kamāl al-Dīn Rif'āt and Kamāl al-Dīn Ḥusayn, all from the original RCC, and Dr. al-Bahai, the spokesman for the government within al-Azhar, attacked stagnation in al-Azhar and told the shaykhs in no uncertain terms that they now had to submit to reform. One of this military triumvirate told the author, "We *gave* reform to al-Azhar because the shaykhs never want it." The meeting dragged on for seven hours, until 3:30 AM, before the shaykhs submitted.

The government indictment against al-Azhar had begun with a statement of that institution's glorious past, during which time it had "stood as an impregnable stronghold against all attempts at our slavery, domination and the destruction of our national and spiritual entity." [18] Traditionally, al-Azhar did not belong simply to Egypt, but to the entire Islamic world. It had spread the light of religion and science over Asia and Africa and was still the goal of Muslim missions which came to Egypt to study Islamic sciences. Kamāl al-Dīn Ḥusayn called it the *Ka'bah* for all Islamic countries.

> However, the fact that al-Azhar has for long years been compelled to stand in the face of all attempts at aggression has made it acquire a sort of reserve which is probably one of the characteristics of the defensive attitude it has adopted all through those centuries. When life revived around it, and the causes that led up to its reserved and rigid

attitude no longer existed it failed to find proper means of renewed activity that would help it adapt itself to contemporary times while retaining its characteristics and assuming its duties of defending the Religion and preserving the heritage of Islām.[19]

Anwār al-Sadāt insisted that from his many travels to other Islamic lands and from his experience with the Islamic Congress, he knew that these nations wanted their sons to learn more than religion so they could be of use in their homelands. Kamāl al-Dīn Rif'āt substantiated al-Azhar's importance for the emerging nations, but declared that Africans trained at al-Azhar could not find jobs when they returned home because they had acquired useless knowledge. But those students trained at the secular Egyptian universities were missing important religious trainings. The solution was to combine the two programs.

> Al-Azhar, being, however, engaged in the training of scholars in religion and the language of the Koran, is not as yet in a position to qualify religious scholars who are specialized in works of experience and production called for by the progress of Moslems in all countries. When certain Moslem states realized this regrettable fact and diverted all or part of their missions to civilian universities in the UAR and other countries, their envoys upon graduation were found to have acquired experience while hardly knowing anything about religion. On the other hand, their envoys to al-Azhar returned with a great wealth of religious and Koranic sciences, but mastered no work and were neither capable of production nor able to participate in any type of progress to which we have referred.[20]

In Egypt *and* abroad, Azharis had become isolated from society.

> A serious unemployment problem had also arisen among them which aggravated their isolation from society: a crisis which had profound effects on the minds of the Azharites and the people at large and did not fail to produce adverse effect on the power of the creed in the minds of both. . . . This feeling, if it spreads, is likely to sever many of our bonds with those countries.[21]

Some shaykhs attempted to say that Azharis could not study *tafsīr* and medicine side by side, the work load being too great. When others boldly asserted that the government was destroying the traditional rôle of al-Azhar as a place to study language and the religious sciences, the government representatives countered by accusing al-Azhar of deviation from its traditional rôle. The government was now *widening* its rôle by *restoring* al-Azhar to its traditional place as a disseminator of *all* sciences, not just the religious ones.

The principles of the law were made to correct all these weaknesses. They were:

1. To maintain al-Azhar's position as the largest and oldest Muslim university in East or West.

2. To maintain its position as the stronghold of religion and Arabism from which Islām will be renewed in its true substance to all levels and every locality in society.
3. To graduate scholars who have a knowledge of religious science, but also of practical knowledge and experience 'so that religion will no longer be their only craft or profession.'
4. To destroy all barriers between al-Azhar and other universities so that Azhar graduates may enjoy equal opportunity in the spheres of knowledge and work.
5. To give a common amount of knowledge and experience to all Azharis so they may be intellectually and psychologically equal with all other sons of the Fatherland.
6. To standardize school and university certificates in all UAR universities and schools.[22]

The reform had been declared in such haste that forces which might have opposed it were never given time to make a defense of al-Azhar. Immediately after the announcement of the law, the press levelled a withering attack against the stagnation and corruption of the men of religion themselves in an effort to justify their revolutionary program for al-Azhar.

The opening gun in the campaign against the shaykhs was fired on June 24, 1961. *Akhbār al-Yawm* on that day declared in a blazing headline, "Religion is not a profession." Its accompanying article stated that:

> The revolution, the banner of which was raised in al-Azhar University, is the first real upheaval which has taken place in that great institution for the past 1000 years. The youth who will be enrolled in al-Azhar will not do so to adopt religion as a profession since religion is not a trade! The feeling of increasing isolation which has been suffered by tens of thousands of al-Azhar students and graduates will come to an end. Moreover, the thousands of the youth who come from all parts of Asia and Africa to study at the greatest Islamic institution will no longer return to their countries to live on the dole or to become a burden on their fellow countrymen, but will return as useful elements in building up their homelands on modern foundations apart from acquiring a deep insight into religion.

On June 25, *al-Ahrām* ran a long article on the importance of the new law for al-Azhar and three days later *al-Jumhūrīyah* had another long explanatory article devoted to questions and answers concerning the new law. On June 29, *al-Akhbār* followed with still another article devoted to the new law.

Ḥusayn al-Shāfi'ī, Vice President in charge of al-Azhar Affairs, carried the government propaganda directly to the shaykhs. In one of his monthly lectures at al-Azhar, he cajoled them with the following thought:

> Al-Azhar became isolated from society and from life. In our effort now to develop al-Azhar, we are but giving expression to our determination to reinstate it in its place of honor and to strengthen the link between its past and present.[23]

These and similar views found their way even into al-Azhar circles. Dr. al-Bahai, in a semi-appendix to a book he had finished, noted that al-Azhar had lost contact with the problems and life of the people,[24] and that it had lost its ability to influence the educated classes.[25] Its separation from reality was already apparent in the 19th century and now, "every day of continuing crisis lessens its value." [26] The twin goals of the new law, now, according to al-Bahai, were the purification of al-Azhar from the effects of imperialism, that is, to bring the graduate back into the society in which he lives, and the destruction of the notion that his call is a profession.[27]

Explanations of the law, of al-Azhar's deviation from its true path, of the need to bridge the social gap between men of religion and the rest of the population, and the necessity of graduating students with practical skills continued to occupy prime space in the nation's papers and journals. But the attacks against the 'ulamā' also continued.

Minbar al-Islām, a newly created government quarterly (now a monthly because of its great success) devoted to the "restoration" of Islām, contained the following words of President 'Abd al-Nāṣir:

> Of course the shaykh does not think of anything except the turkey and the food with which he filled his belly. He is no more than a stooge of reaction, feudalism and capitalism. At that time some shaykhs were trying to deceive us with fatwas of this nature. From the beginning, Islam was a religion of work. The Prophet used to work like everybody else. Islam was never a profession.[28]

To make certain the shaykhs got the message, the first issue of the reformist *Minbār al-Islām* devoted an article to reform. 'Usmān Amīn reviewed Muḥammad 'Abduh's attempts to reform al-Azhar and levelled serious accusations against the shaykhs.[29]

The leading 'ulamā' quickly fell in line and showed an amazing enthusiasm for self-criticism, at least on the surface. *Majallat al-Azhar,* the official Azhar journal, contained the following remarkable statements in its January, 1962 issue.

> The graduates of al-Azhar were considered as only men of religion. As a result of that, they used the religion as a profession with which they can earn their living. Moreover, they lived in complete loneliness far away from their society, because their culture could not meet the requirements of the renaissance era, especially in both fields of work and production.[30]
>
> The new law includes a solution for every problem, it prepares an experience for every field, it brings up preachers and guides to show humanity the straight way of its life. . . . It wants Islam to be revived, ulamas to be of strong faith, living for the *sake* (my italics) and not by means of it. . . .[31]

These are the words of Maḥmūd Shaltūt, Shaykh al-Azhar through the early period of revolutionary reform. Immediately following his article, another comment admitted,

> The reorganization of al-Azhar University will prevent Islamic guidance from being a kind of profession. . . . It will create new kinds of knowledge which enables one to work and earn his living instead of using Islamic guidance as a means of gaining money.[32]

The campaign against the shaykhs has not slackened since 1961. On August 24, 1962, *al-Jumhūrīyah* ran a headline which read, "The state does not submit to a special group in the name of religion." In an important confrontation between the men of religion and the régime, the men of the Revolution refused to name Islām as the state religion in the National Charter, claiming that certain elements were exploiting religion and impeding progress. On February 14, 1963, *al-Ahrām* ran a summary of how the reform was going at al-Azhar. The Rector of al-Azhar University (not to be confused with Shaykh al-Azhar) declared, "In the past there was no *'ālim* known as a man of religion. . . . Religion is not . . . the turban and the *qafṭān!*"

One group within the inner ruling clique wants to push this campaign to the limit, for a few officers believe the shaykhs are "useless, too ignorant to carry the torch of cultural revolution." [33] It is obviously the aim of this group to dissolve the "class" of 'ulamā'. It believes "there will not be a class of 'ulamā' in the future. There will be doctors, engineers and lawyers who are religious. The government is going to destroy the class of 'ulamā'," [34] This extreme view is not held by the majority of the ruling officers who recognize the importance of the 'ulamā' as a direct link between the government and the illiterate or semiliterate majority of Egyptians solidly grounded in their Islamic traditions and between Egypt and other Islamic states. This second group believes the 'ulamā' should be the missionaries of socialism among the people.

As early as November, 1962, the press began calling for the retraining of *Imāms* so they could teach socialism to the masses.[35] Ḥusayn al-Shāfi'ī spoke for the majority government view toward the rôle of the shaykhs in society when he told them,

> I call upon you to transform mosques into centers of radiation. It is not enough that mosques should be devoted to prayers only. The masses have launched a campaign to reorganize their ranks, to strengthen their land. . . . Anyone who stands in the face of justice seeks oppression; anyone who stands in the way of self-sufficiency of his country aims at spreading poverty; and anyone who tries to work for dissension among the people opens the way for the return of political factions, reactionaries and opportunists, who are all as dangerous as infidelity, hypocrisy and polytheism.[36]

These words found an echo in the Azhar official journal. "The task of al-Azhar in its new era," it states, "is to inculcate the new revolutionary thought and understanding in the people's minds." [37]

It is apparent from the government's actions since the fateful reorganization of 1961, that the 'ulamā' and al-Azhar have an important domestic and international rôle to play in the Egyptian Revolution. In the words of the present Shaykh al-Azhar, Ḥasan Ma'Mūn, al-Azhar will continue to act as a beacon casting its light into every corner of the Islamic world.[38]

Al-Azhar provides the régime with an important international instrument for the strengthening of Islamic cultural and political ties with the newly emergent states of Asia and Africa. As such, it has taken up the struggle against imperialism, ignorance and stagnation. Islām has been offered as the religion of freedom, equality, civilization and progress.

Domestically, the 'ulamā' have the important rôle of carrying the Revolution's program of "Islamic Socialism" to the people.[39] Because the 'ulamā' are not as yet conversant with the régime's way of thinking, most of the theorists of "Islamic Socialism" have been from outside the ranks of the shaykhs of al-Azhar. Nevertheless, as the government continues to retrain the 'ulamā' and to wrap its socialist programs in the mantle of Islām, the shaykhs will play an increasingly important rôle. Though they are under firm government control and have suffered a serious diminution of influence, the régime finds them useful in carrying the doctrines of the Revolution to the people in an Islamic garb. But they must be retrained. One of the former rectors of al-Azhar told the author, "Any shaykh that follows only the traditional course of religious instruction at al-Azhar will simply not find a job upon graduation."

IV

After four years, it is possible to see what course reform at al-Azhar has taken. Some aspects of the reform have not as yet been given attention. Others have received too much.

The reform of al-Azhar is a complete reorganization of the system. A new balance of power has been struck within the system in the form of a reduced rôle for Shaykh al-Azhar and greater authority for government agencies. New personnel of a higher calibre have been brought in to occupy important Azhar posts and the type of instruction and subject matter taught in the entire Azhar system has been injected with new vigor. The new law totally integrates the religious system of education with the government system. In a word, al-Azhar has been "nationalized."

Article 8 of Law 103 divides al-Azhar into the following departments.[40]

Supreme Council
Muslim Research Academy
Muslim Culture and Missions Department
al-Azhar University
al-Azhar Institutes

The Supreme Council is charged with the general direction of al-Azhar's entire system, including fiscal matters. (Art. 10) It is composed of the Rector of al-Azhar (President); the Vice-Rector; the Director of al-Azhar University; Deans of the faculties of al-Azhar University; four members of the Muslim Research Academy; an Under-Secretary or Assistant Under-Secretary of State from each of the ministries of Awqāf, Education, Justice and the Treasury; the Director of Muslim Culture and Missions; the Director of al-Azhar Institutes; and three members at most from among experts in university education and public affairs. (Art. 9)

Obviously, government appointed "outsiders" hold the balance of power on the committee. Although Shaykh al-Azhar presides as chairman, his rôle in the general affairs of the whole system has been reduced to an honorary one. He cannot meddle in the affairs of the autonomous departments and is controlled within this Supreme Council by the government appointed members who keep a watchful eye on him. He retains some few privileges, must be "consulted" on some appointments, commands a high salary of £2000 yearly, and continues to receive recognition as the Grand Imām, but his actual influence within the Azhar system is now no greater than that exerted by a reigning king or queen in the British parliamentary system.[41] What influence he does exert is derived from his personal reputation as a pious leader or "knower" of Islām.[42]

Within the guidelines set by the Supreme Council the individual departments have significant autonomy. The Muslim Research Council

> is the supreme body of Islamic research; it undertakes the study of all matters related to such research, and works towards the renewal of Moslem culture, its liberation from intrusion, vestiges and traces of political and ideological fanaticism, its demonstration in its pure and original substance, promoting knowledge of it at every level and in every locality, the expression of opinion on new ideological or social problems affecting the creed, and assuming the responsibilities of the call for the sake of the Religion with wisdom and good counsel. (Art. 15)

The membership of the council numbers 50, representing all Muslim schools of thought. Not more than 20 shall be citizens of the UAR. (Art. 16) This attempt to make al-Azhar an international force for the "purification" of Islām has been half-hearted to date and the work of the Council has been delayed. Its first congress, not held until March, 1964, attracted 100 delegates from 42 countries, but little of importance was accomplished. The shaykhs listened to the presentation of various papers and heard a series of Egyptian dignitaries discuss the need for a reinterpretation of Islām's attitude toward modern problems, but nothing concrete has yet come from the Academy.[43] It has not as yet exerted any significant influence in the Islamic world because its functions overlap with other Azhar departments, it has not been enthusiastically received by Muslim groups in other countries, and has, of course, become a political issue between Arab and Muslim governments.[44] At present it is only represented by a director with an office in the old administration building, but a modern central library is planned for the Academy. The main reason, however, for its inactivity is that the Young Officers have not wished to develop this department at this point. They prefer to continue to support their own highly successful and autonomous Supreme Council for Islamic Affairs. Nevertheless, the possibility of the Academy springing to life at some point in the future should not be overlooked.

The Muslim Culture and Missions Department

> shall be concerned with all matters relating to publication, translation and Moslem relations with regard to missions, preachers, and reception of scholarship students and other persons concerned within the scope of al-Azhar objectives. (Art. 25)

As it is now functioning, the missions arm of the department is the most active. Unfortunately, the autonomy of the five departments is so great that they often work at cross purposes rather than towards a common goal.

This department is responsible administratively for the 4000 Muslim missions studying at al-Azhar, but it has kept them separate from Egyptian students at the university until they are competent enough to compete with their Egyptian counterparts in Arabic. The foreign students live in their own area far from al-Azhar, known as the foreign student city or missions' city (*Madīnat al-Bu'uth*), attend separate classes, and have their own interests and recreations.[45] Yet, when the foreign student has mastered Arabic, to transfer from the Missions Department to al-Azhar University is as difficult, because of bureaucratic inefficiencies and the separate autonomy of the two departments, as transferring from one university to another.

The Missions Department is also active in sending Azhar teachers abroad, but once again, the sharing of responsibility with the Ministry of Awqāf and the Ministry of Education makes it almost impossible for the Azharis themselves to understand just what their actual rôle is. By far the greatest majority of Azharis sent abroad are handled by the Ministry of Education.[46]

The department of al-Azhar Institutes administers all primary and secondary religious training.[47] Of greatest importance is the equalization of religious training in these Azhar institutes with the training given in the government system. Students from these institutes may now receive certificates in industrial, commercial, agricultural and other studies so that they may be accepted into the regular school system upon graduation from the primary or secondary levels. For the time being, however, the flow is in the opposite direction. Government school students have flooded the new faculties of al-Azhar University, almost driving out the Azharis.

The reform has entirely reorganized al-Azhar University, which is now one of the five departments in the Azhar system. Like every department, the university has its own administration which operates independently within the overall system. A Rector of al-Azhar University (not to be confused with Shaykh al-Azhar) presides over the University Council composed of the sub-rector, deans of the various faculties, a delegate from the Ministry of Education, three members of the Muslim Research Academy and three members with experience in university education or public affairs. Since the rector and the sub-rector are appointed by the President of the Republic and the other members by various government agencies, the administration of the university has been taken out of the hands of the traditional Azharis. The past rector, for instance, transferred from Cairo University and all the deans now hold Western Ph.D.'s.

The traditional faculties have been regrouped under the Faculty for Islamic Studies and the Faculty for Arab Studies, but they continue to operate separately as individual faculties and will eventually be moved to Madīnat Naṣr. What will be done with the old quadrangles has not yet been decided.[48] The rest of the curriculum has been revolutionized to include four new areas of study, fields hardly compatible with the traditional interests of the religious scholar. With the creation of the new faculties of Business Administration, Engineering and Crafts, Agriculture and Medicine, al-Azhar has become the fifth Egyptian state university.

All sections of the reformed Azhar will be moved shortly to Madīnat Naṣr (near Heliopolis) though the experimental centers of the Faculty of Agriculture, for instance, will be located elsewhere. Almost without exception, the new faculties have accepted all their students from the overcrowded government universities. The entire faculty for these new departments is also drawn from the secular system. The professors, students and training cannot be any more alien to the traditional Azhar than the fact that instruction within the faculties of Medicine and Engineering is given in *English*.

The announced goal of the reform, to allow the Azharis to receive the same training as their secular counterparts, will thus be several years in coming, for the Azharis are not yet used to the new sciences and are incapable of doing university work in the new faculties in Arabic, much less in English.

The religious sciences have generally been left untouched so as not to stir up undue trouble. Nevertheless, Islām as taught at al-Azhar is becoming increasingly "socialistic" as it is impregnated with the ideas of Arab socialism.[49] Considering the régime's desire to make the religious scholar a "productive" citizen and the trend toward enlightened secularism, one can expect the religious faculties in the future to lose much importance and suffer a serious loss of students, especially under the impact of the reformed primary and secondary education in the rural areas. It will be several years before village boys (and girls) come to al-Azhar for anything but religious training, but the day will soon arrive when al-Azhar will have the characteristics of any Jesuit or Wesleyan university where theology is but one faculty in the total university. The weight of the modern future is pressing heavily on the traditional religious scholar, but it will be his perceived self-interest in seeking satisfactory employment that will finally drive him toward the new faculties at al-Azhar. The turbaned shaykh will give way to the broadly trained religious scholar such as those who already occupy the key posts as deans and rectors in the new system. It is from the ranks of these modern trained shaykhs that any meaningful "restoration" of Islām will come, if indeed it will come from shaykhly ranks at all.

FOOTNOTES

1. For a general survey of the movement to reform al-Azhar, see Bayard Dodge, *Al-Azhar: A Millenium of Muslim Learning,* Washington, D.C., 1961; and *'Abd al-Mut'āl al-Sa'īdī, Tarīkh al-Islāh fī l-Azhar,* Cairo, 1950.

2. See Naday Safran, *Egypt in Search of Political Community,* Cambridge, 1963, for an excellent study of the consequences of the modernization process for Egyptian political orientations.

3. The noticeable withdrawal by al-Azhar from the nationalist movement after 1919 is indicative of the inability of al-Azhar to play a more active rôle in the nationalist movement toward secularism. New groups and institutions, such as political groupings, parliament, the newly emergent nationalist-inspired middle class, and the politicized students of the government schools took over many of the former functions of the men of al-Azhar. To make matters worse, the Azharis continued to withdraw from society under the constant attacks of the nationalists. When religion once more became a factor in Egyptian politics it was the Ikwān al-Muslimun and not the men of al-Azhar who championed traditional Islām.

4. Perhaps "restoration" or "purification" might be a better description than "reform" when discussing Islamic attitudes or doctrines, as A. L. Tiwabi suggests in "English Speaking Orientalists," *Islamic Quarterly* (July–December) 1964, pp. 73–88, for "reform" seems to imply that something is wrong with Islām itself. These are also the phrases that Islamic modernists use.

5. The reformers' position was seriously weakened by the fact that they did not represent an organized group, but a collection of individual reformers, often antagonistic to one another. By their ostracism from the general body of 'ulamā', being in some cases stripped of their title of *'ālim,* the reformers lost the opportunity to work for reform within the religious community. Instead, they had to face the stigma of these who were put in the position of "attacking" Islām.

6. It was for this reason that Muḥammad 'Alī preferred to introduce an entirely new school system rather than institute reform at al-Azhar. Khedive Ismā'īl likewise created Dār al-'Ulūm to avoid a direct confrontation with religious conservatives over any reform within the religious system of education. The old is never destroyed; it is simply allowed to lapse into disuse.

7. Many of the leaders, such as Tāhā Husayn and Sa'd Zaghlūl, were actually graduates of the Azhar system.

8. For an account of the struggle between parliament and the king over the implementation of this law, see Fakhr al-Dīn al-Aḥmadī al-Ẓawāhiri, *al-Siyāsah w al-Azhar,* Cairo, 1945.

9. There was no significant structural change at al-Azhar between 1936–1952. See Dodge, op. cit.; Sa'īdī, op. cit.; H. A. R. Gibb, *Modern Trends in Islam,* Chicago, 1947; and Wilfred C. Smith, *Islam in Modern History,* New York, 1957.

10. *Al-Azhar University,* no author, Cairo, 1950.

11. For published studies on the Ikhwān movement see Christina Harris, *Nationalism and Revolution in Egypt,* The Hague, 1964; Ishaq Husseimi, *The Moslem Brethren,* Beirut, 1956; J. Heyworth-Dunne, *Religious and Political Trends in Modern Egypt,* Washington, D.C., 1950. For the best and most thorough account to date see Richard Mitchell, unpublished Ph.D. thesis, *The Society of the Muslim Brothers,* Princeton University, 1960.

12. Although individual Azharis were fervent members of the Ikhwān, the two organizations fought bitter pamphlet and verbal wars over their respective interpreta-

tions of Islām. An indication of the division between the two organizations is the fact that Ḥasan al-Banna, the Ikhwān Supreme Guide, made only one appearance (December 12, 1947) at al-Azhar. Husseini, op. cit., p. 20 and personal interview with the author.

13. See Naday Safran, "The Shar'ī Courts in Egypt," *Muslim World* 48 (1959) pp. 20–28; 125–135; and Joseph Hajjar, *Proche Orient Chrétien* 5, no. 4 (1955); 6, no. 1 (1956).

14. These men could count only upon the cooperation of a handful of like-minded shaykhs educated in Europe and America who now occupied key positions in the Azhar system.

15. The situation had by this time grown so desperate for the Azharis that students and shaykhs themselves desired reform, though most feared the length to which the reorganization would go. The resignation of the Western trained scholars to government control was summed up by Dr. Maḥmūd Ḥubballah in this crucial period. "Yet, the state that controls the sinews of life has the right, when it wishes, to interfere in religion itself, which becomes dependent on the wish of the state." From "The Challenge of Modern Ideas and Social Values to Muslim Society," in *Islamic Literature* 11 (1959) p. 35.

16. For a comparison of these two bills, see the minutes of the Majlis al-Ummah for June 22, 1961. The amended law as it passed the Assembly can be found in its Arabic original in the same place. An Arabic copy was published in *Majallat al-Azhar* (July, 1961), pp. 237–264. A French translation can be found in MIDEO 6 (1959–1961), pp. 473–484. An English translation can be found in the United Arab Republic publication *Arab Political Encyclopedia: Documents and Notes,* August, 1961, pp. 65–83.

17. These highly revealing unpublished minutes of this meeting were made available to the author in Egypt. They were supported by interviews with several of the key participants at this meeting. Most of the following account of the meeting comes from these minutes and interviews.

18. *Documents and Notes,* p. 79.

19. *Ibid.*

20. *Ibid.*, p. 80.

21. *Ibid.*

22. *Ibid.*, p. 81.

23. *Minbār al-Islām,* English edition (April, 1962) p. 17. This journal published by the Supreme Council for Islamic Affairs, a government-subsidized organ headed by a former army major, has taken from *Majallat al-Azhar* the role of spokesman for a modern or "purified" Islām.

24. *al-Bahai, al-Fikr al-Islāmī al-Hadīth,* Cairo, 1962, p. 488.

25. *Ibid.*, p. 491.

26. *Ibid.*, p. 494.

27. *Ibid.*, p. 496.

28. *Minbār al-Islām,* English edition (November, 1961) p. 13.

29. *Ibid.*, pp. 42–46.

30. *Majallat al-Azhar,* English supplement, p. 17.

31. *Ibid.*, p. 18.

32. *Ibid.*, p. 21. It is also interesting to note that the present Minister of Awqāf and al-Azhar Affairs, Ahmad al-Sharabāssī, is often referred to as "the engineer Sharabāssī," rather than by some religious title.

33. Personal interview.

34. *Ibid.*

35. *Rose al-Yūsuf,* November 5, 1962, pp. 10–11.

36. *Minbār al-Islām,* English edition (November, 1961) p. 18.

37. *Majallat al-Azhar,* English supplement (March, 1962) p. 9.

38. *Minbār al-Islām,* Arabic edition, (August, 1964) p. 19.

39. See *Minbār al-Islām* for the most comprehensive collection of articles rep-

resenting a socialist ideology in Egyptian Islamic thought. President 'Abd al-Nāṣir represented the character of this thought when he told the Yemenis on an important visit, "Islām is based on three principles: socialism as the basis of social justice and equality; popular rule; and unity." *The Arab Observer* (May 4, 1964) p. 12.

40. *Documents and Notes,* p. 66.

41. "The Rector of al-Azhar is the Grand Imam with the final say in all matters related to religious affairs, scholars on the Koran and the science of Islam. He is the supreme guide in all questions connected with Moslem studies in al-Azhar and its institutions. . . ." (Art. 9)

42. The position of Shaykh al-Azhar is much stronger internationally than domestically. The Young Officers support the international travel of this leading shaykh, who has been called by some the "world Muslim leader," for the prestige his dignity brings Egypt. In his own right, for instance, Shaykh al-Azhar annually answers hundreds of questions concerning religious law sent to him from every corner of the Islamic world.

43. For a resume of the Academy's meeting, see *The Arab Observer* (March 16, 1964) pp. 8–9.

44. This department, for instance, shares the duty with the Muslim Culture and Missions Department and al-Azhar University for the "preservation, study, interpretation and dissemination of the Moslem heritage." All three must fulfill "the message of Islām to the people" and take upon themselves "the task of clearing up the truth about Islām and its effect on human progress . . ." (Art. 69)

45. The foreign students also find it difficult to mix socially with the Egyptians. New residential buildings for Egyptian students are now, however, being planned for Madīnat al-Bu'ūth.

46. Of the 3,504 UAR teachers sent abroad in the academic year 1961–1962, only 756 were delegated from al-Azhar. Of these 756, only a very small number were financed by al-Azhar itself. See UAR, *10 Years of Progress,* 1962, Table 1. Figures on Azharis abroad are taken from the records of Shaykh al-Azhar.

47. Article 83 makes possible the creation of more institutes, foreign as well as domestic. Many Muslim countries poor in educational facilities have already requested aid from al-Azhar in setting up religious schools.

48. One innovation is the creation of a new department for Islamic and Arabic Studies at the Faculty of Sharī'ah. Lectures will be given on theology, rhetoric and other Islamic sciences at the mosque of al-Azhar. Anyone may attend, but it is primarily for holders of the secondary certificate and foreign students who are capable of following the courses. At the end of a four-year course, a degree which gives the same rights as any Azhar degree will be awarded. See *The Egyptian Gazette* (March 7, 1965).

49. One of the more important resolutions of the Islamic Research Council conference of 1964 opened the door to Egyptian style "Arab Islamic Socialism." "The government of a country has the right to restrict the freedom to ownership to the extent necessary for preventing corruption and realizing the interests of the country." *The Egyptian Gazette* (April 6, 1964).

Part Six

Language and Education

Languages are learned primarily to communicate meanings, but they can be learned also for other purposes. Second languages, or a first language used "properly," can confer prestige. Auxiliary languages can also be learned as avenues to other cultures.

In schools, the particular vehicle used to convey information can be significant in achieving national goals. Insofar as learning more languages can facilitate the acquisition of knowledge, many countries wish their schools not to be restricted to one language. Economic development aims favor more or less "international" languages like English and French as second languages.

Yet second languages tend to remain no more than auxiliary when mother tongues facilitate the goals of modernization. Schools, concerned with more than economic development, seek to preserve common cultural bonds. Economic goals may suggest the use of "international" second languages in schools, but goals of nationalism and cultural unity often govern the maintenance of vernaculars. It is when group cohesion becomes less valued that mother tongues become amenable to change. In pluralistic nation-states, for example, ethnic groups often find themselves at a socio-economic disadvantage, because their first language is not the primary language of the dominant national society. In highly assimilative environments sub-group allegiances may be sacrificed to secure socio-economic rewards, and national languages, with the aid of schools, may become primary languages for ethnic groups.

This section deals with language as a focus of culture conflict and change in schools. The opening essays, by Erwin H. Epstein and by Arthur C. Rubel, reveal two cases in which a languge is used simultaneously for socio-economic and acculturative ends. English is taught to Puerto Ricans and Mexican-Americans to promote individual and aggregate upward social mobility and to assimilate Latin sub-populations into American society. Not only have the aims of English instruction been similar for both groups, but so have some of the results. Among some Puerto Ricans and some Mexican-Americans, learning English has represented a "selling-out" to North American ways and a rejection of Hispanic tradition, and among a majority in both groups Spanish remains the language of personal relations. English continues to be reserved only for relations of an impersonal type. Yet, in both Puerto Rico and the American Southwest, acquisition of English skills is being viewed increasingly as an instrument for improving the individual's position socially and occupationally.

Although the aims and results of English instruction are largely similar for Puerto Ricans and Mexican-Americans, expectations for the two groups tend to vary. Rubel notes that "Anglos" (English-speaking Southwesterners) deprecate Spanish even as a second language and expect that language to be suppressed in favor of English. Schoolchildren are often punished for speaking Spanish even among themselves. In contrast, English is not expected (at least currently) to be the principal language of the Puerto Ricans. Indeed, Puerto Ricans are expected to be rather bilingual. Schoolchildren are not chastised for speaking Spanish, but they are supposed to have a command of English.

A comparison of the essays on language in Puerto Rico and in the American Southwest suggests that two factors cause expectations to differ in those areas: spatial proximity and political status. Mexican-Americans are in continual contact with English-speaking Anglos and must associate with that dominant group for social and economic purposes. For Puerto Ricans, on the other hand, North Americans are far less visible and English is less predominant and essential. Politically, both Puerto Ricans and Mexican-Americans are United States citizens. Yet whereas Mexican-Americans enjoy privileges identical to those of most Americans, such is not the case for Puerto Ricans. Insofar as Puerto Rico is not fully integrated as a state, North Americans cannot presume the island's principal languge to be the same as theirs. Hence, less is expected of English instruction in Puerto Rico than in the Southwest.

These essays suggest that languages often work at cross-purposes. In pluralistic nation-states mother tongues tend to hold back the tide of assimilation, while national languages, constituting second languages for ethnic groups, promote national integration. By contrast, in less pluralistic societies, second languages are capable of engendering social cleavages at the same time as mother tongues foster national unity. In Lebanese national life, for example, French is a disintegrative force. According to Rosemary Sayigh, that language serves as a window to the outside world, in thought and technology. For those who wish to advance socially and economically, Arabic is not enough. While Arabic represents Lebanese nationality to a greater extent than French, the two languages vie for allegiances, and this contention reflects an "amphibian suspension" between East and West.

The case of Lebanon demonstrates clearly how a conflict of social, economic, and political aims can focus on linguistic aspects of schooling. For Muslims, the role of French is somewhat like the role of English for Puerto Ricans, i.e., to act as a vehicle for knowledge; French is not used to express intimate feelings and is often regarded as a relic of foreign domination. Christians, on the other hand, have viewed French not only as a means of acquiring knowledge, but as a bridge to French culture. Insofar as the school aims to further modernization and associate with a particular Western culture, it must emphasize a second languge. Insofar as the school seeks to maintain national unity, it must elevate the vernacular.

If the dilemmas surrounding language resist solution in bilingual situations, they can become almost unresolvable in polylingual countries. Paul Friedrich notes that India has fourteen languages (a fifteenth, Sindhi, was added recently) for official purposes; most of these official languages are spoken by more than ten million people. Given this extreme degree of linguistic heterogeneity, integration has become perhaps even more salient as a national goal than economic development. Indeed, Indian nationality might well depend on that country's efforts to set a national language over and above its many regional languages.

Discussions of the national language question tend to center on two languages: English and Hindi. Hindi is the most commonly spoken language in India, and, because of linguistic factors, Indian children tend to learn it far more readily than English. Hence, pedagogically and psychologically Hindi is a sounder candidate for India's national language. Politically, however, to adopt Hindi as the national language would be fraught with difficulties. It is but one of several widely spoken vernaculars. Furthermore, relative to some other widespread vernaculars like Bengali, Hindi lacks the prestige of a long and respected literary tradition. English more than Hindi commands the respect of the literati and has already proven to be an integrative force in government.

Inasmuch as English is a "world" language, it is used by the schools to teach modern technology. English must be mastered by individuals who desire to be socially mobile. The greater visibility of English as a tool for mobility may make it more desirable as a second languge among aspiring learners.

Friedrich believes that India's language problem makes unrealistic Western ideals of the "common man" and mass education. Similarly in other countries egalitarian ideals are threatened when languge conflicts are salient. Wherever man learns better in one language when another is available and can better satisfy his aspirations, the school seems destined to be caught in a web of countervailing goals.

Social Change and Learning English in Puerto Rico

ERWIN H. EPSTEIN

A LANGUAGE may be studied in one of two ways; internally, in terms of its structure, or externally, in terms of its roles or functions. Linguists have directed their attention mainly to the study of the *structure* of languages. Their concern has been traditionally with the description of units of sound and meaning and the analysis of interrelationships between them. In contrast, the study of the *function* of languages has been left mostly to sociologists. By language function is meant the way in which language is used to promote individual or societal goals. For instance, an auxiliary language imposed on a multilingual population may "function" to promote cultural and linguistic cohesion. The same language may serve simultaneously to identify members of a social or academic elite, and may be therefore an instrument of social mobility for those wishing to gain entrance to the world of the select.

With technological change, a language, particularly a second language, may change in function for both society and the individual.[1] In former British possessions, for example, English at one time served generally as the communicative link between the metropole and its colonies. For the individual, English constituted largely a means by which one could secure a position that required contact with foreigners. In nations where cultural diversity is extensive, English has served often as an acculturating force as well as a medium of international communication. But perhaps most important, the second language has allowed these nations to be exposed to the literature of science and technology and to values in step with modernization.

The consequences for the individual of an alteration of the function of a language may be significant. If technological change is accompanied by an opening up of the social structure, a language associated with development may be used as an instrument for vertical mobility. Accordingly, a second language may be perceived by the ambitious as an important means of bettering their social position and gaining the benefits of modernization. With the advance of technology, a modern language frequently becomes a prerequisite for the attainment of an increasingly wide range of administrative and technical occupations.

In this paper, we shall examine the role of a second language, English, in Puerto Rico, a society undergoing rapid technological change. More specifically, we shall explore how one age-group of the public-school population, ninth-grade pupils, views English in terms of its socio-economic benefits and in terms of the socio-political implications of learning that language. In addition, an attempt will be made to ascertain whether certain subgroups of the ninth-grade public-school population have generally more favorable attitudes than others toward learning English.

ENGLISH AND THE AMERICANIZATION OF PUERTO RICO

Technological change in developing countries is a potent and disruptive force. In Puerto Rico, it can be seen as a threat to nationality and cohesion or as an avenue to reform and modernization. While it is accompanied by social change and the adoption of new values, it does not prevent many old values from remaining entrenched and unaltered. Change arouses mixed fears and ideological conflicts which threaten to frustrate potential progress. In the wake of change, a once predominant and widely cherished ethos may be viewed by many with sentiment rather than as a guide to everyday behavior.

Language functions as a symbol for those who promote change as well as for those who resist or merely wish to channel it. It is plausible that to persons who emphasize the necessity of rapid technological advance, a widespread learning of English symbolizes an emergence of values in accord with a drive to modernize the island. To others, learning English represents more the displacement of traditional culture. In this regard, language is recognized as being more than a medium of communication; it is a means of defining experience. According to Sapir, a language is in effect:

> . . . a guide to "social reality." . . . Human beings do not live in the objective world alone, nor alone in the world of social activity as ordinarily understood, but are very much at the mercy of the particular language which has become the medium of expression for their society. . . . The fact of the matter is that the "real world" is to a large extent unconsciously built up on the language habits of the group. No two languages are ever sufficiently similar to be considered as representing the same social reality. The worlds in which different societies live are distinct worlds, not merely the same world with different labels attached.[2]

Puerto Ricans are citizens of the United States. To them English is a *lingua franca* insofar as it serves as the linguistic bond with North Americans. There is no one characteristic that better distinguishes a Puerto Rican as an American than his ability to speak English. However, it is possible that many Puerto Ricans fear that learning a new language could at least partially remove the "social reality" to which they are accustomed, thus causing them to be ambivalent if not overtly hostile toward English. Nelita Vientós Gastón, an outspoken critic of the existing school-language policy, has charged the insular Department of Education with not educating Puerto Rican children, but teaching them English with the intention of depriving them of their Puerto Rican character and converting them into Americans.[3] That this criticism should be made relatively recently may appear odd in view of the fact that English is emphasized considerably less in the schools now than it was during the almost fifty years of American influence prior to the end of World War II. In fact, until 1948 English had been frequently the vehicle of instruction for non-language subjects in various grades, even though Spanish had been, as it is now, the language of home and work for the great majority of Puerto Ricans.

Certainly, a concern for minimizing the effect of English is one reason why so much effort has been directed at keeping English as the *second* language in the schools. Puerto Rican educators have long felt that while English has its rightful place in the curriculum as an obligatory subject, it should not be used to force children to become less Latin. The feeling among the educators has been that, most important, Puerto Ricans should receive a good education, and only secondarily should they be "Americanized." And, above all, becoming Americans and being educated are *not* equivalent.[4]

But if Puerto Ricans are alarmed about learning a second language as a threat to their way of life, they also perceive its potential as a prime instrument of self-improvement and of promotion in a rapidly expanding social structure. English in Puerto Rico has come to symbolize a new social order, one resisted and challenged by some because it is different, but more often accepted because it promises new opportunities.

EXPANSION OF OPPORTUNITIES AND THE EMERGENCE OF NEW VALUES

A new value system in step with industrial development is emerging in Puerto Rico. It is one that gives a preferred place to the nuclear family, emphasizes occupational mobility, and is oriented to North American and Western European market traditions. It is also one that emphasizes external success and tangible accomplishment in the evaluation of human behavior.[5] This emergent value system has been fostered by a climate that favors individuals who seek jobs created by industrialization. In contrast to primarily aristocratic societies, in which a social stigma is often attached to business activities (at least in the early stages of industrial development),[6] businessmen in Puerto Rico do not lack social prestige. The most able members of the middle and upper classes are not discouraged from choosing a career in industry.[7] Moreover, the ties between government and elites are not such as to control business opportunity. Artificial barriers are not set deliberately in the path of capitalistic innovation. Whatever political influence was enjoyed by the old upper-class had been lost during the liberal regime of former Governor Muñoz Marín. Furthermore, a new university educated middle-class group has come to staff and influence the government.[8]

But a new system of values has been influenced most by a major shift in the occupational structure, from one dominated by primary and some secondary industry to one emphasizing tertiary, high-level manpower. Between 1950 and 1960, employment in agriculture declined 37 per cent while employment in communications increased 72 per cent, in business services 49 per cent, and in educational services 60 per cent.[9] This occupational realignment clearly signals the increasing importance of education in the social structure. Wherever there is use of proportionately "better" manpower, there must be a concomitant growth in the proportion of educated people (Table I).

TABLE I. YEARS OF SCHOOL COMPLETED BY PERSONS OVER 24 YEARS OF AGE, IN PERCENTAGES[a]

Years of Schooling	*1950*	*1960*
none	33	23
1–8	55	54
9–12	8	15
13+	3	8
Total [b]	100	100

[a] Source: U.S. Bureau of the Census, *Census of Population: 1960, General Social and Economic Characteristics, Puerto Rico,* Final Report PC (1) 53 C, 1962, pp. 53–120, Table 42.

[b] In this and the following tables, figures need not add to totals because of rounding.

The demands made by the industrial revolution in Puerto Rico for highly skilled personnel have resulted in a greatly expanded occupational structure. Opportunities appear to be attracting those who previously had only modest ambitions. Wide opportunity and a social system in which the channels of ascent are relatively unconstricted have made the increased potential for achievement a major sign of progress. In this system, one can no longer stand still and expect to be a complete success. For one of the prime marks of success has become the distance one has moved from a lower position to his present one. And, in the determination to move upward, education becomes increasingly critical.

LEARNING ENGLISH AS AN INSTRUMENT IN SOCIAL MOBILITY

It may be relevant to ask if certain educational components have greater instrumental value than others to vertical mobility and the attainment of emergent goals. English learning in Puerto Rico presents a threat, which may be perceived as such, to the traditional culture. Yet it is also viewed as a means of elevating oneself in the emergent social hierarchy. Since, unlike other aspects of education, language skills are immediately perceptible, it provides an obvious way to demonstrate one's educational accomplishments (and social position).

Those oriented to mobility upward in the social pyramid may be thus more likely to view distinctiveness of language as a means of attaining life goals. Bernstein notes that certain linguistic forms are strategic for success. Specifically, forms embodied in a *formal* language, in which "the speaker is able to make a highly individual selection and permutation [in the] . . . use of structural possibilities for sentence organization," are instrumental in high goal attainment. In contrast, individuals restricted to a *public* language, less expressive of subjective intent, are forced to become oriented "to descriptive rather than analytic concepts." Bernstein maintains that analytic capability is essential for success in educational and business endeavors.[10]

In a bilingual environment, the upwardly mobile individual can make language an instrument for his aspirations in two ways: (1) he can acquire a linguistic superiority in his own language, by mastering its strategic forms, and (2) he can acquire a command of the second language. Of these two ways, the second may be much more subject to technological change. Cultural resistance may be manifested against learning the second language but is unlikely against a mastery of the vernacular. Resistance may be overcome, however, if the second language becomes associated with the emergent sector of the economy and attendant high socio-economic status. In Puerto Rico, as the number of upwardly mobile individuals increases, there appears to be an increasing and parallel demand for education and English skills (Table II).

ATTITUDES TOWARD LEARNING ENGLISH

Several factors may account for the acquisition of English among a rapidly increasing proportion of the Puerto Rican population. Most of these factors relate to a greater exposure to that language. In the first place, there has been a recent upswing in the number of people returning to Puerto Rico from the continental United States. In 1953, the year of greatest migration to the United States, nearly 20,000 Puerto Ricans moved to the continent. Ten years later, the number of people moving back to the island

TABLE II. ABILITY TO READ AND WRITE (SPANISH) AND ABILITY TO SPEAK ENGLISH, FOR PERSONS TEN YEARS OLD AND OVER, FOR PUERTO RICO (IN PERCENTAGES)[a]

Census Year	*Able to Read and Write (Spanish)*	*Able to Speak English*[b]
1960	83	38
1950	75	26
1940	68	28
1930	59	19
1920	45	10
1910	34	4

[a] Source: U.S. Bureau of the Census, *Census of Population: 1960, General Social and Economic Characteristics, Puerto Rico,* Final Report PC (1) 53 C, 1962, pp. 53–121, Table 43.

[b] A disproportionately high number of English speakers may have left the island by 1950, this period coinciding roughly with the huge upswing in migration to the continent, which may account for the absence of an increase in the proportion of the population able to speak English for that year. Persons who were migrating at that time may have been among those with most reason to acquire English. Moreover, those who already knew English may have been more willing to migrate than persons confronted potentially with the considerable difficulties of not knowing the language of the mainland. Persons were reported as able to speak English if they could make themselves understood in the language.

was substantially greater than the number migrating to the mainland.[11] Puerto Ricans who return to their birthplace naturally bring with them an increased facility in English.

Second, the rapid growth in tourism and in continental-based industry increases the demand for English speakers.[12] Opportunities are accelerating for people with English skills, particularly in hotels, restaurants, and shopping centers. Along with the increased emphasis on tertiary, high-level manpower, English has become an essential requirement for a great many managerial, professional, and technical personnel. Besides their often direct contact with North Americans, Puerto Ricans with sophisticated knowledge and skills require English to read the literature of their vocations. Most of the scholarly texts in Puerto Rico are in English, not Spanish—as is evident from a casual browsing of the stacks of the University of Puerto Rico or the shelves in the bookstores serving the University.[13]

But perhaps the most important factor in the increasing spread of English is the expansion of educational services and facilities concomitant with the general development program Puerto Rico is undergoing. The government is making considerable improvements in its educational system. The

Commonwealth, in fact, has become a world leader in the percentage of national income spent on education.[14] Of course, the degree of effort does not yield a complete picture; Puerto Rico is still in the early stages of development, and in absolute amount the resources available for education are quite limited. While the annual per pupil expenditure is roughly twice that for Latin America as a whole, it is a good deal lower than that for any of the poorest states in the Union.[15] Still, a very strong effort is being made to improve public education, and there is notable progress toward giving every child at least a primary-school education.

Ultimately, a question must be raised as to how much these factors relate to the way in which English is perceived by potential learners. Is an increase in opportunities, both economic and educational, reflected in fact in the attitudes of school children toward English? Do pupils who are most oriented to movement upward in the social structure, pupils who most strongly desire the benefits created by new opportunities, have attitudes which are most favorable toward learning English?

To answer these questions, a survey of attitudes of ninth-grade public-school pupils was undertaken. A total of 703 pupils in 21 public schools selected evenly and randomly from three geographical strata—the San Juan Metropolitan area, other urban areas (having 2,500 inhabitants), and rural areas—participated in the study.[16] The results suggest that school children, at least at the ninth-grade level, perceive the value of English quite strongly.[17] The following are some of the more salient findings:

1. Regarding the amount of English pupils felt should be taught in school, approximately 60 per cent expressed a desire to have the language increased above the present amount while less than 10 per cent wanted it decreased. Approximately 80 per cent felt that English should be taught in all grades and to all students at the secondary school level, regardless of ability level or desire (or lack of it) to learn it.

2. Over three-fourths of the pupils found English interesting, while only 5 per cent thought it was boring. Two-thirds of the pupils preferred English "over most other subjects;" 13 per cent preferred other subjects over English.

3. Over half the students indicated that they would often read materials in English had they the opportunity to do so. Only 5 per cent responded that they would seldom if ever read materials in English.

4. Nearly half the students indicated that they would take definite steps to continue improving their English after finishing school (e.g., through night school, daily practice, etc.). Forty-five per cent responded that if English were not taught in their school they would go elsewhere to learn it.

5. Over 90 per cent of the pupils felt that English is useful in obtaining a good job. Less than 5 per cent indicated that English is not useful.

6. Over half the pupils felt that knowing English well earns respect from one's companions; less than one-fourth thought that knowing English is not important in gaining respect.

7. Nearly 60 per cent of the pupils indicated that they would like to marry someone who ordinarily spoke English. Over 80 per cent felt that they would like their children to be able to speak English.

8. Three-fourths of the pupils indicated that they liked to speak English; less than 10 per cent did not like to speak it.

9. Half the pupils felt it essential that Puerto Ricans learn English if their country is ultimately to be advanced. Over 40 per cent thought that English-speaking countries are generally more powerful than others.

Clearly, attitudes toward English among ninth-grade school children are favorable. We shall now consider whether these attitudes are differentiated by an orientation to social mobility.

MOBILITY ORIENTATION AND ATTITUDES TOWARD ENGLISH

To measure mobility orientation, four items were correlated individually with attitudes toward English and then made into a composite index.[18] The items were as follows: (1) willingness to sacrifice immediate pleasures for future gratification, (2) emphasis placed on the importance of having money, (3) desire to have a job better than one's father's, and (4) belief in the importance of working hard for self-improvement.[19] Generally, the individual items related to attitudes toward English in much the same manner as the composite index. This index had four levels which we may term roughly as "high," "high-mid," "low-mid," and "low."

The results of the survey suggest that attitudes toward English are rather strongly associated with mobility orientation. The more mobility conscious a student was the more likely he was to be among the high English achievers (Table III)[20] and also to be among those with generally positive feelings toward English. Some of the most outstanding examples of the latter include the strong relationships between the composite index

TABLE III. GRADE IN ENGLISH, BY COMPOSITE INDEX OF MOBILITY ORIENTATION (IN PER CENTS)

Level of Mobility Orientation	*Grade*					*Total*	
	A	*B*	*C*	*D*	*E*	*%*	*n*
High	15	12	45	25	2	100	(40)
High-mid	8	16	41	31	4	100	(478)
Low-mid	5	15	34	39	8	100	(116)
Low	0	5	38	43	14	100	(21)
Total	8	15	40	32	5	100	(655)

TABLE IV. WAY IN WHICH PUPILS WOULD CHANGE AMOUNT OF ENGLISH TAUGHT IN SCHOOL, BY COMPOSITE INDEX OF MOBILITY ORIENTATION (IN PER CENTS)

	Response			*Total*	
Levels of Mobility Orientation	*Increase English*	*Maintain Present Amount*	*Decrease English*	*%*	*n*
High	70	22	8	100	(40)
High-mid	60	34	6	100	(482)
Low-mid	53	35	12	100	(115)
Low	50	30	20	100	(20)
Total	59	33	8	100	(657)

of mobility orientation and the way in which pupils wished to change the amount of English taught in school (Table IV), the extent to which pupils would read materials in English had they the opportunity to do so (Table V), and the pupils' perceptions of the power of English-speaking countries (Table VI).[21] Table VI is included here to illustrate one attempt to ascertain a symbolic characteristic of English; a language may symbolize power by virtue of the fact that certain countries which use the language predominantly are viewed as great international powers (U.S., Britain). It should be noted that the relationship in Table 6 did not hold consistently. Pupils who were least mobility-oriented were most prone to think that

TABLE V. EXTENT TO WHICH PUPILS WOULD READ MATERIALS IN ENGLISH, BY COMPOSITE INDEX OF MOBILITY ORIENTATION (IN PER CENTS)

	Extent to Which Pupils Would Read English			*Total*	
Levels of Mobility Orientation	*Often*	*Occasionally*	*Rarely if Ever*	*%*	*n*
High	75	20	5	100.0	(40)
High-mid	56	41	3	100.0	(483)
Low-mid	48	42	10	100.0	(116)
Low	43	48	10	100	(21)
Total	55	40	5	100.0	(660)

TABLE VI. BELIEF IN THE POWER OF ENGLISH-SPEAKING COUNTRIES COMPARED TO OTHER COUNTRIES, BY COMPOSITE INDEX OF MOBILITY ORIENTATION (IN PER CENTS)

	English-Speaking Countries Are:			*Total*	
Levels of Mobility Orientation	*More Powerful*	*As Powerful as Others*	*Less Powerful*	%	*n*
High	56	44	0	100	(39)
High-mid	41	55	4	100	(484)
Low-mid	36	53	10	100	(116)
Low	62	19	19	100	(21)
Total	42	53	5	100	(660)

English-speaking countries are either more or less powerful than others.

Although attitudes toward English were found generally to be strongly associated with mobility orientation, it is feasible that the latter in turn may be associated with social status or place of residence. The data, however, suggest that this is not the case. Using an approximate unit-normal-deviate (Z) to test strength of association,[22] the relationship between the composite index of mobility orientation and Hollingshead's two-factor index of socio-economic status (father's occupation given a weight of 7 and father's education a weight of 4)[23] yielded a score of −.40; the relationship between the composite index of mobility orientation and place of residence (by San Juan Metropolitan area, other urban areas, and rural areas) yielded a score of −.74. Both scores indicate negligible association. Moreover, little association was found between attitudes toward English and socio-economic status or residence. For example, no Z scores were found to be above .85 for the relationships between the attitudes toward English shown in Tables 4, 5, and 6 and socio-economic status or residence. In contrast, the Z scores for the relationships between these attitudes and the composite index of mobility orientation were all above 2.50, indicating a very strong association between attitudes toward English and mobility orientation. Thus, although positive attitudes toward English are related strongly to mobility orientation, they are rather broadly diffused in the sample of ninth-grade public-school pupils.

COMMENTS AND CONCLUSIONS

It is clear from this study that languages do not function in a social vaccuum. We communicate by means of language, but also our experiences are defined by the particular vehicle we use to communicate meanings. It may act as a unifying force to promote a more or less uniform "social reality." But it can also function to distinguish members of a gang of toughs, or to set off members of a social elite from the masses. The same language can be used to facilitate movement from a low position to one higher in the social structure.

A man may use his native language variously to define his many social roles; his manner of speech with fellow workers may contrast strongly with that used with his wife or children. The native language is in this sense usually role-diffuse. On the other hand, a second language is not likely to be needed for simple, everyday communication and is relatively role-specific. One learns a second language usually for much more manifest purposes, such as to read technical literature, to communicate with people from other countries, and the like. Moreover, a second language is not often learned naturally. Unlike skills in a vernacular, a person must ordinarily be highly motivated to acquire skills in a second language; he may have to be persistently aware of its potential benefits to master it.

If the culture with which a second language is associated appears very alien, learning it may be strongly resisted. Yet technological change may tend to ease this potential resistance. Although change may arouse fear of the loss of national identity, and a second language may be seen as contributing to that loss, it also creates opportunities for which a second language may be viewed as essential. If the opportunities are attractive enough, they may invite the effort required for learning the second language.

The example of Puerto Rico bears out these points. There change has led to an expansion of the social structure and the adoption of new values. Due to an economic and social transformation, perception of the values of English is becoming increasingly widespread.

Among ninth-grade school children English is viewed favorably. It has been suggested that these attitudes are not differentiated demographically, but tied to mobility aspirations. Children who are most oriented to social mobility were found to have the most favorable attitudes toward English and the highest achievement in that language. Attitudes toward learning English are not strongly related to social status or residence. Why then should they be to mobility orientation?

An unambiguous answer to this question would be unwarranted. It may help, however, to examine briefly the nature of the island and its people. Puerto Rico is a relatively compact, homogeneous society in which regional, ethnic, racial, religious, and linguistic variations are not appreciable. Being a small and densely populated island, Puerto Rico contains virtually no remote areas. The accessibility of communities to the industrial world facilitates the infusion of new ideas and patterns of living. Social change, therefore, may well seep into the roots of "folk" society whose links with the emergent social order may be quite open. Thus, it is not surprising to find values in step with technological change and modernization generally throughout the population, among them the desire to learn English. It is also not surprising that individuals who are more oriented to social mobility have stronger perceptions of the values of learning English. As long as the channels of mobility upward in the social structure remain unconstricted, and as long as social and economic benefits continue to grow, English should become increasingly valued as an instrument in attaining life goals.

In the final analysis, the degree to which speakers become bilingual may depend on three factors: (1) the potential of the second language to become role-diffuse rather than merely role-specific, (2) the extent to which resistance to the second language arising from a fear of culture loss can be overcome, and (3) the extent to which individuals associate their aspirations for a better life with learning the second language. Data collected in Puerto Rico suggest that the island may be moving rapidly toward a bilingual condition. Although these data are limited in that they only touch upon the factors which may lead to bilingualism, they do highlight the importance of language functions in a rapidly changing social order.

FOOTNOTES

1. A comprehensive discussion of the roles of second languages may be found in L. F. Brosnahan, "Some Historical Cases of Language Imposition," in John Spencer, ed., *Language in Africa* (London: Cambridge University Press, 1963), pp. 7–24.
2. David G. Mandelbaum (ed.), *Selected Writings of Edward Sapir* (Berkeley: University of California Press, 1949), p. 162.
3. Nelita Vientós Gastón, "Otra Vez el Biligüismo," *Revista del Instituto de Cultura Puertorriqueña,* XVI (July–September, 1962), 9–10. English is taught as a compulsory subject in all primary and secondary-school grades.
4. Perhaps the best and most concise exposition of this view may be found in Pedro Cebollero, "A Language Policy for Puerto Rico," *Revista de la Asociación de Maestros de Puerto Rico,* XIX, No. 7 (March, 1935), p. 6. It should be noted here that it was only when Puerto Ricans were granted autonomy over their school system that English was eliminated as a medium of instruction for non-language subjects.
5. See Melvin M. Tumin, *Social Class and Social Change in Puerto Rico* (Princeton: Princeton University Press, 1961), p. 472, and cf. Thomas Cochran, *The Puerto Rican Businessman: A Study in Cultural Change* (Philadelphia: University of Pennsylvania Press, 1959), pp. 128–130 and 153–154.
6. British society at the beginning stages of the industrial revolution is a good example. Even in a society still dominated by the landed interests, capitalists were probably second to the royal family in unpopularity. "Stock-jobbers equalled sinecurist tax-eaters in public contempt." G. D. H. Cole and Raymond Postgate, *The British Common People, 1747–1946* (New York: Barnes and Noble, 1961), pp. 146–150.
7. Cochran, *op. cit.*, pp. 73, 74 and 77.
8. *Ibid.*
9. U.S. Bureau of the Census, *Census of Population: 1960, General Social and Economic Characteristics, Puerto Rico,* Final Report PC (1) 53 C, 1962, pp. 53–127.

10. Basil Bernstein, "Social Class and Linguistic Development: A Theory of Social Learning," in A. H. Halsey, Jean Floud, and C. Arnold Anderson, eds., *Education, Economy, and Society: A Reader in the Sociology of Education* (New York: Free Press of Glencoe, 1961), pp. 288–292.

11. See Clarence Senior, *The Puerto Ricans* (Chicago: Quadrangle Books, 1965), p. 39.

12. See William H. Knowles, "Manpower and Education in Puerto Rico" in Frederick Harbison and Charles A. Myers (eds.), *Manpower and Education* (New York: McGraw-Hill, 1965), pp. 111–112.

13. An interesting observation made by a linguist is the following: "To be confined to Spanish is to lag thirty years behind the times in science, engineering, business, and scholarship generally—despite the really vigorous industry with which the Spanish-speaking peoples translate works from many other languages into their own." Robert G. Armstrong, "Vernacular Languages and Cultures in Modern Africa," Spencer, *op. cit.*, p. 65. Since it is assumed that by the time a student reaches the university level in Puerto Rico he should know English, technical literature in English is not ordinarily translated into Spanish.

14. In 1961 approximately 5 per cent of the Gross National Product was spent on public education. The school budget was $96 million in 1962 as compared to $23 million in 1950. Knowles, *op. cit.*, p. 114.

15. Net expenditure per pupil in 1950–60 for Puerto Rico was $120. In Latin America, the annual per pupil expenditure is approximately $70. Expenditure per pupil for Alabama, which has the lowest per pupil expenditure in the United States, was $217 for 1960–61. Osvaldo Rodríguez Pacheco, *Some Aspects of Educational Planning in Puerto Rico* (Hato Rey: Department of Education, 1963), pp. 14–15.

16. For details of the sampling technique and the instrument used in collecting data as well as the results, see Erwin H. Epstein, *Value Orientation and the English Language in Puerto Rico: Attitudes Toward Second Language Learning Among Ninth-grade Pupils and Their Parents*, Cooperative Research Branch, U.S. Office of Education, Project No. S-214, and doctoral dissertation (University of Chicago, March, 1966), Appendices A and B.

17. The steps taken to ensure against biased responses may be found in the full report. *Ibid.*, Appendix A.

18. For details see the full report, *Ibid.*

19. Willingness to sacrifice present pleasures for future gratification is associated with a necessary ingredient in mobility: the will to move toward a distant goal even at the expense of immediate need or enjoyment. The emphasis on money was used as a measure because of the usual requisite of adequate financial resources for attainment of a high social position. The desire for a job better than one's father's is almost a necessary condition for upward mobility. Finally, the feeling of obligation to work hard for self-betterment is a measure of commitment to the ideal of enhancing one's station in life. *Ibid.*, Chap. 4 and Appendix B.

20. In the absence of standardized achievement tests, grades were the only available indicators of English achievement. The chi-square value for the relationship shown in the table is 20.24, slightly outside the .05 level of significance.

21. For ease of illustration, Tables 4, 5, and 6 were simplified from the original by collapsing categories of the variables measured against mobility orientation. Chi-square values for the original tables were as follows: 31.31 (Table 4), 28.89 (Table 5), and 63.53 (Table 6). All had 12 degrees of freedom and were significant at the .01 level.

22. The formula for the unit-normal-deviate is as follows:

$$Z = [(x^2/DF)^{1/3} - 1 + (2/9DF)]/[2/9DF]^{1/2}$$

were *DF* stands for degrees of freedom.

Generally, we may regard a Z score of over 1.00 as indicating moderate strength, over 1.65 as indicating a strong association, and over 2.25 as indicating a very strong association. See Epstein, *op. cit.*, Appendix E.

23. This index was used previously in Puerto Rico. See Lloyd H. Rogler and August B. Hollingshead, "La Clase Social y El Lenguaje Desarticulado en los Enfermos Mentales," *Revista de Ciencias Sociales,* V, No. 4 (December, 1961), 515–528. For an explanation of the occupational and educational categories used, see Epstein, *op. cit.,* Appendix A.

Some Cultural Aspects of Learning English in Mexican-American Communities[1]

ARTHUR J. RUBEL

INTRODUCTION

THE SOCIAL AND CULTURAL FACTORS which influence people's decisions about choice of language are receiving a justifiably increasing amount of attention.[2] There are few areas of the world in which extra-linguistic factors more clearly affect language usage than in the American Southwest. In this region, which comprises the states of Arizona, California, Colorado, New Mexico, and Texas, any discussion about the value of the continued use of Spanish by persons of Mexican descent consistently arouses strong feelings. From this it may be inferred that the use of vernacular Spanish connotes matters of social significance quite apart from the messages the words are intended to convey.[3]

Although the two studies from which most of the primary data for this paper derive were designed to discover the cultural, social, and economic problems which Mexican-Americans confront in their efforts to accommodate to the larger society, neither had as primary emphases the extra-linguistic factors relevant to the use of English as a second language. That topic, however, was often introduced by respondents in the course of formal interviews and informal participant observations of social life. It often stirred heated sentiments, suggesting it to be of at least as much interest and concern to the general public as it has proved to be to educators and social scientists.[4] In these pages, our effort will be directed toward illuminating the role of English as a second language within the larger problem of culture contact and accommodation among those whose native language is Spanish and the so-called Anglos, or native English-speaking people.

The striking determination of the Mexican-Americans to retain Spanish as a spoken language in the face of equally determined efforts by the Anglos to discourage and, when possible, prevent the use of that language exemplifies nativistic responses to acculturation pressures. A nativistic response is a "conscious, organized attempt on the part of a society's members to revive or perpetuate selected aspects of its culture." [5] In his now classic treatment of nativistic responses to acculturation situations, Ralph Linton wrote that there are four forms which a nativistic response could assume.[6] Of these, the one which he describes as a "rational perpetuative nativistic movement" is highly applicable to the importance attributed to vernacular Spanish in the American Southwest. According to Linton, the major function of a rational, perpetuative nativistic movement is the maintenance of the social solidarity of the society or social segment in question. "The elements selected for perpetuation become symbols of the society's existence as a unique entity. They provide the society's members with a fund of commmon knowledge and experience which is exclusively their own and which sets them off from the members of other societies" or social segments.[7] To discuss Spanish-language usage as a nativistic response, it will be necessary first to provide a brief summary of the social history of this region.

SOCIAL HISTORY

The first Europeans to settle the Southwest were Spanish ranchers, clergy, civil administrators, and tradesmen. The earliest settlements were organized at the behest of the Spanish Crown from the end of the sixteenth to the middle of the eighteenth centuries. They were intended to serve as unmistakable notice to Russia, France, and England that these northern reaches of New Spain were in fact, as well as by claim, a part of the Spanish Empire. The hamlets and villages were meant also to lend logistic and military support to the garrisons and missions which were then engaged in efforts to pacify and convert to Catholicism the often hostile Indians.[8]

For the settlers, life was difficult. Long distances over inhospitable terrain separated the northern colonists from such major settlements as Monterrey, Guadalajara, and San Luis Potosí. They could not depend upon the government for assistance, guidance, and leadership. Their relative isolation necessitated having to adapt to an environment which, in several respects, was distinct from that to which they were accustomed and which gave rise to a characteristic way of life.

With the exceptions of the lands given over to mining, the terrain was devoted to the raising of cattle and sheep and subsistence crops. A few wealthy men ruled feudalistically, their lands having been granted them by the Crown.[9] Chevalier notes that the colonizing laws formulated in 1573 made abundantly clear that the northern zone of New Spain was designed "to be *the* zone of powerful individuals, large family circles, housefuls of dependents, and huge estates."[10] Until the arrival of English-speaking settlers, the American Southwest was characterized by two social and economic strata: the rich and powerful on the one hand, the poor and landless on the other.

ARRIVAL OF THE ANGLOS

The introduction of English-speaking families during the last half of the nineteenth century made a considerable impact on the established order of society. Social relations between the two culturally different groups were initially egalitarian, but later changed to dominance of the English-speaking people. Early in the contact period the land-holding gentry lost much of their land to Anglo settlers and speculating land companies, or else sold them at remarkably low cost. Whatever the means by which the land passed from the descendants of the original grantees to English-speaking families or their corporations, it represented a loss of the major source of economic and social power of the Spanish-speaking group.[11] The Anglos then developed large-scale commercial livestock and farming enterprises and constructed elaborate systems of transportation and communication. This effectively transformed a regional economy based on subsistence stock raising and farming to one fully integrated in a national market economy with which the tradition-oriented Mexican-American was not prepared to cope. Furthermore, the Anglos quickly gained political supremacy. In some places, individual Anglos successfully adopted the personalistic techniques which had characterized the Spanish-speaking political leaders, thus enabling the former to build powerful political machines of which they became the "bosses" or *jefes politicos.*

> In becoming masters they [the Anglos] were forced to adjust themselves to the Mexican inhabitant. They learned Spanish and acquainted themselves with the Mexican's psychology, traditions, and habits. In the process they were themselves in a measure Mexicanized. The whole relationship was natural and was not necessarily resented by those who submitted to it; most of them had never been used to anything else either in Texas or Mexico.[12]

The political power of the ascendant Anglos was a function of the fact that they were far more familiar with the processes of representative government which derive from American and English traditions.[13] In addition, in Texas, enactment of legislation which stipulated that citizens must demonstrate literacy and pay a poll tax in order to register to vote effectively disenfranchized many of the Spanish-speaking people. In sum, as a consequence of a number of contributing processes, the distinction which had formerly prevailed between the Spanish-speaking landowner and the landless peón and sharecropper was erased by the overwhelmingly dominant relationship established by Anglos with respect to *any* Spanish-speaking person, rich or poor, landholder or peón.

Unfortunately, information is scarce as to the response of the Spanish-speaking to the increasingly subordinate role assigned them in social, economic, and political life during the latter half of the nineteenth century and the first several decades of the twentieth. However, a study by Mireles clearly suggests that their diminished social status heightened their resentment toward members of the other group.[14]

In 1910 and for several years thereafter, relationships between the two cultural groups were complicated by the arrival of thousands of refugees fleeing the civil unrest and economic uncertainty which was at once the cause and effect of the Mexican Revolution. Many of the new arrivals expected to remain in the United States for only a short while and then, at the end of the Revolution, to return to their homeland. This anticipation made many of them view efforts to learn English as a second language as impractical. Moreover, those who believed their stay to be temporary discouraged their children, relatives, and friends from learning English or in other ways adapting to the new way of life; to learn that language was denigrated as indicative of a traitorous attitude toward Mexico, the motherland.[15] As it turned out, many of those who expected to remain in the United States for only a short time discovered that the hostilities in Mexico lasted far longer than they had anticipated. By the time peace was secured, the immigrants and their children had established strong economic and social ties in the United States. For many it was too late to return to Mexico; yet they remained ill-prepared to cope with American society.

THE PRESENT

Today, there are approximately four million persons of Mexican descent residing in the United States, of whom a million and a half live in Texas.[16] To be sure, the Mexican-Americans are undereducated; yet Texas records the lowest level of education among all Mexican-Americans.[17] According to the 1960 census, among Texans "who were 25 years of age and older, only 1.1 percent of the Anglo group and 5.4 percent of the nonwhite population had had no formal education. In contrast 22.9 percent of the Spanish-speaking group had had none." [18] To some extent the low level of attainment of adult Mexican-Americans can be attributed to an almost total absence of public education in either rural Mexico or rural Texas prior to the turn of the century.[19] A recent assessment of this problem by sociologists Lamanna and Samora yields the distressing prognosis that despite the fact that between 1950 and 1960 the Mexican-Americans made some relative gains on both Negroes and Anglos in Texas, they are likely to remain the least educated segment of the population for some time to come.[20]

Moreover, but hardly unexpectedly, there is a close association among the generally low levels of formal education, disadvantaged position in the labor market, and low levels of income. Mexican-Americans consistently fared worse on these indices throughout the Southwest when compared with Anglos, and they are only slightly better off than the Negroes of this area.[21] Not only is the prognosis for the future poor relative to Anglos and nonwhites, but the much lower level of education among Mexican-Americans gravely affects their ability to adapt themselves to northern industrial cities to which they migrate in search of better employment and social opportunity.[22] The relative youth of the Spanish-speaking group and its high fertility ratio suggest that unless significant new innovations in education among Mexican-American children are introduced, the socio-

TABLE I. DEMOGRAPHIC CHARACTERISTICS OF THE SPANISH-SURNAME POPULATION OF THE FIVE SOUTHWESTERN STATES, 1960

Characteristics	*Arizona*	*California*	*Colorado*	*New Mexico*	*Texas*
Absolute total of Spanish-surname population	194,356	1,426,538	157,173	269,122	1,417,810
Percent of total population	14.9	9.1	9.0	28.3	14.8
Percent growth of Spanish-surname population 1950–60	51.2	88.1	32.9	8.3	38.5
Nativity and percentage	100.0	100.0	100.0	99.9	100.0
Natives of native parentage	49.3	46.0	86.1	87.4	54.8
Natives of foreign or mixed parentage	33.1	34.0	10.4	8.6	31.2
Foreign born	17.6	20.0	3.5	3.9	14.0
Residence	100.0	100.0	100.0	100.1	100.1
Urban	74.9	85.4	68.7	57.7	78.6
Rural non-farm	10.0	10.8	25.2	36.7	15.0
Rural farm	6.1	3.8	6.1	5.7	6.5

Adapted from Table 27 of Harley L. Browning and S. Dale McLemore, "A statistical profile of the Spanish-surname population of Texas," Austin, Bureau of Business Research, 1964.

TABLE II. COMPARISON OF MEDIAN ATTAINMENT AND INCOME OF SPANISH-SURNAME AND OTHER ETHNIC GROUPS, BY STATE, 1960 [a]

Ethnic Group	*Arizona* *Schooling*	*Arizona* *Income*	*California* *Schooling*	*California* *Income*	*Colorado* *Schooling*	*Colorado* *Income*	*New Mexico* *Schooling*	*New Mexico* *Income*	*Texas* *Schooling*	*Texas* *Income*
Spanish-surname	6.7 years	$3,325	8.5 years	$4,381	8.1 years	$3,308	7.7 years	$3,004	4.8 years	$2,400
Total of nonwhite medians	6.8	2,116	10.2	3,951	11.1	3,631	7.0	2,285	7.5	2,161
Indian	5.0	1,500	9.2	3,344			5.3	1,750		
Negro	8.1	2,604	9.8	3,922						
Chinese			10.1	4,141						
Filipino			8.2	3,105						
Japanese			12.4	4,800						
Anglo	12.1	5,168	12.1	5,806	12.1	5,003	11.4	5,573	10.8	4,768

[a] age 25 and over

Adapted from Walter Fogel, "Education and Income of Mexican-Americans in the Southwest," advance report of the Mexican-American Study Project, University of California at Los Angeles, 1965, Table 5.

TABLE III. AGE, SEX, AND FERTILITY MEASURES FOR THE SPANISH-SURNAME POPULATIONS OF FIVE SOUTHWESTERN STATES, 1960

Measure	*Arizona*	*California*	*Colorado*	*New Mexico*	*Texas*
Age distribution					
0–14	42.1	38.6	44.0	43.7	44.4
15–64	54.3	57.3	51.4	51.5	51.7
65+	3.6	4.0	4.6	4.7	3.8
Total	100.0	99.9	100.0	99.9	99.9
Sex ratio					
Total population	109.0	106.2	102.9	101.6	98.4
15–64	113.7	109.2	101.5	100.3	95.7
Child-woman ratio	753	657	738	754	745

Adapted from table 29 of Harley L. Browning and S. Dale McLemore. A statistical profile of the Spanish surname population of Texas, Austin Bureau of Business Research, 1964.

economic distance between them and others will widen and lead to very grave consequences (see Table III).

One of the most important factors contributing to the present educational chasm between Spanish-speaking Americans and other groups in the region is the relatively low proportion of school-age youngsters presently enrolled in school.[23] To a considerable extent, the magnitude of this problem derives from certain characteristics of Mexican-Americans. First, a relatively large proportion are agricultural migrant laborers. Low wages and underemployment in their hometowns induce families to migrate in search of agricultural employment and to remain away from home well into the regular school year, derpiving their children of from one to five months of schooling each year.[24] In the study of New Lots in south Texas, the actual number of Spanish-surname enrollees in elementary school varied considerably according to the migratory work cycle. In the school year 1957-58, four hundred more children were registered and attending classes in the eighth week than in the first week of the school year. There were forty more students during the tenth week than during the eighth.[25] Secondly, the drop-out rates for children with Spanish surnames is disproportionately high.[26] In that same school system, "officials estimate a drop-out rate of 75 percent at the sixth grade level." [27] And, with reference to the state of Texas as a whole, Lamanna and Samora comment: "we see that the Mexican-Americans are much more likely than non-whites or Anglos to drop out of school, and much less likely to go on to higher education." [28] Although the problem in Texas is demonstrably worse than in the other four states of the region, a similar relationship is observed between the Spanish-surname population on the one hand, and Anglos and Negroes on the other in all of the five states of the Southwest.

EXPLANATIONS OF THE PROBLEM

One of the most often advanced explanations as to why Spanish-surname children tend to do less well in school than their Anglo peers and why so high a level of early drop-outs characterizes this population is that they are culturally different and, in a great number of instances come from homes in which Spanish is either the only language spoken or, in the case of bilingual parents, is the preferred language.[29] It is often argued that in a home in which Spanish is either always or sometimes spoken, the way of life differs from the way of life in one where Spanish is never used. Not only is there a problem in verbal communication, but the cultural expectations expressed are often distinctive and, consequently, conducive to conflict between those who represent these two different ways of life.

The rapidly increasing bilingualism in the Southwest is linked directly to acquisition of English as a second language by persons whose primary language is Spanish. With rare exception members of the socially, economically, and politically dominant Anglo segment of the population either reject outright the notion of learning Spanish as a second language, or—among those who have elected to study it in the school system—claim an inability to achieve competence in spoken Spanish.[30] This imbalance between the two languages corresponds to expectations for a society in which the dominance of one group and subordination of the other are such prominent features of social life.[31]

The dominance-subordination relationship between these two ethnic groups has led Mexican-Americans to contend that their situation is analogous to that of Negroes in the deep South. The evidence, however, does not support this argument, largely because the closed caste system which structures Negro-White relations in the South does not apply in the Southwest.[32]

In the former region, social ranking is founded on ascribed racial characteristics; each of the two racial groups comprises a closed caste within which are found a series of ranked social classes. Although channels of upward social mobility are to some extent available to Negroes, it is expected that their mobility will be confined within their own color caste. Those who aspire to better their lot are discouraged from making any effort to equate themselves with Whites of any class level, and severe punishment is meted out to those who try to break the color barrier.

In contrast, relations between Mexican-Americans and Anglos are premised upon an open-class social system, the ideology of which stipulates that individuals be ranked according to achieved social and cultural characteristics instead of ascribed racial traits.[33] In accordance with that ideology, middle-class Anglos expend considerable effort as individuals as well as through civic and religious groups to encourage and help prepare lower- and working-class Mexican-Americans to orient themselves toward upward mobility and a social status equal to that of Anglos. Always implicit and often explicit is an assumption by Anglos that attainment of equal social status is a legitimate goal and one which can be realized. It is also assumed that the upwardly mobile Mexican-American strives for complete assimilation into the Anglo culture. The most often utilized indicator of whether a person is actively attempting to be assimilated is whether or not he becomes a monolingual English-speaker, or remains a bilingual.

SOCIAL MOBILITY AND LANGUAGE CHOICE

The importance imputed by Anglos to monolingualism and their negative attitudes towards Spanish even as a second language may be inferred from the fact that school personnel are directed to prohibit youngsters from speaking Spanish on or near the school grounds; those hapless students caught speaking the vernacular are punished. Punishment ranges from a reprimand to a paddling.[34] Moreover, with the exception of a very few experimental programs, Spanish is taught only as a foreign language, in a manner similar to German, French, Latin, and Greek. It is difficult indeed to exaggerate the symbolic importance which administrators and teachers attach to the acquisition of English and the rejection of Spanish by their young charges. The goal of the schools is a monolingual, English-speaking population. Our research data from Texas speak unmistakably to the point that parents whose primary language is Spanish also are concerned that their children learn English because of the high functional value of that language. With rare exception, Mexican-Americans perceive English-language skill as a means to achieve better education, more and better employment opportunities, and a higher and more reliable income.

But this does not imply that the same parents urge their children to reject Spanish. Barker's findings in Tucson, Arizona, and Scheff's conclusions on the retention of Spanish by immigrants to a northern industrial city are fully supported by our evidence from Texas: Mexican-Americans tend "to preserve Spanish as the language of intimate and familial relations, while reserving English for relations of a more impersonal type. This tendency holds not only for members of the immigrant generation but equally for many . . . [native] born and educated bilinguals."[35]

A few Mexican-Americans are far more oriented to cultural and social assimilation than the average. They make every effort to speak English in all social situations, informal as well as formal, and reject the use of Spanish entirely. Those few who are so oriented are accused by their Spanish-speaking peers as "having turned their backs on their own people."[36] For the average Mexican-American, bilingualism represents a linguistic accommodation to the harsh economic and social realities of an area in which most health, welfare, judicial, employment, education, and other services and opportunities presume competence in English.

While on the one hand interested in mastering English-language skills, on the other Mexican-Americans evidence a marked disinclination to devalue many traditional cultural patterns relating to family life, cliques, political activities, and so on. Traditional ways continue to provide them with satisfying rewards. They remain remarkably well integrated despite acculturation pressures. Consequently, efforts which are made directly or indirectly to modify these basic cultural patterns are very often perceived as a threat to the integrity of the Mexican-American way of life.

The intense interest in retention of the Spanish language by Mexican-Americans in the face of an equally strong Anglo determination to eradicate it, may profitably be seen as an instance of a rational perpetuative, nativistic response. The Mexican-Americans have "selected" their traditional language as a symbol of the continued existence of their way of life. Continued use of Spanish provides members of this group "with a fund of common knowledge and experience which is exclusively their own and which sets them off from the members" of other segments of the same society.[37]

However, continued use of Spanish in this area is becoming less and less effective as a bond between Mexican-Americans and nationals of the Republic of Mexico. Southwestern Spanish is now permeated by vocabulary and grammatical elements which have been borrowed from English. The effects of this borrowing have been such that vernacular Spanish has come to be distinguished from the "standardized" idiom found in either rural Mexico or Mexico City and is characterized by such terms as "Tex-Mex," "border Spanish," "Pocho," and "Arizona Spanish," the descriptives varying from place to place along the border.[38]

Speakers of "border Spanish" are very much aware of and sensitive to the fact that their vernacular is becoming increasingly unique, a truly regional dialect. "Border Spanish" is disparaged by those who speak it and, also, by speakers of more "standardized" Mexican Spanish and by the Anglos whose primary language is English. The deprecatory attitude towards this border idiom is summed up by the often heard statement: "We don't speak either language, neither Spanish or English!" The extensive influence which English has had and continues to have on "border Spanish" contributes to a fast developing sense of social and cultural distinctiveness which an American of Mexican descent feels when he visits in Mexico or is visited by Mexican nationals.

The use of vernacular Spanish identifies a person as a member of a large and important ethnic minority in the American Southwest. On the other hand, intimate borrowing from English is rapidly lessening the sense of identification of the Spanish speaker with Mexico, cradle of his traditional way of life. The continuing controversy over the appropriate roles of Spanish and English in the Southwest must then take into account the larger problem of intergroup relations, of which language usage is but one, although very important, facet.

FOOTNOTES

1. Most of the empirical evidence presented on these pages derives from the author's studies of Mexican-American society in Texas. The study of the small city of New Lots, located on the Texas-Mexico boundary, was part of the Hidalgo County Study, directed by Professor William Madsen, and financially supported by the Hogg Foundation for Mental Health, University of Texas. An on-going study of San Antonio is supported by the Mexican-American Study Project of the University of California at Los Angeles, directed by Professor Leo Grebler. I am very grateful to them for their support and encouragement. I also acknowledge my indebtedness to Professor Joseph Spielberg for his stimulating comments on some of the ideas expressed, and to Mrs. Edeltrud Jolly who so willingly assisted in preparing the ethnographic materials for publication.

2. See the valuable collection of papers, *Language in Culture and Society*, Dell Hymes (ed.), New York: Harper and Row, 1964; Paul Friedrich, "Language and Politics in India," *Daedalus* 91 (3), pp. 543–59; Frank A. Rice (ed.), *Study of the Role of Second Languages in Asia, Africa, and Latin America*, Washington, D.C.: Modern Language Association of America, 1962; John Spencer (ed.), *Language in Africa*, London: Cambridge University Press, 1963.

3. In its present usage, the word "vernacular" refers to a language which is native to a place, rather than to the more specialized meaning given it by the UNESCO special committee: *The Use of Vernacular Languages in Education* (Monographs in Fundamental Education, 8), Paris: UNESCO, 1953.

4. For literature on this subject, see the following: Clyde C. Kluckhohn, "The Field of Higher Education in the Southwest," *New Mexico Quarterly* VII, 1937, 23–30; George C. Barker, "Social Functions of Language in a Mexican-American Community," *Acta-Americana* 5, 1947, 185–207; George I. Sanchez, *Forgotten People*, Albuquerque: University of New Mexico Press, 1940, 30–31; George I. Sanchez, "History, Culture, and Education," in Julian Samora (ed.), *La Raza: Forgotten Americans*, Notre Dame (Indiana): University of Notre Dame Press, 1966, 1–26; John H. Burma, *Spanish-Speaking Groups in the United States*, Durham (N.C.): Duke University Press, 1954, 20–21; William Madsen, *The Mexican-Americans of South Texas*, N.Y.: Holt, Rinehart and Winston, 1964, 106; Herschel T. Manuel, *Spanish-Speaking Children of the Southwest*, Austin, University of Texas Press, 1965.

5. Ralph Linton, "Nativistic Movements," *American Anthropologist* XLV, 1943, pp. 230–40; more recently A. F. C. Wallace has elaborated on Linton's article: A. F. C. Wallace, "Revitalization Movements," *American Anthropologist* 58, 1956, pp. 264–81.

6. Linton, *op. cit.*

7. *Ibid;* for reports of other nativistic responses to accumulation pressures in this area, see Arthur J. Rubel, "Concepts of Disease in Mexican-American Culture," *American Anthropologist* 62, 1960, pp. 795–814; Nancy Solien de Gonzalez "Nativism in New Mexico," an unpublished paper presented at the International Congress of Americanists, Mar del Plata, Argentina, 1966.

8. There is an extensive literature on the history of early Spanish colonization in this area. References which are most pertinent to the settlement of south and central Texas are found in Herbert Eugene Bolton, "Texas in the Middle Eighteenth Century," *University of California Publications in History*, Volume III, Berkeley: University of California Press, 1915; Carlos Castañeda, *Our Catholic Heritage in Texas*, Volume V, Austin: Von Boeckmann-Jones Co., 1942.

9. For good descriptions of this region during the colonial period, see Francois Chevalier, *Land and Society in Colonial Mexico: The Great Hacienda* (Translated by Alvin Eustin), Berkeley: University of California Press, 1963, Chapter 5; Israel Cavazos Garza, "Cedulario Autobiografico de Pobladores y Conquistadores de Nuevo

León," *Biblioteca de Nuevo León* 2, Monterrey (Mexico): Centro de Estudios Humanisticos, Universidad de Nuevo León, 1964, pp. 10–13; Bolton, *op. cit.*

10. Chevalier, *op. cit.*

11. Rubel, 1966, pp. 35–36; Lyle Saunders, *Cultural Difference and Medical Care: The Case of the Spanish-Speaking People of the Southwest,* New York: Russell Sage Foundation, 1954, p. 52; Burma, *op. cit.*, pp. 15–16; Ozzie G. Simmons, "The Mutual Images and Expectations of Anglo-Americans and Mexican-Americans," *Daedalus* (Spring), 1961, p. 287; Florence R. Kluckhohn and Fred L. Strodtbeck, *Variations in Value Orientations,* Evanston: Row, Peterson and Co., 1961, pp. 181–191.

12. O. Douglas Weeks, "The Texas-Mexican and the Politics of South Texas," *American Political Science Review* XLII (August, 1930), p. 610.

13. Interesting discussions of the processes involved in the change from one political system to another are found in: Saunders, *op. cit.*, pp. 77–79; Burma, *op. cit.*, pp. 27–28; Rubel, 1966, pp. 119–40; Kluckhohn and Strodtbeck, *op. cit.*, Munro S. Edmonson, *Los Manitos: A Study of Institutional Values,* New Orleans: Middle American Research Institute, 1957, pp. 49–50.

14. Jovita Gonzalez Mireles, *Social Life in Cameron, Starr, and Zapata Counties,* unpublished M.A. Thesis, University of Texas, 1930, pp. 26–28; *cf.* Vogt, *op. cit.*, pp. 126–127.

15. *Cf.* Americo Paredes, "Texas' Third Man: The Texas-Mexican," *Race* IV (2, May), 1963, p. 55.

16. Harley L. Browning and S. Dale McLemore, *A Statistical Profile of the Spanish-Surname Population of Texas,* Austin: Bureau of Business Research, University of Texas, 1964; *cf.* Donald N. Barrett, "Demographic Characteristics," in Julian Samora (ed.), *op. cit.*, pp. 159–199.

17. Browning and McLemore, *op. cit.*, p. 29.

18. *Ibid.*

19. Lyle Saunders, *op. cit.*, p. 50; Nathan Whetten, *Rural Mexico,* Chicago: University of Chicago Press, 1948, pp. 401–404; George I. Sanchez, *Mexico: A Revolution by Education,* N.Y.: The Viking Press, 1936, pp. 50–51.

20. Richard A. Lamanna and Julian Samora, "Recent Trends in the Educational Status of Mexican-Americans in Texas," Annual Meeting of the Texas Academy of Science, 1965, mimeographed, p. 25.

21. Browning and McLemore, *op. cit.*, Table 33; *cf.*, Walter Fogel, *Education and Income of Mexican-Americans in the Southwest,* Advance Report, Los Angeles: Mexican-American Study Project, University of California at Los Angeles, 1966.

22. Lyle W. Shannon and Elaine M. Kass, "The Urban Adjustment of Immigrants: The Relationship of Education to Occupation and Total Family Income," *Pacific Sociological Review* 6, 1953, pp. 37–42; Lyle W. Shannon, "Urban Adjustment and Its Relationship to the Social Antecedents of Immigrant Workers," *International Review of Community Development* 13–14, 1965, p. 179.

23. The Texas Education Agency estimates that "between 40 and 60 percent of the approximately 100,000 entering non-English speaking first graders each year will have dropped out of school permanently by the end of the elementary grades." Cited in Anne O. Stemmler, "An Experimental Approach to the Teaching of Oral Languages and Reading," *Harvard Educational Review* 36, 1966, p. 43.

24. For efforts to remedy this problem, see *The Texas Project for Migrant Children,* Texas Education Agency, 1964; *cf.*, *Providing Education for Migrant Children,* Denver: Colorado State Department of Education, 1961.

25. Rubel, 1966, p. 10.

26. Lamanna and Samora, *op. cit.*; Stemmler, *op. cit.*; Celia S. Heller, *Mexican-American Youth: Forgotten Youth at the Crossroads,* N.Y.: Random House, 1966, pp. 51–52.

27. Rubel, *op. cit.*

28. Lamanna and Samora, *op. cit.* Surely one of the most sensitive accounts

of the complex social forces which contribute to drop-out problems is an article by Charles Hobart, "Underachievement Among Minority Group Students: An Analysis and Proposal," *Phylon,* Vol. 24 (2, Summer), 1963, pp. 184–96.

29. See for example, "Handbook for the Instructional Program for Preschool-Age Non-English Speaking Children," Texas Education Agency, 1960; Manuel, *op. cit.;* William R. Holland, "Language Barrier as an Educational Problem of Spanish-Speaking Children," in Staten W. Webster (ed.), *Understanding the Educational Problems of the Disadvantaged Learner,* San Francisco: Chandler Publishing Co., 1966, p. 345; Sanchez, 1940, p. 79; Burma, *op. cit.,* pp. 19, 20.

30. An apparent exception to this general pattern is found in Nogales, Arizona. See, Robert C. Stone, *et al.,* "Nogales, Arizona: An Overview of Economic and Inter-ethnic Patterns in a Border Community," *Arizona Review of Business and Public Administration* 12 (1, January), 1963, p. 21.

31. Leonard Bloomfield, *Language,* N.Y.: Henry Holt and Co., 1933, p. 461; A. Richard Diebold, Jr., "Incipient Bilingualism," in Dell Hymes (ed.), *op. cit.,* pp. 496–97. Hans Wolff comments that in an area in which "intelligibility is non-reciprocal, the language or dialect spoken by the culturally dominant group, or the language or dialect with the greater functional value, seems to be the preferred medium for inter-lingual communication." Wolff concludes his article with a query: Is it not "possible to speak of a 'pecking order' of intelligibility?" Hans Wolff, "Intelligibility and Inter-Ethnic Attitudes," in Dell Hymes (ed.), *op. cit.,* pp. 444, 445.

32. Rubel, 1966, p. 20. See also the interesting comment on this topic in Paredes, 1963, *op. cit.,* p. 50. A discussion of the color-caste system in the South is found in W. Lloyd Warner and Allison Davis, "A Comparative Study of American Caste," in Edgar Thompson (ed.), *Race Relations and the Race Problem,* Durham: Duke University Press, 1939; John Dollard, *Caste and Class in a Southern Town,* Garden City: Doubleday Anchor Books, 1957; Allison Davis, *et al., Deep South,* Chicago: University of Chicago Press, 1941; Gunnar Myrdal, *et al., An American Dilemma,* N.Y.: Harper Bros., 1944.

33. Rubel, 1966, *op. cit.,* pp. 4, 12, 18, 20. A most interesting discussion of a change from a caste-like to an open class social system in rural New Mexico appears in E. Z. Vogt, *op. cit.,* pp. 125–130.

34. *Cf.,* Barker, *op. cit.,* pp. 198–99; Stone, *et al., ibid.*

35. Barker, *ibid;* Thomas J. Scheff, "Changes in Public and Private Language Among Spanish-Speaking Migrants to an Industrial City," *International Migration* 3, 1965, pp. 78–86

36. Rubel, 1966, *op. cit.,* p. 244.

37. Linton, *op. cit.*

38. For discussions of this border dialect, see Barker, *op. cit.,* p. 199; Janet B. Sawyer, *A Dialect Study of San Antonio, Texas: A Bilingual Community,* Unpublished Ph.D. dissertation, University of Texas, 1957.

This increasingly divergent regional idiom is not to be confused with an argot utilized by lower-class youths to distinguish themselves from other elements of the larger society, Mexican-American as well as Anglo. See, George C. Barker, *"Pachuco: An American-Spanish Argot and Its Social Functions in Tucson, Arizona,"* Tucson: University of Arizona Press, 1950; Lurline Coltharp, "The Tongue of the Tirilones," (*Alabama Linguistics and Philological Series,* no. 7), University: University of Alabama Press, 1965; Beatrice Griffith, *American Me,* Boston: Houghton Mifflin Co., 1948.

The Bilingualism Controversy in Lebanon

ROSEMARY SAYIGH

THE CARDINAL FACT of Lebanese politics was well expressed by René Aggiouri in an editorial in *L'Orient* on 28 May 1958:

> Le Liban est composé de deux groupes de communautés. L'un des deux se sent toujours lié spirituellement au monde méditerranéan et occidental. L'autre ne peut songer un seul instant à rompre ses attaches sentimentales avec le nationalisme arabe.

This is the Lebanese dilemma. The two communities are close enough to each other in custom and race to form one nation; but because one group looks eastwards and the other westwards, national unity is easily endangered. Everything in the country's life relates to this Janus-like duality, and every controversy, though it may not at first appear political, has confessional-political implications.

Père Selim Abou, whose *Bilinguisme Arabe-Francais au Liban*[1] is the starting-point of this article, remarks that attacks on bilingualism come in times of political tension from the Sunnite lower middle classes "pour qui la confusion du politique et du culturel est à peu près totale." Of course, the "confusion" of cultural and political issues is as common among Christians in Lebanon as among Muslims and indeed the two overlap. It has become habitual in Western countries to *try* to keep religion out of politics; but, as the 1960 election campaign against President Kennedy showed, religion still has political implications in the United States. In Lebanon today (as in the rest of the Middle East) it is impossible to draw a clear line between politics, religion, language, and culture. Religious loyalties inevitably involve political loyalties. A religious minority is always suspected of having "treacherous" political affiliations. Just as in seventeenth-century England the Catholics, loyal to an exiled dynasty, intrigued with England's enemies, so have minorities in the Arab world always looked to outside Powers for support.

This natural law of politics, applied to Lebanon, is complicated by the fact that, in the Arab world at large, Lebanese Christians are a minority, but they are, or feel themselves to be, a majority in Lebanon. Thus, in the eyes of the Arabs, Christian Lebanon is suspected of sympathy with for-

Reprinted with permission from THE WORLD TODAY, Vol. 21, No. 3 (March, 1965), pp. 20–30.

eign Powers (France and the West); while in the eyes of Christian Lebanese it is their fellow Muslims who are suspected of sympathy with foreign Powers (France and the West); while in the eyes of the Christian Lebanese it is their fellow Muslims who are suspected of sympathy with foreign Powers (the Arab world—in 1958 Syria and Egypt). Both can cry that most inflaming of political epithets, "Traitor!"

The civil war of 1958, more damaging to the country's trade than to its population, provided a much-needed lesson, which Lebanon's politicians have been quick to understand, on the dangers of allowing their country's natural divisions to go beyond the point where they can control them. "Chehabism" has meant, among other things, putting national unity first. There has been a general agreement to drop the discussion of awkward subjects, and political aims known to be anathema to the other side have been quietly put in cold storage.

Lebanon's bilingualism, as an indirect reflection of her religio-political division, is a dangerous subject. Père Abou's contribution has been to try to separate the concepts of nation and language. In his view there is no overriding reason why a nation should be monolingual, nor why a linguistic and cultural sympathy for France on the part of Lebanese Christians should not be seen as an advantage for Lebanon. His analysis of the different types of relationship between nation and language shows Lebanon's bilingualism to be unique. It does not arise, as in the case of Belgium, Canada, or South Africa, from different ethnic origins in the population; nor is it, as in many North African countries, merely a legacy of colonial rule, since the use of French in Lebanon preceded the Mandate and has outlasted it; nor is it confined, as in Morocco and Tunisia, to a small educated urban élite but is used by all social classes, in the country as well as the town. French is not needed in Lebanon, as English is in India, as a *lingua franca,* since Arabic is common to all sections of the population, even to relative newcomers like Kurds and Armenians. It has been *adopted* by a certain section of the population, for a variety of reasons whose description varies according to the bias of the observer. According to some the main motive is snobbery. According to Père Abou, the Maronites turned to French "to express their deepest spiritual needs." Probably both interpretations are true.

LEBANON'S SPLIT PERSONALITY

Bilingualism is a particularly useful lens for the study of Lebanon, because its origins are set deep in the country's history and confessional structure, and attitudes towards it tend to follow (sometimes subtly) political-confessional lines. Thus it relates directly to Lebanon's most important political issue, namely, the country's relations with the Arab world (Lebanon's position in the cold war no longer has the importance it had in 1958). Secondly, one's attitude to bilingualism can be taken roughly as an indication of one's faith, or lack of it, in "Arabism." Finally, Arab-French bilingualism has contributed directly to the problem of Lebanon's split personality, her amphibian suspension between East and West, and is thus one of the main themes in her constant search for cultural identity.

As an introduction to Lebanon, Père Selim Abou's *Le Bilinguisme Arabe-Français au Liban*—in spite of the specialization of its title—can hardly be bettered. And it has a particular value for Anglo-Saxon readers because it presents the version of Lebanon of which they are most ignorant. The English usually begin from the premise that Lebanon is part of the Middle East. Lebanese Christians (and the French) start from the premise that Lebanon is essentially a Mediterranean country, a bridge between East and West, belonging wholly to neither. The English tend to see Lebanon as "corrupted" by Western influence. (T. E. Lawrence's dislike of the "bastard French" of the Beirutis is a fairly typical reaction). Lebanese Christians (and the French) see Lebanon as the channel through which civilizing ideas and techniques reach the Arab hinterland. Père Abou's brilliant manifesto of the "Franco-Christian" view of Lebanon is a useful corrective to traditional English prejudice. His case is neither balanced nor impartial, since what he is writing is really a defence of the French language in Lebanon. But it is so ably and comprehensively argued that its defect of partisanship is outweighed by its virtues of consistency, logic, and clarity.

THE BILINGUALISM CONTROVERSY

Arab-French bilingualism in Lebanon has been attacked on several fronts. It has been accused of causing intellectual superficiality (on the ground that it is impossible to speak more than one language really well); of overburdening children's minds and causing linguistic confusion; of undermining Lebanese confidence in their own country and creating a sense of inferiority in them; of detracting from the esteem in which Arabic is held; and of causing a deterioration in both languages. The special Lebanese *patois*, made up of a mixture of French and Arabic, has especially been the object of ridicule.

Père Abou devotes a section of his book to the bilingualism controversy and answers the accusations one by one. It is not proved that precocious bilingualism is harmful to the development of children's minds; if the Lebanese are intellectually superficial, bilingualism is not the cause of it; if French or Arabic is incorrectly spoken, it is not necessarily because of the presence of the other language; and far from detracting from Arabic, the presence of French has caused Arabic to be better taught and better spoken. He claims that the standard of Arabic in schools where French has been withdrawn from the syllabus has actually dropped.

In the case of other bi- or multi-lingual countries, such as Belgium, Switzerland, and Canada, the languages in use are not rivals (though the people who use them may be). What makes the bilingualism controversy so delicate in Lebanon is that the choice of a *foreign* language on the part of one section of the population cannot help seeming like a criticism of the *native* language. The importance of the Arabic language to Muslims is well known and needs no emphasis here. What is worth noting is that Arab nationalists, whether Christian or Muslim, attach as great an importance to the Arabic language, perhaps even more, since language, not territory, is the basis of their creed. They oppose the extensive use by Arabs of any foreign language, and in this their attitude is not very different from that of Englishmen who dislike the influx of Americanisms into their language, or Frenchmen who attack "franglais."

Arabic once was a "language of civilization," and still is one of the world's eighteen most-spoken languages. Arabs have a special reverence for its qualities. But it has not yet developed a vocabulary of science or modern thought and, in spite of the current spate of translations, any Arab who gets as far as secondary school must learn a second language (usually English, French, or German) to pursue his studies effectively. Other difficulties are the gap between classical and colloquial Arabic, out-of-date methods of teaching it, and also its intrinsic difficulty (Arabic is the subject in which Arab schoolchildren most frequently fail). Moreover, the intellectual mediocrity of much that has been written in Arabic in modern times discourages many educated Arabs who have been exposed to modern French or English literature. All these drawbacks have tended to create in many Lebanese a hostility to Arabic, and a desire to escape from its problems into an easier medium such as English or French. The disadvantage of this reaction is that it perpetuates the situation instead of reforming it. In the nineteenth century, Lebanese scholars were foremost in the field of Arabic studies; today there is a noticeable lack of linguists in Lebanon, and too few people seem interested in the work of bringing Arabic up to date. If this is partly due to Muslim conservatism, it must also partly be the result of the ease with which any educated Arab can "escape" into a foreign language to express ideas for which he does not find a ready-made vocabulary in Arabic.

Most people interviewed by the present writer agreed that, although arguments both for and against it may be taken from the fields of linguistics, psychology, or metaphysics, bilingualism in Lebanon is basically a political phenomenon. Père Abou tells in his literary section of a Lebanese writer called Shukri Ghanem, who lived in Paris in the late nineteenth and early twentieth centuries and earned great esteem with his poems and plays on Arab themes. In 1916, fearing the Muslim Arab revivalism of the Hijazian movement, he founded the *Comité de l'Action Française en Syrie*. The story is an instructive one because it shows clearly the law of weights and balances upon which Lebanon's existence rests. The desire of Lebanese Christians for outside support arises from their fear of Arab-Muslim intolerance; but their seeking of foreign support gives rise to the very intolerance which they fear. Moreover, tolerance of each Lebanese community for the other depends partly on Arab policy towards Lebanon, which in its turn depends partly on Western policy towards the Arab world.

Among opponents of bilingualism there are a growing number of French-speaking Christians who, without wanting Lebanon to lose her political independence, believe that the country has a basically Arab character which she should set herself to discover and enrich. In their view, the use of French characterized a period of subservience and lack of self-confidence which should by now be outgrown. Such an attitude is a hopeful augury for future relations between Lebanon's two communities, and between Lebanon and her Arab neighbours.[2]

BILINGUALISM AND LEBANON'S CONFESSIONAL STRUCTURE

In its broadest outlines the connection between Lebanon's bilingualism and the confessional structure is too well known to need description here. Père Abou, who insists that "le clivage des langues ne correspond pas du tout au clivage des religions," at the same time shows that French is far commoner among Christians than among Muslims. In his survey of Central Lebanon he found that of the Arab-French bilingual section of the population 75 per cent were Christian and 25 per cent Muslim.

The reasons for the greater prevalence of French among Christians are several: the historical attachment of the Maronite community to France; the number of French-run schools, mostly clerical, many founded in the nineteenth century, to which Christians naturally tended more than Muslims to send their children; and the fact that the French Mandate and French influence were more welcomed by the Maronite community than by the Muslim.

Until the middle of the nineteenth century, Lebanese Maronite clergy were taught in Italian, but as French political influence grew, the French language gradually ousted the language of the Vatican. The Maronites' own language, Syriac, had died out of use several centuries before, though isolated pockets remained in northern Lebanon as late as the eighteenth century, and it still survives in the Maronite liturgy. The substitution of French for the lost Syriac as the "national" language of the Maronites seems to have been a part political, part cultural phenomenon, a joint product of Maronite aspirations and French encouragement.

Under the Mandate French became the second national language, against the opposition of the Muslim community. Moreover, it was strongly entrenched in the country's educational system. This is not the place to discuss French policy in the Levant nor the reactions to it of different groups of Lebanese. But from the linguistic point of view the Mandate had two distinct effects: one was to *encourage* a small, highly educated, mainly Christian élite to become virtually *monolingual in French,* with Arabic a poor second; the other was to *create,* through a public elementary-school system and through the presence of a large body of French officials, a widespread but superficial bilingualism among many sections of the population. The first phenomenon might well have happened without the Mandate; the second, to which Père Abou attaches great significance, would probably not.

Under the Mandate the Muslim community opposed the official status of French, as they opposed all aspects of French political influence. Yet many wealthy Muslims spoke, and still speak, excellent French. The explanation seems to be that for many generations French has been the language of education and culture. But, as Père Abou points out, the attitude of Muslims to French—or any other foreign language—is basically different from that of most Christians. The Christians needed French "to express their deepest spiritual needs." But for Muslims French was merely a neutral instrument for acquiring knowledge, which could never displace their mother tongue. Arabic, the sacred language of the Koran, must always be the language in which they expressed their deepest thoughts and feelings. To quote Brigadier Stephen Longrigg:

> Although numbers of non-Catholics and even Muslims attended the French colleges and French was widely spoken among the Muslim as well as the Christian intelligentsia, yet such visible signs of French influence outside the ranks of Catholics were in great part illusory; they did not truly indicate devotion to France, though they widely deceived, in that sense, the French public and government.[3]

For Père Abou it is precisely the fact that Christians absorb French culture and humanism along with the French language that gives French its supreme value, both to them and to Lebanon. But this shifting of linguistic and cultural loyalties can never be entirely acceptable to the other half of the country, for whom French, like Turkish, is a relic of foreign domination.

There have been attacks on bilingualism by Muslims, but in the course of conversations which the writer had recently with Lebanese of different religions no strong Muslim hostility to French was found. The usual Muslim attitude was that French is losing ground and will inevitably give place in the course of time to Arabic. The director of an important Muslim educational foundation remarked that bilingualism is basically a Christian problem, since it is the Christians who need to make up their minds where they belong. Muslims know.

Christians, on the other hand, are far from uniform in their attitude to Arab-French bilingualism. One of its strongest opponents is Kamal el-Hajj, a Maronite Professor of Philosophy at the Lebanese University, who believes that it is not possible to have more than one mother tongue and that the use of French has caused a devaluation of Arabic. Another Christian critic, Lucien Bérouti, attacked Père Abou's book recently, mainly on the ground that it was sociologically inaccurate.

Moreover, an important section of Lebanon's Christians, mainly Protestant and Greek Orthodox, use English rather than French as their second language, and look westwards to America or England rather than to

France. They go to Oxford or Harvard for their graduate studies, not to the Sorbonne, and do not, as so many French-speaking Lebanese do, think of Paris as the centre of the world. Lebanese who are bilingual in English and Arabic are frequently hostile to French cultural predominance in Lebanon. "A war of cultures" is fought out in many areas of Lebanese life, from broadcasting to jobs in the Ministries. Only trade seems relatively free of cultural prejudice, and trilingualism among Lebanese businessmen is markedly increasing.

PÈRE ABOU AND THE "FRANCO-CHRISTIAN" IMAGE OF LEBANON

Père Abou's book contains sections on the history and confessional structure of Lebanon; on the origins and structure of its bilingualism; on the social morphology of bilingualism; on the bilingualism controversy, with answers to the critics; and an appendix containing an account of Lebanese writing in both French and Arabic. But all his basic assumptions—as well as many of his conclusions—are to be found in the lengthy Introduction, where he outlines his methodology. It is here that his world view—Latin, hierarchical, European-centred—is most clear, as well as the defensive purpose of his work. His propositions are essentially those of the Lebanese Christian "school," whose writers have over the years built up the image of Lebanon as the "trait d'union entre l'Orient et l'Occident," which is today the most commonly accepted idea that Lebanese Christians have of their country.

Briefly distilled, Père Abou's thesis is this:

i. that French embodies the highest expression of Western civilization, which is now to all intents and purposes world civilization;
ii. that the renaissance of Arab civilization depends on its openness to western civilization, and that it is Lebanon's role to provide the channel through which Western ideas and techniques can pass to the Arab world;
iii. that Lebanon, geographically and traditionally, has two further functions: to interpret the Arabs to the West and the West to the Arabs, and to provide the site for the dialogue between Islam and Christianity;
iv. that bilingualism is essential to the fulfilling of these missions;
v. that Lebanon has always been polyglot. French, historically speaking, has merely replaced Syriac as the "national" language of the Maronites;
vi. that Lebanese bilingualism must be studied anthropologically as an "existential" fact, not subject to scientific criteria, whether linguistic or sociological;
vii. that French is a "fundamental part of Lebanese reality," essential to the spiritual needs of half the population; that it is implicit in the National Pact and that to attack it implies an attack on the National Pact; that far from creating problems, it is "the principle of solution to the problem of an already divided society";
viii. that Lebanon's possession of French has been the means of putting the

country on the map culturally—or "inserting it in the historical present," as Père Abou puts it; that if French is lost the country's relatively high educational and cultural level will decline, to the detriment not only of Lebanon but also of her Arab neighbours.

The position thus summarized is very much that of other Lebanese Christian writers, such as Michel Chiha, Charles Corm, Farjallah Haik, Michel Asmar, Charles Malik,[4] René Habachi. All of them try to define Lebanon in such a way as to sanctify and make permanent her suspension between Asia and Europe. They look resolutely westwards, and either fear, or are uninterested in, the rise of independent nations in Asia and Africa. Michel Chiha expressed their world view when he said, "Nous ne sommes pas disposés à nous résigner au déclin de l'Europe." For him Lebanon, deprived of her Mediterranean personality, would be "jeté dans le chaos et refoulé dans les tenébres." "C'est . . . le devoir du Liban de ne point se prêter à la confusion des continents et des races et d'épargner aux Arabes la décadence qui serait leur sort s'ils se laissaient noyer dans l'ocean indien . . . s'ils subissaient le poids de la masse asiatique ils n'auraient plus qu'un rang de subalterne dans une civilisation asservie." [5]

Farjallah Haik, whose book *Dieu est Libanais* (1946) is of great interest to anyone seeking to understand the special relationship of Lebanon and France, is firm in his insistence that the Lebanese are *white*, "blanc jusqu'a la moelle, d'un blanc inalterable, authentique, ne prêtant à aucun equivoque. Un blanc fanatique, par opposition au Marocain, à l'Algérien, au Sénégalais, à l'Annamite." It is an indication of how far the climate of opinion in Lebanon has changed that a statement of this kind is unthinkable in print today. Contemporary exponents of Lebanon's special position—René Habachi, Charles Malik, Père Abou—are infinitely more careful not to offend the susceptibilities of their fellow Lebanese. But what Michel Chiha and Farjallah Haik wrote yesterday is still verbal coinage today, and very similar ideas can be heard on the lips of Maronite mountain peasants for whom the French language is a palpable manifestation of their kinship with Europe.

In the 1930s the cult of the Phoenicians was one of the ways in which Lebanese Christians tried to put their sense of separateness on a firm historical footing, and add the force of myth to their budding nationalism. Père Abou calls this cult "an incoherent opposition of a Phoenician Lebanon to an Arab Lebanon." Is his own case for a "French" Lebanon open to similar criticism? Certainly it is anything but incoherent, and, whereas the connection of modern Lebanon with the ancient Phoenicians is tenuous, the presence of the French language is indisputable. It remains to be seen, however, whether the "ideology" of Lebanon formulated by these writers has any influence on the country's gradually emerging character. Unfortunately the lack of social surveys leaves public opinion a matter of guesswork; but it seems likely that there is a considerable gap between the formulas of the intellectuals and social reality.

THE SOCIOLOGY OF BILINGUALISM

Most Lebanese take it for granted that Arab-French bilingualism actually exists in Lebanon, and, whether attacking or supporting it, they have shown little interest in discovering its social incidence and forms, the attitudes taken towards it, or the motivation that keeps it going. Père Abou is an exception. One of the most interesting sections of his book describes the incidence of French-speaking in Lebanon, based on surveys carried out under his direction in 1960 and published separately in 1961.

Outside Beirut he found that 23 per cent of adult male respondents, and 40 per cent of children in school, were French-speaking. For Beirut itself he quotes a survey carried out in 1953 by Charles Churchill of the American University of Beirut, which found that 42 per cent of household heads spoke French. An examination of shop signs in several different Beirut quarters showed that 45 per cent were written in French and Arabic, 12 per cent in English and Arabic, and 26 per cent in Arabic only. Tombstones in three Christian cemeteries yielded fascinating figures—French used in 17 per cent, and under the Mandate 24 per cent. According to Père Abou, three government Ministries (Defense, Agriculture, and Foreign Affairs) use French, and French is used with Arabic on stamps, lottery tickets, banknotes, and Régie (government monopoly) cigarette packets.

Evidence of the pre-eminence of French in Lebanon's cultural life was shown by the circulation figures of Beirut's main daily papers, *L'Orient* (8,500-9,000) and *Le Soir* (4,000-4,500). The closest Arabic competitor is *An-Nahar* (c. 4,500).[6] (The English-language *Daily Star* has a circulation of only 2,500 in spite of the fact that English and American residents in Lebanon alone total 12,000.) The most widely read weekly magazine is *Revue du Liban*. Except in one quarter, around the American University, books and magazines displayed in bookshops are predominantly French. The city's only highbrow film club is run by the French "side."

While any casual observer would agree that French is remarkably widely used throughout Lebanon and that it is still, to a large extent, the language of culture, it may be questioned whether it is as deeply rooted as Père Abou believes. In the first place his sociological survey has weaknesses which make its figures somewhat unreliable. Out of the twenty-one villages surveyed, seventeen were in the area called Central Lebanon (the "Petit Liban" of Mandate days) and only four outside it. As Père Abou himself admits, Central Lebanon is predominantly Maronite, and, even more important, it has a very high proportion of the country's schools. Peripheral Lebanon is predominantly Muslim and poorly provided with schools. No one travelling in the Shi'ite South, or in the hashish-growing, semi-nomadic areas of the North or the Beqa'a, would expect to meet a

French-speaking peasant. A further weakness of Père Abou's estimate arises from his taking Beirut as typical of the other coastal cities of Tripoli and Sidon. This is simply not admissible.

Since Père Abou does not admit the relevance of linguistic criteria of bilingualism, it is possible that many of his respondents had only a superficial knowledge of French. He very honestly admits that, of the 23 per cent who said they were bilingual, only 14 per cent had spent more than seven years in school, but he claims that this fact "does not in the least detract from the importance of the phenomenon." But of course it does. It really cannot be claimed that a significant proportion of the Lebanese population speak French with as much ease and correctness as they speak colloquial Arabic. It is remarkable that as many as 23 per cent speak any kind of French at all; but it is not certain that a bilingualism of this kind will prove long lasting.

MOVE TO POLYGLOTTISM

Lebanese social mobility, ambition, business dynamism, and quickness to learn have all in the past been aids to bilingualism. Today, however, the same characteristics seem to be propelling the country towards polyglottism. What seems most likely to happen is that the masses will remain basically Arabic-speaking with a smattering of French and English, while the educated classes will become almost perfectly trilingual in Arabic, English, and French. From the writer's own observation, the tendency to trilingualism among university students, businessmen, and the younger generation of professional men is already marked. French is still thought of as the language of elegance, urbanity, and wit (which it is); but the signs are that it is regarded more and more as a sign of "smartness" among the wealthy of *all* religions, less and less the manifestation of a special relationship between one Lebanese community and the outside world.

People whom the writer interviewed were fairly evenly divided into two groups: those who have complete confidence in the superiority and staying-power of French as the language of culture in Lebanon; and those who have just as complete a confidence that the days of French are numbered, and that Arabic will soon oust it entirely. To the latter, the presence of French in Lebanon is a historical accident; they do not believe that it will long survive the Mandate, which, in their view, was its principal cause. There were few, even among Christians, who believed as strongly as Père Abou that French is a fundamental and inalienable part of the Lebanese scene. As long as the French-run private schools continue to be the most highly esteemed, the French language is unlikely to lose its prestige as rapidly as the Arabists would like to believe; but it is equally certain that, with the growing modernization of Lebanon and the changes in values, the ancient attachment of the Maronite community to France will gradually lose its intensity. The speed with which this change will take place will, of course, fluctuate with events in the Arab world—moving faster when there is prosperity and peace; standing still, or retrogressing, when there is trouble.

CONCLUSION

To argue back and forth across the whole field of Arab-French bilingualism in Lebanon—its meaning, causes, effects, desirability, or harmfulness—is an endless exercise, but a useful one because it covers the entire political and intellectual topography of the country. The fact that it is such an absorbing topic to the Lebanese themselves is in itself revealing. But to arrive at any definite conclusion is quite impossible.

One way out of the maze may be to mark out two propositions as bases for further argument:

i. that the Christian view of Lebanon (as stated by Père Abou) is coherent and convincing. It has intellectual value, and it is necessary to understand it to understand Lebanon;
ii. but that, as an account of what is actually happening or is likely to happen in Lebanon, it is inadequate. The real Lebanon awaits sociological description; but it cannot be done by writers with an ideological case to prove.

FOOTNOTES

[1] Paris, Presses Universitaires de France, 1962. Père Abou is a young Lebanese Jesuit, at present teaching in the University of St. Joseph, Beirut.

[2] It may be significant that, according to a report in *An-Nahar* of 6 October 1964, the Kataeb Party recently issued a statement emphasizing the need for closer relations between Lebanon and the other Arab countries.

[3] *Syria and Lebanon under French Mandate* (London, O.U.P. for R.I.I.A., 1958).

[4] Charles Malik stands apart from the other writers mentioned here, being Greek Orthodox, not Maronite, in religion; English- rather than French-speaking; and addressing himself to a predominantly American audience.

[5] Lecture to the Cénacle Libanaise, 1951.

[6] This was the situation in 1960. Now *An-Nahar* has surpassed *L'Orient* with sales of around 10,000.

*Language and Politics in India**

PAUL FRIEDRICH

OF THE MANY theoretical problems in the rapidly developing field of language and culture, the establishment of a common language for a multilingual state is probably fraught with the deepest political implications. Linguistic unity may conduce to unity in other phases of culture; for example, the presence of an upper class speaking a fairly homogeneous dialect of English certainly increased the national integration of the Congress Party during India's struggle for independence. On the other hand, animosity of political or economic origin may attach itself to the palpable symbols of linguistic difference. Starving Indians in the industrial slums of Bombay have knifed each other "because" one speaks Marathi, the other Gujarati. India today provides an egregious case of linguistic diversity combined with weak chances for any one of the potential national languages. The salient point is that this weakness and diversity appear to be growing. Both the people of the culture and scientific observers consider the combination a disruptive "social problem" about which something should be done. As with food supply and population growth, difficulties are increasing more rapidly than solutions are being formulated or effected. In short, the situation is one of possibly tragic drift.

To examine the problem, we should first define some of the principal terms. "National state" means a fairly large population on a bounded territory, united by a standing government and bureaucracy, by economic organization, some shared customs and values, and most importantly, by a sense of self-identity as a body politic with a tradition. This definition fits India rather imperfectly, because India is composed of numerous seminational states, each with its own dialects, ethnocentric prejudices, and distinctive profile. By "language" is meant a system of mutually intelligible vocal symbols by which the members of a society communicate. "Written language" is a special kind of language. "Dialect" is the speech system of a regionally or socially defined group, marked by a combination of shared linguistic features; such dialects may form a chain, so that speakers of widely separated links cannot understand one another.

Reprinted, with permission of the author and publisher, from DAEDALUS, Vol. 91, No. 1 (Summer, 1962), pp. 543–559.

* This paper derives in part from linguistic research conducted in India during 1958–1959, under the auspices of the Rockefeller Program for South Asian languages. Thus it covers events up through August 1959.

In the anthropological sense, language is a part of culture, because it too is a historically derived system of conscious and subconscious patterns shared and transmitted by the members of a particular society. On the other hand, language is unique because it is a means of communication—in part as a code, in part as a symbolic organization of experience—that is interwoven in the most pervasive way with other cultural subsystems, such as that of politics. Every known society possesses a fully developed language, but many virtually lack other systems, such as music or politics. In addition language plays a singular role in the processes by which individuals and groups define themselves and are defined by others. The rise of nationalism in the modern period is often linked with questions of linguistic status and linguistic boundaries. A primary objective of this paper is to show how language is related to political dynamics in one particular country.

India, which now numbers over 400 million, is exceeded in population only by Communist China. Its social problems have increased in proportion to this quantitative change. Linguistic diversification also tends to increase with the social isolation of speech communities. Most Indians still live mainly in villages, cross-cut by hundreds of subcastes in patterns of sociolinguistic segmentation that have no close parallel elsewhere. Of these villagers, it is the women, linguistically the most conservative, who are responsible for the primary language influences on the children. Even the upper-caste child is often cared for by monolingual, lower-caste ayas. The leading novelist in Malayalam has grown wealthy by his writings and traveled widely in Europe and the Orient; but his wife does not speak English, and has only once gone farther than a mile from her husband's home and her nearby matrilineal household. The extensive migration and labor movement within India does not much counter narrow circumscriptions by caste and region. Linguistic homogeneity may be increased through the mass media, but most Indians have no radio, and are still infrequently exposed to movies or public broadcasts (though the latter are gaining influence).

The problem increases with the number of languages and their relative size and importance; thus Mexico's forty-odd Indian languages, spoken mainly by tiny minorities, do not threaten the national status of Spanish. India, on the contrary, recognizes fourteen languages for official purposes; all but three of them (Sanscrit, Assamese, and Kashmiri) are spoken by over ten million persons, and five are spoken by over 25 million (Telegu, Tamil, Hindi, Bengali, Marathi).[1] In addition, almost one-tenth of the population (32 million) speak dozens of other mother tongues belonging phylogenetically to four categories: Indo-European, such as Nepali; Dravidian, such as Tulu; Austroasiatic (Munda branch), such as Ho; and, fourth, a great number of "non-Indian" languages, notably English and Persian. *The Census of India* cites 24 tribal languages spoken by 100,000 or more, and 720 minor languages and dialects with less than 100,000; of the 63 non-Indian languages, English has the most mother-tongue speakers, with 171,742. At least six nonofficial languages are spoken by over one million, and two of these, Marwari and Sindhi, by only a few hundred thousand less than Assamese. The other big minority groups are, in millions: Santali, 2.8; Ghondi, 1.2; Bhili, 1.2; Mewari, 2; Jaipuri, 1.5.

The big official languages are absorbing the minority languages and also impeding the development of a national one; the Ho agriculturalist is learning a regional dialect of Hindi, but the Tulu is learning Kannada, while neither is learning English. Many who speak India's minority languages, especially the refugees from Pakistan, are now in various stages of transitional multilingualism marked by a reshuffling of dialects, considerable linguistic interference, and increasing submergence to the official languages. These minorities often resent the lack of official recognition; their case contrasts unfavorably with that of Rhaeto-Roman, a national language in Switzerland, although spoken by only one percent of the population.

The neglect of the minority languages on the part of the Indian government has further political implications. It is known pedagogically that children learn more rapidly and with less inner conflict if they first acquire literacy in their mother tongue. The present policy of immediate assimilation to the alien official language is bound to engender ambivalence and status conflict, for linguistic factors become inextricably enmeshed with political ones. India's sense of national unity might be reinforced by using minority languages in the elementary grades, by research into the geography of dialects and by the reconstruction of linguistic protohistory; but comparatively little is spent on such activities. This is not to mitigate the significance of the stop-gap government programs for intellectual exchanges between states, or the mushrooming interest in scientific linguistics, strongly supported by many universities, state governments and financial magnates.

Linguistic problems tend to emerge as a symbolic reflex of almost any other conflict. Many Indians feel that the so-called "linguistic question" is itself abnormal and counter to the ethos of their culture; people are hungry and anxious about getting employment and providing for their families, so they get exasperated by language differences. The necessity of struggling for jobs with persons of different speech communities intensifies economically based animosities. Naturally, the Communist Party of India has frequently exploited linguistic differences, since they weaken the Central Government and allow the Communists to identify themselves with "the people"; but the party line has varied greatly the last twenty years.

A spoken "natural" language is far more likely to attain national status, since the majority of a population is seldom sufficiently familiar with dead languages to make these immediately practical. But two extraordinary cases provide a contrary precedent. Hebrew, primarily a liturgical language for over 2000 years, was re-instituted politically by the Israeli state in 1948. At least three factors account for this and none of them obtains in India: first, the presence before 1948 of a Hebrew-speaking base population; second, the high literacy rate; third, the extraordinary patriotism bred of a profound sense of national mission, shared suffering under the Nazis, and a common Arab enemy of overwhelming numbers. Finally, modern Israeli Hebrew is strictly speaking a constructed dialect with a Biblical base and many recent accretions from other languages.[2] The second contrary case is presented by China. Written Chinese serves as a national code for the literate section of 618 million people speaking various dialects of at least seven mutually incomprehensible languages (for example, Cantonese, Peiping), as well as dozens of other Sinitic and non-Sinitic dialects. But special factors account for the vitality of the complex system of written ideographs: militant patriotism, the practicality of an existing supraregional language, the link of China's ancient, verbal culture, the esthetic and moral connotations of calligraphic training.

Sanscrit is sacred to most Hindus. Since the Vedic hymns (c. 1500 B.C.) it has served in various related forms as a vehicle for metaphysics, the national epics, the laws of Manu, or the immortal poetry of Kalidasa. All literate Indians are more or less familiar with this spiritual lore and most revere it; orthodox Hindus know some by heart and may devote their declining years to reading and reciting aloud from the *Bhagavad Gita* and other repositories of wisdom. The grammarian who formulated the rules of Sanscrit over two thousand years ago today enjoys the status of a saint in the Hindu system. To a limited extent, written Sanscrit unites the educated Indians, especially the literati; hundreds of words and phrases are comprehended from the Indian Ocean to the Himalayas, and a much smaller scatter of items are understood even by those who cannot read.

The case of Sanscrit, however, while analogous to Hebrew and written Chinese, differs significantly on many counts. India exhibits a degree of cultural pluralism that staggers the imagination. The Christians and the Muslims, who constitute about 15 per cent of the Indian population and up to half the population in the deep south, are sharply divided into innumerable subgroups. But they generally join to oppose Sanscrit. Even the Hindus are pitched against one another on the Sanscrit question; numerous copies of the sacred *Ramayana* epic have been publicly burnt by lower-caste organizations because of a racist interpretation of the dark-skinned monkeys in the text. Many Tamil intellectuals will not even consider studying Sanscrit because of its "Aryan" connotations. Hatred of the Brahmins because of their economic and political role is often linked with animosity toward Sanscrit, as in Bengal, Maharashtra, or Mysore. In addition, only a tiny subculture is really conversant with the language, and only a few thousand, centered in the Sanscrit colleges, can communicate freely using its complex inflections and luxuriant vocabulary. Since the great majority of Indians are still illiterate even in their mother-tongue, it would seem a purely scholastic fantasy to suggest making Sanscrit *the* national language. Nevertheless, an influential nation-wide society is devoted to the cause.

A language may be established feasibly in direct proportion to its structural distance from other languages which it will partially supplant. One of the more convincing arguments cited by Indians in favor of Hindi over English is the affinity of the former to other Indian languages. Most Indian languages share features such as distinctive aspiration, a series of retroflex sounds, four or more nominal case endings, considerable morphological synthesis, and syntactic patterns such as the modifier-modified order in phrasal attribution. These traits more or less unite them and, conversely, set them off from English. Recent testimony from schoolteachers indicates that Indian children learn Hindi almost twice as fast as they do English. Pan-Indian semantic categories may also account for this differential in speed.

But typological affinity can be a two-edged sword. Actually, minute differences can mobilize hostile sentiment almost as effectively as some typological abyss. Many Tamilian dialects lack the voiced, aspirate sounds, retroflex sibilants, and some other generally pan-Indian features. Tamilians, strongly opposed to the "imposition" of Hindi, may feel comparatively apprehensive about using Hindi in New Delhi precisely because of the absence or insignificant function of these subtle features in their own mother-tongue. And South Indian military history provides a striking analogy to the Biblical shibboleth, because many Tamilians found it impossible to pronounce in a satisfactory manner the retroflex, liquid nonocclusive phoneme in the speech of their medieval foe, the Malayali. On the other hand, prestige and power can overcome almost any degree of linguistic space. For example, the medieval Koreans discarded an eminently simple alphabet of twenty-five letters for the sake of writing Korean with the prestigious Chinese characters and to some extent for using Chinese itself for official purposes, despite the vast differences separating their language and Chinese in both spoken and written forms.

The foregoing considerations lead to what might be called the problem of the feasible degree of multilingualism. Just how many tongues can the average citizen be expected to control? Is multilingualism simply another type of lingualism or a qualitatively different phenomenon? Proficient, correct multilingualism on the part of individuals seems to be accompanied by a certain minimum of general intelligence, verbal aptitudes and code-switching ability. At the societal level, it usually involves special familial or subcultural patterns for inculcating vocabulary and automatic translation habits, as exemplified by the intelligentsia of Bombay, who often speak English, Marathi, Gujarati, Hindi, and sometimes Sanscrit, or those of the Polish Jewry, speaking Yiddish, German, Polish, Russian, and Hebrew, with high fluency in at least three out of five. Multilingualism appears to be especially workable between typologically and genetically close languages, such as Tamil and Malayalam, Marathi and Gujarati, or Danish, Swedish and Norwegian. On the other hand, widespread multilingualism between drastically different languages is rare—for example, the combination in much of Samarkand of Russian, Uzbek (a Turkic language) and Tadzhik (a variety of Persian). Many educated Malayalis in government service actually practice such an extraordinary range (e.g., Malayalam, Hindi, English, and Sanscrit), but their versatility can be explained through special schooling and career goals. All these aspects to the psychology of language learning suggest that one national or common language over and above the regional language might reasonably be considered the absolute maximum.

The basic fact remains that every member of every known culture speaks at least one language, but that no national state with full bilingualism—to say nothing of trilingualism—has ever existed. Thus, Switzerland, almost one-hundred-percent literate, deserves its illustrious reputation for language planning. But most Swiss villagers speaking French as their mother tongue are actually monolingual, and many educated Swiss know little Italian. Similar limitations to bilingualism may be adduced from other multilingual states, such as Paraguay (Spanish-Guarani), Canada (French-English), and the non-Russian republics of the U.S.S.R. Many Indians optimistically advocate a schedule of national trilingualism, combining the regional mother-tongue with some combination of Hindi, English, or Sanscrit. But India will eventually have to combine the mother tongues with Hindi *or* English *or* Sanscrit. Even then she will experience difficulties in maintaining adequate competency, and she will be constantly threatened by communication breakdowns.

The general level of literacy also determines the acceptance of any language for national purposes. The demonstrable fact that all languages are equally perfect symbolic systems (with respect to phonology and grammar), and are equally capable of expressing any denotative information, should not be confused with the equally demonstrable fact that illiterate masses, whether primitive, peasant or proletarian, are semantically hindered from playing a full role in the economic, social, and political life of a large nation. The presence of hundreds of botanical terms in some remote Hindi dialect does not mean that the speakers of it can make sense out of a governmental regulation. Educated Indians are passionately discussing what the average man—meaning the coolie, the peasant—wants to learn. But since the teeming masses are largely illiterate, even in their lower-caste dialects, the question of what second language they might want to learn is partly speculative, at least for the immediate future.

Some internal contradictions would be eliminated by focusing on the multilingualism to be promoted among the 100 million literates and the 15 million spiritual, political, and business leaders who must communicate between regions and nations. Politicians wax vociferous about the "common man" and hesitate to mention an "elite," partly because of the guilt and fear which they themselves feel about their own upper-caste status. Yet upper-caste leadership will probably endure for some time, irrespective of political transformations; the top leaders of even Kerala's well-known Communist Party are all Nayars or Brahmins. In the modern West the ideals of the "common man" and of mass education have led to policy about a language for the entire population of a national state. Such democratic vistas are realistic in comparatively educated countries, but they seem unwise and illusory in India.

Elitist considerations are connected with status anxiety in a second way: that "speakers imitate the habits of their superiors" is a fruitful if somewhat uncritically accepted assumption in sociolinguistics. A standard language may evolve from a dialect of great geographical dispersal, much of it rural, so long as it is sufficiently prestigious; literary Russian in the nineteenth century exemplifies this. Standard Malayalam has developed largely over the past forty years from the dialect of the socially and intellectually dominant (but largely rural) Nayar caste; here, as with Russian, the literary work of certain prolific and popular writers has played its influential role. But the standards of a language usually derive from urban dialects, such as Parisian French or New Delhi Hindi; indeed, the sheer density of population in the cities makes them foci for linguistic change.

Hindi falls short of the mark as a standard national language because it lacks sufficient prestige. The official figure of 160 million "Hindi" speakers actually includes a plethora of Hindustani, Urdu, Punjabi, and other dialects, mostly spoken by illiterate peasants and often having less affinity with one another than with the neighboring dialects of other languages. As one of India's most influential writers on the question of a national language puts it: "The fact is that Hindi is not even a good *regional* language. There is a lot of synthesis yet to be done among the dialects of Hindi." [3] Many southerners feel that the Hindustan area itself is backward and dirty and that New Delhi is comparatively corrupt. To the average Bengali intellectual, Hindi is a lingo of the bazaars, although more status is accorded to its standard forms. As Tagore wrote in a short story, "But the hard fact was that my little Hindi happened to be picked up from the porters and bearers and would scarcely enable me to enter into intelligent controversy with the Badraon princess." [4] In an analogous sense, Berliners would not accept Munich Bavarian as standard German.

To the educated person, especially a man of letters, the prestige of a language is inextricably associated with the literature in which the writers of the past have given expression to the genius of the tongue. Sparkling metaphors and sensitive characterizations can soften the resistance of proud minorities. For example, many Soviet citizens of minority states have eagerly learned Russian, the language of Pushkin and Tolstoy, despite their resentment of ethnic and political domination. English has also been appreciated in its own right by many Indian intellectuals; today Romantic poets such as Byron are more fondly read in India than anywhere in the English-speaking world. Shakespeare is widely read in the schools. Once I was interviewing a prominent Malayali novelist who has always despised grammar in general and Sanscrit grammar in particular. He alluded to the value of the "most unkindest." As I did not immediately grasp the reference, my Nayar companion chimed in, "You know, the famous Shakespearean cut."

According to an almost universal consensus, the foremost literary language of contemporary India is Bengali, above all because it was the vehicle and in part the creation of Rabindranath Tagore. The Tamilians, on the other hand, possess one of the longest unbroken literary traditions of any of the world's living languages.[5] During the fifth and sixth centuries syndicates of bards in the principal cities created a glorious romantic and devotional poetry, full of imagination and realistic perceptions, and largely free of the deadening influence of Sanscrit models. A high point in this literature is signified by the two thousand poems of the *Eight Anthologies,* attributed to the "Third Academy" of Madras. The medieval poetry of Tamilians such as Ramanuja still occupies a primary place in Hindu traditions. On the other hand, although some date Hindi as a literary language by the fourteenth-century poems of Kabir, there are many others who claim that "as the channel of the main stream of poetry it was established only with the beginning of this century."[6] Hindi does have a literature that includes well-known contemporary names such as Prem Chand. But objective and weighty criteria tend to rank it below at least Sanscrit, Tamil and Bengali. Certainly most Indians having non-Hindi mother-tongues would rank Hindi beneath at least one other Indian language as well as English.

For the same reasons there is a reaction today against the imposition of an "inferior" recent idiom. Rajagopalachari, speaking before a packed and cheering mass meeting in Calcutta in 1959, said, "The new Hindi, as it continues to develop, is not a language but a burlesque. Self-styled Hindi lexicographers and self-appointed Hindi purists have been competing with one another in evolving all manner of fantastic and unfamiliar words and phrases."[7] To quote another leader: "The strength of a language is as large or as poor as its literature. Precision and flexibility are essential for a language to be great and useful. It is well known that Hindi fails in these respects. The claim to greater political importance is absurd . . . if people speaking other languages prefer English and Sanscrit as furnishing greater knowledge, greater wisdom, greater enjoyment and greater continuity of enlightened life."[8]

Up to now the emphasis has been on the spontaneous acceptance of national languages. But they may be established also through political and military pressure; in Mexico the Spanish language was forced on the Indian population, linguist-friars following closely on the iron heel of the conquistador. The Russification of minorities in the U.S.S.R. has been consistently backed by the power of the central government—not to be confused with the linguistic sophistication of Soviet policies on nationalities. But prestige and power never guarantee permanency, since a shift in political hegemony can lead very rapidly to linguistic change. Persian has virtually disappeared from India since its heyday under the Moguls, and English may eventually go the same way.

Political power and the national language are uniquely interrelated in India. Hindi was voted in *de iure* by a congressional majority of only one during the wave of patriotic fervor and anti-British sentiment that swept the country in 1947. The main factors in this victory for the Hindi faction were the geographical extent and numerical plurality of Hindi speakers, and the location of the capital in Delhi (Hindi dialects extend approximately from the Western Punjab to Bihar, and from the Nepal border south to Andhra Pradesh). All over India people responded to the passionate appeals of Mahatma Gandhi and others by studying Hindi. Today, with a considerable change in public opinion, the Indian Central Government is faced with the predicament of insufficient power and will to carry through a program that has been legalized.

Various events reflect these contradictions. The nominally powerful Language Commission has issued pronouncements on complete Hindization by 1965. On the other hand, Chatterji, India's most distinguished linguist, has produced a widely read dissenting opinion that resulted in a reconsideration of the majority report in 1959 and the appointment of Chatterji as president of a Sanscrit Commission, presumably to weaken the "Hindi fanatics" through this indirect line of attack. Delhi is influenced by numerous extremists, many incapable of discussing the language question in a rational manner, whether they are linguists, journalists, or political leaders. Indian fighters for national independence from the British have subsequently been insulted on the public rostrum as traitors because they were standing against Hindi. Many of the Dravidians and Bengalis who occupy key roles in the central government are exerting their influence against Hindization. Non-Hindi adults all over India are passively resisting Hindi for all practical purposes by not taking any active steps to acquire it. A final example of inner conflict comes from the All-India Summer School for Linguistics held in Madras in 1959, twelve years after the Independence. About half the students favored Hindi, most North Indians passionately so. Nevertheless, fewer than one quarter could understand the Hindi speeches, and a public clash over the language question resulted in a social schism that ultimately affected most of the student body and some of the faculty. These disputants were linguists, supposedly enlightened as regards language. Some Indians say privately that they feel some dictatorial power is necessary to solve the language question, among others. But such power and the strategic vision to go with it are as yet absent.

Various fissures in India's culture may be growing rather than decreasing. One aspect of her linguistic pluralism has thrown into relief certain connections between language and politics. During British rule the political provinces almost never coincided completely with language boundaries. Thus Madras State included not only Tamilians but many people speaking Telegu, Malayalam, and Kannada, not to mention minority languages. The Bombay Presidency included speakers of at least four major languages. The principal result of this lack of congruence was that persons of differing speech communities were forced to interact and therefore to apply the principles of intergroup tolerance that underlie so much of Indian life. Second, English tended to emerge almost automatically as the *lingua franca*, in politics especially. English enjoyed a comparatively neutral status, since it was for the most part the prerogative of a supraregional elite, members of which are often scattered over many states in a network of subcastes, reaping the benefits as political mediators and leaders. They usually control some combination of Dravidian languages, or Indic languages, and English; one fairly representative Mysore Brahmin knows Kannada, Tamil, Telegu, English, and some Hindi (plus Kodaku, his childhood language). Many such polyglot intellectuals and administrators have opposed the organization of "linguistic states," believing that the public support was basically the reflex of a provincial chauvinism that would rapidly accelerate the introversion of India's culture areas. But against this fading intelligentsia stand the lower-caste leaders, rising rapidly in the democratic atmosphere, and more prone to incite the largely monolingual, voting masses by exploiting symbols of linguistic difference.

Gandhi and his followers had already harnessed linguistic self-determination to the Independence movement. This opened a veritable Pandora's box with which Nehru and others have not been able to cope very successfully. In 1948 the Linguistic Provinces Commission, appointed in the same year, stressed in its annual report the dangers of narrow regionalism. But by 1953 the Central Government had to organize the first "linguistic state" of Andhra (Telegu-speaking), after ceding to tremendous pressures that were climaxed by serious riots organized by the Communists after the fast to death of a Gandhian leader in Andhra—one of the first little whirlwinds of "passive resistance" that the Congress Party may continue to reap in the future. A States Reorganization Commission was appointed in 1954, submitted its report the following year, and recommendations began to go into effect after 1 November 1955. Despite various cautions and qualifications, it could be said that the cause of linguistic autonomy had won the day: the number of states was cut to fourteen, or one-half the original number, plus six centrally administered territories.

Since the "reorganization of linguistic states," the feared consequences have indeed followed with great rapidity. English instruction has weakened, notably in greater Hindustan. The partial maintenance of standards is limited to non-Hindi areas, since it was stimulated by reaction against Hindi. The Hindi program has almost come to a standstill in some southern areas. More and more states are instituting their regional languages; in 1959 the Mysore universities went over to Kannada; almost all instruction at all levels in Uttar Pradesh, including Delhi, is or soon will be in Hindi. This is the academic side of India's more generalized and largely regional self-discovery that continues to be a profound national experience, leading at best to what might be called "constructive nativism," as in the resynthesis of areal dance forms, but coupled at its worst with provincial bigotry and cultural discrimination. Leaders have played increasingly on linguistic prejudices against intrusive job-seekers from other states, leading indirectly to ramifications of a more serious character. Thus great numbers of (mainly Nayar) officials, expelled from Madras after the "reorganization," had to return to their native Kerala. The consequent piling-up of ambitious and frustrated leaders in Kerala significantly influenced the Communist victory in the elections of 1957 (won through Nayar support), and also the defeat of the Communists in 1959 (after the Nayars withdrew their support).

The "reorganization of linguistic states" has raised a series of additional long-range problems. First, on a per-capita basis the little states such as Assam (five million) are drowned out by Hindi-speaking aggregates such as Uttar Pradesh. Second, a political drift aptly called "the balkanization of the South and the consolidation of the North" [9] has been set in motion. Specifically, each of the four southern, Dravidian states is turning more to its own language—Tamil, Telegu, Kannada, or Malayalam. On the other hand, the huge Hindi-speaking states (Uttar Pradesh with 63 million; Bihar with 38 million, Madhya Pradesh with 26 million) are becoming consolidated and tend to be joined politically by other states where Hindi is either spoken also or easily learned (Punjab, Rajastan, Jamnu and Kashmir, and Bombay).

The combined process of balkanization and consolidation rests in part on a logical *non sequitur* that has been conveniently overlooked by politically interested persons. The comparatively tenable principle of "one language for each state" (because of efficiency in administration, and so forth) does not mean that one must create a single state or an arbitrarily small number of states for each language. One leader has suggested a plan for breaking up the great northern states into two or three smaller units each, centered around large cities serving as new regional capitals. As things stand at present, however, the organization of "linguistic states" has exacerbated the question of a national language while at the same time it makes some of the reasonable solutions less likely of success.

Finally, the principle of linguistic autonomy has proved unfeasible in Bombay and the Punjab because of the intense antagonism and inextricable intermingling of speech communities of commensurate strength; the Sikhs have been agitating with characteristic vigor for the official recognition of their writing system. The close juxtaposition of linguistic minorities does not necessarily produce fusion, despite the heat and friction of the urban industrial pot; thousands of caste groups living in diaspora in the big Indian cities have retained their mother tongue, endogamy, and religious practices for hundreds of years, in accordance with the deep-lying values that support social segregation, combined with various types of social interdependence. In 1958, for example, I took part in a "test for dialect distance" between a Marathi and the member of a Marathi subcaste whose ancestors moved down into Andhra over six hundred years ago. India's multilingual cities, notably Bombay, would provide excellent laboratories for the study of linguistic interference.[10] Such interference, however, might be found to differ markedly from the same process in other parts of the world, where the tendency to form colonies and "quarters" is not reinforced by the values of a pervasive caste system (admittedly, there are some parallels in the Near East). The extreme "ghetto-ization" of India's cities means that urbanization and industrialization are not as favorable to the development of linguistic uniformity as is usually the case.

Perhaps the most compelling force for the spontaneous adoption of a language is its relation to political values. In some cases a speech community may lack such a political substructure and may be segmented into two or more political bodies (e.g., the linked dialects of Austria, German Switzerland, East Germany, West Germany, and Holland). Or a state with more or less homogeneous political values may lack a single national code; thus the German in Switzerland is closer to Swiss French with respect to a partly covert system of political meanings than it is to Berlin German. But as a usual rule national and linguistic boundaries tend to coincide; indeed, these two domains of culture may powerfully reinforce each other's development. India's linguistic pluralism, on the other hand, is paralleled by a political disjointedness that has largely the same causes. She was never united before the British conquest; even the Mauryan and Guptan dynasties brought together only various portions of the country, and a consciousness of "national unity under Akbar" is vague indeed in the Dravidian South. A superstratum of British legal and political ideas, while genuinely espoused by many Indians, still lacks much in the way of integration with the various regional cultures. Also, any state or national government remains threatened by the possibility of massive mob action and the self-directed aggression of Indian "passive resistance."

What is the relation of the English language to Indian political values? Contrary to a widespread impression, the British followed a rather enlightened policy, without explicitly "imposing" their tongue. As early as 1832, however, they were seeking to produce individuals who would be Indian in blood, but English in opinion, morals, and intellect. During the late nineteenth century an anglicizing fashion swept upper-caste India because of the political and economic advantages of English, or because of ethnic shame (e.g., about nakedness, polygyny), and in part because of the intellectual appeal of English culture. An extensive system of non-progressive schools achieved high proficiency in English through a combination of memorization by rote and active use in the classroom.

Today many Indians fully appreciate the advantages of this "window to the outside world." The regional languages themselves have become suitable for higher instruction only because of the new European learning. The languages of the mass media reflect public attitudes; over 1,000,000 copies of English-language newspapers are sold daily, in contrast to fewer than 400,000 in Hindi. English enables Indians to attend international conferences with "dignity" (meaning elegance, sophistication). Even the Communist intellectuals are grateful for the "English language experience," which has brought them translations of Tolstoy and Gorky. But all these patterns are ironically counteracted by certain feelings. During a recent convention Malayalam writers were bitterly accused of "knowing all about world literature but completely ignoring their Tamil neighbors."

Some Malayali defended themselves by blaming "the British yoke" for their ignorance. But both the accusation and the defense were couched in the language of Byron.

Above all the practical and logical advantages stands the unforgettable association with British rule. The great majority of Indians, from the illiterate *harijan* to the cultivated polyglot, feel that the national language must be Indian and not the flat, denotative code imported by a people who, despite their democracy and their Shakespeare, were primarily conquerers, imperialists, and exploiters of the native land. After one hundred and fifty years, less than two million Indians speak English (more have some smatterings). Powerful, informal pressures affect many Indians who prefer English to their regional languages; a brilliant Tamilian poet of my acquaintance is frequently made to feel uneasy by his fellows because English is the language "of his excitement." And bitter indeed is the psychological predicament of the young Anglicized Indian who can speak only English. "It is doing violence to the manhood and especially to the womanhood of India to encourage our boys and girls to think that an entry into polite society is impossible without a knowledge of English. It is too humiliating a thought to be bearable." [11] Thus we see a negative value decisively influencing India's political destiny.

In conclusion: some Indians feel that the least harmful way out of the present difficulty might be an improved education in the regional languages and also in Hindi and English (selected according to circumstances), combined with a general attitude of tolerance and patience. Pressurized programs could stir up nativistic reactions beyond government control. Multilingualism itself should be regarded as a goal and a form of knowledge. It is hoped that language skills will continue to develop and be tried out in an experimental spirit, with leeway for the spontaneous drift of personality and culture. During the interim English might be explicitly rejected as a national language, while continuing in the status of an existing code, useful for national and international purposes. It would certainly accord with the Indian traditions of tolerance and religious reverence for "The Word" to adopt as a motto for the present: "Speak and let speak!"

REFERENCES

1. The states are (with the population in millions as of the 1951 census, and the language, in parentheses): Andhra (31, Telegu); Assam (5, Assamese); W. Bengali (26, Bengali); Bihar (38, Hindi); Bombay (46, Marathi and Gujarati); Madhya Pradesh (26, Hindi); Madras (29, Tamil); Orissa (14, Oriya); Punjab (16, Punjabi, Hindi); Uttar Pradesh (63, Hindi); Rajaston (15, Rajastan, Hindi); Jamnu and Kashmir (4, Kashmiri, Urdu); Mysore (19, Kannada); Kerala (14, Malayalam). Note that five states are all or mainly Hindi-speaking. Telegu and Kannada, Malayalam and Tamil form two sets of closely related Dravidian languages. Most of the Indic languages listed are also very closely related, about as far from one another as the Scandinavian languages. Bengali has about 80 million speakers if we count the

community in Pakistan. S. Sarkar, *Hindustani Yearbook* (Calcutta, 1959), pp. 402–407.

2. E. Y. Kutscher, "The Role of Modern Hebrew in the Development of Jewish-Israeli National Consciousness," PMLA, 1957, pp. 38–42.

3. C. Rajagopalachari, in *The Hindu,* 20 May 1959.

4. Rabindranath Tagore, "Episode of 1857," in *Stories from Bengal,* translated by S. Dutt (Bombay, 1959), p. 14.

5. A. L. Basham, *The Wonder That Was India* (London, 1956), p. 476.

6. S. H. Vatsyayan, "Hindi Literature," *Contemporary Indian Literature: A Symposium* (New Delhi, 1957), p. 73.

7. C. Rajagopalachari, *Tamil Culture,* 1959, p. 210.

8. *The Hindu,* 20 May 1959.

9. B. R. Ambedkar, *Thoughts on Linguistic States,* Aurangabad, 1955.

10. U. Weinreich, *Languages in Contact,* New York, 1953.

11. Mahatma Gandhi, *Young India,* 2.2.12.

Bibliography

PART ONE: CULTURE CONTACTS AND EDUCATIONAL TRANSFER

Bilinsky, Yaroslav, "Education of the Non-Russian Peoples in the Soviet Union," *Comparative Education Review,* Vol. 8, No. 1 (June, 1964), pp. 78–89.

Clignet, R. P., and Philip J. Foster, "French and British Colonial Education in Africa," *Comparative Education Review,* Vol. 8, No. 2 (October, 1964), pp. 191–198.

Foster, P. J., *Education and Social Change in Ghana* (Chicago: The University of Chicago Press, 1965).

Kawai, Kazuo, *Japan's American Interlude* (Chicago: The University of Chicago Press, 1960).

Lerner, Daniel, *The Passing of Traditional Society: Modernizing the Middle East* (The Free Press of Glencoe, 1958).

Lindsay, Rao H., *Nineteenth Century American Schools in the Levant* (Ann Arbor, Michigan: The University of Michigan, School of Education, 1965).

McDonald, Ellen, "English Education and Social Reform in Late Nineteenth Century Bombay: A Case Study in the Transmission of a Cultural Ideal," *The Journal of Asian Studies,* Vol. XXV, No. 3 (May, 1966), pp. 453–470.

Medlin, W. K., and W. M. Cave, "Social Change and Education in Developing Areas: Uzbekistan," *Comparative Education Review,* Vol. 8, No. 2 (October, 1964), pp. 166–185.

Minogue, W. J. D., "Education in a Dependent Culture—New Zealand: Some Problems Relating to the British Influence in New Zealand Education," *Comparative Education,* Vol. I, No. 3 (June, 1965), pp. 203–209.

Peshkin, Alan, "Education, the Muslim Elite, and the Creation of Pakistan," *Comparative Education Review,* Vol. 6, No. 2 (October, 1962), pp. 152–159.

Ruttner, Ralph, "American Educational Aid for National Development," *Teachers College Record,* Vol. 62, No. 5 (February, 1961), pp. 348–355.

Sizer, Nancy F., "John Dewey's Ideas in China—1919 to 1921," *Comparative Education Review,* Vol. 10, No. 3 (October, 1966), pp. 390–402.

PART TWO: EDUCATION AND THE POLITY

Almond, G. A., and S. Verba, *The Civic Culture: Political Attitudes and Democracy in Five Nations* (Boston and Toronto: Little, Brown and Company, 1965).

Azrael, Jeremy R., "Soviet Union," in James S. Coleman, ed., *Education and Political Development* (Princeton, New Jersey: Princeton University Press, 1965), pp. 233–271.

Chauncey, Henry, "Education for National Power—Soviet Style," *Orbis,* Vol. III, No. 2 (Summer, 1959).

Comparative Education Review, Vol. 10, No. 2 (June, 1966)—Special Issue on Student Politics.

Curle, Adam, "Education, Politics, and Development," *Comparative Education Review,* Vol. 7, No. 3 (February, 1964), pp. 226–245.
Easton, David, "Function of Formal Education in a Political System," *School Review,* Vol. LXV, 1957, pp. 304–316.
Eisenstadt, S. N., "Education and Political Development," in Don C. Piper and Taylor Cole, eds., *Post-primary Education and Political and Economic Development* (Durham, N.C.: Duke University Press, 1964), pp. 27–47.
Georgeoff, John, "Nationalism in the History Textbooks of Yugoslavia and Bulgaria," *Comparative Education Review,* Vol. 10, No. 3 (October, 1966), pp. 442–450.
Greenstein, Fred I., *Children and Politics* (New Haven, Conn.: Yale University Press, 1965).
Hess, Robert D., "The Socialization of Attitudes Toward Political Authority: Some Cross-National Comparisons," *International Social Science Journal,* Vol. 15, No. 4 (1963), pp. 542–557.
Jordan, A. C., "Apartheid and South Africa's Student Refugees," *Teachers College Record,* Vol. 66, No. 5 (February, 1965), pp. 387–398.
Kazamias, A. M., and B. G. Massialas, *Tradition and Change in Education: A Comparative Study* (Englewood Cliffs, N.J.: Prentice-Hall, Inc., 1965), pp. 130–144.
LeVine, Robert, "Political Socialization and Cultural Change," in Clifford Geertz, ed., *Old Societies and New States* (The Free Press of Glencoe, 1963), pp. 280–303.
Price, J. W., "Education and the Civil Service in Europe," *Western Political Quarterly,* Vol. X (December, 1957), pp. 817–832.

PART THREE: EQUITY, EFFICIENCY AND EDUCATIONAL PLANNING

Anderson, C. Arnold, "Educational Dilemmas in the U.S.S.R.," *School Review,* Vol. 67, No. 1 (Spring, 1959), 26–44.
Balough, Thomas, "The Economics of Educational Planning: Sense and Nonsense," *Comparative Education,* Vol. 1, No. 1 (October, 1964), 5–17.
Bowman, Mary Jean, "The Human Investment Revolution in Economic Thought," *Sociology of Education,* Vol. 39, No. 2 (Spring, 1966), 111–137.
Foster, Philip J., "The Vocational School Fallacy in Development Planning," in C. Arnold Anderson and Mary Jean Bowman, eds., *Education and Economic Development* (Chicago: Aldine, 1965), pp. 142–166.
Hansen, W. Lee, "Human Capital Requirements for Educational Expansion: Teacher Shortages and Teacher Supply," in C. Arnold Anderson and Mary Jean Bowman, eds., *Education and Economic Development* (Chicago: Aldine, 1965), pp. 63–87.
Harbison, Frederick, and Charles A. Myers, *Education, Manpower and Economic Growth: Strategies of Human Resource Development* (New York: McGraw-Hill, 1964).
Harburger, P. F., "Experiments in Vocational Education in a Developing Country," *International Labour Review,* Vol. LXXXIX, No. 1 (January, 1964), 29–42.
Hovne, Avner, "Manpower Planning and the Restructuring of Education," *International Labour Review,* Vol. LXXXIX, No. 6 (June, 1964), 529–550.
Phillips, H. M., "Economic and Social Aspects of the Planning of Education," *International Social Science Journal,* Vol. XIV, No. 4 (1962), 706–718.
Schultz, Theodore, *The Economic Value of Education* (New York: Columbia University Press, 1963).
Sizer, Theodore R., "Educational Planning and Individual Freedom," *Comparative Education Review,* Vol. 10, No. 3 (October, 1966), 381–389.

Vaizey, John, and Michael Debeauvais, "Economic Aspects of Educational Development," in A. H. Halsey, Jean Flood, and C. Arnold Anderson, eds., *Education, Economy, and Society: A Reader in the Sociology of Education* (New York: Free Press, 1961), pp. 545–557.

Weisbrod, Burton A., "Investing in Human Capital," *The Journal of Human Resources,* Vol. I, No. 1 (Summer, 1966), pp. 5–21.

PART FOUR: SUB-CULTURAL VARIATIONS AND EDUCATION

Abu-Laban, Baha, "The Impact of Ethnicity and Occupational Background on the Aspirations of Canadian Youth," *Sociological Inquiry,* Vol. 36, No. 1 (Winter, 1966), pp. 116–123.

Arasteh, R., "The Role of Intellectuals in Administrative Development and Social Change in Modern Iran," *International Review of Education,* Vol. IX, No. 3 (1963–64), 326–335.

Cameron, John, "The Integration of Education in Tanganyika," *Comparative Education Review,* Vol. XI, No. 1 (February, 1967), 38–56.

Elder, Glen H., "Achievement Orientations and Career Patterns of Rural Youth," *Sociology of Education,* Vol. 37, No. 1 (Fall, 1963), 30–58.

Goldthorpe, J. E., "Social Class and Education in East Africa," *Transactions of the Third World Congress of Sociology,* Vol. 5 (1956), pp. 115–122.

Gouveia, Aparecida J., "Preference for Different Types of Secondary School Among Various Ethnic Groups in São Paulo, Brazil," *Sociology of Education,* Vol. 39, No. 2 (Spring, 1966), 155–166.

Jenks, Christopher, and David Reisman, "The American Negro College," *Harvard Educational Review,* Vol. 37, (Winter, 1967), pp. 3–60.

MacLaine, A. G., "Educating the Outback Child in Australia," *Comparative Education* Vol. 3, No. 1 (November, 1966), 33–39.

Siegel, Bernard J., "Social Structure, Social Change, and Education in Rural Japan: A Case Study," in George D. Spindler, ed., *Education and Culture* (New York: Holt, Rinehart and Winston, 1963), 530–560.

Rose, Brian, "Bantu Education as a Facet of South African Policy," *Comparative Education Review,* Vol. 9, No. 2 (June, 1965), 208–212.

Turner, Ralph H., "Sponsored and Contest Mobility and the School System," *American Sociological Review,* Vol. XXV, No. 5.

Whiteford, Andrew Hunter, *Two Cities of Latin America: A Comparative Description of Social Classes* (New York: Doubleday, 1964).

Wylie, Laurence, *Village in the Vaucluse: An Account of Life in a French Village* (New York: Harper & Row, 1964).

PART FIVE: RELIGION AND EDUCATION

Adams, Don, "Rebirth of Moral Education in Japan," *Comparative Education Review,* Vol. 4, No. 1 (June, 1960), pp. 61–64.

Bereday, G. Z. F., and Joseph A. Lauwerys, eds., *The World Year Book of Education,* 1966 (New York: Harcourt, Brace and World, Inc., 1966).

Brickman, W. W., "Church, State and School in International Perspective," in W. W. Brickman, and Stanley Lehrer, eds., *Religion, Government, and Education* (New York: Society for the Advancement of Education, 1961), pp. 144–247.

Erickson, Donald A., "Religious Consequences of Public and Sectarian Schooling," *The School Review,* Vol. 72, No. 1 (Spring, 1964), pp. 1–21.

Freund, C. J., "Muslim Education in West Pakistan," *Religious Education,* Vol. 56, No. 1 (January, 1961), pp. 31–37.

Hans, N., "State and Church in Italy and France," *Comparative Education Review,* Vol. I, No. 3 (February, 1958), pp. 10–12.

Latourette, Kenneth S., *A History of Christian Missions in China* (New York: Macmillan, 1929).

Pike, Frederick B., ed., *The Conflict Between Church and State in Latin America* (New York: Alfred A. Knopf, 1964).

Rodhe, Birgit, "Religious Education in the State Schools of Sweden," *Theology* (July, 1965), pp. 332–339.

Scanlon, David G., ed., *Church, State and Education in Africa* (New York: Teachers College Press, 1966).

Small, J. J., "Religion in the Schools of New Zealand," *Comparative Education Review,* Vol. 9, No. 1 (February, 1965), pp. 53–62.

Wilson, Norman H., "Dutch Schools and Religious Segmentation," *Comparative Education Review,* Vol. 3, No. 2 (October, 1959), pp. 19–23.

PART SIX: LANGUAGE AND EDUCATION

Bernstein, Basil, "Aspects of Language and Learning in the Genesis of the Social Process," *Journal of Child Psychology and Psychiatry,* Vol. 1 (1961), 313–324.

Bull, William E., "The Use of Vernacular Languages in Education," *International Journal of American Linguistics,* Vol. 21 (1955), 228–294.

De Sola Pool, Ithiel, "The Role of Communication in the Process of Modernization and Technological Change," in Bert F. Hoselitz and Wilbert E. Moore, eds., *Industrialization and Society* (UNESCO-Mouton, 1963), pp. 279–295.

Denny, Neville, "Languages and Education in Africa," in John Spencer, ed., *Language in Africa* (Cambridge: Cambridge University Press, 1963), pp. 40–52.

Epstein, Erwin H., "National Identity and the Language Issue in Puerto Rico," *Comparative Education Review,* Vol. II, No. 2 (June, 1967).

Fishman, J. A., and V. C. Nahirney, "The Ethnic Group School and Mother-Tongue Maintenance in the United States," *Sociology of Education,* Vol. 37, No. 4 (Summer, 1964), 543–559.

Hymes, Dell H., "Functions of Speech: An Evolutionary Approach," in Frederick C. Gruber, ed., *Anthropology and Education* (Philadelphia: Univ. of Pennsylvania Press, 1961), pp. 55–83.

Katz, Joseph, "Bilingualism and Biculturalism in Canada," *Comparative Education,* Vol. 2, No. 2 (March, 1966), 113–118.

Le Page, R. B., *The National Language Question: Linguistic Problems of Newly Independent States* (London: Oxford University Press, 1964).

MacNamara, John, *Bilingualism and Primary Education: A Study of Irish Experience* (Chicago: Aldine, 1966).

Ong, Walter J., "Latin Language Study as a Renaissance Puberty Rite," *Studies in Philology,* Vol. LVI (April, 1959), 103–124.

Soffietti, James P., "Bilingualism and Biculturalism," *Journal of Educational Psychology,* Vol. 46, No. 4 (April, 1955), 222–227.

Index

DATE DUE

FE 5 '73			
MY 19 '77			
AP 19 '79			
AP 13 '81			